Effective

Practices

in

Starting Co-ops

About the Effective Practices Series

Developing co-operatives can be a challenging task. Every step and every decision can be surrounded with questions and an array of options. The Effective Practices series of publications from New Rochdale Press is designed to guide those who endeavour to take on, or support, this collaborative adventure. In this series, we do not provide uniform answers – as no two co-ops are exactly alike – here you will find information to help co-operators make informed choices. In these publications we have documented the insights and experience of other co-operators and co-op developers on how to optimize the use of time and resources, and how to best design the internal structures of the co-op, to create successful and vibrant enterprises.

Publications in the Effective Practices Series

- Co-ops by Design: Building Blocks for Co-op Development – (Eds) Lyn Cayo, Kathleen Gableman, Sol Kinnis
- Effective Practices in Starting Co-ops: The Voice of Canadian Co-op Developers (with DVD) – (Eds) Lynn Cayo and Joy Emmanuel
- Effective Practices in Starting Co-operatives – Two Part DVD
- Effective Practices in Starting Co-operatives (Volume 2) – Joy Emmanuel

For more information on other publications by New Rochdale Press, see the end of this publication.

Effective Practices resources and tools can also be located on the BCICS website at: http:// bcics.org/

⌐21059 (24)

EFFECTIVE PRACTICES

IN **STARTING CO-OPS**

The Voice Of Canadian Co-op Developers

JOY EMMANUEL

LYN CAYO

EDITORS

 NEW ROCHDALE PRESS

University
of Victoria

Cover design and layout by Colin Swan.

Printed in Victoria, Canada

Library and Archives Canada Cataloguing in Publication

Effective practices in starting co-ops : the voice of Canadian co-op developers / Joy Emmanuel, Lyn Cayo, editors.

ISBN 978-1-55058-361-8

1. Cooperative societies--Planning. 2. Cooperative societies--

Management. I. Cayo, Lyn II. Emmanuel, Joy, 1955-

HD2963.E44 2007   334.068   C2007-906417-5

British Columbia Institute for Co-operative Studies
University of Victoria
University House 2 – Room 109
PO Box 3060 STN CSC
Victoria, B.C. V8W 3R4
Tel. (250) 472-4539
rochdale@uvic.ca
http://bcics.org

B C I C S

Co-operatives Secretariat
Secrétariat aux Coopératives

Contents

Section Two: Financing Co-ops

Section Three: Working Together to Make Co-ops Work

Acknowledgements

The primary purpose of the British Columbia Institute for Co-operative Studies (BCICS) is the development of the field of Co-operative Studies. A fundamental characteristic of that field is effective engagement between research activities and the actual operation of co-operatives, whether new or old. The underlying belief is that research and action need to inform each other and, on some level, to mutually validate what is done and what is understood. This book is one example of how such collaboration can take place and what the benefits of it might be.

It began with three simple premises: that there is a small but growing band of people with considerable experience and expertise in the development of co-operatives, that recording what they have learned and are learning is important for understanding how the movement can grow, and that recording such knowledge could make a significant contribution to the body of knowledge that those interested in Co-operative Studies need to develop. This book, as well as other publications and resources developed from the project, clearly demonstrate the correctness of these premises; the consequences of mingling research and practices can be beneficial in diverse ways to all involved or interested.[1]

BCICS would like to thank the Co-operative Development Initiative (programme of the Co-operatives Secretariat, Government of Canada/Secrétariat aux coopératives, Gouvernement du Canada) for its financial support for this project and its officers, particularly Alain Roy, for their encouragement, understanding, and assistance.

We would like to thank Professor Daniel Côté of HEC at the Université de Montréal for his work in helping to design the project and in organizing

---

1 Additional resources from this project include: Two educational DVDs (included with this publication), Effective Practices web resources (available winter 2008, accessible from the BCICS website: http://bcics.org, also through CoopZone www.coopzone.coop and other co-op websites), a second Effective Practice book (due out spring 2008), in addition project collaborators made many presentations at national and international conferences.

the work among Francophone colleagues. We wish to express our gratitude to the Canadian Worker Co-operative Federation and especially its executive director, Hazel Corcoran, for her assistance and enthusiasm. We hope this book and the other resources emanating from the project will be useful for the development of CoopZone, the very valuable information hub of the Co-operative Development Initiative – Advisory Services.

BCICS began this project by asking developers across Canada who should be included in the project as authors of papers. They identified: Glen Fitz-patrick (Newfoundland), Peter Hough (Nova Scotia), Russ Christianson (Ontario), Christian Savard (Québec), Joël Lebossé (Québec), Marie Joelle Brussard (Québec), April Roberts (Saskatchewan), Lynn Hannley (Alberta), Greg O'Neill (Alberta and NWT), Melanie Conn (British Columbia), and Marty Frost (British Columbia). These developers met with us in Toronto (spring 2006) for an intense two-day meeting, which was video-taped and has become the basis for the development of two educational videos. Following the meeting, each of the developers wrote a paper for this book and the results follow.

In addition, we undertook two sets of interviews with other developers. Daniel Côté interviewed the following co-op development experts from Québec for the development of Chapter Five and we would like to thank them for their collaboration: Armand Lajeunesse (Executive Director, CDR de Lanaudière), Guy Bisaillon (Senior Advisor and former Executive Direc-tor, CDR de Montréal), Guy Provencher (Senior Advisor, CDR du centre du Québec – Mauricie), Patrick Duguay (Executive Director, CDR Outaouais – Laurentides), Claude Dorion (Executive Director, MCE conseils), Richard Lapointe (CSN), Pierre Lamarche (CSN), Yves Létourneau (Financial Ana-lyst, Capital régional et coopératif Desjardins, and former Senior Advisor, CDR de Québec), and Sylvain Parenteau (Treasurer, Sixpro, Board member, CDR centre du Québec – Mauricie).

Joy Emmanuel, the Research Co-ordinator at BCICS, supervised this project, wrote several chapters for this book, and edited it with great care and dedication. BCICS is much indebted to her for her leadership and ef-ficiency in carrying the project through to its conclusion. Among the tasks she undertook, a particularly pleasant one, was interviewing developers in English-speaking Canada for the development of Chapters Three, Four, and Thirteen. They included Peter Hough (Financial Officer and Fund Manager - CWCF, Developer, Nova Scotia), David Daughton (Developer, Prince Edward Island), Jim Winter (Newfoundland and Labrador Federation of Co-op-eratives), Sheelagh Greek (former co-op developer, CWCF, Co-op Atlantic), Victor Teumo (Conseil de la cooperation de l'Ontario - CCO), Ethel Côté (Ontario – developer, community economic development and social economy expert), Sally Miller (Director, Community Power Education, Ontario Sustainable Energy Association), Terri Proulx (Community Business Counsellor, Seed, Winnipeg), Blair Hamilton (Dungannon Consulting Services, Manitoba), Russ Rothney (Manager, Community Economic Development, Assiniboine Credit Union, Winnipeg, Manitoba), Hazel Corcoran (Executive Director, CWCF, Executive Director CoopZone) Yvonne Chiu (Multi-Cultural Health Brokers Co-op), Gulalai Habib (former settlement counsellor, Immigrant Services Society of B.C.), Nicole Chaland (CCEDNet), Lee Fuge (International Women's Catering Co-op, Victoria), Lyn Cayo (former Developer), Stéphane Audet (former Director of Co-operative Development, BCCA, Fall 2006), and Vanessa Hammond (Developer, Victoria, British Columbia).

Finally, I would like to express the gratitude of BCICS to Lyn Cayo for her careful and informed help in editing the book, Colin Swan for his remarkable skill and care in laying it out, and Sandy Polomark for her administrative support.

We hope you will agree that what follows is a model of one kind of project that can help build the field of Co-operative Studies. We hope particularly that it will demonstrate the value of building bridges between the researchers/*acteurs* in the academy and the *acteurs*/researchers in communities. They have much to contribute to each other.

Ian MacPherson

Director, BCICS

Introduction

Joy Emmanuel

S tarting co-operatives is a challenging task. Fortunately, Canada has a rich treasury of experienced co-op developers whose insights and advice can be called upon to help people who want to start co-operatives in order to meet their economic and social needs. However, despite decades of Canadian experience with co-ops, the efforts of many developers, and the large Canadian co-operative movement, little information has been available on the most effective practices for developing new co-operatives under diverse conditions in Canada. With financial support from the Co-operative Secretariat, the British Columbia Institute for Co-operative Studies (BCICS) has attempted to address this gap through documenting the insights of co-op developers across the country.

In order to learn from their experiences, we asked developers to identify effective practices in developing new co-ops. Through meetings and interviews we explored with them such questions as: What are the crucial issues in the start-up phase of new co-ops? What factors hinder the growth of new co-ops? What creative solutions have you found to address these challenges? What factors contribute to the success of new co-ops? Beyond this we also explored the various roles developers play, what for them is most challenging, and what personal/professional insights they had for the next generation of developers.

In these discussions we covered a range of issues that surfaced at the micro level in meetings between developers and co-op members and also examined macro level factors such as government policies, economic factors, and environmental conditions. The timeframe examined ranged from conditions prior to the pre-feasibility study, to the importance of after-care, and what issues show up in later years if certain items are not addressed in the foundational period.

Collectively, the developers who have contributed to this volume have worked in every province and region of Canada. They have between 2 and 30 years of experience doing co-op development work. They represent both genders and various ethnic groups. Some of these developers work as private consultants, others work for various organizations (economic development associations, co-operative organizations, and non-profit groups), and some are members or workers in the co-ops they discuss.

Our interest has been to focus primarily on new co-ops in their formative years when they are perhaps most vulnerable and when developers are most likely to be involved. This journey has allowed us to map out many intricate details, and some of the major contours, in the domain of developing new co-ops. This inquiry has also been instrumental in revealing the inter-connections between all the layers (micro to macro), the many players (members, developers, organizations, government, etc.), and the many issues and factors that affect the success of new co-ops. We had originally intended to zero in on the work developers do at the community level engaging with members of new co-op initiatives; however, the web of meaning that emerged quickly showed us that all dimensions needed to be part of the discussion to truly map out effective practices in co-op development - thus a broader canvass was most appropriate.

Our Purpose

Mature co-operatives can be said to pass through five stages, these are named within a "life cycle model" as: formative, stabilizing, building, strategizing (either because of significant growth or because of a crisis caused by internal or external factors), and reformulating (when a co-operative takes on a markedly different purpose or structure).[1] The later two stages are frequently cyclical in nature. Models of co-operative development that account for these five stages examine how co-operators interact with one another as members, how they relate to their communities, to the co-operative sector, and to the state, as well as the ways in which they carry out the activities of the co-op (e.g., visioning, developing a business plan, raising of capital, marketing, etc.). Those relationships invariably change as a co-operative proceeds through the various stages. The shape of each stage is also influenced by culture, class, contact with others in the co-operative movement, the conception of the co-operative, and other factors.

---

1 In his years of studying co-operatives, Dr. Ian MacPherson developed such a model to examine the life cycle of the co-operative as a changing, evolving organization.

While various aspects of co-op development have been previously examined, there has been little documentation around the role of developers and their perspectives on the process. Their views are an invaluable part of the picture. Undertaking a collaborative enquiry such as this not only adds new dimensions to the above described life cycle model, which will be of interest to those in the field of co-operative studies, it can also benefit people who are starting their own co-ops, greatly enhance the work of the next generation of developers and community organizers, as well as offer concrete direction to professionals and policy makers who work with new co-operatives.

Thus, our intent has been to ensure that valuable insights gained from years of practical field experience as a co-operative developer are documented so this vital knowledge can benefit others in the sector and those partners who work closely with members of the co-operative movement. In documenting these insights, we also hope to contribute to the field of co-operative studies and to the leadership within the co-operative movement.

Why the Co-op Model?

While the very existence of human beings has depended on co-operation and every culture exhibits various forms of co-operative social arrangements, co-operatives are a relatively new type of social structure that has been around for less than 200 years. Co-operatives grew out of the efforts of a group of working class artisans who sought to have a collective measure of control over their economic and social situation, which in their day, reflected the harsh conditions of the industrial revolution. A group of weavers in Rochdale, England are credited with starting the first modern day co-operative when they formally incorporated in 1844. Through pooling their meager savings they became co-owners of a small store, allowing them to have control over the quality and cost of their food. Eventually the model was adopted in the work place as a form of economic enterprise, and over the next few decades the co-operative model rapidly spread to countries around the world.

Today, more than 800 million people belong to co-operatives in countries around the world and the model has been adapted to many forms of social enterprise, large and small, ranging from agricultural co-ops to credit unions, from housing to social co-ops, and transportation to worker co-ops. The International Co-operative Alliance (ICA) defines co-operatives as "an autonomous association of persons united voluntarily to meet their common economic, social, and cultural needs and aspirations through a jointly owned and democratically controlled enterprise."[2]

Wherever co-operatives are found, and no matter for what purpose the model has been adopted, they reflect the will of people to work together in order to have a measure of control over their future, improve some aspect of their lives, and to contribute to the betterment of their communities. Key to the growth of co-operatives as a worldwide movement has been that they are firmly rooted in a body of co-operative principles and values, which reflect the lessons of the original Rochdale pioneers. These principles are:

1. Open and Voluntary Membership: Membership is open to all.
2. Democratic Control by Members: Co-operatives are democratic organizations. At the community level, primary co-ops follow the rule of one member, one vote.
3. Member Economic Participation: Members contribute equitably to, and democratically control, the capital of their co-op.
4. Autonomy and Independence: Co-operatives are autonomous, self-help organizations. If they enter into contracts with other parties, they do so in a way that ensures democratic control by the members.
5. Co-operative Education, Training, and Information: These are on-going activities within the co-op to ensure that members understand how a co-op works and can play an active, informed role in the life of the co-op.
6. Co-operation among Co-operatives: Individual co-operatives and the co-op movement are strengthened when co-operatives work together for mutual support and benefit.
7. Concern for Community: Co-operatives are about more than meeting the needs of their member. Co-operatives also foster a concern for the broader community.

Differences between co-operatives and private enterprises arise precisely because these principles form the foundation of every co-operative. Co-ops are collectively owned and operated social enterprises that allow the owner-members to have a direct say in the operation of the co-operative, to directly benefit from the services offered through the co-op, and in many cases, to benefit from any surplus earnings that are generated. The co-operative model provides a means for people to work together to meet their own needs. Co-operatives encourage collective action for mutual benefit, in addition, they strengthen and extend democratic processes within the economic sphere.[3]

---

2 For more information see: http://www.coop.org/coop/index.html
3 For more information on the basic principles and characteristics of co-operatives and to

In the 150 plus years that formal co-operatives have existed, they have played an important economic and social role in communities around the world. Co-operatives were first formed in Canada in 1861,[4] and are now well established in every province and territory, and exist in many economic and social sectors. Estimates are that 4 in every 10 Canadians are members of at least one co-op.[5]

Co-operatives are not just an "alternative" way of creating employment and providing services. Co-operatives are a time-tested model of a collective enterprise that embraces the importance of ensuring ordinary people are empowered to meet their needs in a just, fair, and sustainable manner. That being said, it should also be noted that co-operatives have their own set of challenges to becoming established viable enterprises. While co-op developers are not involved in the start-up phase of every co-op, they provide an invaluable contribution toward the growth of the co-op movement. The role and the importance of developers in guiding new co-op initiatives through some of the initial hurdles is the thrust of this book.

Why "Effective Practices?"

We began this project with the intent of exploring "best practices" in co-op development. Over the last few decades the concept of "best practices" has surfaced in various disciplines. Although the particulars of what "best practices" means are defined differently within various sectors, at the core of the discussion is a focus on improving the way we do our work to influence the outcome of our efforts.

In some approaches to identifying best practices the emphasis is on a scientific examination where research is employed in a systematic manner to determine statistically which practices most often produce the optimum or desired results. A second approach is to draw on the collective, experiential knowledge of practitioners and identify points of agreement around practices that enhance one's work objectives. A middle way is to draw on the strengths of both scientific and experiential knowledge to determine best practices.

---

learn more about the differences between co-ops and private businesses visit any of the following sites: The International Co-operative Alliance: http://www.coop.org/coop; The Canadian Co-operative Association: http://www.coopscanada.coop/; The Co-operative Secretariat: http://www.coop.gc.ca; British Columbia Institute for Co-operative Studies: http://bcics.ogr

4 The first co-operative business in North America was a consumer co-op established in Stellarton, Nova Scotia, by British immigrant coal miners in 1861. At about the same time, the Britannia Consumers Co-operative was set up in Sydney Mines, Cape Breton.

5 See Co-op Statistics on the Canadian Co-operative Association website: http://www.coopscanada.coop/

As is often the case with any journey however, what one anticipates and how the expedition unfolds can be quite different. In the course of our research and generating this book, we found the practitioners involved preferred the concept of "effective practices" rather than "best practices" for reasons described below.

The Journey

In undertaking the task of documenting effective practices in co-op development, we first sought to bring together a group of peer-nominated, experienced co-op developers who might act in some advisory capacity and as direct contributors to this work. Requests for nominations were sent out through co-op organizations across the country and through co-ops and CED networks. In the end, we were able to bring together 11 co-op developers, including 3 co-op development experts from Québec. We sought to have a diverse group of developers who reflected a high level of geographic, gender, and sector diversity. We met for two days in Toronto in the spring of 2006 for a rousing exchange around the best practices affecting the formative stage of co-op development. We explored such questions as: What was most critical? What was most challenging? What was most helpful? And, how did they approach their work?

One of the most taxing aspects of the discussion was how to locate the perimeters of the topic. We found there were different interpretations of the questions themselves. Some came at it from the particulars of the steps in the process; others took a broader view of the factors that must be in place to support new growth. We explored key issues and stages. We talked about the various players and their roles. We came back many times to examining the differences between co-op development within and outside of Québec, and asked, "What are the lessons that can be learned from the Québec experience?" We explored personal challenges, success stories, and times when things did not go well. We scrutinized the concept of "best practices," explored other terms, and considered how co-ops were themselves a best practice even if the term did not seem to fit within our discussion on the development process.

We listened intently to all the comments that surfaced. The emotional tone of the discussion was as important and as tangible a dimension as the particular issues. There was indifference for the term best practice; some tension around the researcher-developer relationship; frustration around feeling that developers receive little support and acknowledgment for their work; and feelings of camaraderie, passion, and commitment surfaced around working in a field of personal and social transformation where values and principles are considered important. Humour broke forth and lightened the burden of finding answers, and tingeing the parameters of the discussion was always a purposeful questioning of ourselves, of the process, and of naming what truly has an impact and can be called a "best/effective" practice.

At some points the discussion became too broad and abstract, at other times it was too narrow and off the mark. We listened, we debated, we disagreed on points, we explored and meandered down many paths, we worked through points of uncertainty, we digressed over meals, slept on what came up, and allowed a process to unfold that demanded there be no clear boundaries to the discussion.

In our discussions, the relevance of the term "best practices" was questioned in relation to how these developers viewed their work. While some were comfortable with the term, others had reservations. They noted that at a sector level (e.g. housing or worker co-ops) it might be appropriate to talk about a best practices formula, but at the level of separate co-ops from diverse sectors this did not apply. At the root of their hesitation was the view that every new co-op has unique features that must be considered; what works in situation "A" might not be appropriate in situation "B." They emphasized that there are many ways to do this work. These developers were also concerned that the term "best practice" might send a message that there is a certain standard or optimal practice by which to compare and evaluate people's work.

From their perspective, there are many factors to consider and countless strategic decisions to make along the way. At the same time, this is not to say that "anything goes" or that there are no guideposts to help determine the most appropriate approach in a given situation. There was recognition that the more familiar a developer is with the co-op model, the more experience and resources they will have to draw on in guiding new co-ops. Also, the more familiar one is with understanding how co-ops are a viable business model and how they differ from private enterprises, the more effective one's efforts may be in working with and promoting new start-ups.

An additional concern that must be brought forward is that not only must one consider the particular conditions and practices in relation to the new co-op, but this dialogue must also be understood in the context of a broader, multi-layered canvass of factors that contribute to the success of new co-ops. In other words, it is not just the actions and interventions of developers that make a difference and influence the well being of new co-ops. At the micro level, developers noted the key role that co-op members play – in many cases individuals within this core group carry the development process forward between consultations with developers. Some called the members the true developers. On another level, developers emphasized that the role of the co-op sector in actively promoting and advocating for co-op development is just as important to consider as the particular work that developers do in the field. From their perspective, if we were to focus on just the developer's actions, the lens would be far too narrow to capture the full picture.

Terms other than "best practices" were considered. Some that surfaced were: root practices, successful practices, effective practices, and useful practices. We knew we wanted to capture an array of perspectives and insights that were grounded in the experiences of developers and focused on what interventions and factors make a positive difference in the success of new co-ops. In the end, it was agreed that "effective practices" was an appropriate and acceptable term to name the interventions and practices we wanted to document.

Following our consultation, each developer was asked to identify his or her area of expertise and passion and set down their insights on that aspect of development work in relation to how it influences the success of new co-ops. These reflective pieces form the basis of the chapters in this publication.

To complement and expand on the insights coming from this small group, we arranged in-depth interviews with other developers in English-speaking Canada and co-op development experts in Québec. This allowed us to tap the broader wealth of experience and expand on the diversity of communities and distinct conditions under which co-op development takes place.

In Québec, interviews were done with eight senior officials and financial advisors who have years of experience working within the co-op sector in that province. A summary of the insights from these interviews is presented in chapter five. Another eighteen co-op developers outside of Québec were interviewed by telephone. The results of these interviews form the body of chapters Three, Four, and Thirteen.

Our final task has been to bring all of these articles, reflections, interviews, tools, and resources together in this publication. This has been a challenging task. Even though this is a weighty volume of material, we recognize it is really the tip of the iceberg and only another layer of the discussion on best and/or effective practices in co-op development.

How this Volume is Organized

Just as there are many ways to approach this subject, there are many options for how to present this material. As mentioned above, we asked the core group of developers to write on what they were most passionate about and express how they view what is helpful to know about that aspect of co-op development. We then took this collection of articles and, in light of the stream of thought emerging from our earlier consultation, determined what order and grouping seemed most appropriate.

The articles in Section One, *Guideposts for the Journey*, present an orientation to co-op development. Chapter One provides a framework of terms of reference and typologies for thinking about different conditions under which co-op development happens. In Chapter Two you will find a useful overview of the development process. Chapter Three contains insights and comments from the interviews with developers and provides an introduction to the developers themselves, the various ways they are positioned to do development work, and their varying perspectives on co-op development. In Chapter Four we examine co-operative processes and structures that are critical in nurturing a "co-operative culture" within the new collective. Chapter Five offers a contrasting, yet complementary perspective on the macro level, top-down approach to co-op development that has evolved in Québec.

Section Two, *Financing Co-ops*, focuses on issues of financing new start-ups and the importance of developing funding strategies that support co-op development and co-op developers and promoters. Chapter Six provides an examination of the difference between financial capital and social capital and explores how social capital is an under-valued asset for securing funding for new co-ops. The thesis found in Chapter Seven elaborates on the importance of developing macro level funding strategies for supporting co-op development. In Chapter Eight the approach to financing co-ops in Québec is set out and explained.

In Section Three, *Working Together to Make Co-ops Work*, the concepts of Governance and Partnerships are explored. In Chapter Nine the processes of decision-making and good governance are examined. In Chapter Ten the formation of partnerships as an effective practice in co-op development at a regional and provincial level is discussed. Chapter Eleven provides an in-depth look at how partnerships are formed within the Québec model of co-op development.

The articles in Section Four, *Collaborative Strategies – Addressing Specific Needs*, illustrate effective practices in co-op development when working with particular populations. Chapter Twelve provides a detailed look at the process of developing a women's co-op in an urban based, low-income, immigrant community. In Chapter Thirteen we offer two short case studies of other co-ops whose members are also immigrant women living in an urban setting. Chapter Fourteen takes us to a rural setting and reviews some of the challenges and lessons learned in developing agricultural co-ops on First Nations reserves.

The chapters in Section Five, *Co-operating into the Future*, offer an eclectic and expansive view of co-op development and brings together some of the main themes in the book. Chapter Fifteen offers a review of the primary challenges facing new co-ops in the critical first three years of operation. Chapter Sixteen brings our attention to the difficulties of creating a culture of co-operation and developing new co-operatives in the midst of the dominant, competitive culture. The broader context of environmental changes is also explored in terms of challenges, opportunities, and embracing co-operative values. In Chapter Seventeen the concept of best practices is taken up from the perspective of making co-operatives a best practice. Examples are explored that illustrate how co-operatives have been adopted to address the triple bottom line of respecting economic, social, and environmental concerns, and how they can and do offer a viable and sustainable alternative in an economic milieu that is both competitive and at times unstable.

The second part of the book provides two additional case studies, as well as examples of resources and tools that developers use in their work.

Who might Read this Book?

Anyone interested in knowing more about co-ops, what makes them tick, and most importantly, how to nurture a fledgling co-operative enterprise will find this volume full of practical knowledge, thoughtful reflections, useful ideas, and an expansive view of approaches to co-operative development in Canada. While the focus of this volume is to provide concrete ideas on co-op development grounded in the experience of those who do this work, it is also an examination of the "growing edge" of the co-operative movement and raises questions about how we care for and promote the co-operative model as a viable and important alternative means of meeting economic and social needs.

Through this project we have worked closely with developers in order to document what they have learned from years of working with new co-ops. Part of our intent has been to ensure this vital knowledge is available for another generation of co-op developers. Whether one is working within the co-operative movement or is already fairly knowledgeable about co-ops, we expect that this book will offer valuable suggestions to enhance your future co-op development work.

If you are doing community economic development work and/or working with particular populations such as new immigrants and do not have a strong background in co-op development, this book will provide you with an orientation to specific critical issues that are important to be aware of, help you understand the broader dimensions in the life of a healthy co-op, and suggest how you can better support and promote co-op development in your community. For community organizers who may want to sponsor a co-op start-up within a particular population, Section Four will be of particular interest.

Many times the question was raised: who are the true developers? It was acknowledged that, for a variety of reasons, many new co-ops start without the assistance of a developer. Even if a developer is involved, they may feel the real "developers" are the core members of the co-op who are truly committed to the co-op, are on the front lines making decisions, carrying the responsibility, and sharing the future benefits of the co-op. For those who are members of a co-op, whether or not you are working with a professional who is knowledgeable on co-ops, this book will offer practical guidelines, as well as a broader orientation to dimensions in the life of a co-op. We encourage you to find what is most helpful in your circumstances and leave the rest for another time.

One of the concerns that surfaced in the course of this work was the vital role existing co-ops play in contributing to the development of new co-ops. Indeed, the active support of the co-op sector is viewed as a critical factor to the growth of new co-ops. If you are a member of an existing co-op – large or small – we expect you will find constructive ideas here on how your co-op can make a difference, as well as how you may contribute more effectively to the healthy life of your own co-op.

For professionals, such as lawyers, accountants, and representatives of government agencies, this volume offers a deeper understanding of some of the inner workings of co-ops and the particular challenges for which they require your support and services.

This book should also hold special interest for administrators, both within and outside the co-op movement, who may be in a position to fund new co-op developments and/or set policies that affect their promotion and regulation. Chapter Seven raises particular concerns on how more resources can be channeled to future co-op development growth, while Chapter Seventeen advocates for a more proactive approach to promoting co-ops.

Whether you belong to one, all, or none of these groups, if you are interested in co-operatives, we hope this book inspires new ideas on how the co-operative model can be successfully adapted to local circumstances and more effectively nurtured for the benefit of all concerned.

Closing

While co-op developers have written most of the articles in this book, as a researcher who has also contributed articles there is the awareness of being an "outsider" to the development process and at the same time influencing the direction of the dialogue and presentation of this information. In a sense, the role of the researcher, like the village scribes of old, is to preserve and care for the process of collectivizing this knowledge and experience in such a way that nurtures and respects the co-operative roots of this work. As one way to strike a balance between the domain of the developer and researcher, this volume was co-edited by Lyn Cayo, a co-op developer. We hope that in the end it is the developers' views and voices that are most prominent in shaping the ideas and suggestions presented here.

The key to the success of this project has been working together with developers to generate a document that reflects their experiences and that may enhance the work of future generations of developers. We recognize that what works in one situation will not work in all others, but we can learn from experiences and be stimulated by the insights of others so that no one has to re-invent the wheel – especially not the co-operative one.

While starting new co-ops will doubtless continue to be a challenging task, this collection of essays may at least provide more insights, tools, and resources for the journey.

Section One: Guideposts for the Journey

Chapter One

How Do We Start Our Co-op? Let Me Count the Ways…

Peter Hough

This paper outlines a way of classifying the different types of initiatives that can lead to the creation of a co-operative. Hopefully this will have a number of uses for people interested in starting a co-op, or those who are mandated to support the development of co-ops.

I also offer some guiding principles for the relationships between all parties involved in the co-op development initiative. In my experience, these principles can guide the development of the appropriate roles and responsibilities which various people play in different types of co-op initiatives. They help the players orientate themselves as to what kinds and types of authority, responsibility, and accountability various players can, and should, have.

My goal is not to be definitive regarding what roles various players should take and why, but rather to highlight how co-ops are developed under various conditions and, keeping that in mind, present a set of principles which can be a stimulus for reflection in any particular case when working in a collaborative manner to create a successful co-op. I define a successful co-op as one with "a knowledgeable, committed membership working within a viable, self-sustaining co-operative, following the co-operative principles and values."

Useful Distinctions

Different Players

To begin, I would like to set-out the distinction I make between co-op promoters, co-op entrepreneurs, and the co-op developer/supporter/facilitator/et al. It is important the differences between the categories are clear and understood as these distinctions are at the heart of the co-op development process. They determine what level of authority, responsibility, accountability, and risk one has or is taking. They also determine the source, type, and length of commitment one has to the co-op.

The co-op promoter is a person who makes it their business to promote the co-operative option within their communities. They may be co-op volunteers who are committed to seeing the co-op movement expand. They are sometimes paid staff of co-op or Community Economic Development (CED) organizations, or government employees with a co-op promotion mandate as part of their job responsibilities. People playing the role of co-op promoter do not normally become members or leaders of the new co-op. They help identify opportunities and introduce the idea to potential co-op entrepreneurs and will often connect them to co-op development facilitators. It should be noted that co-op promoters can and may go on to have a role as co-op development facilitators at the next stage of development, depending upon their interest, skills, and/or professional mandate, or even become members of the co-op if it is within their community and meets their needs.

The co-op entrepreneur stands inside the developing co-op. Whether as member, director, or manager, the co-op entrepreneur has some area of authority and responsibility for making decisions on behalf of the co-op. Co-op entrepreneurs are the primary beneficiaries of the co-op's success, and they are the ones who generally have the most to lose if the co-op fails. Their dedication and capacities are the driving force behind the activities of the co-op; its sustainability ultimately depends upon them and their open-ended commitment to making the co-op a success.

Co-op development facilitators (also referred to as co-op developers), in contrast, have no inherent authority or responsibility to make decisions for the co-op. Their usual contribution is to provide guidance, technical services, training, etc. without the authority or responsibility to make decisions. Typically, they work as independent contractors or as staff of dedicated co-op development organizations. As such, they often have a mandate and are accountable to other authorities outside the developing co-op (of course they may have a contractual relationship with, and be accountable to, the co-op for specific services) and their personal benefits are not directly tied to the outcomes produced by the co-op. However, to some extent their future professional reputation and opportunities may be tied to the success or failure of the co-op as an initiative. Their commitment to, and involvement with, the co-op may be limited in length by their non-member status, the co-op entrepreneurs' decisions regarding their role, and the co-op's capacity to meet their need for remuneration – whether by the co-op directly or by external funders who support the co-op development process.

Grassroots or Top-Down

Another distinction which is often made is between grassroots/bottom-up co-op development and top-down initiatives driven by a CED or co-op organization. For the purposes of this paper, "grassroots" means a co-op initiative started by a group of individuals on their own initiative based upon their common vision and resources. "Top-down" means a co-op initiative envisioned and developed by an existing organization that then seeks out potential co-op entrepreneurs with whom to work in the creation of the co-op. These selected co-op entrepreneurs will ultimately assume ownership and control of the developed co-operative.

The grassroots approach is often endorsed as "good" or necessary, because it is assumed to demonstrate the potential members' needs and commitment – all it necessarily shows is members' interest. As we all know from our love life, interest is a long way from commitment. In a top-down development initial interest is generated in a different way. In principle, this approach has just as strong a chance of developing member commitment as the bottom-up approach, especially if there is a thoughtful selection process that clearly identifies a potential member group with common needs and aspirations that the co-op can meet.

The difference between top-down and bottom-up development is two-fold: first, the starting point of the members' involvement, and second, the different preliminary development work required in the early stages of the creation of the co-op. Both must move from interest to commitment. For most members, whether from grassroots or top-down processes, commitment can only be developed and demonstrated through long-term engagement with a co-op that meets their needs, expectations, and aspirations. The road to member commitment is indeed the road of the successful co-op development process.

Proactive or Reactive

Another distinction often made when describing a co-op development project is to say it is either a proactive initiative or a reactive one. Proactive is usually spoken of in a positive light and reactive as inadequate. Although there is some use for the distinction it can be misleading. The choice of description simply describes where one is sitting. Below are four examples that illustrate variations on how parties may engage in the co-op development process from a proactive or reactive stance.

Example One

From the group's perspective, proactive means future members want to create the co-op because they have a common vision of how it will meet their needs. This common vision often provides the interest with the emotional drive to start and carry on a self-directed co-op development process. In this situation, the co-op development facilitator's involvement is reactive, i.e. the co-op development facilitator is responding as an outsider who has been contracted by the group to engage in the co-op development process and who can be un-invited at any time. Essentially an outside "pair of hands," the co-op development facilitator carries out requested technical assistance as directed by the co-op entrepreneurs. To label the role of the developer as "reactionary" is not to disparage the activity but simply to note that the co-op development facilitator is responding to, not initiating, the development initiative. How they interact with the group should, of course, be thoughtful and creative.

Example Two

From the perspective of a co-op development facilitator, proactive development means taking the lead in initiating a co-op project using a model which the co-op development facilitator(s) has the experience and resources to successfully develop. It is important to note that, although I am using the term co-op development facilitator, most top-down developments are initiated by organizations that have mandates to support the creation of new co-operatives. In these situations the co-op development facilitator(s) are often part of a team of two or more people working on the development under the direction of their organization. The co-op development facilitator(s) creates the vision for the development initiative and has the responsibility and authority to design and carry it out. Initially, the co-op's potential members are in a reactive mode as an external party introduces them to the co-op initiative being supported by the co-op development facilitators. The potential members are reacting to an opportunity presented to them, not one created by their own initiative and vision. However, as co-op entrepreneurs, the potential members will eventually have to engage proactively as they assume responsibility for the developing co-op.

Example Three

When there is a meeting of common agendas and the development of a formal relationship for the duration of the development process between co-op entrepreneurs and co-op development facilitators, a proactive situation exists for both parties. A group of people independently envisions a co-operative that can meet their needs and aspirations, and their vision fortuitously meets with an appropriate co-op development facilitator (often working for an organization with a co-op development mandate) with dedicated resources and a mandate to develop this type of co-operative. Here there is a different relationship between the co-op entrepreneurs and the co-op development facilitator than noted in the previous examples; the co-op entrepreneurs provide the vision and the co-op development facilitator, while still providing technical assistance, is involved with the whole development process in partnership with the co-op entrepreneurs.

Example Four

There is also a situation which may be reactive for both co-op entrepreneurs and the support parties. An example of this is a plant or store closing where the potential members and co-op development facilitator(s) respond to an external crisis generated by the decision of another party (e.g. the owner of the business). For the potential members this is reactive because they are not responding to a self-generated creative vision with an innate interest. Rather, they are reacting to an imposed situation; one response to the circumstances, though not necessarily the most favourable or easiest, is the development of a co-op. For the support parties, it is reactive in that they are also responding to circumstances they didn't generate. In addition, neither party may be able to determine if and how the project will continue as the control over the key assets required for the co-op are often controlled by a party (such as the current owner) who has no inherent accountability or commitment to the development initiative.

Table One: Useful Distinctions

The Players

Co-op Promoters increase awareness of the co-op option and help to identify co-op development opportunities.

Co-op Entrepreneurs are the member/owners of the co-operative.

Co-op Developers/Facilitators are individuals who provide co-op development expertise to co-op entrepreneurs.

Different Origins

Grassroots refers to co-op development initiatives envisioned by a group of potential co-op entrepreneurs.

Top-Down Initiatives are driven by co-op development facilitators from within an organization mandated to develop co-operatives.

Different Contexts

Proactive refers to a project envisioned and initiated by the co-op entrepreneur(s) or co-op development facilitator(s) or both.

Reactive is when one is responding to an initiative and context created and controlled by others.

I believe these distinctions are important for a number of reasons. The grassroots/top-down distinction clarifies whether it is the co-op entrepreneurs or the co-op development facilitator who is the initiator of the project and what authority they have in determining how the development process will be carried out. The grassroots initiative often creates a fairly conventional client/consultant relationship between the co-op entrepreneurs and the co-op development facilitator. Although the co-op development facilitator shares the end goal of assisting with the development of a successful co-op, they have limited authority, responsibility, or control in the situation. The relationships in the top-down initiative are much more complex. The co-op development facilitators formally control the development process, and yet, through the process, the co-op entrepreneurs must ultimately be the ones who embrace/modify the vision of the co-op, make it their own, and assume full responsibility for its future. The relationship here is not of client/consultant but rather that of an evolving partnership with a common goal. The end-point is to have a successful co-op fully controlled by the co-op entrepreneurs.

The distinction between proactive and reactive is important, because it highlights the relationship of the co-op initiative to the external developmental context. Whether the project is proactive or reactive influences what level of control the various players have not just to internal factors (such as the group's vision, organizational development, etc.) but also the external context (such as funders or owners of critical assets) and therefore, the scope and types of challenges which must be addressed within the particular context.

A Caution

These distinctions – grassroots/top-down or proactive/reactive – although helpful in highlighting some different characteristics of different types and contexts of co-op development initiatives, all gloss over, or even submerge, the crucial common element. All co-op development projects are *creative* activities that take place within a context of limited knowledge and resources with no guarantee of success. Each developing co-op faces challenges that are uniquely its own. Both co-op entrepreneurs and co-op development facilitators must recognize this and work together to create a co-op organization that can successfully overcome its unique challenges within the context of these limitations.

Typology of Co-op Development Initiatives

Having discussed the different players, the different starting points, and the differences in how the players are positioned in the co-op development process, I now turn to the classification of development initiatives. The general typology of co-op development initiatives presented below is derived from looking at the above distinctions in the players involved, identifying the various processes that bring the potential members together, and highlighting the general relationship the co-op development facilitators and co-op entrepreneurs have to the initiative. The following six types of co-op initiatives are not prescriptive; they function as ideal types. I hope a review of these types of initiatives by co-op development facilitators and co-op entrepreneurs will enhance their understanding of the many variations in relationships that may arise between the parties. A good understanding of these relationships is an effective foundation for organizing the development process with greater clarity on the appropriate roles and responsibilities of all parties involved.

1. Self-Selecting Groups

Self-selecting groups are generated through the informal process of friends and acquaintances chatting. Through their conversations, an idea is developed that appears to have merit and meets a common need or aspiration of the group. It is grassroots and proactive, as outlined above. Virtually every type of co-op can be, and has been, created in this way.

The level of co-op knowledge and experience within a self-selecting group may vary from very little to extensive. Within the groups, leaders are often identified though the initial discussion. The co-operative idea may be just a gleam, or it may be substantially thought out. It may be based upon an existing co-op type or model, or be a unique one-off. These groups usually see it as their responsibility to secure funding to pay for technical assistance and for capitalizing the co-op.

If the members of a self-selecting group are experienced co-operators, they may have little need of co-op development facilitators. However, groups where knowledge of co-operatives is very limited will benefit from substantial involvement with co-op development facilitators. Some key challenges for the self-selecting groups are to come to a clear understanding of what is involved in creating a successful co-op, to identify what assistance they need and where to find it, and to find good co-op development facilitators and use them effectively.

2. Constructed Groups

These are groups created at the initiative of an external party – a Community Economic Development organization, a Co-op Development organization, a non-profit group, or even a for-profit organization owned by an independent entrepreneur who has secured funding from foundations or government to support a co-op development program. These organizations provide the co-op development facilitator(s) and play the role of the overall administrator/director of this top-down initiative.

Co-op development organizations here include dedicated resource groups for a particular type of co-op, associations or sector federations with a mandate to do co-operative development, as well as existing co-operative enterprises or federations of co-op enterprises that desire to create new co-op enterprises.

The potential members may be brought together from various starting points. There may be a specific co-operative enterprise already identified for which they are recruited. Sometimes the potential co-op members are recruited simply for a skills training program which is to be used as a foundation for developing and operating a co-op which uses their newly acquired skills. The recruitment and selection of potential co-op entrepreneurs is carried out by the initiating organization, and the potential co-op entrepreneurs may have little or no knowledge of one another at the beginning of the process.

At the beginnings of these initiatives, it is never certain that a committed and capable membership base will be developed as potential members are simply being introduced to one another and the proposed co-operative enterprise. The internal co-operative leaders must be identified and developed through the development process. Because of the co-op development facilitator's control of the resources and the process, the potential members usually have limited control or financial responsibility for the development process. However, at the implementation stage they are normally required to contribute capital to the co-op and to assume control of the co-op's governance and operations.

For the co-op development facilitators, one inherent challenge is to foster the capacities of the co-op entrepreneurs so they become ready to assume full responsibility for their co-operative. This doesn't necessarily mean there won't be an ongoing relationship, but that there is a necessary process of withdrawing the authority the co-op development facilitator has had as the initiator of the co-op.

The quality of these initiatives can vary dramatically. At the two poles there is the sophistication of the Mondragon Co-operative's approach with its near perfect level of success, and at the other pole, there are initiatives led by some CED organizations or independent entrepreneurs with little knowledge or understanding of the challenges in creating successful co-operatives and an often poor record of success. Between these two extremes, of course, lie the majority of development initiatives.

3. Replications or Model-Driven Development

The origin of a replication can be either a self-selecting group or a constructed group. The key characteristic of this type is a successful co-op prototype that the development initiative sets out to replicate. The knowledge of the model's key characteristics and challenges are available both to the potential members and to the co-op development facilitators. The prototype is largely free of contextual variation and doesn't require fundamental redesign because of the development context. An example is traditional non-profit housing co-operatives. Other examples include industry-specific consumer or worker co-ops, such as a gas bar or café. However, it is important to note that simply starting a co-op in the same industry doesn't necessarily imply that it is a replication as there are significant alternative approaches to developing co-operative enterprises in the same industry and with different groups of members. This type of initiative can be either grassroots based or top-down and, depending upon the circumstance, be proactive or reactive for either the co-op entrepreneurs or co-op development facilitators. However, it is most likely to be a top-down initiative led by a co-op development organization with the co-op entrepreneurs as a constructed group.

The benefits of a co-op replication approach are that successful systems, approaches, and the external context are known in advance. They can be clearly articulated and understood at the beginning of the process. Both co-op entrepreneurs and the co-op development facilitators can rapidly develop the expertise to make the co-op a success. Clear approaches for member development, members' control of the co-operative, and the role of the co-op development facilitator are known, understood, and accepted by all parties to the development.

The big challenges for the co-op entrepreneurs and co-op development facilitators are to find an appropriate context for the replication; to carry out the necessary training to ensure a thorough understanding of the governance, management, and operational systems; and to secure the required financing for the development process and the co-op's capitalization.

4. Common Interest (or Host) Organizations

Many co-operative initiatives are generated from common interest organizations. Examples include women's centres, immigrant support organizations, independent living organizations, farmers' associations, environmental organizations, etc. that bring together people with common needs, interests, challenges, and opportunities.

In these types of organizations, through the natural processes of meeting together, sharing, and discussing issues the desirability of creating separate organizations with specific mandates to meet particular needs of at least a limited number of participants from the mother organization can arise. These initiatives are sometimes conceived as co-operatives. This choice is made for a variety of reasons that may be value-based, practical, or both. Sometimes this is an informed choice and sometimes based only upon the notion that co-ops seem to be a good way of working together – whether or not the co-op model may be the most appropriate in the circumstances.

The starting point for this type of initiative has a mixture of both top-down and grassroots elements. For the co-op development facilitator, this approach may have either a grassroots orientation in which the facilitator is usually in the reactive mode, or it may have a proactive orientation where the co-op development facilitator has had a long-term association with the host organization and been proactively involved in designing the initiative.

The unique feature of these initiatives is that they are conceived and supported through the regular activities of the existing host organization. The organization doesn't have co-op development as its primary purpose and may have little or no experience in this field. Through their common participation in the host organization, co-op entrepreneurs and self-selecting groups often have prior relationships with one another and possibly some identified leaders. They will also likely continue to have a relationship with the common interest organization regardless of the success or failure of the co-op. However, there is also some similarity with top-down constructed groups as the co-op develops within a predetermined and supportive organizational context.

Co-op development facilitators in these situations often have two relationships to manage: one with the common interest organization and the other with the co-op entrepreneurs. This three-way relationship adds complexity to the process and can create challenges in organizing and supporting the initiative. As with self-selecting groups, the involvement of the co-op development facilitator is formally determined by the other parties. As noted above, in some situations the co-op development facilitator may be a full partner in developing the initiative - regardless of the formal authority.

These types of co-ops are often incubated under the legal/organizational umbrella of the mother organization, and the operating co-op may not formally incorporate. The staff of the mother organization and the designated co-op members may both be considered co-op entrepreneurs in this context. Indeed, the co-op may become simply an integral part of the mother organization and an ongoing tool for addressing the needs of members in a transition phase of life. Questions such as if, how, when, and why the informal co-op should become incorporated and autonomous may not be transparent in this context. The discussion regarding the desirability and benefits of incorporation can be facilitated by an openness to the various options with informed input from all three parties.

5. Crisis Response

Co-op development initiatives may be formed in response to a crisis situation, such as plant, bank, or store closings, or the withdrawal of government-funded local services. This type of initiative often doesn't fit either the grassroots or top-down type, because the actions of an external party are the catalyst for generating the need for the co-op. In the beginning, both co-op entrepreneurs and co-op development facilitators are in the reactive mode.

Here the decision which precipitates the crisis and the need for the co-operative is taken by a person or organization (e.g. business owner, government, etc.) that may have little or no interest or concern regarding the effects their decision has on the local parties (e.g. workers, community, etc.) who are suddenly thrown back upon their own resources. Often the potential co-op entrepreneurs would prefer for the situation to simply revert to the status quo or for a new buyer to come in and rescue the plant, store, etc. Beyond that first preference, the response to the co-op option may range from seeing it as an exciting opportunity to take on a locally controlled initiative to that of a necessary evil and the only available option.

Of course, each crisis situation has its own context. A crucial difference in crisis situations is whether or not the response must be immediate with a clearly delimited   membership base or whether a long-term response is an option with a membership open to all within the community. A large plant closing in a single industry town is dramatically different from the last bank deciding to close its local branch.

With the large plant closing, the opportunity to mount an effective co-op response is limited; the existing owners of the plant control the required assets and have their own strategic purposes for closing the facility. In addition, there are many other short-term organizational and business challenges for an unprepared group and co-op development facilitators to undertake, such as capitalization, co-op promotion to employees, etc. Significant resources must be readily available and quickly put into place if there is to be any hope of success. Hanging over the project is also the fact that the fate of crucial assets required for a positive outcome is determined by the original owners of the assets. In the worst-case scenario, the owners may actively oppose the co-op initiative, and in the best case, they will need to be brought to an understanding of the option and see it as not conflicting with their strategic objectives.

Another crisis situation, such as a bank branch closure, may allow for a more long-term response as the necessary physical assets required can be secured from sources other than the closing business. In this situation, people are not forced to leave the community, and the leadership and the necessary support for a co-op response can come from any source. A co-op start-up in a year's time will still meet the community's needs in the long-term. The co-op entrepreneurs and co-op development facilitators may begin in a reactionary mode but may soon move into a proactive mode, either through a self-selection process or constructed group process led possibly by the provincial credit union system, another co-op, or CED organization.

6. Conversion of Existing Businesses or Organizations

Another type of co-op development initiative is the conversion of an existing enterprise (not one in a crisis and/or threatened with closure) into a co-operative. Conversions can start from existing market corporations, non-profit corporations, or even government-run services. Depending on which type of organization is undergoing the conversion, the motivation and the identity of the players will vary.

A common characteristic of the conversion situation is that the source of potential co-op entrepreneurs is from within the original structure of the converting enterprise. This membership could typically include employees and customers, although other players, such as suppliers or community-based investors, may also join. Another characteristic is that the conversion must meet the diverse goals of the original owners/trustees and the needs of the potential co-op entrepreneurs. Here, as in the common interest organization type, the co-op development facilitator will have relationships with two parties and, in all likelihood, relationships with many other parties brought into the development by the original owner/trustees of the converting organization.

Conversion as a type of co-operative development highlights the role that co-op promoters play. The key to developing conversion opportunities is to communicate the co-op option to the owner/trustees and the potential co-op entrepreneurs. In doing this, the opportunities for grassroots initiatives can be generated. This is essential, as there must be strong buy-in from both owner/trustees and co-op entrepreneurs if the conversion is to move forward.

In this situation, co-op development facilitators may be in the reactionary mode. However, in circumstances where co-op development organizations have the mandate, experience with, and resources for carrying out conversions, a mutually proactive situation for all parties can be created by developing an integrated approach amongst all the parties: owner/trustees, co-op entrepreneurs, and co-op development facilitators.

Guiding Principles For Organizing the Co-op Development Process

As noted in the above typology, there are many different perspectives and starting points for co-op development initiatives. Those starting points create/indicate different relationships between the potential members and co-op development facilitators. Different needs, capacities, and access to resources of the potential members, co-op development facilitators, and key external parties must be understood and addressed through the work and its organization.

These variable starting points require that one of the first steps in a co-op development process is to understand the particular context of the initiative. Who are the potential members? What is their background, experience, skills, etc? What interests bring them together? What do they hope to get from the co-op? What can and will they commit to the process if it moves forward? What questions, hesitations, must be addressed? What do they expect from co-op development facilitators? What do external parties require? What influence do external parties have on the outcome of the initiative? What is the required timeline? Who are the potential co-op development facilitators? What is the source of their commitment? What resources do they have to offer and under what terms? Who is to do what, be accountable to whom, based upon what authority? With these realities in focus, the development facilitator can determine the parameters of the initiative and set out to organize the particulars of a specific initiative.

As apparent from the above, I believe the successful co-op development process can be understood as the journey from member interest to member commitment – members developing the skills, knowledge, virtues, and co-op structures needed for them to take responsibility for the success of their co-op and become accountable to one another for that success. It is not a given that this will happen; indeed frequently it does not happen, with the resulting non-start or failure of the co-op. To succeed requires ongoing creative action which responds to the particular challenges and circumstances of the developing co-op and its members and, of course, good fortune regarding circumstances beyond the knowledge or control of the co-op entrepreneurs and their co-op development facilitators.

The following principles are offered as a stimulus for reflection in the creation of a co-op development initiative that will enable the co-op entrepreneurs' movement from interested parties to committed members through a creative process.

1. Through all actions, ensure the co-op members are developing the needed knowledge, skills, and virtues to make their co-op a long-term success. (Love)
2. Ensure your response or guidance to the group is based upon a clear understanding of the group's needs, expectations, and aspirations at both the collective and the personal levels. (Prudence)
3. Be entirely honest (with tact) to the groups and individuals in your reactions to the proposed project. (Honesty, Integrity, Courage)
4. Assume the future doesn't have to duplicate or be limited by the past. (Faith) However, seek to expose wishful thinking, yours or the group's, and potential pitfalls. (Diligence, Courage)
5. Ensure the experience of all the parties is brought to bear on issues to assist potential members to engage and understand the situation. (Humility)
6. Work to enable members to recognize and embrace their personal responsibilities in making the co-op a success. (Love)

7. Don't let your desires and needs determine your role (Sacrifice), but rather your capabilities and the needs of the project. (Determination)
8. Provide what is needed when it is needed and nothing more. (Service, Humility)
9. Don't usurp the role of others. (Humility, Prudence)

I believe these virtues (in brackets) are required to creatively fulfill each specific guiding principle. They illustrate that co-operatives are the coming together of people in equality for mutual benefit, and this coming together is best enabled if we set the highest standards for our character and behavior in all our actions as co-op promoters, co-op entrepreneurs, and co-op development facilitators.

Starting a Co-op

Russ Christianson

C o-operative development is a complex and creative activity. This article describes five key issues in starting a co-operative: 1) identifying a real economic, social, and/or environmental need; 2) evaluating whether the propensity to co-operate outweighs individual self-interest; 3) developing an economic model to co-operatively fulfill the need; 4) ensuring leadership and management are in place; 5) raising adequate capital, and protecting and conserving cash. Ideally, just like the ideal co-op group, all of these key areas will work together as an integrated whole. If any one of these key issues is not properly addressed the co-op will likely fail. As people begin to truly grapple with the dramatic impacts of climate change and fossil fuel depletion, our need to co-operate with each other and the natural environment will become more pronounced. This could provide the opportunity for the co-operative organizational structure to become the premier model for human activities in the future.

Introduction

Shortly after completing a Masters of Industrial Relations degree in the early 1980s, and unable to find suitable employment in a labour market shutdown by an economic depression, I became an over-qualified unemployment statistic. I felt frustrated that I had "done everything right," and had not been rewarded with the promised plum job.

After months of searching, I was faced with the choice of taking an executive position with a large corporation or accepting a job offer as an underpaid manager with a small wholesale food co-operative. I chose the co-operative fork in the road and, while the financial rewards were not great, the emotional, intellectual, and experiential rewards were. That was 1984. Ever since, I have committed my time and energy to building as many co-operative businesses as possible.

Over the past twenty years, I have worked with over one hundred co-operative businesses, mostly start-ups. The majority of them are still operating; a remarkable feat (particularly when compared to the 80% failure rate of conventional businesses) for which I credit the perseverance and ingenuity of their founders, and the co-operative organizational structure, principles, and values.

This article shares some of the learning I have benefited from over the past two decades of working as a co-op developer. I feel strongly that the co-operative organizational structure will become the predominant one in this century. As we face the unprecedented challenges of climate change and fossil fuel depletion we will simply have to co-operate to survive.

Overview

Co-operative development is a creative process. It is more like a circle or a spiral than a straight line. There is no one right way to do it. Each development situation, like each co-operative and each co-operative member, is unique. A co-op developer has to be sensitive to the culture, priorities, values, and needs of the proponents. A developer needs to nurture the ability to:

- listen carefully,
- closely observe body and facial communication, and
- intervene appropriately when a group is going off track.

And a developer needs to have a sense of humour. Co-op development can be fun. If it feels like a chore, then you know something is missing.

The long-term goal is to support and encourage the co-op group to become self-reliant, take appropriate risks, and learn from their mistakes. Unlike many mainstream consultants, good co-operative developers transfer skills and knowledge to their clients. This fulfills two of the most important co-operative principles that contribute to long-term success:

- Principle Five: Co-operative Education and Training, to promote ongoing member education.
- Principle Six: Co-operation amongst Co-operatives (which I am suggesting could be interpreted in this case as: co-operation with a co-op developer).

When people think about co-op development, they usually think of a grassroots group of people who get together with an idea to start a co-op. It could be a housing co-op, a food co-op, a worker co-op, a marketing co-op, a childcare co-op, an energy co-op, or any other type of co-op. This core group of people has already determined that they would like to work together to meet a common need. At some point early on in the development process, they usually end up contacting a co-operative association or government department that in turn puts them in touch with a co-op developer.

The degree of support that a co-op developer provides a grassroots group can vary greatly. Depending on the skill level and resources of the proponent group, it can range from simply answering a few questions and pointing the group in the direction of facilitating a visioning session, writing a feasibility study and business plan, helping raise capital, or even managing the business on a temporary basis.

As a co-op developer, I think of this type of grassroots or "bottom-up" organizing as "reactive" co-op development — because I react to the group's needs once they contact me.

There is another type of co-op development that I call "proactive." Proactive co-op development describes a situation where a need has been clearly identified by a developer or a sector organization. The co-op developer completes the necessary market research, feasibility study, and organizational model and may even have written a draft business plan. Or an existing successful co-op model may be chosen for replication — kind of like a business franchise.

Housing co-ops provide a good example of a successful model that has been replicated across Canada and worldwide. The Mondragon worker co-ops and the proactive co-op development role taken by the Entrepreneurial Division of the Caja Laboral Popular (Working People's Savings Bank or Credit Union) in Spain are two other examples. Many of these proactive co-op developments have a high success rate because they draw on a proven model, professional expertise, and access to adequate capital. Mondragon has a 95% success rate.

Starting any business, whether a co-operative or a private business, is a complex human activity. It requires vision; leadership; perseverance; courage; risk taking; the ability to sell; and organizational, interpersonal, negotiation, and management skills. A single individual rarely exhibits all these qualities. However, a group of people who pool their skills, experiences, and resources will likely find all of these qualities amongst themselves. This is the fundamental reason co-operatives work so well — people work together to accomplish something they could not accomplish as individuals.

Starting a Co-operative

In the following pages, I have attempted to distil the ingredients for starting a co-operative into five key areas:

1. Identify a real economic, social, and/or environmental need.
2. Evaluate whether the propensity to co-operate outweighs individual self-interest.
3. Develop an economic model to co-operatively fulfill the need.
4. Ensure leadership and management are in place.
5. Raise adequate capital and protect and conserve cash flow.

I. Clearly Identify a Real Economic, Social, and/or Environmental Need

The starting point for any successful co-operative development project is the clear identification of a real economic, social, and/or environmental need. In most cases, co-operatives (by their very nature) fulfill economic and social needs. And, as the negative impacts of climate change, habitat destruction, and environmental pollution escalate increasing numbers of co-operatives are also focusing on environmental needs. Indeed, co-operative organizations are pioneers in fulfilling a triple-bottom line: economic, social, and environmental.

Identifying a need is often as simple as observing a gap. Usually it's quite straightforward, because it's a physiological need that is not being fulfilled – food, shelter, childcare, health care, or meaningful work. Often people have a gut feeling, or they simply know from personal experience that there is an unmet need.

On a more formal level, this intuitive or experiential feeling can be affirmed using rational models of decision-making based on the more "scientific" tools of market research, demographic analysis, and consumer research. Environmental scans or a *situational analysis*[1] can provide a framework for understanding the various factors that may influence the development of a co-operative.

In the case of proactive co-op development, the need has already been confirmed by a sector organization which may then publicize the idea to communities that may benefit from such an initiative. If the co-op is developing from the bottom-up, it is ideal to reach a group consensus that the

---

1 A *Situational Analysis* includes an evaluation of the "business" environment within which the co-operative will operate. The co-operative, competitive, economic, social, political, legal, and natural environments are all considered from the point of view of effects on the co-op's potential success and how the co-op may develop strategies to take advantage of these.

need is a real one. Reaching this consensus is a good initial (and low-risk) test of the group's capacity to work together.

2. Evaluate Whether the Propensity to Co-operate Outweighs Individual Self-Interest

While it is clear that human beings have always co-operated to survive, our dominant culture believes in *survival of the fittest*. To successfully organize a co-operative within this competitive cultural milieu, and ensure the members stick with it, requires another way of thinking and another way of doing things. Rather than base their economic model on the neo-liberal assumptions of self-interest and competition, co-op proponents need to focus on equitable co-operation. For some people this is a great leap. If people join a co-op and maintain a competitive, individualistic modus operandi, they will cause grief for the co-op and their fellow members.

If co-op proponents are only motivated by money then the co-op model is not the way to go. No one will get rich by being a member of a co-operative. There is no potential (nor should there be) for a co-operative corporation to run an IPO on the stock market and make millions for its founding members.

Co-op developers who have worked for years in the field know there are significant barriers to co-op development, including the assumptions or beliefs of neo-liberal capitalist ideology.

In addition to ideological barriers of belief, our economic and political systems have built-in biases and rewards that favour individual private property ownership, individual entrepreneurship, hierarchical and autocratic organizational structures, and short-term thinking. It is no small challenge to overcome these attitudinal, behavioural, and systemic barriers to co-operation. It takes strong individuals and a collective will to confront these barriers and insist on investigating the possibility of starting a co-operative.

If the proponents of starting a co-operative realize they have a basic need that they cannot fulfill on their own (maybe they've tried and it's been too hard) and they are willing to seriously consider working together with others, then they have the opportunity to tap into the intrinsic co-operative motivation that human beings have developed through eons of evolution.

In a grassroots situation, where founding members share a high propensity to co-operate, they will be ready to evaluate the feasibility of applying the co-operative model to their situation. Given this propensity, a real need, and a real advantage to co-operating the model will fit – in any industry or sector of activity.

There are a number of tools that developers and nascent groups can use to test the group members' propensity to co-operate. Through group process exercises and consensus decision-making, developers can work with the proponents to hone their skills and abilities in running meetings and making collective decisions. These practices can alert the developer to additional skills individuals or the group may need to develop further, or they may provide other valuable insights into the dynamics and potential success (or failure) of the group.

The group members need to:

- build trust, and determine whether they have a shared vision for the future of the co-op;
- agree on the co-op's main role or purpose; and
- share similar values and goals.

The ICA Statement on Co-operative Identity is a good educational tool and may be used as a discussion topic in the early stages of development. Another useful tool is comparing the essential elements of various organizational models – sole proprietorships, partnerships, corporations, and co-operatives.

Evaluating the group members' propensity to co-operate is the most crucial stage in bottom-up co-op development. First of all, if the group continues past this point, the investment of time, energy, and money in developing the co-op (market research, feasibility studies, legal costs, and business plans) increases substantially. Secondly, if the group moves through this stage prematurely, without truly exploring its propensity to co-operate, it may implode as a group in a later stage as the pressure increases. At this early stage, the group may benefit from training in group dynamics, democratic decision-making, consensus building, and conflict resolution. If the group continues to struggle with interpersonal conflict, it may be better to make the conscious decision to halt the development than to continue on and risk a much more expensive and public failure. Or some of the original proponents may drop out and new ones may join if the idea is sound and some members exhibit a willingness and ability to co-operate.

3. Develop an Economic Model to Co-operatively Fulfill the Need

If one views co-op development as putting together the pieces in a complicated jigsaw puzzle, this stage would be like building the outside frame of the puzzle. In some cases the pieces come together easily, in other situations it's more difficult – on first glance some pieces seem to fit, but then it becomes clear that other pieces need to be tried.

The economic model for the co-operative needs to answer a number of questions:

1. Who will the members be? What is the potential size (and demographic characteristics) of the membership and the market the co-op will serve?
2. Exactly what role or function will the co-op play in fulfilling its members' needs?
3. Are there existing competitors, and if so, what significant advantage is the co-op planning to offer?
4. What human resources will be required to run the co-op's business? What are the key roles or responsibilities that will need to be fulfilled, and how much will this cost?
5. What level of sales and expenses (a forecasted income statement) will be required to fulfill the needs of the members, break-even, and hopefully generate a positive cash flow?
6. What are the start-up costs or capitalization requirements? What will the members be expected to invest (time and money), and what are other potential sources of capital?
7. What type of co-operative is the best fit? For example, a for-profit share co-operative or a non-share not-for-profit co-operative, a worker or employee co-operative, a producer co-operative, a consumer co-operative, or a multi-stakeholder co-op?
8. What level of confidence do the co-op's proponents and the co-op developer have that the co-op will be successful?

The basic idea is to work things out on paper. If the co-op's economic and organizational model works on paper, then it's much more likely to work in reality. There are many tools to use in determining the co-op's feasibility; many of these are used by conventional businesses.

Reality Check: Many co-op proponents, like many entrepreneurs, are overly optimistic about their chances of success. It's a fine balance for a co-op developer to continue to encourage the group members and not dampen their enthusiasm, while ensuring they understand the realities of developing their co-op.

Ideally, in grassroots co-op development, the core group and potential members will participate directly in the development and evaluation of the feasibility study. In addition to testing the feasibility of the business concept, the process will also test the group's solidarity and productivity. If the co-op proponents (together with the professional support they may require) can't confidently and efficiently complete a feasibility study, it's not likely they'll be able to successfully start and operate a business together.

If the feasibility study meets the criteria or benchmarks set by the co-op proponents (together with the developer), then it can be used to form the foundation of a full-blown business plan. In addition to the economics of the business, the plan must also clearly spell out the organizational model, which in turn can be used as the basis for incorporating the co-op.

At this stage, the co-op developer and other professionals can play a key role. They can bring the experience and expertise required, as well as an objective critical eye. However, the co-op proponents need to maintain control over the process and ensure they and their professional consultants have written agreements that clearly spell out the expectations and deliverables.

4. Ensure Leadership and Management are in Place

In grassroots co-op development, the leadership abilities and skills that the co-op proponents bring (and enhance) throughout the development process (with its inevitable ups and downs) are crucial. More important than the words they espouse, co-op leaders need to prove through their actions that they have what it takes to start and oversee the operation of the co-operative.

The co-op proponents need to exhibit the character required to make the start-up and operation of the co-operative successful, including:

- Providing and encouraging the development of a shared, inspiring vision for the co-operative's future.
- Building relationships (based on effective communication, mutual respect, and trust) with key stakeholders – including members, suppliers, employees, government representatives, financial institutions, etc.
- Using good problem solving and conflict resolution skills.
- Exuding well-founded confidence that the co-operative will be successful, and using the best intuitive and rational decision-making tools to back up their confidence level.
- Exhibiting the qualities and values of co-operative leaders – honesty, transparency, accountability, democracy, equality, equity, solidarity, and humility.
- Being open-minded and creative, willing to change one's mind, and admit mistakes.
- A willingness to take appropriate risks.
- Ensuring the co-op has the necessary expertise required to move forward (including hiring external professionals when appropriate).
- Showing the tenacity and perseverance required to deal with setbacks in an effective and timely manner.

The leadership of the co-op must provide the driving force for its development and successful operation. As mentioned earlier, one of the key strengths of the co-operative model is its ability to draw together the requisite mixture of leadership qualities that are held by a group, rather than a single individual. The leadership also has to support and build the co-operative's capacity for democratic governance.

Co-operative management becomes essential in moving the organization successfully through the entrepreneurial start-up stage to the managerial, or operational/consolidation stage. The board of directors and the manager need to work together as a team to ensure the co-operative fulfills its organizational mission and purpose.

Co-op management poses a significant challenge to co-operatives within a capitalist economy. On the one hand (or so the theory goes), in order to attract "the best and the brightest" co-operatives have to compete with private sector firms for management talent. On the other hand, these managers are not likely to have any affiliation with or knowledge of co-operatives or co-operative principles.

To recruit good managers, co-operatives have to appeal to a wholistic set of internal motivations, such as the need for achievement, recognition, responsibility, advancement, and growth.[2] Enjoying the work itself is often a key motivator for managers. Good co-op managers like dealing with people, organizing operations, and solving problems together with others. An important recruitment advantage is that co-operatives appeal to the human urge to contribute to something meaningful, something larger than oneself.

Like any business, co-operatives need to provide adequate compensation to their managers. However, there is no reason to copy the ridiculously extravagant executive compensation practices of private corporations. During the 1990s, CEO pay soared by 535%, rising to 531 times that of the average employee.[3] In the words of Adam Zimmerman, former CEO of Noranda, "executive compensation is completely out of balance."[4] Co-operatives cannot, and should not, attempt to compete against private-sector firms strictly on the basis of executive compensation. Doing so would be a violation of the co-operative principles and values. The most important criteria for compensation systems within co-operatives is that they are perceived to be fair.

---

2 These motivators are a summary from Frederick Herzberg's classic article, "One More Time: How do you Motivate Employees?" *Harvard Business Review*, January-February 1968.

3 David Olive, "Many CEOs Richly Rewarded for Failure," *The Sunday Star*, August 25, 2002, p. A1.

4 *CBC Radio One* – The Sunday Edition, May 9, 2005.

When a co-operative recruits external management candidates, the interviewers should try to determine the candidates' propensity to co-operate and their openness and interest in the co-operative principles, in addition to ensuring candidates have the required skills and experience. Once the manager is hired, the co-operative will need to provide ongoing co-operative education.

Ideally, co-operatives will be able to find and nurture managerial talent within their organizations – people who already support the co-operative principles and have the quality of managerial experience, aptitude, and education necessary.

5. Raise Adequate Capital and Protect and Conserve Cash Flow

Raising capital for any start-up business is challenging and raising capital for co-operative businesses offers additional challenges and some advantages. The advantages include:

- In a co-op, members pool their resources (including knowledge, cash, and sweat equity).
- Patronage rebates (dividends to members based on the amount of product or services purchased from or supplied to their co-op) are treated as a before tax expense on the co-op's income statement. Dividends to members of agriculture co-ops are also tax free in the hands of members.
- To raise significant amounts of capital, co-operatives must have their Offering Statements approved by the applicable provincial government. In comparison, private corporations' must meet much more stringent and expensive prospectus requirements.

Like other economic enterprises, co-operatives have to raise enough capital to run their business well. Co-operatives also need to make a profit (or a surplus from operations if they are a not-for-profit) to generate the working capital and cash flow required to fulfill the co-op's objectives, replace aging equipment, and finance growth. Like regular businesses, the best and most common way to finance co-operative growth is through retained earnings.

However, it is often challenging for co-operatives to raise adequate capital in the start-up phase. While there are limited amounts of capital through co-op friendly sources (including members), the mainstream capital markets are designed for conventional corporations. Canada's investment and tax regimes do not adequately recognize co-operatives' unique structure and contribution to the common good and fall far short of the benefits showered on private corporations. Some benefits private corporations have access to include:

1. Corporations have easy access to the single largest pool of capital in Canada – the tax-free inherited wealth of Canada's richest families. These rich families spend millions each year to hire the finest (and most expensive) corporate lawyers to create complex legal structures as a way to avoid liability and minimize income taxes.
2. Corporations have access to speculative capital through the stock market.
3. All levels of government support private corporations with billions of dollars in grants, loans, contracts, tax incentives, and free business consulting advice and support.
4. Financial advisors and investment regulations strongly encourage speculative investment in private corporations.

Harry Glasbeek, a Professor of Law at Osgoode Hall, University of Toronto, and a corporate lawyer, summarizes the role of private corporations as "the primary, permanent, and very concrete tools that wealth-owners use to satisfy their never-ending drive to accumulate more riches and power at the expense of the rest of us, the majority."[5]

Unlike private corporations, whose sole purpose is to maximize shareholders' wealth, co-operatives have a triple bottom line for their members and their communities:

- Economic,
- Social, and
- Environmental.

Even with the tax and policy advantages that private corporations enjoy, people continue to organize co-operatives. Given the widely dispersed economic, social, and environmental advantages that co-ops bring to communities, tax and policy changes that encourage co-operative development are long overdue. Citizens deserve an investment environment that strongly encourages co-operative development.

Summary

The table below summarizes the five key issues I have identified for successful co-operative development and the related requirements, tools, and skills. As I stated early in this article, co-operative development is a creative process. It is not linear. If any one of these key issues is not properly addressed, the co-op will likely fail. Ideally, just like the ideal co-op group, all of these key areas will work together as an integrated whole.

---

5 Harry Glasbeek, *Wealth by Stealth* (Toronto: Between the Lines, 2002) p. 7.

Table One: Keys to Successful Co-op Development

Key Issue	Requirements, Tools, and Skills
A real economic, social, and/or environmental need is identified	• Intuition, experience, sector knowledge • Market research, formal and informal; secondary (demographics, industry publications, etc.); and primary (whole systems feedback, focus groups, surveys) • Environmental Scan – Co-operative, Competitive, Economic, Social, Political, Legal, and Natural Environments; SWOT(Strengths–Weaknesses–Opportunities–Threats) – though I find this too limited on its own • Evaluate organizational/group capacity
Evaluate the propensity, ability, and commitment to co-operate	• The co-op model is more effective fulfilling the identified need than the potential members could individually • Propensity to co-operate; co-op self-assessment • Focus on process – consensus decision-making, democratic governance • Group dynamics and trust building exercises • Shared values and objectives/goals • Co-operative identity – principles and values • Organizational comparison charts – co-operative, sole proprietorship, partnership, corporation, for-profit or not-for-profit • Second tier co-operative organization support
Develop an economic model to co-operatively fulfill the need	• Feasibility study – template outline, spreadsheet; "What if?" analysis • Market research – formal or informal • Human resource requirements and expectations regarding roles, responsibilities, and compensation • Membership benefits and responsibilities (equity investment) • Risk/return ratio makes sense (financially, socially, environmentally) • Business Plan, Incorporation, and Bylaws
Leadership and Management Capacity	• Leadership training and development • Business education and sector experience • Entrepreneurial characteristics and temperament • Shared vision, mission, purpose and values – Whole Systems Feedback • Trust building exercises and experiences • Communication skills and techniques • Clear definition of roles and responsibilities • Accountability Chart • Co-operative/democratic governance
Adequate Capitalization and Cash Flow	• Business Plan • Offering Statement • Member equity, commitment, perseverance • Legal/financial documents – member share certificates (member loan certificates for non-share co-ops), preferred shares, bonds, debentures • Financial control systems – variance analysis • Member education, outreach/communication strategies, and materials

Conclusion

Most human beings have a natural propensity to co-operate. When a community is faced with a challenge, it often finds innovative ways to work together to fulfill its needs. Sometimes these collaborative efforts lead to the formation of a legally structured co-operative. Co-op developers can play an important role in educating and supporting co-op proponents to navigate their way through the maze of starting a co-operative.

When co-op developers are working with a group, it is important to let the members know they are not alone. The co-operative model has been chosen by eight hundred million people worldwide; making it the fastest growing socio-economic movement in the world.[6] In addition to serving their members, co-operatives also provide over one hundred million jobs around the world – twenty percent more than trans-national corporations.[7] One in four Canadians is a member of a co-operative or credit union.[8]

As the human species begins to truly grapple with the dramatic impacts of climate change and fossil fuel depletion, our need to co-operate with each other and the natural environment will become more pronounced. The most important technology in this adaptation will not be hydrogen fuel cells, wind turbines, or nanotechnology; rather, it will be the social technology of creative collaboration. Co-operative organizations have led the way in co-operative theory and practice for over 160 years and have the potential to become the premier organizational structure for human activities in the future.

---

6 International Co-operative Alliance <www.ica.coop> 2007.

7 <http://www.ica.coop/coop/statistics.html> Aug 2, 2006.

8 <http://www.coopscanada.coop/aboutcoop/statistics/> 2007.

Chapter Three

Co-operative Developers: A Rare and Special Breed

Joy Emmanuel

I n our exploration of effective practices in co-operative development, we would be missing an important piece of the picture if we overlooked an introduction to developers and the variety of conditions under which they work. The domain of co-operative development is a complex web involving many players (members, developers, funders, various community organizations, customers, etc.). All of these parties must work together within varied and changing environments and engage an array of decisions and factors, both favourable and unfavourable, to support the growth of new co-ops. The way co-op developers are positioned within the field to do this work, and how they see their role, can vary substantially - both within the profession and from one co-op project to the next.

To complement the other articles in this book written by individual developers, another group of developers from across Canada were interviewed in the fall of 2006.[1] In this chapter, I present a snapshot of these eighteen

1 Although some of these developers work in francophone communities, their development work is outside of Québec. As the approach to co-op development is quite different within Québec, Daniel Côté interviewed another eight co-op

developers, including what led them to this work, how they are positioned in the field, their approach to co-op development, and a look at the many roles they play in the development process.[2] While this is not a statistically representative group, these developers were peer-nominated based on their reputation as developers. They also reflect different regions of Canada, both genders, a mix of ethnic backgrounds. They work in different sectors and they are positioned in a variety of ways to do co-op development work.[3]

As a profession, it is hard to classify co-op developers as a distinct stand-alone group; rather, they are a special mix of people who have a commitment to working with others using the co-operative model to address various economic and social needs.

Co-op development stemmed from my educational experiences and training, but it was always a passion.[4]

Preparation for Being a Developer

Canada is fortunate to have a host of highly experienced co-op developers. Although three developers in our survey had less than 6 years of experience, the remaining group had between 10 and 30 years of experience. The preparation developers had for doing this work reflects a patchwork of training opportunities ranging from the personal arena, to academic fields, to lived experiences.

Three developers claimed they were "born into the co-operative movement," as their families were deeply involved in co-operatives.

---

development experts from Québec. Their insights are presented in Chapter Five: *Best Practices and Co-operative Development in Québec.*

2 The BC Institute for Co-operative Studies thanks the following developers for their generous donation of time and insights offered in this survey. From east to west they are: Peter Hough in Nova Scotia; David Daughton in Prince Edward Island; Jim Winter in Newfoundland; Sheelagh Greek in New Brunswick; Victor Teumo, Ethel Côté and Sally Miller in Ontario; Terri Proulx, Blair Hamilton, and Russ Rothney in Manitoba; Hazel Corcoran and Yvonne Chiu in Alberta; and Gulalai Habib, Nicole Chaland, Lee Fuge, Lyn Cayo, Stéphane Audet, and Vanessa Hammond in British Columbia.

3 Co-opZone, a national co-op developer's network, lists a total of 52 co-op developers from across Canada (including Québec) (www.coopzone.coop – accessed April 5, 2007). This is not an exhaustive list but it does give some indication of the small number of people who are actively and regularly engaged in co-op development work in Canada.

4 Quotes from the interviews will be generously inserted into this article to bring the reader into close contact with the developer's true perspective. Most quotes are assigned directly to a particular individual, others are not, either because this information does not seem necessary or due to the sensitive nature of the comments and wanting to ensure developers felt free to share their thoughts and feelings.

I come from a co-op family. My first bank account was at the local Caisse Popular; it was part of a tradition of thinking collectively. I truly believe in the co-op approach. Co-ops for me are a kind of model that has been developed and tested. All the tools are there, not only to incorporate, but all the tools to help people manage properly, there are the principles, the values, the steps. We have been through more than a 150 years of co-op development experience in Ontario. Those tools don't exist in other social businesses. I truly think it is one of the best, or the best, concept out there because we have so much history and so many tools. You can be inspired by so many practices.

Ethel Côté – Ontario

No one in this group had formal training specifically to become a co-op developer,[5] however, everyone had post-secondary degrees and/or some professional training. Several people had training in community economic development (CED), community development, or a related field; others had a background in business, law, or management. Two people had experience in international development.

People come to co-op development from all different walks of life; some people have business degrees or that experience; other people may have been into social work, sociology, and a whole broad range of things; some have international development. And there are some who actually have experience doing it from the 'inside' as a member of a start-up co-op, because that's another way development happens. You come together and you figure it out, you might re-invent the wheel but you learn in the process.

Hazel Corcoran – CWCF, CoopZone

Some people upgraded their education after becoming a developer specifically to enhance their skills as a consultant.

I worked with about 30 different co-ops that incorporated. By the time I got to the end of that, I decided I should try and get some business background. I was totally self-taught. I was accepted in an MBA programme and that's when I became more knowledgeable on the business side.

Peter Hough – Developer, Nova Scotia

The most common path that led people toward becoming a developer was the experience they had in being a member of a co-op. Two-thirds of the developer's in this group had been a member of a co-op in early adulthood – while they were obtaining their formal education. Several were members of one of the early housing co-ops in the seventies; food, consumer, and worker co-ops were also mentioned. Over half of these developers were

---

5 Many, if not all in this group, have since taken professional training and workshops to enhance their skills as a developer, but the point here is that no one took training specifically to become a developer.

involved in founding a co-op to address some of their own economic or social needs and preferences. Bit by bit, their involvement in co-ops grew; they helped others form them, and at some point, it became a more-or-less official job title.

> I guess I began my life as a co-op developer without realizing it. When I went to university, the food was unimaginably bad. I fell in with a group of people who were into good food. We negotiated with the university and collectively we opened a good food place, and that was done as a co-operative.
>
> David Daughton – Developer, P.E.I.

> In the beginning it was not through an organization, but we were a group of people who started our own co-op. It was an artists' co-op at the university and we were living in a housing co-op. We ended up helping and providing technical assistance to other groups. There was a day care and a few groups like that. And through the process, I maintained my membership and I have been a member of two co-ops ever since.
>
> Ethel Côté – Ontario

Two people mentioned actually working in a co-op as a manager as part of their on-the-job training for doing development work. Eight people in this group worked, at some point, for a regional or national co-op organization – five of them still do. This further enhanced their co-op development experience, offering a more macro view of the development process.

Only two people specifically mentioned being mentored in the early period of becoming a developer.

For anyone interested in becoming a co-op developer or studying co-ops, there are few training options available in English-speaking Canada. Only a handful of courses at the post-secondary level are specifically on co-operatives. In some business and law courses, co-ops may be briefly mentioned. Thus, little formal training is available for anyone interested in becoming a co-op developer. As we see from this group of developers, while post-secondary courses may help prepare one in some respects, most people who do co-op development work learn through their direct involvement with co-ops. CoopZone, a national network of developers, is looking into ways to enhance and supplement the training of developers. Below, Hazel Corcoran, the coordinator of CoopZone, describes some of the current training options:

> There are some specific training opportunities that developers may take advantage of; for example there is programming at Simon Fraser University offering a Community Economic Development certification. There are relevant workshops offered in locations across the country. Another option is the Co-operation Works group in the U.S. They hold training sessions a couple of times a year and it leads to a certification programme. It is

fairly intensive and there's an online component. Some of the regional associations also offer training sessions from time to time. All these opportunities are listed on the CoopZone website. [www.coopzone.coop] CoopZone also hosts training conference calls throughout most of the year. Another place that people can go for some training and resources is to the Canadian Worker Co-op Federation [www.canadianworker.coop]. Both CWCF and CoopZone also hold an annual conference with workshops that are relevant for co-op developers.

How are Developers Positioned to do Co-op Development Work?

If the group we interviewed are indicative of how co-op developers in English-speaking Canada are positioned to do this work, then new co-ops benefit from the support of developers under a great variety of conditions. Before reviewing how these developers are positioned in the field, three points should be acknowledge: first, the intent here was not to provide a complete review of all the conditions under which co-ops developers work, but rather to give some indication of the wide range of circumstances in which co-op development does occur; second, because the particulars of their co-op development careers changed over time the descriptions below reflect these variations; and third, many fledgling co-ops do not even have access to a developer for technical support.

Three dominant trends surfaced in the way these developers have been, and are, positioned to do co-op development work:

1. As an independent consultant,
2. As a representative of an organization, and
3. From the "inside" as a member and/or worker in a co-op.

1. Doing Co-op Development as an Independent Consultant

Seven of these eighteen developers have worked as independent consultants doing co-op development work; some are doing so now, for others this was a particular point on their journey. These individuals have been working in the field long enough that their reputation as developers means that people often approach them to ask for assistance. However, developers were quick to point out that, like any small business operators, they must actively do promotional work to let people know of the services they offer. And, as with other small businesses, these people offer a variety of services to make sure they can get by between co-op development contracts.

If you can develop some kind of continuity with a co-op you are probably of more use than if you are doing a few days here and a few days there. If you can manage to go back and do some work every six months or so then you can see the progress. You are far enough out of it that you can actually notice the changes, but you have enough background that you can have the relationships to support them.

Vanessa Hammond – Developer, Victoria

Can I make a living as an independent consultant? The broad answer to that is yes, but it depends on the week, the month, the year. Last year, I was making a living doing co-op development and the year before - but this year I won't be. I'll be making my living doing that and a number of other things. But then I compare myself more to the sort of farming and artist community than to the civil servant community. If you're a farmer there are good years for grain, there are good years for pork, and then other years you have to drive a school bus. But you don't necessarily get out of farming. The same with being an artist. Co-op development is pretty much my vocation and I won't stop doing it just because it falls out of favour with the current administration or it's tougher to make a living at some time.

David Daughton – Developer, P.E.I.

You can't make a living at it full time, you have to have other irons in the fire. Maybe there are some people who are on staff somewhere as full-time co-operative developers, but I tend to think not. Sometimes people get a grant and so someone creates the position for a year, but on an ongoing basis it tends to be part of either a CED staff position with broader responsibilities or in the self-employed scenario, like myself. I've got a broader practice and this is one component of it. So recognizing that reality, it's not the only thing you're going to be doing, that's really important. There has to be a lot of spheres of activity.

Blair Hamilton – Developer, Manitoba

2. Doing Co-op Development while Working for an Organization

Another way that co-op development work happens is when one works for an organization whose mandate is strongly, or peripherally, oriented toward co-op development. These organizations include: regional or national co-op associations; sector co-op organizations, such as the Canadian Worker Co-op Federation (CWCF) or worker co-ops set up to do co-op development and/or community economic development (CED) work; those employed by CED or related organizations; credit unions; host organizations involved in sponsoring the growth of a co-op; and, finally, organizations with a specific mandate within which co-op development is an option (such as the Ontario Sustainable Energy Association). All but one of the developers interviewed has been, or presently is, positioned to do co-op development work from this vantage point.

One of the biggest differences (and possible advantages) of doing co-op development work as an employee of an organization is that one may be able to assist with many aspects of the development of each co-op and follow that co-op for a longer period of time. This is not to say that such is always the case, perhaps far from it, however, in general more resources are available to both the developer and the co-op as the "meter" is not continually running and inhibiting what is requested or controlling what can be offered. As one developer referred to it, this can be the "deluxe package."

> I was a full time staff person who was responsible for all kinds of things. One of the core things was to be the co-operative advisor, giving organizational, strategic and/or technical support sometimes to do with things like bylaws and incorporation processes. Really there was a wide range of things over 20 years. There is not much I haven't had a go at.
>
> Jim Winter – Newfoundland

> The whole deluxe start-to-finish scenario – taking them from a disorderly rabble to a big co-op with a huge policy manual and finally honed skills as directors – I used to do more of that when I worked in co-op housing because at the time the Canada Mortgage and Housing Corporation paid handsomely to have resource groups work with housing co-ops through that whole process.
>
> David Daughton – Developer, P.E.I.

Working for a regional or national co-operative association, or a sector federation such as CWCF, has provided many of these developers with an opportunity to view co-op development from a broader scale and ask questions around how strategies for co-op development could be advanced on a regional or sector scale rather than working one co-op at a time.

> Right now, I don't feel I am a developer in this position. I see developers as people that are involved on very specific projects. I think this position, Director of Co-op Development dwells less on the details and should be more focused on larger strategies to build the movement and the sector and create the framework that makes co-operatives grow and facilitates the emergence of many new co-ops in many sectors.
>
> Stéphane Audet – Former Director of Co-operative Development, BCCA

> We have created a movement and one of the co-op principles is to be engaged in the community, but also to be engaged in the movement. People 100 years ago or 150 years ago, when they started thinking about co-ops, they were creating one co-op and then another co-op. We are creating a movement of people who can learn from each other, or a group who can teach each other, a group who can provide the technical assistance to each other, groups who can build up the voice to be heard by government and in social society.
>
> Ethel Côté – Ontario

For Vanessa Hammond, a developer from Victoria B.C., doing contract work for the Canadian Co-operative Association allows her to work on international projects and extend her work as an independent co-op development consultant, while playing a part in supporting the growth of the co-op movement.

> One of the big differences in the work I have done in Mongolia and I will be doing in Ukraine is that I have far more input into the early planning at these huge distances than I do for something up the road. I think part of that is that there are very strong national organizations that understand the whole picture and co-ordinate the work. I think here a lot of people don't know that co-op developers exist. I think it is more haphazard here than in many other places.

One of the models for doing co-op development is the formation of worker co-ops formed by developers for the purpose of developing other co-ops and doing CED work. Three of these developers have been involved in setting up this form of co-op. In these situations, the worker/developer has an intimate knowledge of co-operatives, has access to the experience of others who also have that first hand knowledge, is able to pool resources and efforts rather than carry the full responsibility of an independent consultant, has a broader network to draw on, can build up their expertise in one area of development while their co-workers advance in other areas, and can be positioned to mentor new developers who assist with various projects. However, these co-ops can have their challenges too, such as finding compatible and experienced partners, devoting many long hours to determining the approach for their work, many of the same challenges other co-ops face, navigating the lack of funding for co-op development so that new co-ops can hire them, and there are no guarantees of overnight success. Creating these collaborative businesses has given some developers another potential channel for doing co-op development work while doing other community development work also.

> Right now, we are trying to pilot what we are calling a 'collaboration co-op,' which is a co-operative management service that is pooling management resources for a number of co-ops to work together. It is an attempt to pick up something like they've got in Mondragon in Spain where they've got large capacity that's shared in the movement and saying, 'Okay, taking that down to the microscopic level, how might it work locally?' And so just trying to take the principles and see if we can design something that we can get some traction from.
>
> Blair Hamilton – Developer, Manitoba

> Right now there are about eight service providers working with what we call the Collaboration Co-op. The co-op is basically controlled by the co-ops that benefit from the services, although there are also minority voting privileges for the service providers; so it's

a multi-stakeholder co-op. In an organizational, institutional sense, it reflects the model of trying to create co-op development supports in the context of long-term engagement and using a shoulder-to-shoulder member approach, rather than being an advisor on a short-term basis and then moving on. It's particularly significant in the inner city context that we are heavily involved in.

Russ Rothney — Assiniboine Credit Union, Manitoba

I am a chair of a new organization created a year and a half ago. It is a non-profit organization that is mobilizing the co-op movement, the municipalities, everybody involved in co-ops and CED in Ontario. But as a CED and co-op practitioner, I am a consultant working for myself. We have filled out all of the papers to probably transfer from non-profit to a worker co-op ... so that is where we are. We don't stop - till we drop.

Ethel Côté — Ontario

Working for a credit union can sometimes be another way to approach doing co-op development. Many credit unions have community investment programmes. Not all of these funding arrangements are specifically targeted toward co-ops; however, in some instances, new co-ops are included. Russ Rothney works as CED Manager at Assiniboine Credit Union in Winnipeg. Through his work he is involved with several co-ops.

I'm located in what's called the Business and Community Financial Centre at Assiniboine Credit Union, but I don't do the lending myself. One of the tricky things about that is when one staff person is providing mentorship and support of that type and then next door they are providing loans. If I was to give advice to somebody about who they might turn to for marketing advice and then that doesn't seem to work out, they could go to the other office and say, 'Why should we pay back this loan? We followed the advice of somebody else in the credit union.' So it's a fine line, but there haven't been any serious problems.

Two of the people interviewed work for a community organization and are positioned to do co-op development. Gulalai Habib[6] is a "settlement counsellor" with a background in community development and co-ops. She is doing development work as a "co-op co-ordinator" in a new co-op for immigrant women. This co-op is sponsored by a host organization that employs Gulalai to help co-ordinate the co-op.

This is more of a project co-ordination role drawing on my background as an experienced settlement counsellor with a background in community development and being a person from within the culture. My role was volunteer co-ordinator, but officially I became involved in the project in the category of my organization, Immigrants Services Society of B.C. This was totally, for us, a new area for the whole organization. To accommodate the

---

6 See the co-authored article written by Gulalai Habib and Melanie Conn on Malalay, the Afghan Women's Sewing and Craft Co-operative (Chapter 12 in this book).

job description, the title became community economic developer. .... At the same time, we are part of the national network of immigrant co-operatives, which is called ICAN, Immigrant Co-operatives Action Network. So that is part of the seed and it's a support in creating and developing this national network of immigrant co-ops. It is another area of involvement that we are working on, joining hands together to support new co-op developers based on the lessons learned from each other, we are supporting their efforts.

Sally Miller works for the Ontario Sustainable Energy Association. Their mandate is to support the generation of a sustainable energy economy in Ontario through the development of community-based sustainable energy initiatives. Sally's job title is "education director," she works with new community groups to help them set up community power associations. Although a group may form as a non-profit organization, she encourages them to move toward becoming a co-op, because it "makes sense."

We have two different categories [non-profits and co-ops]. .... The goal is that once a group really has a project underway and then figures out what form they're going to do, they tend to incorporate as a co-op. We don't have any members that have chosen not to be a co-op, because it doesn't really make sense to do community owned renewable energy unless you're a co-op. .... One of the things I do is help renewable energy co-ops get off the ground. .... I am the education director and I work with new members as they go through the various stages. That means both helping them understand...by doing trainings on community owned renewable energy and answering questions and giving them support with the incorporation and development of "Offering Statements," that kind of thing.

Across the country, many people who are positioned to do CED work may do some co-op development as part of their job. Four people in this group have worked for a CED organization.

I have worked for SEED Winnipeg (Supporting Employment and Economic Development) for three years, as a business councillor with the community and worker ownership programme. We help to develop social enterprises and worker co-operatives.

Terri Proulx — Developer, Manitoba

Although Nicole Chelan assists new co-ops in their start-up phase through her works for CEDNet in Victoria, she defines her job as a "co-op educator."

I see co-op development as a much bigger process. I would be more comfortable calling myself a co-op educator than a co-op developer. I definitely think there is a need for co-op educators out there.

Even while working for an organization — whether a co-operative association, a CED organization, or otherwise — co-op development is never a straightforward path. There may be more resources available when working for an organization; however, there may be other constraints that an independent developer will not have to deal with.

After many years of trying to support myself doing co-op development and promotion of co-ops, I officially took a 'real job' in the co-op movement. (laughter) I was as an executive director. But at that time we had few staff and were mainly managing projects. So I was executive director, but I was also involved in the technical efforts that would support co-op development. During that time it was crazy, we were managing and providing technical assistance to between 20-50 groups a year.

Sheelagh Greek — former Developer, New Brunswick

The good thing about working with an organization is that you can take on groups that have long-term development needs, so that's the advantage, but you are much more susceptible to having them become dependent on you. You have to guard against that possibility. You have to have a plan for some sort of orderly transition or skill transfer that is realistic. A lot of times we make incredibly naïve assumptions about how quickly someone who didn't finish high school may learn management skills and be able to run their own business. It can happen that we make a lot of assumptions around that. As a self-employed person now, I tend not to get into the long shots as much. You don't want to take money just for taking it. The tasks [in either position] are fairly similar, there's just a lot more clarity. When you're on staff, you're the guy who does everything, you bring all those technical pieces or you find the person who's going to bring them. When you are fee-for-service it's like, 'Well what can you afford to pay me for?' and you have a contract for services, it's fairly delineated. That makes it cleaner and you can do the same things. You can do bylaw development, articles of incorporation, group development, business planning, finance planning, and whatever else needs to be done.

Blair Hamilton — Developer/Consultant, Winnipeg

If you have a formal relationship where you're required to talk to each other once a week or once a month, that helps; the door is open and you're building that. But in many cases, particularly as an independent developer, you're getting paid for what you do for them. You might tell people, 'Call me anytime and if you've got something to chat about give me a call, there's no charge, it's part of what I'm doing for you. I'm always happy to take 10 or 15 minutes of my day and chat about any issue you've got and provide a little guidance if I can do that.' Many times people don't take you up on that. ... When I worked for the federation, I speak with people who are members, they're paying dues to the federation, then there's some expectation that they should be able to phone you up as part of your job and you're going to talk to them. As an independent developer, they just don't think about it or they don't want to bother you, so they don't. Then you get a call and discover that the reason they're calling is that they've run out of money. Well, 'You should have called me two months ago saying, we're having a real challenge in terms of making our sales, do you have any suggestions?'

Peter Hough — Developer, Nova Scotia

3. Doing Co-op Development as a Member of a Co-op

While some co-op developers work from the "outside" as independent consultants or for an organization, some developers work from the "inside," as members, and in a few cases, as employees of a co-op.

Many of these developers spoke about their early years as a developer helping to form co-ops in which they were also members. The early housing co-ops and food co-ops of the 1970s and 1980s were examples, but worker co-ops are another prominent example of this hands-on learning environment. A number of developers in this group have also been involved in developing a second-tier, national co-operative federation, the Canadian Worker Co-operative Federation, which allowed them to bring all their former training to bear in creating a model co-op that would be beneficial for developing that sector. (See the Case study on CWCF later in this volume.)

In some instances, the distinction between developer and member or employee becomes more complex and less distinct. This might occur in a worker co-op where a member is a member/worker and happens to have previous co-op development experience or is quite knowledgeable about co-ops.

As a member of a worker co-op, Yvonne Chiu of Edmonton is both a member and a worker (the co-executive director) and plays an important role in helping the co-op develop. Yvonne began as the project co-ordinator 10 years ago, and although she has played a key role in the development of the co-op, she does not call herself a developer.

> I wouldn't call myself a developer purely because I am a member of a local worker co-op. If there is any development work it is purely our own unfolding of the organization and our own efforts to truly live and operate as a worker co-op. In a way, I am a little bit of an indigenous developer, but it is often the case that my learning comes more out of my experience with the challenges and the growth issues that I have a little bit of insight to share.

Growing small-scale community co-ops from the inside-out is a process with which Lee Fuge of Victoria is familiar. Her first experience in developing a co-op came when a natural food store she frequented was going under. She and a few others came together to form a co-op and kept the store going as a consumer co-op. In that experience she became both the developer and the manager of the co-op. Presently she is involved in a management capacity with three co-ops she helped found as community development initiatives.

> Early on there was an agreement struck, that I would look after administrative things; I would be the interface with bureaucracy and potential clients, and those kinds of things. It's only been in the last couple of years in our process that some of the other members

of the co-op have stepped forward and taken on some of the responsibility for those kinds of things. I think it depends on the individual personalities involved and their skills and limitations. And it's the same from the developer's side. There are a lot of things that are needed to make the co-op work that come from people other than myself. So it's a matter of recognizing who's the appropriate person to take a leadership role in a particular situation and everybody being comfortable with that.

Although the manager of a co-op is employed by the co-op and normally takes direction from the board, several people mentioned that they have, under challenging circumstances, been called in to be the manager of a co-op during a period of transition.

Right now, I'm providing interim-management and direction for a co-operative that we helped develop through the federation. ... They were left without any management and they were in need of a lot of proposal writing and business plan writing and all kinds of things. It was quite an unfortunate moment, but I was also between things so they asked if I would take this over. For years I have provided advice to others on what to do, and now I must take my own advice. It is an interesting perspective because the relationship of advisor is always a tentative one. You're trying to sometimes persuade, sometimes direct, sometimes just be there, and sometimes do technical things for them but usually making some suggestions as to how they might proceed. Sometimes they take your suggestions and sometimes they don't. In this case, I have to take my own suggestions. So that part of it is kind of interesting. I am having to work more directly with the membership and some of it has been a little more personally rewarding to be hands on and not have to say, 'Here is what I suggest you do' and then wait to see if they do it.

Jim Winter – Newfoundland

We can see from all the above examples that there is no one pattern for how co-op development happens. The circumstances of development can be as varied as the number of developers. However, the on-the-job flexibility and ingenuity highlights the special traits required of anyone who takes up the role of co-op developer.

Developers on Co-op Development

Not only are developers positioned differently to do co-op development work there are also variations in how their role as developer is defined and how they see their relationship with new co-ops. Below Hazel Corcoran provides an overview of many of the common tasks a developer undertakes in the field.

A co-op developer is like a business counsellor who has a really good understanding of co-ops and can help a group that wants to start a co-op work through the various things that need to be done. At the start of a co-op, people are basically starting a business that's running on co-op principles. You need to be sure the business piece is going to work out; you need to be sure that the group can function as it needs to, as a co-operative, as co-op members; and that you carry out the incorporation and get the bylaws and policies in place. So those are the three key areas that a developer works in. The developer typically helps out in the early stages to get the co-op off the ground and maybe briefly afterwards giving "after-care," such as support for team management and governance once the co-op has started. But a really important thing about the developer is that they are there to facilitate the group knowing how to run its co-op and not to be there forever. That's a key part of the knowledge — how to make sure that those members understand what they need to do to run their co-op successfully in the long-term.

Having said that, I can also add that not all co-ops get started with the help of a co-op developer. In some cases people have the ability on their own and/or they can't find a developer to work with, so they just go out and do it. The only issue with that is they may be reinventing the wheel and could save a lot of time and trouble if they had some support in doing that. It's not in every case, but I think it's easier, substantially easier, and it's more likely that they're going to succeed if they can bring that experience in from somebody who's done this a number of times before, maybe has taken some relevant training, or even just training in comparable areas so they can get that support.

Victor Teumo works with a francophone co-op organization in northern Ontario. As a developer who works for an organization, his duties to promote and support co-op development are even more extensive than described above.

In my capacity as Co-operative Development Officer of the Conseil de la coopération de l'Ontario (CCO) [Co-operative Council of Ontario] my work consists mainly of supplying the technical support required by community entrepreneurs and co-operative project promoters at every stage of their projects' implementation. The duties of the co-operative developer position also include identifying which policy principles of co-operative development are applicable in the francophone communities of remote areas, especially the rural communities of northern Ontario. . . . We see preliminary evaluation as a fundamental step in assessing the technical support that will be required in order for us to provide project-promoting groups with assistance that is tailored to their needs.

En tant que Agent de développement coopératif du Conseil de la coopération de l'Ontario (CCO), mon travail consiste surtout à apporter l'appui technique nécessaire aux entrepreneurs communautaires et promoteurs de projets coopératifs à toutes les étapes de mise en oeuvre de leur projet. Ce travail de développeur coopératif consiste aussi à identifier les principes d'action en développement coopératif applicables dans les communautés francophones des régions éloignées, surtout rurales du grand nord de l'Ontario. . . . La première évaluation est fondamentale à nos yeux pour apprécier l'appui technique nécessaire afin d'offrir aux groupes promoteurs de projets une aide spécifique et adaptée à leur besoin.

As mentioned earlier, it is not uncommon for developers to hold positions within the co-op and work alongside the members to get the co-op off the ground. Below, two developers describe their role working from "inside" the co-op. In both cases, they are employed by another organization and do co-op development as part of their broader mandate to do community development.

> I do not always carry the title of developer. I consider the people in those co-ops to be the true developers. I tend not to use expressions like CED practitioner and co-op developer; I'm the treasurer and so on. I think of myself as facilitating, helping to facilitate, rather than being the developer in itself. A slight difference in the emphasis but it can have implications in terms of the style of interacting with the members of the co-ops. It means that I try to take myself more as working shoulder to shoulder in a mutual process as opposed to being an outside consultant brought in. And it's also the evolution of a management development support model, which is where you participate and you are part of the co-ops you're working with. Instead of being outside the group, you have to be part of the co-op you're working with.
>
> **Russ Rothney — Assiniboine Credit Union, Manitoba**

> I'm not a big "D" developer. … I think what I bring to the table is probably different from what most co-op developers bring. My involvement is always on the ground and long-term. I think what's missing in the system is the on-the-ground support for the long haul, the day to day participation with the people who are developing the co-op. Because we don't have a huge co-op presence in the education system of this country, most people are unaware of the co-op model. Most people aren't in a position where they can look at it and say, 'Oh yes, this is something that I understand and that I can work with.' I think it takes a long time to overcome the novelty aspect of what they're getting involved into, and some people never overcome that.
>
> I think another thing that's missing in the system is the valuing of the small bits and how their connection can be more significant than the big pieces. For instance, I think most people, when they're thinking about a business start-up think that you need a significant amount of capital, you need formal planning, and you need a lot of resources. The kind of work that I'm involved in is a matter of working with what's there and trying to leverage what's there into something greater. So you don't need the 'something greater' up front.
>
> **Lee Fuge — Victoria**

Below, an independent developer consultant echoes the view of the developer taking a moderate role and encouraging the members to take the lead.

> Often what happens is that you are called in to do a specific thing. … It would be whatever they specified. I think it is really nice if they say, 'We are thinking of doing the following, do you have any comments?' I think it is good for them to take the initiative.

I think it is good for the developer to take an outside look at it. Sometimes you might say, 'Think about doing the following in the future.' I don't think it is good for the developer to make too radical a change, but sometimes there is a bit that you notice is missing.

Vanessa Hammond — Developer, Victoria

While some developers work with separate co-ops and tailor their work to the specific requests of the group, others work with several co-ops but adopt a particular orientation in their overall approach. Below we hear from Sally Miller, who assists in the set-up of community power groups. Sally is engaged with several groups at a time and works to find ways of providing generic, in-depth information and support to each group, yet work efficiently and effectively to ensure she has time for all the groups.

I think that I am probably a little odd in that I train people and give them the tools to do it themselves. I sometimes wonder if that's really a co-op developer. . . . I think that the personal challenge is that I have to make sure to remind myself that I don't always know the answer. In order to really own it I think that people have to figure it out themselves. So even though I can make recommendations, what I try to do is give people choices when they are dealing with a problem. And to give them examples of other co-ops that have solved the problem in different ways and let them decide which one of those ways makes sense to them. One of the things that I do is listen carefully and try to figure out ways to solve a bunch of co-ops' problems at once. That's why I am doing the financing guidebook, because everybody talks about it, and its really enormously complicated. So rather than trying to learn it all myself and explain it to each of them, we have a few financial wizards who have been in the sector for a while. I am trying to squeeze the information out of them and put it in my guidebook so I can give it to everybody.

We close this section with a lengthy passage from Nicole Chaland of CED-Net in Victoria, B.C. talking about the importance of co-op educators and the potential to bring about systemic changes through the growth of new co-ops.

The way I see the type of co-op development that we need is very different from what currently exists in Canada. Let's say there are three ways to develop co-ops, there are probably fifty, but let's say there are three ways. One way is to allow for spontaneous co-op development. So somehow people find out about co-ops — that they exist. Somehow people learn how to organize themselves on their own and get to the point where they are able to write a grant application and get money and then hire a professional consultant to assist them to develop their co-op. That is one way. If I go back to the reason why I got interested in co-ops, which is sustainable economies, then to me this approach is not going to get us out of the mess we are in right now.

A second approach that I find really interesting is like incubating or spinning off co-ops. Say you have a worker co-op and the worker co-op members saw themselves not just having a mandate to employ their members but they had a mandate to create employment opportunities for community members. Say they had a business of graphic designers and in their governance plan they said, 'The maximum number of worker owners we want is 7. That's our ideal number and we are going to continually take on and mentor new people into our co-op. Not only will we train them in the work we do, we'll train them in how to run a co-op and once there is three we'll push them out the door with $500 and co-op #2 will be formed.' That is another way to develop co-ops. That's how they do it in Italy with social co-ops, they spin off new ones.

The third way to do co-op development, which is kind of the 'Moses Cody way,' is the adult education approach, which is like an extension agent. That to me is the modern day version of Community Futures [a CED organization] – if only they all had a little co-op development centre, and knew about co-ops. I would see anywhere that there is support for small business development there should be support for co-op development. I feel it is important to say that because, to me, co-op development is a much bigger process than where you hire someone to take you through the steps. I would be more comfortable calling myself a co-op educator than a co-op developer. I definitely think there is a need for co-op educators out there. ...

The point is, it is really important to ensure when a person develops a co-op it is a successful co-op, that is one really important thing. But my point is about how to create a co-operative economy. I think that is more where my interest lies. To do that you definitely want successful co-ops, but you are not satisfied with just responding to interests to develop individual co-ops. ... To me there is a need for co-op educators, to be able to go out and mentor and assist people. This is how you organize, this is how you go through a process. 'These are the conditions in our community. We are facing poverty. We are facing language barriers. We are facing lack of secure housing and these are the assets.' Do an economic analysis. 'We all spend $500/month on food. We all spend $250 on transportation. We all spend $300/month on childcare.' Do an economic analysis of the community. 'OK, let's do a food buying club which may grow into a co-op, or ok, let's start a child care co-op.'

That to me is the type of work that is missing from the co-op development field, which I call a co-op educator or community animator. ... It's that adult education piece. It is getting people to go through the steps to where they decide, 'We are a collective, we see we have a common economic problem and we have committed to a solution.' It's being able to go into a community and talk with people about their situation, their conditions, their dreams and going from there. ...

We have to get people to accept that even if they have learned English that isn't going to get them out of poverty. An individual living in poverty often will think to themselves 'I'm poor because I...' Whereas there needs to be a community organizing process that allows people to see that their situation is not an individual situation, it is part of a group, a systemic situation. So that's the community organizing process. Once people say, 'OK, so even if I learn English, I'm not going to escape poverty. This is actually our problem as a community.' Then to go from that to, 'OK, we have the ability to change our situation.' Which is another whole process. 'We are a committee. We now see ourselves as a group of people rather than a bunch of individuals. We see ourselves as a group that is able to change our situation.' Then to go through a good process - that is the piece that is missing in my view, someone who can help do that. At that point, then I see the co-op development part, the learning how to make group decisions, learning how to elect a board of directors, learning how to trust each other. I see that as all part of the co-op development process that developers do as part of their work. But it is that pre-development, that community organizing part, that needs to happen first. It is difficult because the co-op sector is interested in developing co-ops, but if you acknowledge that community organizing process is a true process where a community is empowered to make its own decisions, they may choose a co-op and they may not. So you're asking the co-op sector, who wants to see more co-ops, to invest in a community education process, which may or may not lead to more co-ops. That is one of the problems.

The Many Roles Developers Play

HELP WANTED: Seeking individuals experienced in developing co-operatives. Must be a self-starter, good at networking, and willing to advocate for others. Skills at finding money (for your salary and for the business) and locating other scarce resources are a definite asset. Being a sensitive, patient, and encouraging person who can get along with most everyone, is vital for this work. Send resume and be prepared to be on call, ready to start, when the funding comes through.

While developing co-ops has many rewards, it also has many challenges that necessitate developers be multi-talented with an array of tools in their kitbag. Helping the co-op find funding to pay you is not a joke. Many consultants must deal with this short fall. Below, a developer speaks about this concern and reveals some of the personal attributes required to creatively work under these circumstances.

One thing I wanted to expand on is when you asked me about whether I make a living as a co-op developer. I'm sitting in an office talking to you. The office rent is paid by a co-op that I helped to develop; the phone bill is paid by a co-op that I helped to develop; my car is parked in the parkade, being paid for by a co-op that I helped to develop; and my computer was bought by a co-op that I did some work for. My cell phone is the same thing. So there are a lot of in-kind resources that you can access within the field, and I believe that part of the job of a co-op developer is to develop their own role. Again, it's great if you can find a job that pays you to be a co-op developer; but if those jobs aren't around, how

> can you still be a co-op developer? What are the resources that you need? How can you
> access them without necessarily having somebody cut you a big cheque? I see my job is
> to find the money to permit me to work as a co-op developer. Groups who need the help
> of a co-op developer usually need me to figure out how to get paid for it, rather than me
> saying, 'Great, I can help you, if you can figure out how to pay me.'

While some developers may be adept at generating their livelihood in this
manner the reader should not assume that all developers are prepared to live
on such a creative cusp; however, the passage shows the ingenuity that is
required at times when working in the field. In the quote below, another developer speaks about accessing other types of resources in the community.

> In my particular case, and I'm thinking very specifically, this is a community that I've
> been in for a long time and I've become very familiar with, I think part of the value I
> have is that I am well connected. I know where a lot of resources are. I know a lot of the
> right people to call if something should come up. I'm familiar with the political systems
> and I'm familiar with the communities and the sector. I think I'm seen as being fairly
> connected here and have access to many different resources.

Networking is another aspect of finding resources and connecting people
with others for their mutual benefit. However, networking does not always
translate into direct employment for the developer. Indeed it may be more
unpaid work that they take on, yet it is a common task in which many
partake. Perhaps, as a community oriented person, it is a natural role for
developers and a definite asset. Below, Ethel Côté describes the networking
role she has embraced and how this benefits many co-ops.

> Every time I find information that could be useful to somebody in the co-op movement,
> I'm trying to send it out to them. I'm trying to connect people to save them time, to be
> more efficient. When I see an immigrant co-op in Toronto and another one in Ottawa
> who are different but have similar elements, I try to connect them, because they could help
> each other go through the different steps. ... I found out the importance of connecting the
> dots. Sometimes it could be a provincial body to a local co-op, or a big co-op with a small
> co-op, or a thinker and a doer. Just connecting the dots, I have seen how we could have
> a lot more impact if we work together than if we stay in our little silos. If people have
> access to information it could help accelerate their progress, inform them better about the
> next step, help them become inspired by another story. So that's it, be proactive to connect
> people who might take years to find each other. That's also part of the co-op principle of
> sharing and inter–co-operation.

Actively promoting co-ops may be viewed as another dimension of finding
necessary resources for new co-ops.

> My role as a developer essentially consists of presenting the co-operative model to commu-
> nity entrepreneurs and to public and private organizations, as well as to the associations

we deal with. This requires me to participate in the different social economy tables, local development tables, and economic development tables so that I have a global vision and can better share my experience with all our partners and support the co-operative promoters as best I can.

Victor Teumo — Developer, Northern Ontario

While some developers speak of the need to be "co-op promoters," others described their work as "prospecting" for co-op opportunities.

I work with a lot of projects. I'm usually prospecting and kick-starting; that's my primary role, prospecting, kick-starting, and then mentoring.

David Daughton — Developer, P.E.I.

Developers must have strong people-oriented skills. The ability to work with others from many different backgrounds and in different group configurations is key to the developer's job. Creating harmonious groups from a collection of strangers or helping people develop their own communication skills is an everyday part of the job.

As a developer, you really have to get a sense of each individual that you're working with and understand their level of knowledge and be hyper-aware of that because the rest of the group is going to have their own level of knowledge. So you are the one that is watching everybody and saying, 'I think the question here being asked is this,' or, 'I think that perhaps so and so is not understanding.'

In one group I worked with, they didn't know each other very well at the beginning and so it was easy for me to be able to be the one saying, 'I think what is happening here is this.' They ended up being comfortable with themselves and each other, but I had to do a lot of group facilitating and really get to know each person individually, and they weren't focusing on that so much because they were trying to get their own opinions across. . . . Some people just don't know how to work in a group and some people can if they're shown how to do it. They really want to, they just don't know how. Of course, the people that absolutely can't, they won't be in that group for too long.

Terri Proulx — Developer, Manitoba

Being a "bridge for people" is how Russ Rothney defined his role of engaging people in a positive manner and helping to build supportive relationships within the co-op.

Often I am introduced as being a treasurer or helping with financing for the co-op. So people often assume that basically that's my major accomplishment and I often end up being a bridge between people within the co-op along the human relationships side. The challenge is, there are so many things that get peoples' backs up that can undermine a co-op or any other situation, and so it's understanding why people get stressed out and what can be done about it or approaches that can help out. It becomes a personal challenge to me if other people that I'm working closely with are struggling because of either work relationships or personal stress, which typically has nothing to do with the co-op at all. That is the challenge, to stay on board with people who are sometimes struggling in personal relationship situations and encouraging others to help them as well in the same way. I never thought of my work originally in that way, but when I stand back I have to say that helping, bridging, and encouraging other people to bridge, you can't really say there's anything more important than that, even though people think of me as I said, more going in with technical skills.

One developer relates these people skills to bringing the co-op values and principles into the core of the co-op relationships.

Trying to develop that community spirit. Trying to help people work through how they are going to live out those seven international co-op principles, I find that a really useful tool.

Vanessa Hammond — Developer, Victoria

While connecting people to one another may be a rewarding part of the job, being the one who feels they have to say, 'This isn't going to work' is a difficult role to fulfil. Several developers spoke about this challenge.

There are a lot of consequences to every decision and it is really important that the developer knows what they are. I am always looking forward to see the consequences and having to say the hard truth. It happens in a lot of co-op groups, but I've also seen many local proprietors and partnerships as well. It is just such an idealistic mindset that you're not being honest with yourself. 'Here's the business and I can make this work. I am going to give it my everything. I love my co-workers and I am going to make sure they are treated well. I am going to have all this respect for them.' I think that you've got to always be providing information and saying, 'I think you guys should have an employment agreement in place. I think that you should have a termination agreement in place.' I think you always have to be realistic. ... You've got to really be the person who's really grounded and really looking at all possibilities and providing everybody with as much information as possible. A lot of that can only come from experience; it can only come from doing the work itself to say how groups have worked. I think you've always got to be the realistic one.

Sometimes it is hard for me to deal with this as the reality. I would rather just say, 'Yes you can do it' and be their cheerleader and be their friend. But I think sometimes you really have to be the realistic one and say, 'This is not going to work you guys. You can't just get this loan from here, because what happens if you don't have a solid business plan in place yet or you don't have the capacity to be accepting this order, and that sort of thing?' You really have to be the one that understands the business from the beginning until they do.

Terri Proulx — Developer, Manitoba

Below, developer Peter Hough elaborates further on the concern of being the "realist" by framing this role within the ethical context of being "professional."

> *I've been a trainer. I've been a mentor. I've been a business planner. But basically my first role is always as a professional. And that has ethical requirements in terms of how I should deal with people. That role always requires me to be honest with them about what I think of what they're proposing to do. Be honest with them over whether I even think a co-op is a good idea for them. That professional attitude is essentially the one that I try and bring to the table in dealing with any of the issues that I am working with as a developer. That's kind of the overriding foundation for what I would do.*

Another way that being a professional was described was the sense of always working to upgrade one's training and credentials.

> *I try to be as professional as I can. I buy books like crazy, everything that's coming out. I'm trying to continue to train myself, inform myself. I just want to try to do my best in different ways to support development and promote co-ops as best as I can. I try to be more professional, be more aware, be more informed, be more educated - it's a self-development process.*
>
> Ethel Côté – Ontario

How can one find resources for the co-op, for your salary, build people skills, promote the co-op, be the one who makes the tough calls, be professional in all matters, and still be there to support the co-op members at the end of the day? The last passage touches on the mentoring role developers play in encouraging the group along but guiding them from their vision toward their future goals.

> *I think the first thing is validating what people have already done – unless there is something absolutely appalling. If people have made a decision to do something and they are doing it, then a lot of what people need is encouragement. That is the mentoring aspect. There is no particular need for me to prove that I know more about co-ops than somebody else does. They know more about their business and what they want to do, so I think supporting that is really important.*
>
> *Along with that is always looking at the task from their point of view and what else you can do to be useful. Take the opportunity to say, 'Do you have any other questions?' or, 'What do you think you will be muddling over in the next six months?' Always leading them into the future and always leading them back to their vision. 'What was your vision? The questions you are asking right now, will they help bring reality to that vision?'*
>
> Vanessa Hammond – Developer, Victoria

In some ways developers may be the unsung heroes of the co-op movement as they help to advance a cause they believe in and are deeply committed to – whether resources for doing this work are plentiful or come out of their own pocket. When you stop to take the full package into account, developers are truly a rare and special breed.

Chapter Four

Critical Issues in the Life of a Co-op

Joy Emmanuel

I have always felt there is an inside and an outside to the co-op movement. I liken it to a book called 'The Little Prince.' In the early part of that book the prince is trying to describe perceptions and how people see into things - or not - depending on their capacities. He draws a picture that looks like a hat, and it turns out to be an elephant inside of a boa constrictor. Co-ops and the co-op movement are like that, the snake from the 'inside' and the snake from the 'outside' look very, very different. All the principles, philosophies, sense of community, and all those things that are frightfully important, are usually only perceived as important by those who are inside the movement. People on the outside of the movement don't see that. I find this a bit of a stress ... and yet, the values and principles are often not useful when trying to work with people who <u>need</u> co-operatives. They're much more practical and self-serving, and say, 'What is in it for me? Will I sell more? Do I get something cheaper? Where is the economic benefit?' It is only after you've had the experience that you start to feel all warm and fuzzy; it's like Church - almost. So, I find there is always this tension amongst people involved with the development side, as to whether the values and principles rule or the business requirements dominate.

— Jim Winter – Developer, Newfoundland

hat is the process by which a group of people come together and moves from a conglomerate of assorted individuals into a collective unit working effectively and harmoniously toward a common goal? What are some of the key characteristics of co-ops that set them apart from other social economy organizations? What makes a new group grow up into a co-op rather than a non-profit society or a corporation? What is the "glue" that holds the co-op together through the formative period and sets out the foundation for a healthy enterprise? How are the co-operative principles and values, that are "frightfully important," integrated into the business side of the co-op in such a way as to be intricate to the structure of the collective enterprise? This chapter focuses on the "inner life" of the co-op and the intricate relationship between co-operative processes and co-operative structures, which intersect to form the foundation of the co-op model. We examine the inside workings of co-operatives and explore many of the "soft skills" of group development, as well as the "hard skills" of operating a business or collective venture – keeping in mind that a co-op is a certain type of social economy organization and thus has unique features and particular challenges.

Throughout Canada, co-op developers are positioned in various ways to work with new groups; they may work as independent consultants, be employed by co-operative or community organizations, or work in the field of community economic development.[1] Those who do co-op development work have a great variety of skills, experience, and perspectives on how to work with a group and assist in the process of shaping the group into a successful and effectively run co-op. This chapter brings together the insights of eighteen developers from across the country who were interviewed in the fall of 2006.[2] As was commonly acknowledged in the interviews, there is no "one way" to work with a group – every start-up is different and the circumstances surrounding the development can vary a great deal. This material is set forth as one plausible and cohesive way to approach understanding the intersection of co-op processes and structures.

In the interviews, developers were asked what they felt were three critical issues that affected the success of new co-ops. The first part of the interview was open ended, allowing them the opportunity to identify what they felt was most important. The second part of the interview offered a list of areas in the life of a co-op, any of which they were invited to elaborate on if they felt it was important to do so. The survey provided hundreds of pages of notes that were then sifted through to identify common critical issues that affect start-ups and creative solutions to address these concerns.

This chapter focuses on critical issues that pertain to the inner life of a co-op. Unlike an acorn seed, which always grows up to be an oak tree, there

---

1 For more on the different ways co-op developers are positioned to do development work, see Chapter Three in this book - Co-op Developers: A Rare and Special Breed.
2 See footnote 2 in Chapter Three for a list of developers who were interviewed.

is no guarantee that a group of people united by a seemingly common goal will go on to be a co-operative, let alone an effective and successful one. In "listening" to the responses of the developers who participated in the survey, a subtle, yet vital, thread kept surfacing around the interconnection between co-operative processes and co-operative structures in the very early stages of the group's development. That thread is flushed out in this chapter by synthesising the various insights and comments offered by developers.

The Context is Always Different

The context within which each group forms is unique. A particular group of people are coming together at this time, within a specific set of circumstances, in the hopes of achieving a certain goal – and they are considering using the co-operative model as the vehicle to embody their vision. This is where culture, geography, conditions, type of co-op, experiences of potential members and the developer, how the developer is positioned to work with the group, and so much more all comes into play and makes a difference in the process and the outcome. The model has to be tailored to the particular group and the specific context to ensure there is a good fit and the seeds of co-operation take root. The process and formation of the same type of co-op (i.e. a worker co-op) can vary substantially from one group to the next. Even two co-ops in the same community can be very distinct.

It takes skill and foresight to bridge the experience and expertise of the developer with what the members of the group are ready for and can appreciate; keeping in mind that the group itself is not homogeneous and people bring different things to the process and take away different information; in other words, the "inside" and the "outside" are very different.

> Doing co-op development is a contextual thing. It depends very much on many factors. The context that I have worked in and have puzzled over and theorized about forever is a challenging one. Newfoundland is a population of dispersed people. An afternoon gets me barely a third of the way across the province. There are many isolated communities that do not have much contact with each other, and therefore, the sense of community is very different.
>
> Jim Winter – Developer, Newfoundland

Each co-op has its own path to follow; the developer is the guide who helps discern part of the trail but s/he must also listen closely to the group and take other factors into account to help them discover their particular path. Although many developers claim they have no "established practices," meaning a set order of things to do in the same way every time, they did caution that there are certain steps that do need to be covered. The order of the steps, group development, particular policies, timing, process, these are the types of things that will vary from group to group.

> *The right path is their own path. It is important that they follow their own path but going step-by-step and having the technical expertise that is needed, yet adapted to their reality. Sometimes as technical assistants we try to fit everybody into one model, when each co-op initiative is different. The context will be different, yet the concepts will be the same.*
>
> Ethel Côté – Developer, Ontario

Even in instances where someone is working with a number of co-ops that are all in the same sector, the process of implementation can be quite different. Sally Miller helps develop community energy initiatives in Ontario – many of which adopt a co-op model for their organizational structure. Sally has developed a series of training sessions and a package of materials she offers to each group; however, she cautions that a recipe won't do the trick. Her "model" is more about process.

> *They have to do a lot of it on their own and figure out their own way of doing it. I think co-ops are very strong and work really well because they are community based, but that means that they have to do a lot to make their own decisions and figure out their own way of doing it. I believe in providing them with more of a process approach so that they can make good decisions, rather than telling them that they have to do it like all the others. If we look at all of our co-ops, they are quite different. They are even structured differently. Some of them are not-for-profit and some of them are for-profit.*

Housing co-operatives across the country and many natural food co-ops in Ontario were also started by providing potential members with a "whole package" of excellent suggestions and tools on how to make it work. Future co-op members could then tailor the resources to the particulars of their group.

A Tale of Two Co-ops

I find it very different from group to group. It always surprises me. I had a group really struggle with how much their membership shares should be. This group really wanted to find a way to keep out people they didn't want. Another group really wanted to find a way to not give any patronage back to members. With the first group, I wasn't sure if a co-op suited them, while the second group wanted a strong democratic process with all the money going back to their co-op so they could develop it further and follow the principle of co-operation among co-ops by helping set-up another worker co-op. The two start-ups were very different – polar opposites.

Terri Proulx – Developer, Manitoba

Motivation

Every group has a beginning point – a moment when a spark is ignited that sets things in motion and eventually draws a group together. What has brought this group of people together at this time? What motivates individuals within the group, and what is the seemingly common motivation that has brought them together to work on this initiative? Just as the circumstances surrounding each new group varies and needs to be taken into account, the motivation of the group is also important. Over one-third of the developers we interviewed noted the importance of motivation as a factor affecting the development of a group.

Is this group of people coming together to resolve some economic issues they are facing? Is this group coming together because they like each other? Are they coming together even though they do not know one another or might not fully trust one another and have even been competitors prior to this? Are they coming together because they need each other and feel they have no other option if they are going to address their individual needs and concerns? Co-operatives are well known for helping people meet their economic and social needs; however, if the people who come forward are in difficult economic circumstances, their focus may very well be on addressing their immediate needs, which may take precedent over long-term planning efforts and strategic decisions that will be required to build the co-op.

As one developer said, "There is no need for judgement; however, unless you know why they are coming together, you might not be able to make sure that you tap into all of the reasons co-ops work or don't work." For example, the group may benefit from more consensus type decision-making, but they may feel they cannot take the time to really develop the skills of working in this way. Or, their motivations might influence decisions around how much money to put in reserve for the co-op before patronage funds are paid out. Unexamined assumptions about what motivates people to form the co-op can surface with unexpected consequences later in the group process. "All of a sudden, you have a whole diversity that could be detrimental. It doesn't mean it is but this is where the developer really has to be able to put everything on the table in ways that people are comfortable and willing to share what is really going on."

Within a capitalist economic model, competition and individualism are promoted and rewarded far more than co-operation. Developers noted that "fierce" individualism, placing a high value on independence, and a lack of experience in working co-operatively are culturally inhibiting factors when it comes to pursuing collective goals. Although many people turn to the co-op model, perhaps "because they like it ideologically or in theory,"

> **Decision-making Exercise One**
> We give everyone two different cards with two different colours. We invite people to say, 'In expressing my opinion, I'm coming from a green card,' which is a worker's perspective. Then when someone holds up a purple card, 'Now I'm talking as an owner.' Why do we do this? Despite our success in the last few years, we are still struggling with financial security. Most of my colleagues are still working part-time with the co-op while maintaining a day job to survive. As a worker, often the hours that are distributed to us are scarce and uneven. When we talk about hours or talk about putting more resources to one community vs. the other, it does require us to step up a bit and to understand the differences among the communities. Because as human beings our tendency is to really only recognize our own reality, saying, 'OK, my community has these issues and I need to be recognized.' That is important, that is a reality, but as an owner you have to step up a little and look at all of the communities.
> Yvonne Chiu — Multicultural Health Brokers Co-op, Edmonton

many people find that it is not always a straightforward process. Indeed, the crack in an over-idealistic image of how co-operatives work can bring some people to "turn their backs on co-ops in frustration and say, 'Ah, nobody wants to share, nobody wants to co-operate,' and walk away from it."

This scenario comes as no surprise to many experienced developers. Some recognize the coaching element that is important in the development process and take steps so that setbacks, personality clashes, and disillusionment do not sour the process. At times, the role of the developer is to "facilitate the development of momentum" and knowing what important steps the group needs to address next, and what skills and resources are required, allows the developer to ease the group over difficult spots.

Several developers spoke about the importance of the group having positive experiences early on in the project as a way to build a feeling of success and trust and to counteract the pull of individualism and competition.

> Many people have had no collective experience. Somewhere in the early stages of the project, it is critical for people to have some positive experience — that sense of, 'We did this together and it worked.' In my view, co-operation is not necessarily a natural matter and creating a co-operative success early on in the process goes to levels of trust and building common goals.
>
> Jim Winter — Newfoundland

Another developer emphasized the importance of having fun as a way to build community and create positive experiences to offset the difficulties along the way.

We are often so serious as a group because we are struggling. We are addressing difficult issues in the community. We are knocking on doors working with the system, trying to effect change. Change comes slow and we feel like we are running out of time. It is not helpful for our relationship that whenever we come together we are always solving problems. It doesn't really help. We do much better when we have fun activities and more time for joy. That is true.

Yvonne Chiu — Multicultural Health Brokers Co-op, Edmonton

David Daughton, a co-op developer from P.E.I., feels there are two critical issues influencing the successful start of new co-ops; they are: being encouraging of the groups ideas and helping them access start-up funds so they can explore the possibilities further. He cautions against pre-maturely dismissing the new group by using guidelines that are too rigid.

What I try to do is be a resource to the group in terms of maintaining their motivation, encouraging them, and finding the resources they need to move forward. Essentially, I find that new groups need somebody to be encouraging and helpful. Once they're able to move to the next stage, you can shoot down their ideas with all due diligence, but if somebody walks through your door and says, 'We're thinking of doing this thing that we think would be really neat,' and you say, 'Oh great, come back to me with a 30-page business plan' — you never hear from them again. So I try to facilitate and encourage as my first step.

Russ Rothney, CED Manager with Assiniboine Credit Union begins from the starting point of uncovering the passion in the group and leveraging that force as a motivating factor for individuals and the group.

There's no point in starting any business, let alone a co-op, unless you've got a team of people who have real passion for the particular roles, not just a co-op, but for the particular roles that they will play in that co-op. ... The basic logic is that nobody excels at something unless they love doing it; that goes for every specific role within the co-op, whether it's the financial role, product development, customer relations, marketing, or whatever. ... Everybody has different orientations and a team approach is needed. If you haven't got that and people are being misled into thinking, 'You can do it, you can do it,' without stopping to think what it really means - it can be trouble. So my number one focus is to figure out who is there to sustain and drive this business. Without that, it's a no-starter to me - even if you've got the most beautiful business plan in the world.

Following on that note, other developers echo the view of the merits of screening initiatives that are proposed to them. While it can be difficult to tell a group that one does not think this project has the right mix of people, resources, and a sound business plan to get off the ground, many developers recommend this forthright approach rather than generating false hopes and hardships after valuable time, money, and resources have gone into the initiative. Gulalai Habib, former Settlement Counsellor with the Immigrant Services Society of B.C., looks for the strength in the group and the broader community support for the co-op initiative.

> Of course, there are many, many ideas, but we need to be sure which ideas have a future, which ideas have the support of the community and service providers, and the right time and momentum, and the strength within the community.

Co-operative Values and Principles

Central to the co-operative model are values and principles that are defining features of co-ops around the world. These core values and principles have been identified as key to the successful life of co-operative ventures since formal co-ops began in the 1840s. They have also been important in shaping and defining relationships within co-operative movements from the local to the international level. According to the International Co-operative Alliance, "Co-operatives are based on the values of self-help, self-responsibility, democracy, equality, equity, and solidarity. In the tradition of their founders, co-operative members believe in the ethical values of honesty, openness, social responsibility, and caring for others."[3] In addition to these values there are seven "principles," referred to as the "Co-operative Identity Principles," which are guidelines for how co-operatives put their values into practices.[4] While Co-operative Acts and Regulations go into much greater detail about how a co-op functions, legislation should not contradict these defining principles and should allow co-operatives to be autonomous, self-governing organizations that have a unique internal structure different from other social enterprises.

Adoption and incorporation of these values and principles into the processes and structures of a new co-operative is an art and a true test of the developer's understanding of the intricacies of the co-op model. As you will hear in the excerpts below, it is a challenge to keep the balance between the business demands of the enterprise and alignment with the core values and principles; however, there is consensus among the developers that this is what makes the co-op model not only unique but a positive force in our society. Some developers introduce the co-op values and principles right from the beginning; others find ways to incorporate them each step along

---

3 http://www.ica.co-op/co-op/principles.html (October 2007).
4 These seven principles are elaborated on in the Introduction to this book. Briefly they are: (1) Open and Voluntary Membership, (2) Democratic Control of the co-op by Members, (3) Member Economic Participation, (4) Autonomy and Independence, (5) Co-operative Education, Training, and Information, (6) Co-operation among Co-operatives, and (7) Concern for Community.

the way. From time to time, co-operative organizations have been able to offer training workshops and programmes specifically on the connections between the values and principles and everyday actions and policies of the co-op.

If I'm doing an introduction to the worker co-op model, the first thing I do is actually talk about what a worker co-op is, just in terms of very basic structures, and then I talk about the co-op values and principles and have them relate these back to a worker co-op. There is no question that co-operative values and principles play a role in terms of articulating the issues and educating people around those issues.

Peter Hough — Developer, Nova Scotia

I keep coming back to this balance between weaving in the co-op values and principles and making sure there are solid business practices. How do they relate? That is missing all over the place. I bring that to the table when I am doing development work because I don't want them managing in the same old ways. I want them looking at their decisions about how they hire, how they fire, how they choose their suppliers, everything with: How does that fit with being a co-op?

At one point when I worked in co-op management and educational training, we created a management development programme. It was four days. We took the co-op values and principles as threads and took it from the individual, to the one-on-one, to the group, to the intra-group, to the corporate level. Everything had the co-op values and principles as the thread. I've never seen anything else like it since then.

It is a constant battle within every co-op, no matter what type. But it has to eventually have a strong sense on both sides. At one moment you might have to make some choices that you are not really happy with, you have to make them knowing you are making them against something you believe in. People forget they have to be a viable business, too. I think we can change a lot in our world, but until it is changed, and as we keep working at changing it, we have to keep things afloat too. It is the balance between good business practices in today's business environment and the co-op values and principles.

You have to go both with the co-op side and the business side in my opinion, but without the values and principles you just end up doing things the same old way.

Sheelagh Greek — Former Co-op Developer, Atlantic Canada

There is a lot to nurturing the right relationships within a co-op. There is so much about internal development, too. Of all of the organizational types that exist, co-ops require us to be more spiritually mature human beings than any other organizational format. That takes support. I don't think too many of us realize, once you become a member of a co-operative it is about committing yourself to spiritual growth because it is about a shared community, it is not about singularly — myself doing well. It is about us all doing

well. For that part, I haven't seen much support or existing technical resource or processes.
I think we have a gap in the sector around that.

Yvonne Chiu – Multiclutural Health Brokers Co-Op, Edmonton

Initial Meetings – Preparatory Work

From forming the initial vision, through to the feasibility study, the business plan, and eventually opening the doors of the new co-op there are many steps and details that must be worked through. While there may be the temptation to jump right into action or make the decisions that seem easiest, developers caution that it is important to take the time to go through all the steps rather than adopt a "fast food mode." If steps are skipped there may be problems that will not show up until later and then they may cause more havoc than if the appropriate time is taken early on. While all of the steps are considered important, developers also affirm the importance of the steps being adapted to the particular group.

Having good process from the start and developing clarity around the vision of the co-op are viewed as critical pieces in laying the foundation for the new venture. Some developers advise that if the group can establish a conscious decision-making process they will save a lot of time and "not get bogged down in the first stage." Having a process up front where they "really identify the vision, mission, and values" is viewed as one of the criteria between successful co-ops and those that struggle to address everything that comes up.

Understanding from the start what a co-op is, the values, the principles, and the history helps the group to discern if this model is right for them, what their roles and responsibilities might be, gain a sense of the different mode of operation that makes a viable co-op work, and become acquainted with the notion that they are not reinventing the wheel but they are becoming part of a whole movement that exists with resources, success stories, and experiences that may benefit them. When it comes to doing the prefeasibility study and business plan, not only will the group have a better grasp of how the co-op model works but this understanding can be built into each step. Some steps might take a short time or a long time, the key is that it is the right time for each group and that all the steps are taken.

What influences success? I think it is really to understand the different steps as a collective that they have to go through before they establish their co-op. In a co-op, you are building from the first day that people are sitting at the table. ... Sometimes we jump from the step of creating the group to a business plan. Then we notice, going through the business plan, that we are not sure if this is the right structure, when we should confirm that in the feasibility study. Honestly, all the steps are important. It has been documented in many books and through many trainings. If they skip the first step, then maybe they will skip some others. Then they incorporate a co-op and they figure out it is not what they really need. That is the worst enemy of the co-op movement - when a new co-op has been created but it is not active because it was not the right venture to realize that mission or that mandate. Those failed ventures leave scars. It is very hard after that to explain what a co-op really is and how it should be implemented. Yes, all the steps are important.

Ethel Côté — Developer, Ontario

Developers emphasize the slow but thorough approach as a way to acclimatize new members to a "culture of co-operation" and help establish a way of working together that is different from their previous workplace culture.

There is a great misconception about what co-operation is, especially the discrepancy between co-operative theory and co-operative practice as it applies to managing collective projects. Communities present real problems to the start-up of new co-operatives. Even though co-operatives may be well established in the community, there is still the very real problem of education about co-operation.

Victor Teumo — Developer, Northern Ontario

Nicole Chaland has done Community Economic Development work with marginalized populations in B.C. and other parts of Canada. To solidify the group and affirm common values and priorities, she advocates a "community education" approach in the early interactions with potential co-op members.

There seems to be a gap in raising awareness. It's not like there is a programme to let people know what co-ops are. It's that adult education piece that is needed. It is getting people to go through the steps to where they decide, 'We are a collective. We see we have a common economic problem and we have committed to a solution.' It's being able to go into a community and talk with people about their situation, their conditions, their dreams, and going from there.

Early Assessment

The Early Assessment Stage provides an opportunity to determine what factors may hinder or support the success of the new co-op. It can be beneficial in a number of ways. It provides the developer the opportunity to become better acquainted with the potential co-op members; to assess the skills, aptitudes, and interests of the group; and to determine the needs and resources for the co-op that might come from within the group. Working together, the developer and the new members have the opportunity to assess the viability of the co-op's vision, assess the market for the co-op, identify resources and technical support, determine the legal structures for the new co-op, decide if this is the best model for what the group wants to do, identify benefits for co-op members, and test the waters to see if the co-op can attract the number of members it needs.[5] Developers vary in how they name this stage and how many separate stages the process is broken into, both CoopZone (a developer's network) and the Co-operatives Secretariat refer to a seven-step process. In this section, we present helpful comments and insights developers offered on critical aspects of the early assessment stage.

Self-Assessment of member's skills can be a good way to get a feel for the strengths of the group and the interests of members. Russ Rothney, CED Manager, Assiniboine Credit Union, adopts a self-assessment approach by identifying a list of ten or eleven key areas (some of which are sub-divided). Members then rate themselves on a five-point scale. Key to this approach is that people feel the safety and support to acknowledge what they are good at and what they like to do.

> We have had great experiences with this approach, including where we think people might be embarrassed because they won't show high. Actually, some people have been really moved to — almost allowed to — acknowledge that in certain areas that's just not them. Yet they've been expected to perform in that capacity. What it means is, if you take that approach, often people shift where they might go and then they can function much better. If it's a shift that goes right outside of the business context, well, it's better to have a friendly parting early on and they don't have to feel that there are these expectations on them and that's just not them. So it works well. The way I look at it, you can deal with a skill shortage through training and you can deal with experience shortage through mentorship, but you can almost never deal with an aptitude or passion shortage — if it's not there, it's not there.

This approach parallels the Sirolli model,[6] which emphasizes "not pushing people," but being "responsive" to them. It is very different from a top-down job creation approach.

Developers talked about the importance of having an array of skills within the co-op, particularly at the board level. Having people with a finance background, people who are good with the media, people with business and

5 There are various on-line resources to help members and those working with new co-ops determine the various areas that need to be assessed in the early development of the co-op. Common resources are: CoopZone: http://www.CoopZone.co-op/en/developmentpath, Co-operatives Secretariat: http://co-op.gc.ca/index_e.php?s1=guides&s2=kit&page=intro, Provincial Co-operative Associations, The BC Institute for Co-operative Studies (BCICS) has on-line resources and a Manual called: Co-operatives by Design — see: www.bcics.org, also see the Tools section of this book.

6 For more information on this approach see the Effective Practices web page resources at http://bcics.org, under Research.

marketing skills, or people with co-op experience brings valuable resources directly into the co-op. Some developers suggest the array of skills they feel will be helpful and some brainstorm about this with the whole group. Why do this intentionally? "Because people who are struggling to start a new co-op often don't think of it proactively, they just kind of wait to see what comes along." Suggesting the group approach someone from the local credit union to be on the board is also a recommended practice. If there is no one on the board with certain skills the co-op needs, the new co-op might look at hiring someone with those skills.

> I think that you have to have some skills in the group. They have to have some compe-
> tency either in the work that they are going to be doing, whether it is farming or the arts
> or whatever, and there has to be some business competence too. ... In a big corporation
> you have specialists who do different things. So it makes a lot of sense in a small business
> to let people do what they are passionate about, then hire someone who is passionate about
> bookkeeping to do the bookkeeping rather that expect someone who is a brilliant cobbler
> to also do the website.
>
> **Vanessa Hammond – Co-op Developer, Victoria**

Another asset that is important to have in the group is people with leadership skills. It was noted that a sound leadership practice involves going beyond relying on one charismatic leader. People spoke about effective leadership and times when they have encountered a leadership vacuum. It was recommended that the early assessment stage is a good point to provide encouraging and constructive feedback on the leadership capacity in the group. (Leadership is discussed in greater detail later in this chapter.)

As well as the internal strengths and weaknesses of the co-op, a key aspect of early assessment is to survey the external environment that may affect the new co-op's growth.[7] What opportunities will support the development of the co-op? What are the barriers or blocks that might threaten the new initiative? What government polices support and promote co-operatives? What programmes support co-ops, particularly in the sector of the new co-op?

The Canadian Worker Co-op Federation (CWCF) recommends the early assessment step as a viable way for the group to see if their business idea has merit. What do people involved hope to get out of the co-op? Do they have a realistic view? Are there sufficient resources within and outside the co-op to support the idea moving forward? The assessment process provides the group with critical information to decide together if this initiative can work for them. CWCF offers a pre-feasibility checklist to assist new groups

---

7 This can be the appropriate time to do an environmental scan. See the Tools Section of this book.

and has some funding available for worker co-ops to do a pre-feasibility study. If the results are good, the group can apply for additional funding to proceed to the next stage. If the assessment shows mixed results, the group is encouraged to consider making amendments before proceeding.

Working with francophone co-ops in northern Ontario, Victor Teumo, acknowledges the importance of the early assessment as an indicator of what support his organization (Conseil de la co-operation de l' Ontario) can offer new groups.

> We see preliminary evaluation as a fundamental step in assessing the technical support that will be required for us to provide project-promoting groups with assistance that is tailored to their needs. For this reason, we created a framework document (Cadre d'intervention du CCO dans les projets co-opératifs — Framework for CCO Action in Co-operative Projects) which allows us, as co-operative developers, to target our actions appropriately according to the promoters' needs and the resources the co-op already has to develop their projects.

> La première évaluation est fondamentale à nos yeux pour apprécier l'appui technique nécessaire afin d'offrir aux groupes promoteurs de projets une aide spécifique et adaptée à leur besoin. C'est ainsi que nous avons crée un document cadre (Voir en annexe le document : Cadre d'intervention du CCO dans les projets coopératif) qui nous permet, en tant que développeur coopératif de cibler nos interventions en fonction des besoins des promoteur et des ressources qu'ils disposent déjà pour développer leurs projets.

Making sure there is a match between the people, a realistic vision for the co-op, the business or activity plan, and the expectations and rewards of those involved is an important benefit of the early assessment process and can test the skill and wisdom of the developer.

If the feasibility step reveals that there are problems, this does not mean that the co-op should not proceed; it may be an opportunity to revise the plan for the co-op or address shortcomings before proceeding. At least, the co-op members have information to help them make an informed choice at this point. If steps are skipped and the co-op starts anyway, "after two or three years they may still feel they are at step one because they never honed the process."

The Business Plan

When the co-op has clarified their vision, mission and values, and gathered sufficient information, it will be time to develop their business plan. Development of the business plan can be a real test for the co-op members to move from the broader vision of the co-op into the practical, grounded reality of a workable plan. "There are often times when people get really jazzed about the co-op values and decide to start a co-op without thinking through what the business is. A sound business idea is definitely a key factors in the success of the co-op."

Cautions were raised against moving too quickly and jumping ahead to the business plan before earlier steps were solidly in place. While it is viewed as beneficial to involve people with an expertise in business planning and have the technical support of a developer, the importance of all board members having a grasp of the business plan and operations of the co-op was strongly recommended. "It is a key tool but when it is done by a consultant, and people don't know what is in the plan, it could be a tool that just stays on the back burner and nobody will use it. They won't have that very good tool to make sure people in the co-op work together to make it happen."

Building Community – The Group Process

Completing the above steps with any group is not a mechanical or straight-forward process. It is not sufficient to have a list of the development steps and follow them religiously. To assist a group in truly forming a collective enterprise that is able to effectively function as a co-operative requires that co-operative processes are utilized and adopted along with building co-operative structures. Developing a highly effective co-operative involves the artful practice of community building. The business plan may work perfectly, but if the group is unable to implement it because they are not working together as a homogeneous unit, things may quickly fall flat.

The inter-personal and communication skills involved in working together cannot be underestimated. As the above example points out, this dimension in the life of the co-operative is often the Achilles' heel that disrupts the smooth, perhaps successful, functioning of the group.

> The issue of group dynamics is to me both fascinating and challenging and essential. . . . People operate differently in a group situation than they do individually. And you need to understand how that works and to work with it and build the group rather than allow things to break down. . . . Those skills to me, in the context in which I have worked over the last 20 years, have a tremendous amount to do with the success or failure of a co-op.
>
> Jim Winter – Developer, Newfoundland

Confronting our own internalized patterns of competition, individualism/separatism, or our (un)comfortable familiarity with hierarchical structures is never easy. Developing the capacity of a high functioning group takes time and patience on the part of everyone.

I find the skills of working together are a huge issue. Lots of people have either worked for people where they've been told more or less what they're supposed to do, or they might have been self-employed where they essentially decided what they wanted to do. Suddenly finding one's self in a situation where your are trying to decide collectively what to do and how to make a collective decision is challenging and requires a whole set of skills and the ability to communicate and listen and problem solve — for many people it's a brand new experience.

Terri Proulx — Business Counsellor, SEED, Winnipeg

How does one promote a co-operative culture? What are some of the essential components that must be present? For some developers, effective practices in co-op development means paying as much attention to building "people skills" as one gives to the practical and technical domain. How people treat one another and the language they use can be indicators of the norms that are operative in the group. Making the assumption that co-operation comes naturally, may not always work in the best interests of the co-op.

What makes a co-op work is the people involved and their level of commitment. What makes co-ops not work is the people involved and their level of disfunctionality. ... Those people skills are the real skills that we need. Yes, we need to know how to write a contract, we need to know how co-op law works, and we need to know other stuff, but, just as important, we need to be able to listen.

Lyn Cayo — Former Developer, B.C.

Creating a co-operative culture is a very important and complex part of the life of the co-op. Developing "corporate responsibility where everyone has

I worked with a co-op start-up once - one of the loveliest projects I ever had. It was a group of eight or nine workers who were displaced and they decided they wanted to start a little dairy goat industry. One of their members, who was very much a leader, was really interested in doing the processing (the making of the mild cheese). They thought they might be able to learn the animal husbandry involved in raising goats. It was a sweet project. They produced some of the most beautiful goat cheese I ever tasted. But their inability to work together and to build amongst themselves the skills they needed was what basically brought their downfall. We struggled so hard trying to get them to trust each other. How do we build consensus? How do you build respect for each other? Using 'I' when you should instead of always saying 'you.' Ultimately they just became paralyzed with this and couldn't move forward. And that was such a lovely project, and three or four years of work, and a lot of money spent.

Jim Winter — Developer, Newfoundland

the right to contribute and everyone takes responsibility for contributing" is part of the goal. Taking small steps to bring people together who have formerly been competitors, or who may not even know one another at all, requires a lot of care and attention. Some developers adopt a strategic approach, going slowly, step-by-step through the stages, building community spirit along the way. Testing the waters early on is also recommend as a way to get feedback on how strong the collective spirit is within the group.

> Take small steps at first, making sure everyone is on-side and feels a sense of accomplishment, then take further steps. Have a 'test' to see if there truly is a shared vision and commitment, or whether people are just going along with things because they don't want to be left out - especially in cases where the co-op is intended as an alternative economic venture following the closure of a major employer or the decline in a resource sector. Better to test and assess this early on rather than after a lot of time and money has been invested in the co-op. ... Mutual self-interest is what this is about, but self-interest is a big part of the 'mutual.' We all have to agree that we are all going to benefit from this, and they have to say it to each other as well. That is a whole world of group development.
>
> Jim Winter – Developer, Newfoundland

Leadership

Leadership can make or break any group – co-ops are no different. Strong leadership can be a critical factor in the success of a new co-op; a lack of leadership, poor leadership, domineering leaders, and power struggles can undermine the progress of a new group. Developers must be prepared to assess and work with the leadership dynamics in the group.

Because co-operatives are set-up as democratic institutions and draw on the co-op identity principles, what defines leadership within a co-operative can be a little different than in other organizations. Developers noted that leadership styles within a co-operative must be "inclusive and participatory." They described co-operatives as a place where everyone has a responsibility to share, and given the need for an array of skills on the board, it is most beneficial if leaders emerge in different areas of the co-op. Other important leadership traits that were noted include having someone who people feel comfortable with and trust and someone with the "ability to stand behind others" while they go through their own growing experiences.

In assessing the leadership in the group, some developers look for people who already have leadership experience at the community level and/or people who have the depth and capacity to grow in that area.

Two roles that were highlighted were the need to have "advocates" and "moderators." Spokespeople are often required for co-ops, people who are capable, confident, and able to meet with community leaders, the media, and potential funders. On the other hand, having someone who is able to moderate discussions, encourage sharing, and draw the group together to find solutions is important. Sometimes the group doesn't develop because they choose their most dynamic leader to be the chair and expect that person to "be charging forward on the white steed and speaking on their behalf; however, eliciting the ideas from others is often missed out. Yet, moderating, sharing, and finding solutions together is essential to the co-operative collective approach."

When there is a lack of leadership within the group, developers must assess how to best encourage the development of leadership and ensure the group is not overly dependent on them. It is important to have momentum and direction come from within the group, because "at some point this burgeoning little group has to be set adrift on its own and somebody has to be at the helm that they trust, otherwise it won't move, it will just fall in on itself." In situations were there is an obvious leadership vacuum, one developer takes the approach of discussing the roles and responsibilities of the co-op with the group and clearly pointing out what is needed; "you try to turn the idea of the co-op into a series of strategic moves that are doable for them." He then leaves it with the group to talk over and get back to him – if no one contacts him, it is a clear indication the group was not ready to proceed.

While lack of leadership is a concern in some groups, the other extreme is when the leadership is domineering, even abusive. This can be a personal challenge for the developer as they are often the ones who know that things are amiss and will address the issue. One developer encountered circumstances where the leader "acted like a little king." Another developer was called in to help a co-op and found a situation where one person had decided they wanted to set up a co-op to accomplish personal goals and then ran the co-op like a private enterprise. When the developer attempted to clarify how a co-op operates, she was verbally attacked and dismissed. Before long the co-op dissolved. Member education, especially at the board level, emphasizing that there are different roles and shared responsibilities in the co-op may help to address these situations.

While self-confidence is a key trait of leaders, it was noted that self-esteem is often missing in groups of people who have been marginalized in society. Being sensitive to how discriminatory social barriers may have impacted group members, and then providing opportunities to bolster their self-confidence, are key practices when working with some co-op start-ups.

Leadership and power relations – that's huge and complex – and can involve dynamics like colonialism, racism, sexism, classism. People who are not from middle class back-

grounds often do not have connections to fall back on if they go wrong. They're not always use to being expected to be leaders. They can walk away when a door opens for them, leaving some middle-class CED practitioners terribly frustrated, but at the same time, the same people can be very determined and strong in their own way and creative. It is really important in working with groups that involve that sort of diversity, to make sure the people who are perhaps least likely to step forward in a formal leadership role, that their thinking is supported and encouraged to a maximum as a very deliberate strategy. Otherwise, the inequalities of our society will just play themselves out in the co-op. . . . If one goes in and is looking for someone who's got the normal middle-class orientation, being able to talk at meetings and all that sort of stuff, those people are going to get left behind. They really are towers of strength if you can work with them, but also realize they are putting up with a lot of pressure that we are not.

Russ Rothney — Assiniboine Credit Union, Manitoba

To address leadership development and help members identify the skills and attributes required in different roles, some developers hold a brainstorming session with the group to get all the ideas on the table about what is needed. One developer recommends rotating the position of "chair" early on to give various members a feel for what this role requires. For some developers, it is a standard practice to do sessions on leadership skills and governance. "You give it all to them and sometimes people will absorb it and sometimes they won't. But my job is to make sure that they are aware that these are the roles that need to be fulfilled." In one instance, a "train-the-trainer" model was used with women's groups (some of which were co-ops) to make the most of limited resources and overcome the challenges of reaching many small groups spread over a broad geographic area.

As people find the role that is right for them they may increasingly "feel good about themselves, and what they're doing, and they will become leaders." Whatever approach is used, member education around leadership and how a co-op works can be a vital, on-going aspect of the developer's work. The point that developers emphasize the most is the value in educating people that "in a co-op everyone is entitled to an equal voice, and sarcasm and abusive language is not appropriate."

Governance Matters

The governance structure is one of the key features that makes a co-op distinctive from other social economy organizations. This is where the values and identity principles are internalized into the operational structure of the co-op. It takes time to understand and appreciate all the intricacies of the many bylaws, policies, and decision-making processes; however, if structures are adopted in a routine fashion, the project may end up being a co-op primarily in name and the inner life of the co-op may be stifled. It can be a temptation to quickly push through bylaw development for the purpose of early incorporation and funding, or overlook the opportunities here for member education because it is considered to be too complex and dry. Many co-ops end up mechanically adopting the "default rules" set out in the governing legislation without the benefit of understanding how those rules and policies embody the larger vision of what a co-op is all about.

> Everyone should understand what is needed in governance. That is not emphasized enough. There is a lot of emphasis on marketing and management, and that is important, but they are aspects of implementation. It's the governance aspect that holds the vision of the co-op. The governance is the glue that holds it all together.
>
> **Vanessa Hammond – Victoria Co-op Developer**

> Governance is key. Some co-ops are not co-ops any more because either they are managed only by staff and the members don't play an active role, or the opposite, the staff are struggling with a board who is trying to micromanage and they can't move, they can't breathe.
>
> **Ethel Côté – Developer, Ontario**

One important aspect of governance is clarifying roles and responsibilities so that everyone knows what is expected of them and what they can expect of others. Even though co-operatives are about "the collective bus," it is important to clarify specific roles and decision making power pertinent to those roles in regards to the operation of the co-op. For example, the governance structure helps clarify the distinction between the role of the board and role of the executive director or manager. As mentioned above, being clear on the domain of the director in relation to the board is very important. One developer pointed out, often people do not realize how important good governance and good decision-making processes are until something goes wrong. (See Chapter Nine for more on Co-op Governance.)

Consensus Decision-making

One aspect of governance is decision-making. A mode of working together that is commonly adopted in co-operatives is the consensus approach. However, developers caution that it is a common misconception that all decisions must be made this way. Indeed, that would be cumbersome, even detrimental, for most co-ops. Sometimes people may think the co-op is going to "have some great big love-in and people will make all these mutual decisions together" or people feel that "everybody should know every aspect of the co-op," but that is not always the most practical way of working, or the most sustainable.

When and why should co-ops adopt a consensus approach to decision making? Peter Hough, a developer with over 20 years of experience – particularly with worker co-ops – offers these guidelines:

> It depends on the circumstances. Achieving consensus is the best approach for moving forward, particularly in worker co-ops. But it really depends on the issue and how fundamental the issue is. On fundamental issues it's extremely important that you've got the support of your membership. If that means a consensus process to get there, then I think it's definitely worth going that route. One of the great things about co-ops is that the members get to decide what they think is best for achieving their goals and objectives. The issue is: how can the members understand the relationship between making effective decisions – however they're going to do it – and producing effective results? If you create a decision-making process that produces ineffective results for the co-op, whether it's consensus, whether it's democratic, or hierarchical, that's not a good result.

Sheelagh Greek, another long time developer, echoes this position. She adds:

> Ultimate consensus is almost an impossibility. However, the first step is knowing what consensus is, the next step is knowing what kinds of decisions they need to make by consensus. ... Sometimes people get really hung up and think, 'If we don't do consensus then we are not really a co-operative.' It is important to help them understand it is a process that takes time and exposure to consensus decision making in a safe environment first is helpful, and then in the practical environment that they are working in. I have used a number of tools that help them realize how little they access each others knowledge and skill. This is where the co-op developer needs to be there as a coach.

In worker co-ops it can be particularly challenging to make some decisions, especially around the allocation of hours and benefits when members are both owners and workers. Yvonne Chiu, who works with and is a member of the Multicultural Health Brokers Co-op in Edmonton, outlines some of their challenges.

> When we are engaging in a decision-making process, of course it has to start with our own individual sense of reality as we experience it, but once we move on in the decision making, we have to balance that out with thinking about the needs of all. It can be very difficult. We are often more comfortable with a clear hierarchical structure and sometimes we just want to give up and say, 'Put this policy or this decision in place and we will just live with it.' But because we are operating in diversity, it is my personal view, it is dangerous to apply only one black and white policy or have only one way of deciding.

While developers recommend consensus for some decisions, there seems to be agreement among those who participated in this study that co-ops do not need to use consensus all the time. A healthy co-op is structured such that a manager can make decisions that pertain to the day-to-day operations of the co-op, decisions can also be made by committees, and the board can make decisions using various democratic procedures – including the consensus model.

Member Education and Training

Member education is another aspect of governance. Each step along the way is an opportunity for member education and training on what a co-op is and what it means to work co-operatively and effectively together. Developers emphasize that education about the different stages of development, roles, responsibilities, values, and principles is something that the co-op should do on an on-going bases. Educating the founding members is one stage, but members will come and go over time, and "if we've got new parents coming in and they haven't signed on with their heart and soul to those old agreements, then guess what? We're in for a shake-up!" On-going member education and new member orientation is one way to maintain the stability, strength, and vitality of the co-op.

If the developer or someone working with the co-op does not do foundational education around what a co-op is and how it functions, then, where will members get this essential information? There are few courses at university or in business schools on co-operative structures and processes. If we rely on the assumption that we all

> ### Decision-making Exercise Two
> I have a couple of exercises I like to use to help people understand the different types of decision making processes. One of them involves putting jelly beans in a clear plastic jar, then you have a big string of beads, and you get a big stack of paper. You have to know how many beads are on the string, how many pieces of paper are in the stack, and how many jelly beans are in the jar. You break the large group up into three small ones. Then to Group A you say, 'Ok, this jar of jelly beans represents your decision to moving your operations from Winnipeg to Brandon. You have to use consensus and determine how important that is.' Then with the group that has the stack of paper, 'Ok, you are a committee and the stack of paper represents this decision ….' And the beads represent another kind of decision and, 'You have to make this decision using majority rules.' At the end you talk with the group. 'How did you feel? Did you feel pushed to move this decision forward and implement it right away? Did you feel heard? Did you feel respected? It is a fun way to help people understand different ways of making decisions.
>
> Terri Proulx – Developer, Manitoba

know how to co-operate – the co-op will, at times, be on shaky ground. One developer recommends that to preserve the integrity of the group as a healthy functioning co-op, there may be a need for member education for seven or more years – at least until the co-op is able to host their own training workshops.

> As far as governance and understanding the co-op structures, members need to have regular education. They need to really want to know how co-ops work. They need to want to be curious about co-ops in other places, and find out what the best practices are, and how they can adapt those for their own co-op. They have to have a co-op curiosity. When you see people who are fascinated with co-ops as a business form, they are absorbing and integrating things that other people have done, and they are avoiding pitfalls that other people have fallen into.
>
> Vanessa Hammond – Developer, Victoria, B.C.

Member education is viewed as a key reason why it is important for new co-ops to work with a developer. Member education covers all aspects of the set up and operation of the co-op, plus an introduction to co-operative processes and to the movement itself – of which they are now a part. If this foundational education "doesn't happen, you really don't have a co-op."

Conclusion

In this chapter we have covered many aspects of the inner life of a co-op. There are certainly many other areas and layers to developing healthy, effective co-ops that could have been discussed; some of those topics are covered in other chapters of this book.

All of us have been a part of many social groups and organizations: some more formal and structured than others, some more effective than others, and some with more positive life experiences than others. Although as human beings we do act co-operatively to varying degrees – at least most of the time – to truly work co-operatively and be effective requires training and awareness to develop a "culture of co-operation." The co-operative model, which has developed from decades of experience and experimentation, provides not just a framework and a set of structures but a body of knowledge that nurtures the social element of co-operative practice.

What makes a co-op a healthy functioning collective enterprise is more than a formula for structuring and adapting the co-op model. The inner life of the co-op has many layers and dynamics that, if carefully nurtured, can enhance the co-operative spirit in each of us and lead to a healthy and successful new co-op.

Chapter Five

Best Practices and Co-operative Development in Québec

Daniel Côté

A discussion of co-operative development practices in Québec must begin by situating itself within a broad perspective. Doing so will allow for the identification of major practice types and their related competences, such as facilitation, stakeholder dialogue, and accompaniment/support. In order to enhance our reading and understanding of these practices, it is also important to go from a global view to a closer look at specific models and experiences; the discussion of this second aspect will involve an examination of the practices of distinct co-operative models, such as solidarity co-operatives and worker-shareholder co-operatives (WSC). These two co-operative models are not well known as they were only recently created (the late 1980s for WSC and the mid-1990s for solidarity co-operatives); however, they account for the majority of co-operatives created in Québec in the last few years. A third area of co-operative development in Québec also requires a more detailed analysis. This is the practice of converting capitalist enterprises into (worker) co-operatives, which is based on unique practices that need to be documented and explored.

In order to provide an in-depth examination of effective practices, two applications of the co-op model are discussed in-depth: health co-operatives and ambulance co-operatives. The case of health co-operatives offers the dual advantage of shedding light on both the development of the solidarity co-operative model and the emergence of co-operatives in the health sector. For their part, ambulance co-operatives shed light on a sector that has been reorganized by favouring a co-operative formula and has witnessed the conversion of several private companies into co-operatives, made possible because of the involvement of workers' unions as partners.

Best Practices: An Overview[1]

To ensure co-operative development three core practices need to be considered—facilitation, partnership and dialogue, and accompaniment. There is also a fourth core practice, namely the development of appropriate tools (models, laws, fiscal, etc.). The Co-opératives de développement régional[2] (CDR) embrace these four core practices.

Facilitation

In Quebec, there have always been people in the field working to make the co-operative model known. CDRs organize galas and events, publish newsletters, and give talks (to such organizations as the Chamber of Commerce). In doing so, they inform, sensitize, and educate others about the co-operative formula.

The first two target audiences are the co-operative sector and economic and social development actors.

1 The author would like to thank Armand Lajeunesse (Executive Director, CDR de Lanaudière), Guy Bisaillon (Senior Advisor and former Executive Director, CDR de Montréal), Guy Provencher (Senior Advisor, CDR du centre du Québec – Mauricie), Patrick Duguay (Executive Director, CDR Outaouais – Laurentides), Claude Dorion (Executive Director, MCE conseil), Richard Lapointe (CSN), Pierre Lamarche (CSN), Yves Létourneau (Financial Analyst, Capital régionale et coopératif Desjardins, and former Senior Advisor, CDR de Québec), and Sylvain Parenteau (Treasurer, Sixpro, Board member, CDR centre du Québec – Mauricie). These resource people generously agreed to answer many questions and share their vast experience in co-operative development.

2 The CDRs are co-operatives aimed at co-operative development. Their membership is composed of those co-operatives evolved in their territory. They have existed since the mid-80s and count on a budget of several millions dollars to support their activities. The provincial government provides most of the budget for the CDRs; however, the programme they belong to is being managed by the «conseil de la cooperation du Québec».

The attitudes, behaviours, and skills required for facilitation begin with respect for people. Each person's limits and talents must be recognized. It is necessary to be able to generate interest and to share information and ideas. It is thus not a case of doing "sales." Facilitation work requires a lot of energy as the co-operative formula, which remains poorly understood, needs to be continually explained.

Successful facilitation requires a mastery of presentation techniques. A key element of this success is a pedagogical approach. Facilitators must know how to plan their interventions. They have to target their public well and make the distinction between responding to a request and initiating a solicitation activity. The main audiences are made up of development agents, such as Local Development Centres (*Centres locaux de développement* – CLD) and Community Development Societies (*Sociétés d'aide au développement de la collectivité* – SADC),[3] professionals (lawyers, accountants, consultants, and so on), business associations, various sectors, and the general public. For example, the facilitators have to participate in Chamber of Commerce lunches as speakers, as well as in meetings with CLD agents.

Facilitators must also rely on various tools such as fliers, information kits, PowerPoint slideshows, documents, etc. These facilitation techniques require systematic development and training.

Stakeholder Dialogue

It is also crucial to participate in resource pooling and network synergy, in other words, bringing together all the actors concerned with community development. Co-operative developers must create a dialogue with representatives from CLDs, SADCs, regional elected officials, etc. There are two "natural sites" for dialogue (regional and sectorial sites) and it is absolutely necessary to participate in them. The facilitators from the CDRs play a role and participate in the dialogue as experts in the area of co-operative development, and they are recognized as such.

"Dialogue sites" can be territories or sectors (such as health, education, tourism, etc.). Representatives from all of these "sites" call upon partners to help with the success of their undertakings, and CDRs must participate in this effort. There is a danger of devoting too much energy to various undertakings. However, doing so is unavoidable at times; otherwise, less can be done. Everything intersects. As such, it is necessary to be involved in various actions. It is necessary to be present when major issues are defined

---

3 The Réseau des SADC du Québec was born of the merger, on May 6, 1995, of the Community Business Development Centres (CBDCs) and the Community Futures Committees (CFCs), which became, for the most part, Community Futures Development Corporations (CFDCs).

and decided upon, both to exercise influence and to be influenced. When the question of co-operative development arises, all these actors will know to turn to CDRs as the major player. Partnerships are thus fuelled by the various stakeholders, which leads to mutual help and collective development in which all parties have a place and a role.

Dialogue requires sitting down with the major actors to discuss common projects which are not necessarily co-operative in nature. All the actors concerned by the project in question (leisure, tourism, industrial, commercial, etc.) have to be involved.

The expertise needed to play a key role in dialogue begins with creating a broad vision of development. This can be difficult. This vision has to be multi-sectoral and territorial. It is also necessary to show the relevance of proposals, suggestions, etc. The individual who represents the co-operative sector has to be acknowledged as a relevant, complementary resource. This co-op expert must also demonstrate a capacity for understanding the concerns of the other stakeholders. Otherwise, they will not be attentive to the CDR's concerns. This is a win-win context. There is thus a required presence in all sectors and regions.

Accompaniment – Support

It is also necessary to accompany or support co-operative entrepreneurs. In this context, it must be understood that few experts (notaries, lawyers, accountants, industrial commissioners, etc.) have a good understanding of the co-operative model. It is thus essential that co-operative development experts assume this support role. As such, it is necessary to develop relevant expertise in the area of accompanying collective entrepreneurship.

The act of accompaniment should also be conducted in dialogue with other stakeholders since it requires their support for the project (co-operative in this case) to be successfully implemented. It is thus important to seek out those who can help the project succeed.

Here as before, successful accompaniment requires that the co-operative expert display a mastery of facilitation skills. It is important to have a good understanding of the project in question, as well as to ensure that the co-operative formula is adapted to and meets the needs of the entrepreneurs. In short, the facilitator must quickly assess whether or not this is a case of, and for, collective entrepreneurship. The expert must then present the different co-operative models that might apply (producer, consumer, worker, or solidarity), co-operative principles, and the capital structure specific to the co-operative formula. After this, the creation stages can begin.

The first step is a prefeasibility study. It is important for the co-operative project's promoters to gather information and conduct the necessary analyses of the market, production costs, profit margin, and so on. Otherwise, there is no viable enterprise. The second step involves an application to incorporate a co-operative and the formulation of a set of bylaws. Lastly, the co-operative's founding general meeting is held.

While CDRs do not conduct feasibility studies, they will assist the project's promoters and point them to available competent experts. The latter's contribution will help develop the project.

The writing up of the bylaws is done by the project promoters, with help from the CDR team. This is an important step because they have to justify the choices they make. They also have the opportunity to begin the learning process (and the discipline that goes with it) about meeting agendas, electing a meeting chair, etc. In this way, they begin to practice implementing the co-operative formula.

On average, it takes three to six months to get to the stage of setting the project in motion. The expert from the CDR and the project promoters meet every two or three weeks.

Roughly one in ten projects makes it to the start-up phase. This 1:10 ratio corresponds to the ratio for collective entrepreneurship in general. Before determining whether a project is genuinely co-operative, the co-op development expert needs one or two meetings, which help eliminate subsidy seekers, promoters looking for "fiscal dodges," and so on.

On-going accompaniment support can last one or two years following the start-up. The facilitator ensures that meetings are properly held. He or she steps in if needed to ensure that practices are observed and to help implement work discipline. This can easily take an entire year. Following this, the co-operative actors should be up to speed and able to assume responsibility for preparing statements, reports, projections, elections, etc. In other words, an entire cycle is needed. In the ensuing years, support occurs as a function of the co-operative's needs. Because of uneven resources, the different CDRs have different practices for follow-up. This is an obvious weakness given the risks in the first five years. It would also be quite appropriate to offer training activities to various members of the co-operative. Indeed, some CDRs have a resource person whose only responsibility is to follow up on co-operatives created with their help. As well, there are programmes to help defray the costs of this kind of follow up.

There are roughly 160 co-operatives in the territory covered by the Québec-Mauricie CDR.[4] Advisors do the follow up for co-operatives that have been in operation for fewer than two years. During this period, the CDR representative participates in a few board of directors meetings. The CDR has a resource person who checks up on these co-operatives. They are called

---

4 For more on this CDR, see the paper by Christian Savard in this book.

in once every six months. A co-operative diagnosis is performed, which focuses both on the associative and the financial aspects. Outside resources are called in when the co-operative experiences difficulties and a recovery plan is formulated.

The CDR must also invest in the development of the "associative life" of the co-operative (education, information, consultation, and decision making). This requires the CDR to provide training about the roles and responsibilities of co-operative directors and members. This training should cover the bylaws, management of member contracts, the founding general meeting, annual financial reports, and remittance of documents to appropriate bodies. The CDR has to ensure that the board of directors quickly becomes autonomous.

The expertise required for effective accompaniment includes:

- Mastery of the introduction and application of the co-operative formula,
- Mastery of the components of an effective enterprise (i.e., business plan, functions, etc.),
- The ability to go beyond the literal legal aspects (co-operative law and status), even though accompaniers (CDR experts) are references in legal matters,
- Accompaniers (CDR experts) must also be able to draw on all the expertise needed by the project promoters, and
- Facilitation skills, as well as a variety of training skills are also important.

Development Practices and New Co-operative Models

Over the past 20 years, Québec has witnessed dynamic co-operative development. This development was made possible by the creation of Regional Development Co-operatives (Coopératives de Développement Régional – CDR), which led to the development of a high degree of expertise in co-operative development. The global approach detailed in the foregoing section is the reflection of field-validated practices. However, the global approach on its own is not enough. Québec's co-operative development was also enhanced by new co-operative models – solidarity co-operatives and worker-shareholder co-operatives. These two models have added new depth to the existing models (producer, consumer, housing, and work co-operatives). It is thus worthwhile to dwell on the practices developed to support these new models. Finally, co-operative development was also helped by the emergence of a "worker's union approach," which enabled the creation of specific expertise and appropriate tools to foster the conversion of private companies into co-operatives. These three general trends were major forces underlying co-operative development over the past 20 years. The practices observed in their deployment are presented in this present section.

1. Solidarity Co-operatives

The solidarity co-operative formula is especially appropriate for local development. It is often the best model. Workers, users, and the region's development officers can become members. It is also used when worker co-operatives seek to expand. This formula enables the inclusion of support members, access to additional capital, and greater expertise. It has three kinds of members: users, workers, and support members. From 50% to 60% of new co-operatives opt for the solidarity co-operative model. It can be adapted to all situations and sectors.

We are now witnessing the transformation of non-profit organizations into solidarity co-operatives. This formula allows for partnerships (since solidarity co-operatives can allow membership of non-profit organizations, and public organizations) and diverse members (since solidarity co-operatives can bring in members as users, employees, and partners), something which is not possible in the non-profit organizational model. The solidarity co-operative is better able to mobilise its members as it responds to significant needs shared by a large portion of the community. However, when many people become members it is important to ensure that the co-operative does not deviate from its founding mission, especially when there is a high number of support members (such as non-profit organizations and public organizations). There is a danger that they will influence the decision-making process. Whereas there may be five or six user members, there can be as many as a 100 support members. The latter can lead the co-operative business discussions far from strategic issues.

A Practical Example of Solidarity Co-operatives: Health Co-operatives

One way health co-operatives begin is with a citizens' group protesting the absence of health services and making appropriate demands on elected officials. Things are usually kindled by an announced closure of a physicians' office that wants to sell its clinic because of heavy management responsibilities. Thus, an opportunity is created.

Citizen involvement is an essential condition for the success of a health co-operative. It takes shape via local leaders and concerned citizens.

The first step consists of a feasibility study that encompasses the problem in its entirety. This study can take up to six months. The demand evolves into a proposal. The market study involves the CLDs, economic actors (such as the Chamber of Commerce), local leaders, etc. The study's results are presented at a meeting of citizens who are asked to vote on the co-operative's creation.

Recruitment of members for the co-operative is set in motion at the outset. To ensure the co-operative's success, a significant number of citizens must decide to become members. Citizen mobilisation is a very important criterion. Following the meeting in which the study results are presented, a provisional committee is created.

Citizen support for the co-operative project has to be measured. This can be done informally by observing the apparent interest and presence at the information meeting. More formal measures involve surveying the population.

Over and above technical and financial feasibility, conditions for success includes 1) willingness on the part of the citizenry, 2) acceptance by health professionals that the co-operative is a viable solution (it is important for physicians to participate in information meetings, to give their ideas about the project, and to manifest their interest in being associated with it), 3) the support of other professionals is also important (i.e., physiotherapists, dentists, workers at local community service centres and hospitals, etc.), and 4) acceptance of and commitment to the project on the part of public authorities and economic leaders is also a winning condition (i.e., the municipality, CLD, SADC, the Chamber of Commerce, etc.). These various actors have to be met within the framework of the feasibility study to ensure that their point of view is heard.

There will be local project promoters who must ensure that they are responding to a collective problem. It is essential to be informed by public debates in the community, especially when city councillors are faced with a void in services and there is an attendant wave of panic. It is at this moment that the project promoters turn to the CDR to find a solution.

The project is often conceived so that the co-operative takes over the building and can involve other workers in addition to physicians and users. Opting for a solidarity co-operative is thus a logical choice for opening the co-operative to various types of members.

In addition to physician services, the co-operative also works to develop other kinds of services. In these health co-operatives, the emphasis is on prevention and the assumption that the responsibility for health is with the citizens of the community.

The CDR can offer accompaniment support to the co-operative for several years.

Best Practices in Development of Solidarity Co-ops

The best practice remains that of being attentive and connected to the communities concerned. It is thus essential to remain connected with elected municipal officials and committed citizens. It is also important to be flexible and to adopt a strategic approach.

The best way to connect with elected officials is to highlight past accomplishments of the CDR team as experts on these matters. These successful accomplishments serve as important references for the communities concerned. It is also important to be present in these communities and to develop personal relationships. Credibility is very important.

More precisely, it is important to go towards people in need of key services, such as health care, and begin with the local conditions and community leaders. In this regard, the local credit union can play a key role since it can facilitate the work of collecting shares and soliciting the population. If the project's promoters had to develop this part of the project on their own the difficulty would be much greater.

Business Model

The choice of a solidarity co-operative allows various stakeholders of a health co-operative to become members (they may be: users, physicians, nurses, or workers) and provides more stability to the co-op.

This model enables the consolidation of medical personnel. It allows for operating a clinic with physicians, and eventually with related services and an approach based on health prevention and promotion. Health care providers are freed up from management and investment responsibilities (building, equipment, etc.). The money earmarked by the Québec Medical Insurance Plan and usually sent to the physicians is redirected (by the physicians) to the co-operative. The co-operative takes care of the administrative aspects (i.e., appointments, relations with the Board of Health, personnel management, supplies, building maintenance, etc). Physicians no longer have to invest their time in operating and managing the clinic. In this model, they have a turnkey service and can concentrate on their medical practice. In certain communities, the number of physicians has increased after a co-operative opened. Some physicians opt for setting up a practice in a community that already has a co-operative because they have the support of the population.

Additional income is generated by the development of related services and diverse activities. The co-operative can in this regard develop activities such as physiotherapy, acupuncture, or a travel clinic, etc. Renting space to professionals who provide these services extends the co-ops services and brings in additional income.

It often takes around 12 months from the initial stirring until the opening of the clinic.

Obviously, the number of users varies from one community to another. The cost of being a member (the share in the co-operative), ranges from $50 to $100. However, it is not necessary to be a member to receive health care from the co-operative. Becoming a member is above all a gesture of solidarity; otherwise, the community would be in danger of losing services (due to the closure of local clinics). The advantages of being a member are related to peripheral services. Members can call during the no appointment hours of the clinic and see a professional within 60 minutes. The co-operatives also have agreements with local businesses and professionals, thereby enabling members to get discounts (at a physical conditioning centre, or a health food store, etc.).

There is also a feeling of belonging, because the co-operative made it possible to counter-balance a feeling of powerlessness in light of a looming loss of medical services. The users can develop privileged links, be recognized at the co-operative, and have access to a family physician.

The "associative life" of the co-operative (co-operative education, information, consultation, and decisions) has to be dynamic. In Aylmer, the CDR provided a training programme for all members of the co-operative. This training programme provided participants with a better appreciation of their rights and responsibilities and incited them to think about their role as members. A training programme was also provided for directors. This ongoing training process facilitates the development of strong internal ties. Aylmer also has a community nurse who is responsible for special projects. She is attentive to local needs and maintains links with the community.

Difficulties to Overcome

Initially, this type of co-operative was viewed as a kind of privatisation. Now it is seen more as the collectivisation of a private service. Former opponents of this type of co-operative acknowledge the importance of citizen mobilisation. They have come to realise that it is not merely a financial transaction in which physicians transfer ownership of a building to the community.

The emphasis on health promotion converges with current trends and seeks to give back a role to individuals. The state is concerned more with the curative dimension while co-operatives are focused on prevention. As such, a new paradigm has been set in place.

Public sector actors have a better grasp of the health co-operative formula and even though they have a control reflex they do not control the co-operative. As such, there is a malaise between the two. Thus, the contractual agreement is not between the co-operative and the Health Ministry, the link is more with the physicians involved.

There is often a need for greater harmonisation of services between the public and the co-operative, even though the co-operative is more attentive to the community's expectations and needs. This is particularly obvious with FMGs (family physicians' groups).

At present, there are around a dozen health co-operatives in Québec. The next step is to make it easier for them to network via the creation of a federation. Indeed, the potential for more health co-operatives in Québec is quite high – at least by MRC[5] – which could well lead to the creation of more than 60 health co-operatives in the next five years.

2. Worker-Shareholder Co-operatives (WSCs)

There have been many failed attempts at WSCs. Only around 60 of them are still in operation because the formula is too often viewed as a solution to save a business. To be able to use this formula effectively, it is crucial to understand the model and to know how to use it.

A WSC is not a tool for replacing a business in difficulty because the workers (grouped together in a shareholder co-operative) are a minority of shareholders and do not have control. As such, it is not a tool for saving a company. Often, in the context of a failing business, not recommending the WSC formula may be viewed as a best practice.

The WSC formula is an excellent tool for participation, interessment, and company development. It is also an excellent tool for teaching workers how to invest in their own work place. It is thus an excellent school for empowering workers.

The key to successfully starting a WSC is the choice of company.

How to successfully get a WSC underway:

1. First of all, an implementation analysis that examines the business aspect has to be carried out. For example, human resources and labour relations have to be diagnosed to ensure that the entrepreneur/owner is not merely seeking to avoid unionisation.

2. It is also important to make sure that there is a development plan that will call for the collaboration of a third party investor. This will allow not only for bringing workers together, but also for involving a partner sensitive to collective and co-operative investment (e.g., Capital régional et coopérative Desjardins, Investissement Québec, le FondAction, la caisse de solidarité, Filaction, etc.). Their involve-

---

5 Municipalités régionales de comté—bodies that group together all the municipalities in a given region.

ment will ensure that in the event the investor pulls out, it will favour selling its shares to the workers via the WSC.

3. Conducting publicity campaigns around the WSC should be avoided. It is more effective to use word of mouth among businesses, as well as among financial partners already involved in various WSC projects.

4. It takes time before a WSC can get operational in the right way. First, there needs to be a meeting with the employees to give them an overview of what is going on. Next, it is important to meet with the employees twice on an individual basis. The employees will no doubt have personal questions to ask (e.g., their capacity for investing, which they might not want to ask in front of their colleagues). The first meeting serves to inform them and to ensure they ask all the important questions. Following this meeting, they can discuss matters with other people they work with and ask, or be asked, other questions. The second meeting revisits all these questions.

5. The implementation analysis requires an understanding of the company's history, an analysis of the financial statements with a view to demonstrating what would happen if the employees invested in the company, and meetings with the employees.

6. Based on these analyses and meetings, the CDR should be able to make a recommendation about the overall situation and about the relevance of going ahead with establishing a WSC in the company. A copy of the implementation analyses must be provided to the employees.

7. The next step is to begin the process of applying for a charter. This step also involves employee training, a founding general meeting, and a general meeting. It is also important to prepare shareholder agreements and to have shares purchased by the WSC. Lastly, there is the constitution of the WSC's Board of Directors.

8. To purchase shares, the WSC can either borrow the necessary funds or secure financing from the company itself. Even if the share purchase occurs gradually, the WSC will have all the rights associated with the block of shares it will eventually own. This step provides a good indication of the company's attitude and intentions with regard to employee participation in its capital.

If the WSC's objective is to take over from the entrepreneur, the objective is different. Although a WSC is also appropriate in this context, the workers will have to invest to buy the company's total assets.

3. Conversion and Co-operative Development

The conversion of private companies into co-operatives involves meeting significant challenges that require distinct practices. Québec's experience in this area is largely concentrated at MCE Conseils (a consultant firm associated with the CSN[6] that works with various partners). What follows is the approach it favours.

At the outset, the standard conditions of feasibility for an economic project must be in place. In this perspective, the co-operative is a means and not an end in itself. As such, there must be assurances of economic viability and a balance between skills and the market.

Evaluating these conditions involves the following question: Is it a good idea to convert this company into a co-operative? It is thus necessary to find a business whose situation is bad enough that it has to be sold, but which is still able to survive and improve. In this regard, MCE Conseils prefer to see people unemployed now rather than later if it turns out that the economic project is not viable. It takes a very critical, responsible approach and the risks are calculated. This is all the more important because MCE works with different partners who do not have contact with one another. It works with CSN members and always does business with the same financial partners. Before a conversion project gets the go ahead, there have to be two *Yeses*: from MCE and the workers.

During the conversion process, MCE assigns considerable importance to worker training. They are first trained about how co-operatives operate and then about managing a business. As such, MCE assigns significant importance to economic training so that all the workers have a good understanding of the business side of things. The Board of Directors must have a good grasp of all aspects of its business plan. This is a precondition to the start-up because it will be in a better position to anticipate how it will manage the operation afterwards. In sum, a significant educational effort must be made.

MCE Conseil's chief co-operative conversion concerns are respectively techno-economic viability, training, complicity, and complete transparency with financial partners. It is important that the partners view MCE as being responsible. MCE begins with a technical audit (market and production) followed by a human audit (expertise and culture). It is important that the workers be able to fully take up the co-operative model, something which is achieved throughout the training activities and the formulation of the bylaws. MCE consultants present the workers with choices and observe how they react. Doing things this way takes longer but produces more solid

6 Confédération des syndicats nationaux (*National Union Confederation*).

results. Emphasis is placed as much on the economic dimensions as on co-operative ones.

It takes around six months to bring a project to fruition. While it can be done in three months if everything quickly falls in place, it can also last up to 15 months if unexpected difficulties arise.

As a consultant firm, MCE's responsibility is larger because the workers have never envisioned ownership. They have to be more motivated than simply wishing to avoid unemployment.

MCE's success rate is quite good and the survival rate of the created co-operatives is very high. These rates are the result of an important screening process at the outset. Indeed, MCE only takes on 50% of the projects submitted to it. It then successfully follows through with 40% of the projects, with the balance being abandoned along the way. When the process is completed, 20% of the initial projects are converted into worker co-operatives. Of these, there are very few that go under and fail.

Over the past 15 years, MCE Conseils and its network of partners have developed a set of tools to facilitate co-operative development. Whereas financing was a problem in the late 1980s, it is no longer the case today. Financing for the solidarity economy is well established in Québec and collective ownership is accessible.

After having completed a project, MCE takes care to add winning conditions in the years that follow. The co-operatives for which this works the best are those that invite MCE back to participate in general meetings and board of directors meetings. This kind of intervention, which can receive financial support from Emploi-Québec (*Employment Québec*) and thus cost nothing for the co-operative, helps co-operatives to avoid crisis situations.

MCE Conseils also take care of training new members. They also participate in board meetings focused on updating the business plan.

Preventive maintenance is thus quite important. MCE Conseils can provide in-depth assistance to the co-operative if necessary, whereas follow-up work is largely funded by Emploi-Québec. To obtain this funding, a joint application is made by the co-operative and MCE Conseils. In this case, Emploi-Québec can participate. Around 30 hours a year of preventive maintenance is typically anticipated. A more serious intervention requires around 200 hours. It is thus important to follow the correct procedures to ensure EQ help is available for co-operatives. The CLDs can also support this kind of intervention.

A Conversion Example: The Ambulance Sector in Québec - The Emergence and Development of a Co-operative Approach in a Union Context

At present (Feb. 2007), there are eight ambulance co-operatives in Québec. Among these, two have also taken the form of a worker-shareholder co-operative. The remainder are worker co-operatives.

In total, there are about 850 employees in these ambulance co-operatives. If we exclude Montreal, which is served by Urgences Santé (public sector), ambulance co-operatives handle around half of the ambulance interventions in the rest of the province.

Co-operative development in this sector originated with the beginning of the unionisation of ambulance workers in 1983-84. Following this unionisation, ambulance workers wanted to negotiate directly with the government rather than with private companies that held the ambulance permits.

At that time, there were serious congestion problems in emergency wards. Ambulance workers played an important role in dealing with this problem because their activities could generate as much as 80% of emergency ward volume. As such, there was a need for better dispatching of ambulance-borne patients among the various emergency wards. This need for greater coordination had become problematic since there were 23 private ambulance companies across the province. Calls were being managed inefficiently. A reorganization of the industry was in the best interests of the government (so as to be able to rely on a more efficient and effective ambulance structure), it was also in the best interests of ambulance workers whose working conditions were quite unsatisfactory (very low wages, no training, outdated equipment, etc.). The idea of unifying the ambulance network to increase efficiency became a very important issue.

From the perspective of private companies, the emergence of a strong union voice that wanted to negotiate with the government would strip them of control of over 80% of their costs (labour). In this light, they stood to lose their profit margin. They quickly came to the conclusion that they would be better off selling out.

Apart from the government, the only potential buyers were the workers, and the idea of creating a co-operative gradually took hold. At the time, ambulance workers earned $6 an hour and did not have the means to invest in the purchase of permits and equipment. Moreover, interest rates were oscillating between 15% and 20%. At the same time that unionisation was spreading throughout the province there were a few attempted buyouts in various places in Québec. In this context, unionisation and co-operation came to be seen as the two complementary ingredients for implementing a more efficient and better organized ambulance structure. As such, with the exception of major urban centres, the co-operative model was adopted and turned out to be the most efficient model.

Prior to the sector's unionisation-co-operativisation, the industry was characterised by unsafe vehicles, inadequate equipment, and an almost complete absence of training. At present, vehicles meet BNQ[7] quality standards, equipment is adequate, and all ambulance workers must have college-level training. Enormous progress has thus been made in ambulance services. As well, there is better coordination with physicians, who have gone so far as to create elaborate intervention protocols for ambulance workers. There has thus been a professionalisation of the entire ambulance worker field.

In present co-operatives, workers can hold, on average, around $50,000 in privileged shares. This capital has been accumulated since the beginning of 1983. Ambulance workers now earn $22 an hour. As well, returns to members can be quite high and amount to around $8,000 per year.

Without union action the ambulance co-operative sector would not exist. It could not take advantage of the economic intervention tools that have enabled the sector's reorganization. It could not take advantage of the various actors specialised in co-operative development accompaniment. The success experienced in this sector is thus due to the network of actors within the umbrella of the CSN.

Three-Phased Development of Ambulance Co-operatives

1) The development of the co-operative

The technical expertise necessary for completing phase One is made available and supplied by the CSN via MCE Councils. They also provide employee supervision and training. Start-up financing is also supplied by the CSN's solidarity financing network, in particular by the Caisse d'économie solidaire (Solidarity Credit Union).

At present, it is very difficult to get an ambulance co-operative underway if the promoters are not unionised (CSN). Unionised ambulance workers only have to give the mandate to their union, who will call upon MCE for technical, economic, and co-operative expertise as well as the CSN's solidarity financing network (FondAction, Solidarity Credit Union, Filaction) for the required capital.

2) Day-to-day management

It is important to find the right model to ensure a good balance among the stakeholders in an ambulance co-operative. Three key parties are in-

---

7 Bureau national de qualité (National Quality Office)

volved—unionised workers, co-operative workers, and the government. A fourth party, financial players (the CSN's network) is also involved. Even good day-to-day management can encounter significant difficulties when there is confusion between the union and the co-operative. The government is also involved via professional practices. The day-to-day management of these entities is rendered more complex in the case of the largest co-operatives since a large number of members are involved (200 and more).

Although the co-operative's revenues are guaranteed (by the government), it is important to exercise good control of spending to ensure the co-operative's long-term survival.

3) Expanding the model

Phase Three involves expanding the model. The tools that the CSN's network has set in place (such as financing, consultation, union's support, etc.) provide technical expertise and advice with regard to the economic, co-operative, and financing aspects of the project. It is thus quite realistic to envision expansion.

The co-operative formula is advantageous for the government and ambulance workers alike. The other actors in the health system have changed their view of ambulance workers. As the efficiency of the services improves, they are increasingly viewed as partners in the health network.

Although there is still room for consolidation involving private (family) companies, it is also possible to look to a related sector, namely adapted transportation of handicapped people, which is quite inefficient because it is poorly organized. This inefficiency has repercussions for the ambulance sector when it is called upon as a replacement, because ambulance transportation is more expensive.

Financing: Capital régional et coopératif Desjardins

Financial backers play a key role in co-operative development. Co-operative stakeholders routinely decry the absence of capital as a major cause of "co-operative non-development." Over and above the actors and models presented earlier, this last section revisits practices with a financial point of view in mind. What are the best financial practices? How can they be harmonized with those of co-operative developers? In this connection, it is important to note that Québec has witnessed the emergence of several financial actors dedicated to co-operative financing over the past 20 years. They have a partnership approach that respects co-operative development.

Let us examine the approach used by Capital régional et coopératif Desjardins.

Capital regional et coopératif Desjardins (CFCD) accords minimum financing of $250,000 for each co-operative project it accepts. The accorded financing is in no way linked to guarantees and serves to complement the required initial investment support after traditional financial backers have agreed to become involved.

Because of its internal policies, the co-operative sectors financed by CRCD are largely those in the agricultural, forestry, and manufacturing sectors. It does not finance consumer co-operatives unless they operate several service outlets. The sectors and co-operative projects not covered by the CRCD can secure financing for other elements of the Desjardins network (e.g., Business Financing Centres).

The types of possible financing include: equity (and quasi-equity), non-convertible debentures, privileged capital, and lending. The CRCD offers a variety of tools that cover most of the co-operatives' current needs. The CRCD can also be associated with its partners, such as RISQ, FondAction, Filaction, Caisse de solidarité, Investissement Québec, etc.

Rather than a lack of funds, it is the quality of co-operative projects that limits co-operative development. This can be explained in part by the fact that co-operative development has focused more on social projects in the past few years.

The CRCD finances five to six projects a year. To do so, it analyses 25 to 30 projects. The rates charged are competitive and can fluctuate between 6¾% and 13%. To ensure profitability, it has to charge average rates of around 8% to 9%. Of the 17 projects financed to date by the CRCD there have been no bankruptcies and only three projects are considered to be at risk. The other projects are in good to very good shape.

Criteria for Obtaining Financing

Three precise points are taken into consideration: 1) a promising market, 2) competence of the management team, and 3) vitality of the associative dimension (such as member's involvement, co-operative education, information, and consultation). This latter point is also viewed as being very important and is systematically analysed.

Due diligence of the verification process is quite rigorous. The co-operative's strategic positioning is analysed. As such, its business plan is thoroughly studied. If the CRDC feels there is a danger for the members, it will let them know. When financing is accorded, a CRDC representative is delegated to sit on the co-operative's board of directors. This individual is an expert who can "add value."

The CRDC has an extensive team of experts in management, recovery, market development, communication, and so on who can be made available for the co-operative. These services are available at no extra cost to the co-operative. This team of experts is not available at Investissement Québec and FondAction has fewer resources to be able to offer the same service quality.

Projects can be financed with the help of partners such as Investissement Québec, FondAction, and, to a lesser extent, the Caisse de solidarité.

The CDR's analysis of the associative dimension covers many areas and goes into great depth. The CRDC wants to assure itself that the members are involved and are present at the general meetings. It makes an effort to have direct contact with the members. Meetings are thus held with the members, the directors, and the partners. The CRDC wants assurances that it is dealing with a genuine co-operative. The diagnostic tools used for this analysis are very well developed.

The analysis of the co-operative dimension is very important because if problems arise, the CRDC will have to invest more money. It thus wants assurances that the members can (and will want to) invest in their own co-operative.

The CRDC never gets involved in the project at the beginning. It is called upon only when a business plan has been established.

Conclusion

This chapter began by exploring issues related to effective co-operative development practices from a broad perspective. Three practice areas were identified: facilitation, dialogue, and accompaniment/support. The context within which they best apply is that of a region because proximity to the various actors is a key element. The permanence of the network of actors dedicated to co-operative development is a critical factor. The early work by co-operative actors (CDR) is thus very important, even though we tend to focus on the accompaniment practices.

The second section of this chapter discussed two new co-operative models that spearheaded the dynamism of co-operative development in Québec over the past 20 years. Solidarity co-operatives and worker-shareholder co-operatives are important drivers of co-operative renewal, going beyond traditional models (consumption, production, worker, and housing). Solidarity co-operatives have made a multi-party approach possible, one that involves three types of members—users, workers, and support members. This model's flexibility has propelled it to become the most adopted formula, particularly when there is a need to deal with local development challenges. The particular case of health co-operatives in Québec (the great majority of which adopted a solidarity co-operative status) is a good example of the possibilities inherent in this formula. In addition, WSCs have the great advantage of enabling co-operative development in economic sectors that were often inaccessible to traditional co-operatives. Indeed, WSCs were conceived to facilitate the grouping together of workers in a given company to enable them to purchase shares in the company they work for. With this kind of formula, it is possible to envision co-operative development in more demanding areas of capitalisation.

These two new models call for distinct development practices that go beyond basic, traditional practices. This explains the importance of describing their particularities. The third dimension discussed in the second section concerns the conversion of private businesses into co-operatives (typically worker co-operatives). Here again, distinct practices are required. Unions and associated partners play a determining role in this kind of setting. The example of ambulance co-operatives illustrates the complexity of this process. We can also observe not only the conversion of private companies into co-operatives, but also the almost complete reorganization of an economic sector.

Finally, this chapter discussed issues related to the financial dimension of co-operative development. In this regard, it is interesting to note the importance assigned to the associative dimension (member involvement, governance, etc.) of co-operative vitality.

Meilleurs pratiques et développement coopératif

Daniel Côté

L a réflexion sur les pratiques de développement coopératif doit reposer d'abord sur une perspective large. Ceci permet d'identifier les grandes axes de pratiques, et les compétences qui y sont rattachées, tels l'animation, la concertation des intervenants et l'accompagnement. Par ailleurs, pour approfondir notre lecture et compréhension de ces pratiques, il importe également de quitter le point de vue global pour jeter un regard plus pointu sur des modèles et expériences particuliers. Pour mener à bien ce deuxième volet de l'analyse, nous dégageons les pratiques de modèles coopératifs distincts, particulièrement les coopératives de solidarité et les coopératives de travailleurs actionnaires. Ces deux modèles coopératifs ont le mérite d'être moins connu parce que plus récents (fin des années 80 pour les CTA et milieu des années 90 pour les coopératives de solidarité) alors qu'ils constituent la majorité des coopératives créées au Québec depuis quelques années. Un troisième champ de développement coopératif demande à être analysé plus en détail. La conversion d'entreprises capitalistes en coopératives (de travail) repose sur des pratiques uniques qu'il est également important de documenter.

Pour davantage approfondir l'analyse des meilleures pratiques, deux applications sont documentés : les coopératives de santé et les coopératives ambulancières. Le cas des coopératives de santé offre le double avantage d'éclairer à la fois l'application du modèle de coopératives de solidarité tout en documentant l'émergence de coopératives dans un secteur stratégique. Finalement, le cas des coopératives ambulancières nous éclaire sur un secteur réorganisé en privilégiant la formule coopérative (ambulances), qui a connu plusieurs conversions d'entreprises privées en coopératives, le tout ayant été rendu possible grâce à l'implication des partenaires syndicaux.

Meilleures pratiques de développement coopératif : un point de vue global[1]

Pour assurer le développement coopératif, il y a trois noyaux de pratiques à considérer, d'abord l'animation, deuxièmement, le partenariat et la concertation, troisièmement, l'accompagnement. Un quatrième noyau peut être identifié, à savoir le développement d'outils appropriés (modèles, lois, fiscalité, etc.). Les CDR couvrent ces trois champs de pratiques.

l'Animation

Au Québec, de toujours, il y a eu des gens de terrain qui étaient préoccupés à faire connaître le modèle coopératif.

En matière d'animation, les CDR organisent des gala, des événements, publient un journal (Coopoint), un bulletin, prononcent des conférences (chambre de commerce, etc.). Ce faisant, elles informent, sensibilisent et éduquent à la formule coopérative.

Les deux premiers publics visés sont la famille coopérative et les acteurs du développement économique et social.

Les attitudes, comportements et compétences requises pour participer à l'animation commencent par le respect des personnes. Il faut reconnaître les limites et talents de chacun. Il faut savoir susciter l'intérêt et pouvoir partager les choses. Ce n'est donc pas d'un travail de «vendeur» dont il

1 L'auteur souhaite remercier MM. Armand Lajeunesse (directeur général, CDR de Lanaudière), Guy Bisaillon (conseiller senior et ancien directeur général, CDR de Montréal), Guy Provencher (conseiller senior CDR du centre du Québec – Mauricie), Patrick Duguay (directeur général, CDR Outaouais – Laurentides), Claude Dorion (directeur général, mce conseil), Richard Lapointe (CSN), Lamarche (CSN), Yves Létourneau (analyste financier, Capital régionale et coopératif Desjardins et ancien conseiller senior à la CDR de Québec) et Sylvain Parenteau (trésorier chez Sixpro et administrateur à la CDR centre du Québec – Mauricie). Ces différentes personnes ressources ont généreusement accepté de répondre à des nombreuses questions et ainsi partager leur vaste expérience en matière de développement coopératif.

s'agit. Participer à ce travail d'animation demande beaucoup d'énergie alors qu'il faut continuellement expliquer la formule coopérative...encore mal connue.

Pour bien réussir cette activité d'animation, les techniques d'animation doivent être maîtrisées. Une approche pédagogique est une des clés de la réussite. L'animateur doit savoir élaborer une planification de ses interventions. Il doit bien cibler son public et distinguer lorsqu'il répond à une demande, comparativement aux sollicitations qu'il devra initier. Les principaux publics sont les agents de développement tels les CLD, les SADC, les professionnels (avocats, comptables, consultants...), les regroupements tels les gens d'affaires, les différents secteurs, et le grand public. À titre d'exemple, il devra participer aux dînés de la chambre de commerce à titre de conférencier, également aux rencontres des agents de développement des CLD (Centre locaux de développement).

L'animateur doit également pouvoir compter sur différents outils tels dépliants, pochettes, présentation Power points, documents, etc.

Ces techniques d'animation devraient faire l'objet d'un développement et d'une formation plus serrée.

Concertation des intervenants

Il est également essentiel de participer à la mise en commun des ressources et à la synergie des réseaux, i.e. l'ensemble des acteurs préoccupés par le développement du milieu. Les développeurs coopératifs doivent donc se concerter avec les agents des CLD, SADC, la conférence régionale des élus, etc. Il y a des lieux de concertation naturels et il est absolument nécessaire d'y être. La CDR joue ce rôle et participe à l'exercice de concertation à titre d'expert en développement coopérative, et reconnu comme tel.

Les lieux de concertation concernent non seulement le territoire, mais également les secteurs (santé, éducation, tourisme, etc.). Tous ces acteurs font appel aux partenaires pour faciliter le succès de leurs propres dossiers, et la CDR doit participer à cet effort. Il y a donc là un danger de consacrer trop d'énergie à des dossiers divers...mais c'est incontournable sinon, il n'y a rien à faire. Tout se croise. Il faut donc participer à l'action. Il faut être présent, là où les grands enjeux se dessinent et se décident, pour influencer et être influencé. Lorsqu'il est question de développement coopératif, tous ces acteurs sauront faire référence à la CDR comme acteur de premier plan. Le partenariat est donc nourri par les différents intervenants, ce qui conduit à l'entraide et au développement collectif alors que chacun a sa place, son rôle.

La concertation requiert de s'asseoir avec les principaux acteurs et d'échanger autour de projets communs, par nécessairement coopératifs.

Tous les acteurs préoccupés par le projet en question (loisir, tourisme, industrie, commerce, etc.) doivent être impliqués.

L'expertise requise pour jouer un rôle clé en matière de concertation commence avec le développement d'une vision large du développement. Ceci s'avère difficile. Cette vision se doit d'être multisectorielle et territoriale. Il est également nécessaire de savoir démontrer la pertinence des avancés, suggestions, etc. Le représentant coopératif à ces exercices de concertation se doit d'être reconnu comme une ressource pertinente, complémentaire. L'expert doit également démontrer sa capacité à comprendre les préoccupations des autres intervenants…sinon, ceux-ci ne seront pas là pour celles de la CDR. Dans ce contexte, tous sont gagnants. Il y a donc une présence obligatoire auprès des secteurs et des régions.

l'Accompagnement

Finalement, il faut également procéder à l'accompagnement des entrepreneurs coopératifs. Dans ce contexte, il faut réaliser que peu d'experts (notaires, avocats, comptables, commissaires industriels, etc.) ont une connaissance du modèle coopératif. Il est donc essentiel que des experts en développement coopératif puissent jouer ce rôle d'accompagnement. Il faut donc développer une expertise en accompagnement de l'entrepreneurship collectif.

L'accompagnement doit également se faire en concertation puisqu'il requiert la contribution des intervenants pour soutenir le projet (coopératif dans ce cas). Il faut donc aller chercher ceux qui peuvent aider à la réussite du projet.

Pour bien réussir le défi de l'accompagnement, l'expert coopératif doit encore une fois bien maîtriser les qualités d'animation. Il s'agit de bien comprendre le projet soumis. Il faut également s'assurer que la formule coopérative est adaptée et répond aux besoins de l'entrepreneur. Est-ce qu'il y a matière à entrepreneuriat collectif? Par la suite, l'expert doit présenter les différents modèles coopératifs qui peuvent s'appliquer (production, consommation, travail, solidarité), les principes coopératifs et la structure de capital propre à la formule coopérative. Par la suite, les étapes de création peuvent être enclenchées.

La 1e étape est celle de l'étude de préfaisabilité. Il est donc nécessaire que les porteurs de projet coopératif aient procédé à la cueillette d'information et à l'analyse permettant l'étude de marché, des coûts de revient et marges de rentabilité, etc…sinon, il n'y a pas d'entreprise viable. Par la suite (2e étape), il y aura la demande de constitution d'une coopérative et la rédaction d'un document de régie interne. Finalement, il y aura l'assemblée de fondation de la coopérative.

La CDR ne fait pas d'études de faisabilité, mais elle va accompagner les porteurs de projet vers les experts compétents et disponibles. Cette contribution des experts pourra permettre l'approfondissement du projet.

L'étape de rédaction du règlement de régie interne est fait par les porteurs de projet, encadrés par l'équipe de la CDR. Ceci est important puisque ces derniers doivent justifier les choix qui sont faits. Ils ont également l'occasion de débuter l'apprentissage (et la discipline) des ordres du jour, l'élection d'un président de réunion, etc. Ils commencent donc à se pratiquer à la formule coopérative.

Le temps requis pour se rendre jusqu'à l'étape du démarrage du projet prend en moyenne de 3 à 6 mois. L'accompagnateur (expert de la CDR) et les porteurs du projet se réunissent à toutes les 2 ou 3 semaines.

Pour un projet coopératif qui se rendra à la phase de démarrage, il faudra voir +/- 10 projets. Ce ratio de 1/10 semble correspondre au ratio observé pour l'entrepreneurship collectif dans son ensemble. Avant de déterminer si le projet est vraiment de nature coopérative, l'expert accompagnateur aura besoin d'une à deux rencontres, ce qui permettra d'éliminer les chercheurs de subvention, les promoteurs à la recherche de «passes fiscales», etc.

L'accompagnement pourra se poursuivre sur une période de une à deux années par la suite. L'accompagnateur devra s'assurer que les réunions sont bien tenues. Il devra resserrer les pratiques au besoin, aider à implanter la discipline de travail. Cela prend facilement une année. Par la suite, les coopérateurs devraient avoir pris le rythme et pouvoir procéder à la rédaction des bilans, rapports, projections, élections, etc. Il faut donc faire un tour complet. Pour les années suivantes, l'accompagnement se fera au gré des besoins de la coopérative. La CDR de Lanaudière ne fait pas de suivi faute de ressources. Mais il y a un manque évident à ce niveau compte tenu des risques des 5 premières années. Il serait également très pertinent de proposer des activités de formation aux différents membres de la coopérative. Par ailleurs, la CDR centre du Québec – Mauricie compte une ressource qui ne fait qu'assurer le suivi auprès des coopératives créées avec son support. Il existe d'ailleurs des programmes permettant de supporter les coûts associés à un tel suivi.

Sur l'ensemble du territoire couvert par la CDR centre du Québec - Mauricie, il y a environ 160 coopératives. Pour les coopératives de deux ans et moins, ce sont les conseillers qui font le suivi. Lors des 2 premières années, la CDR s'assurer d'assister à quelques réunions du conseil d'administration. Ils ont une personne ressource à la CDR qui ne fait qu'un suivi auprès des coopératives de deux ans et plus. Un appel est fait aux 6 mois. Un diagnostic coopératif est fait, autant sur le volet associatif que sur le volet affaires. Des ressources externes sont appelées au besoin lorsque la coopérative connaît des difficultés. Un plan de redressement est développé.

La CDR doit également investir dans le développement de la vie associative. Ceci requiert de fournir une formation sur les rôles et responsabilités des administrateurs et des membres de la coopérative. Doivent être couverts les règlements de régie interne, la gestion des contrats de membres, l'assemblée de formation, les rapports financiers annuels, l'envoie des documents aux instances concernées. La CDR doit viser à ce que les conseils d'administration soient rapidement autonomes.

L'expertise requise pour procéder à l'accompagnement est :
- La maîtrise des applications de la formule coopérative;
- La maîtrise des notions des composantes de l'entreprise, i.e. plan d'affaires, les fonctions, etc.
- Il faut pouvoir et savoir aller au-delà de l'aspect légal, alors qu'ils sont la référence en matière de loi;
- L'accompagnateur doit également s'assurer de pouvoir regrouper les expertises qui seront requises par les porteurs de projet;
- Les qualités d'animation s'avèrent également importantes, ainsi que celles de formateurs.

Les pratiques de développement et nouveaux modèles coopératifs

Le Québec a connu un développement coopératif dynamique au cours des derniers 20 ans. Celui-ci fut rendu possible grâce à la création des Coopératives de Développement Régional (CDR) qui ont permis le développement d'une expertise pointu en matière de développement coopératif. L'approche globale développée dans la première section de ce texte reflète les pratiques validées sur le terrain. Par ailleurs, la seule perspective globale ne suffit pas. En effet, le développement coopératif québécois fut également enrichi de nouveaux modèles coopératifs, les coopératives de solidarité et les coopératives de travailleurs actionnaires. Ces deux modèles sont venus enrichir les modèles traditionnels, i.e les coopératives de production, de consommation, d'habitation et de travail. Il est donc pertinent de s'arrêter sur les pratiques développées pour supporter ces nouveaux modèles. Finalement, le développement coopératif fut également porté par l'émergence d'une approche syndicale qui aura permis la création d'une expertise unique et d'outils appropriés de manière à favoriser la conversion d'entreprises privées en coopératives. Ces trois courants lourds furent des forces majeures à la base du développement coopératif au cours des 20 dernières années. Les pratiques que l'on y observe sont brièvement présentées dans cette deuxième partie.

1. Les coopératives de solidarité

La formule de coopérative de solidarité est particulièrement pertinente pour le développement local. C'est le meilleur modèle. Peuvent être membres, les travailleurs, les usagers ainsi que des agents de développement de la région. Elle sert également lorsque les coopératives de travail veulent prendre de l'expansion. Ceci permet l'inclusion des membres de soutien, l'accès à des capitaux additionnels ainsi qu'une plus grande expertise. Nous retrouvons donc 3 types de membres, les utilisateurs, les travailleurs et les membres de soutien. De 50 à 60% des nouvelles coopératives choisissent le modèle de la coopérative de solidarité. Elle s'adapte à toutes les situations et tous les secteurs.

Nous assistons maintenant à la transformation d'OBNL en coopératives de solidarité. Cette formule permet d'associer des partenaires et d'aller chercher du membership ce que ne permet pas le modèle de l'OBNL. La coopérative de solidarité peut davantage mobiliser ses membres.

Par ailleurs, il importe de s'assurer que la coopérative ne s'écarte pas de sa mission d'origine lorsque beaucoup de personnes deviennent membres, particulièrement des membres de soutien. Il y a donc un danger que ceux-ci influencent le processus décisionnel. Alors qu'il y a de 5 à 6 membres utilisateurs, il peut y avoir environ une centaine de membres de soutien. Ces derniers peuvent faire dévier les débats loin des enjeux stratégiques.

Un exemple pratique de coopératives de solidarité : les coopératives de santé (level 3)

Il y a d'abord un regroupement de citoyens voulant dénoncer l'absence de services de santé et revendiquer auprès des élus. Le déclencheur est habituellement alimenté par l'annonce de la fermeture du bureau de médecins qui veulent vendre leur clinique, trouvant la gestion trop lourde. Il y a donc une opportunité qui se manifeste.

L'implication citoyenne est une condition essentielle pour le succès d'une coopérative de santé. Elle prend forme via les leaders locaux et les citoyens concernés.

La 1e étape consiste en une étude de faisabilité permettant de couvrir l'ensemble de la problématique. Cette étude peut prendre jusqu'à 6 mois Il y a donc une évolution de la revendication à la proposition. L'étude de marché implique les CLD, les acteurs économiques tel la chambre de commerce, etc. Les résultats de cette étude sont présentés en assemblée des citoyens à qui il sera demandé de voter pour la création de la coopérative.

L'objectif de recrutement des membres de la coopérative se met en branle dès le départ de la démarche. Pour assurer le succès de la coopérative, un nombre significatif de citoyens devra prendre la décision de devenir membre. La mobilisation citoyenne est un critère très important. Suite à l'assemblée de présentation des résultats de l'étude de faisabilité, un comité provisoire est mis sur pied.

Il faudra mesurer l'appui des citoyens à ce projet de coopérative de santé. Ceci sera fait informellement en constatant l'intérêt soulevé et la présence à l'assemblée d'information. De façon plus formelle, un sondage sera conduit auprès de la population.

Au-delà de la faisabilité technique et financière, les conditions de succès sont : (1) la volonté citoyenne, et (2) l'adhésion des professionnels en santé à l'idée que la coopérative est une solution. Il importe que les médecins soient présents aux assemblées d'information et puissent s'exprimer sur le projet, manifester leur intérêt à y être associé. (3) L'appui des autres professionnels sera également important, i.e. physiothérapeutes, dentistes, CLSC, centre hospitalier, etc. (4) L'adhésion et l'engagement des pouvoirs publics et leaders économiques seront également une condition gagnante, i.e. municipalité, CLD, SADC, chambre de commerce, etc. Ces différents acteurs devront être rencontrés dans le cadre de l'étude de faisabilité pour s'assurer que leur point de vue est entendu.

Il y aura donc des porteurs de projet à l'échelle locale qui devront s'assurer de répondre à un problème collectif. Il est donc essentiel de s'inspirer des débats publics au sein de la communauté, particulièrement lorsque les conseillers municipaux font face à un vide dans les services…et qu'une certaine panique s'installe. C'est à compter de ce moment qu'ils viennent rencontrer la CDR pour trouver une solution.

Le projet est souvent conçu de manière à ce que la coopérative reprenne la bâtisse et puisse impliquer les autres travailleurs en plus des médecins et des usagers. Le choix de la coopérative de solidarité devient donc logique pour donner accès au membership à ces différents types de membres.

Au-delà des services de médecin, la coopérative travaille également à développer d'autres types de services.

Dans ces coopératives de santé, l'emphase est placée sur la prévention et la prise en charge de la santé par un mouvement citoyen.

La CDR pourra accompagner la coopérative pendant une période de plusieurs années.

Les meilleures pratiques

La meilleure pratique demeure la capacité d'écoute et de proximité des milieux concernés. Il est donc essentiel de connecter avec les élus municipaux et les citoyens engagés. Il faut également être souple et adopter une approche stratégique.

La meilleure façon de connecter avec les élus est de mettre de l'avant les réalisations passées. Il y a là une référence importante pour les milieux. Par la suite, il faut être présent dans ces mêmes milieux, entretenir des liens très personnels. La crédibilité est très importante.

De façon plus précise, il importe d'aller vers les gens et démarrer avec la dynamique locale. À cet égard, la caisse joue un rôle capital puisqu'elle facilite le travail de collecte des parts sociales et la sollicitation de la population. Si les porteurs de projet avaient à concevoir ce volet du projet sans la caisse, la difficulté serait nettement accrue.

Le modèle d'affaires

D'abord le choix de la coopérative de solidarité qui permet aux différentes parties prenantes de devenir membre (usagers, médecins, infirmières, travailleurs), et apporte plus de stabilité.

Ensuite, l'exploitation d'une clinique...d'abord de médecins, mais éventuellement avec des services connexes et une approche axée sur la prévention et la promotion de la santé.

Ce modèle permet vraiment la consolidation des effectifs de médecins. Ces derniers sont débarrassés des responsabilités reliées à la gestion et aux investissements (bâtiment, équipements...). Les sommes d'argent prévues par la RAMQ et normalement versées aux médecins pour l'administration sont redirigés (par les médecins) vers la coopérative. Cette dernière verra à s'occuper de la partie administrative, i.e. la prise de rendez-vous, les rapports avec la Régie de la Santé, la gestion du personnel, les approvisionnements, la gestion du bâtiment, etc. Les médecins ne veulent plus investir dans des cliniques. Dans ce modèle, ils bénéficient d'un service clé en main, et peuvent se concentrer sur la pratique de la médecine. Dans certains milieux, le nombre de médecins a augmenté après l'ouverture de la coopérative (Aylmer). Certains médecins choisissent de s'installer dans un milieu où il y a une coopérative. Ils ont le support de la population.

Des revenus additionnels sont générés par le développement de services connexes et la diversification des activités. La coopérative peut ainsi développer les activités de physiothérapie, d'acupuncture, de clinique voyage, etc. La location d'espaces aux professionnels offrant ces services permet ainsi l'élargissement de l'offre de services et l'apport de revenus additionnels.

Il faut environ 12 mois pour passer des premiers balbutiements à l'ouverture de la clinique.

Le nombre de membres usagers va évidemment fluctuer d'un milieu à l'autre. Le coût d'adhésion (part sociale) à la coopérative varie entre $50 et $100. Par ailleurs, il n'est pas nécessaire d'être membre pour recevoir des soins à la coopérative. Devenir membre est donc d'abord un geste de solidarité...sinon, la communauté risque de perdre les services (fermeture de la clinique). Par ailleurs, les avantages à devenir membre sont liés aux services périphériques. Les membres peuvent appeler pendant les heures de clinique sans rendez-vous, et passer dans l'heure qui vient. La coopérative fait également des ententes avec des commerçants locaux et des professionnels, permettant ainsi aux membres d'obtenir des rabais (centre de conditionnement physique, magasin d'aliment naturel, etc.).

Il existe cependant un sentiment d'appartenance alors que la coopérative a permis de lutter contre un sentiment d'impuissance face à la perte éventuelle des services d'une clinique de médecins. Les usagers peuvent développer un lien privilégié, être reconnu à la coopérative, avoir accès à un médecin de famille.

La vie associative se doit d'être dynamique. À Aylmer, la CDR a entrepris un programme de formation auprès de l'ensemble des membres de la coopérative. Cette formation permet aux participants de mieux apprécier leurs droits et responsabilités, mais également de réfléchir à leur rôle comme membre. Une formation est également donnée aux administrateurs. Ce processus de formation continu facilite le développement d'un lien d'usage assez fort. Aylmer a également une infirmière communautaire, responsable des projets spéciaux. Elle est à l'écoute des besoins locaux et fait le lien avec la communauté.

Les embûches à surmonter

Au début, ce type de coopérative était perçu comme une forme de privatisation. Maintenant, il est davantage perçu comme étant la collectivisation d'un service privé. Les (anciens) opposants à ce type de coopérative ont reconnu l'importance de la mobilisation citoyenne. Ils ont ainsi réalisé qu'il ne s'agissait pas d'une simple transaction immobilière où les médecins transféraient la propriété de la bâtisse à la communauté.

L'emphase mise sur la promotion de la santé rejoint les tendances actuelles, et vise à redonner un rôle à la personne. L'État est davantage tourné vers le curatif alors que la coopérative est dans la prévention. Il y a donc là un nouveau paradigme à implanter.

Par ailleurs, les acteurs du secteur public comprennent mieux la formule coopérative de santé, mais le réflexe en est un de contrôle…alors qu'ils ne contrôlent pas la coopérative. Il existe donc un malaise entre les deux. Il n'y a aucune entente contractuelle entre la coopérative et le ministère de la santé. Ce lien est davantage avec le médecin.

Il y a un besoin d'une plus grande harmonisation des services entre le public et la coopérative alors que cette dernière est plus à l'écoute des attentes et besoins de la communauté. Ceci est particulièrement évident avec les GMF (groupes de médecins familiaux).

Il y a environ une douzaine de coopératives de santé actuellement au Québec. La prochaine étape est de faciliter leur réseautage via la création d'une fédération. Par ailleurs, le potentiel de coopératives de santé au Québec est élevé...au moins une par MRC, ce qui peut conduire à la création de plus d'une soixantaine de coopératives dans les 5 prochaines années.

2. Les coopératives de travailleurs actionnaires (CTA)

Il y a beaucoup d'échecs dans le domaine des CTA. Il en resterait à peine une soixantaine actuellement parce que cette formule est trop souvent vue comme une solution pour sauver l'entreprise. Pour pouvoir utiliser cette formule, il faut bien connaître l'outil et savoir l'utiliser.

La CTA n'est pas un outil de prise en charge. Ce n'est pas l'outil pour remplacer l'entreprise en difficulté parce que les travailleurs (regroupés en coopérative actionnaire) sont minoritaires au sein de l'actionnariat et ne détiennent pas le contrôle. Ce n'est donc pas un outil de sauvetage. Dans ce contexte, il ne faut donc pas craindre de ne pas recommander la formule CTA.

Par ailleurs, la CTA est un excellent outil de participation, d'intéressement et de développement de l'entreprise. C'et un excellent outil pour apprendre aux travailleurs comment investir. C'est donc une excellente école.

La clé pour réussir le démarrage d'une CTA est le choix de l'entreprise.

Comment s'y prendre pour réussir l'implantation d'une CTA...

1. Il faut d'abord procéder à une analyse d'implantation, et aller assez loin sur le volet de l'entreprise. Il faut diagnostiquer le volet ressources humaines et relation de travail pour s'assurer que l'entrepreneur ne veut pas simplement éviter la mise en place d'un syndicat par exemple.

2. Il est également important de s'assurer qu'il y a un projet de développement qui va demander la collaboration d'un 1/3. Ceci permettra non seulement d'associer les travailleurs, mais également d'impliquer un partenaire sensible à l'investissement collectif et coopératif, i.e. Capital régional et coopératif Desjardins, Investissement Québec, le FondAction, la caisse de solidarité, Filaction...L'implication de ces partenaires permet de s'assurer qu'en se retirant, ceux-ci vont privilégier la vente des actions aux travailleurs via leur CTA.

3. Il faut éviter de faire de la publicité autour de la formule des CTA. C'est davantage le bouche à oreille entre les entreprises qui est intéressant. Également entre les partenaires financiers impliqués dans divers projets de CTA.

4. Il faut du temps pour que la CTA puisse démarrer de la bonne manière. Il faut d'abord rencontrer les employés pour leur expliquer globalement de quoi il s'agit. Par la suite, il est important de rencontrer les employés deux fois sur une base individuelle. Ces derniers auront des questions personnelles à poser, ex. leur capacité à investir, qu'ils ne voudront pas poser devant leurs collègues de travail. La première rencontre est donc pour les informer et s'assurer qu'ils se posent bien toutes les questions importantes. Suite à cette rencontre, ils auront le loisir de consulter diverses personnes de leur entourage, poser/se faire poser d'autres questions. La 2e rencontre privée permet de refaire le tour de toutes ces questions.

5. L'analyse d'implantation requiert une compréhension de l'historique de l'entreprise, une analyse des états financiers de sorte à pouvoir démontrer ce qui pourrait arriver si les employés allaient investir dans cette entreprise, et les rencontres avec les employés.

6. Sur la base de ces analyses et rencontres, la CDR doit être en mesure de faire une recommandation sur l'ensemble du dossier et sur la pertinence de procéder à l'implantation d'une CTA dans cette entreprise. L'analyse d'implantation doit être remise aux employés.

7. Par la suite, la démarche de charte peut être enclenchée. S'ajoute la formation des employés, la tenue de l'assemblée de fondation et l'assemblée générale. Il faut également préparer les contrats d'actionnaires et l'achat d'actions par la CTA. Finalement, il y a la constitution du conseil d'administration de la CTA.

8. Pour l'achat d'action, la CTA peut procéder par emprunt ou sur la base d'un financement fournit par l'entreprise elle-même. Même si l'achat d'action se fait graduellement, la CTA aura tous les droits attachés au bloc d'action qu'elle compte détenir. Ce volet relié à l'action d'actions apporte beaucoup d'indice sur l'attitude et les intentions de l'entreprise en regard de l'implication des employés dans le capital de l'entreprise.

Si l'objectif de la CTA est d'assurer la relève à l'entrepreneur, l'objectif est différent. Quoique la CTA soit également pertinente dans ce contexte, les travailleurs auront à investir pour acheter le passé de l'entreprise.

3. Conversion et développement coopératif

La transformation d'entreprises privées en coopératives présente des défis importants qui requièrent des pratiques distinctes. L'expérience au Québec est principalement concentrée chez mce conseil. Ce groupe d'experts conseils est associé à la CSN et travail de concert avec les différents partenaires de ce syndicat de travailleurs. Voici l'approche qu'ils préconisent.

Au point de départ, les exigences traditionnelles de faisabilité, le projet économique, doivent tenir la route. Dans cette perspective, la coopérative est un moyen et non pas une fin en soi. Il faut donc s'assurer de la viabilité économique et de l'équilibre entre les talents et le marché.

Ceci permet de répondre à la question suivante : est-ce une bonne idée de convertir cette entreprise en coopératives. Il faut donc trouver une entreprise assez mal en point pour devoir vendre, mais également capable de survivre. De ce point de vue, mce conseil préfère avoir des chômeurs maintenant plutôt que des chômeurs plus tard…s'il s'avérait que le projet économique ne soit pas viable. Ils adoptent une approche très critique et responsable alors que les risques sont calculés. Ceci est d'autant plus important qu'ils travaillent en vase clos avec différents partenaires. Ils interviennent auprès des membres de la CSN et font toujours affaire avec les mêmes partenaires financiers. Avant qu'un projet de conversion aille de l'avant, il leur faut deux oui, le leur comme expert conseil et celui des travailleurs concernés.

Lors du processus de conversion, mce conseil accorde beaucoup d'importance à la formation des travailleurs, d'abord sur le fonctionnement démocratique coopératif, ensuite sur la gestion de l'entreprise. Ils accordent donc une grande importance à la formation économique pour que tous les travailleurs comprennent bien le volet affaires. Le conseil d'administration doit s'assurer de maîtriser tous les aspects de son plan d'affaires. Cela est un préalable avant le démarrage parce qu'ils peuvent mieux anticiper comment ils vont gérer par la suite. Il y a donc un gros travaille de vulgarisation qui doit être accompli.

La viabilité technico-économique d'abord, la formation ensuite et finale-ment la complicité et la transparence totale avec les partenaires financiers, voilà les préoccupations fondamentales de mce conseil dans une approche de conversion en coopératives. Il est important que leurs partenaires les trouvent responsables. Ils procèdent donc à un audit technique (marché et production) suivi d'un audit humain (expertise et culture). Il importe que les travailleurs puissent s'approprier le modèle coopératif, ce qui se fait à travers la formation et la rédaction des règlements de régie interne. Les experts de mce conseil les placent devant des choix et observent comment les travailleurs réagissent. Cette démarche prend davantage de temps mais permet d'arriver à des résultats plus solides. Ils insistent donc autant sur les volets économiques que coopératifs.

Le temps requis pour mener un projet à terme est d'environ 6 mois. Ils peuvent boucler le projet en 3 mois si tout tombe en place rapidement, mais l'ensemble du parcours peut s'étirer à 15 mois si des difficultés imprévues sont rencontrées.

Leur responsabilité, comme groupe conseil, est donc plus large parce que le travailleur n'a jamais envisagé la propriété. Ce dernier doit avoir une motivation plus grande que de simplement vouloir éviter le chômage.

Le taux de succès de mce conseil est très bon alors que le taux de survit des coopératives créées est très élevé. Par ailleurs, ces taux sont le résultat de la forte sélection des projets dès le démarrage basé sur un «screaning» important puisqu'ils ne retiennent que 50% des projets qui leur sont soumis. Ensuite, ils vont réussir 40% des projets alors que 60% seront abandonnés. À l'arrivée, ils auront procédé à la conversion de 20% des projets initiaux en coopératives de travail. Sur la vingtaine de coopératives créées, il y a très peu de cas d'échec (2). Sur les taux obtenus, mce conseil se pose la question de la sévérité associée à la sélection de projets soumis...

Depuis une quinzaine d'années mce conseil et son réseau de partenaires ont complété le développement des outils requis pour faciliter le développement coopératif. Alors qu'à la fin des années 80, la question du financement posait problème, ce n'est plus le cas aujourd'hui. Le financement de l'économie solidaire est en place au Québec...et la propriété collective est accessible.

Après avoir mené le dossier à terme, mce conseil voit à rajouter des conditions gagnantes au cours des années. Les coopératives où cela fonctionne le mieux sont celles qui les invitent par la suite. Ils sont ainsi invités à participer aux assemblées générales ainsi qu'aux conseils d'administration. Ce genre d'interventions peut être supporté financièrement par Emploi-Québec et ne coûte ainsi rien à la coopérative alors qu'elle permet d'éviter des crises.

mce conseil voit également à ramener la formation coopérative lorsqu'il y a des nouveaux membres. Ils assistent également les conseils d'administration sur la mise à jour de leur plan d'affaires.

L'entretien préventif est donc d'une grande importance. mce conseil a donc la possibilité de rejoindre la coopérative pour une assistance plus lourde si besoin est, alors que le suivi conseil est en grande partie financé par Emploi-Québec. Pour obtenir ce financement, une demande paritaire est formulée par la coopérative et mce conseil. Dans ce cadre, Emploi-Québec pourra participer. Il est prévu environ 30 heures / année «d'entretien préventif». Si une intervention plus substantielle est à prévoir, il faut compter environ 200 heures de travail. Il est donc important de trouver les moyens d'être accessible aux coopératives par l'entremise d'Emploi Québec et des CLD qui peuvent également supporter ce genre d'intervention.

Un exemple de conversion : le secteur ambulancier au Québec... émergence et développement d'une approche coopérative en contexte syndical

À ce moment-ci, il y a 8 coopératives ambulancières dans la province de Québec. Parmi ces dernières, 2 ont pris également la forme d'une CTA (coopérative des travailleurs actionnaires). Les autres sont des coopératives de travail.

Au total, nous retrouvons environ 850 employés dans les coopératives ambulancières. Donc, si nous excluons Montréal où intervient Urgence Santé (secteur public), les coopératives ambulancières réalisent environ la moitié des interventions ailleurs en province.

Les origines du développement coopératif dans ce secteur remontent aux débuts de la syndicalisation des ambulanciers en 1983-84. Suite à cette syndicalisation, les ambulanciers ont voulu négocier directement avec le gouvernement plutôt qu'avec les entreprises privées qui détenaient les permis d'ambulance.

Il y avait à cette époque de sérieux problèmes d'engorgement des urgences. Les ambulanciers avaient un rôle important face à cette problématique puisque leurs interventions pouvaient générer jusqu'à 80% du volume d'activités dans les urgences. Il y avait donc un grand besoin d'une meilleure répartition des patients amenés en ambulance entre les urgences. Ce besoin d'une plus grande coordination était rendu difficile à cause de la structure de l'industrie alors que nous retrouvions 23 entreprises privées d'ambulances à travers la province. Il y avait donc une gestion inefficace du traitement des appels. Une réorganisation de l'industrie était donc dans le meilleur intérêt du gouvernement (compter sur une structure ambulancière plus efficace et performante) ainsi que dans le meilleur intérêt des ambulanciers qui subissaient des conditions de travail très difficiles, à commencer par les salaires très bas, l'absence de formation, les équipements désuets, etc. L'idée d'unifier le réseau ambulancier pour plus d'efficacité devenait donc un enjeu d'une grande importance.

Du point de vue des entreprises privées, l'émergence d'une force syndicale où s'exprimait la volonté de négocier avec l'État les privait du contrôle sur 80% de leurs coûts (main d'œuvre). Ces dernières voyaient donc disparaître leur marge de profit et en sont rapidement arrivées à la conclusion qu'il valait mieux vendre.

Alors que les entreprises privées souhaitent vendre, le seul acheteur potentiel (à part l'État) était les travailleurs...L'idée de créer une coopérative s'est donc graduellement imposée. Par ailleurs, les ambulanciers (à l'époque) gagnaient $6/heure, et n'avaient donc pas les ressources pour investir dans l'achat des permis et équipements ambulanciers. De plus, les taux d'intérêts oscillaient entre 15% et 20%...Il y eu des tentatives de rachat à quelques endroits au Québec, au même moment que la syndicalisation s'étendait à l'échelle de la province. Dans ce contexte, la syndicalisation et la coopération étaient donc vues comme les deux ingrédients complémentaires à l'implantation d'une structure ambulancière plus efficace et organisée. Donc, à part pour les grands centres, c'est le modèle coopératif qui s'est imposé et s'est avéré le plus efficace.

Avant la syndicalisation/coopérativisation du secteur, l'industrie souffrait d'un manque de sécurité associé aux véhicules, d'équipements inadéquats et d'absence quasi-totale de formation. Maintenant, les véhicules respectent les standards de qualité du BNQ (bureau national de la qualité), les équipements sont très adéquats alors que tous les ambulanciers doivent recevoir une formation de niveau CEGEP (formation collégiale). Il y a donc eu des progrès énormes dans les services ambulanciers. Nous assistons également à une meilleure coordination avec les médecins qui vont jusqu'à rédiger les protocoles d'intervention des ambulanciers. Il y a donc eu une professionnalisation de l'ensemble de la profession.

Dans les coopératives actuelles, les travailleurs peuvent détenir, en moyenne, environ \$50 000 en parts privilégiées. Ce capital fut accumulé depuis les débuts (1983). Actuellement, les ambulanciers ont un salaire horaire de \$22 / heure. Par ailleurs, les ristournes versées aux membres sont importantes et peuvent s'élever à environ \$8 000 / année.

Sans l'action syndicale, le secteur coopératif ambulancier n'existerait pas. Il ne pourrait profiter des outils d'interventions économiques ayant permis la réorganisation du secteur. Il ne pourrait profiter des différents acteurs spécialisés dans l'accompagnement. Le succès dans ce secteur repose donc sur le réseau d'acteurs dans le giron de la CSN.

Trois phases dans le développement des coopératives ambulancières

1) Le développement de la coopérative

L'expertise technique requise pour mener à bien cette 1e phase est disponible et fournit par la CSN via mce Conseils. Ces derniers fourniront également l'encadrement et la formation des travailleurs impliqués. Le financement requis au démarrage est également fourni par le réseau de finance solidaire dans le giron de la CSN, au premier chef par la caisse d'économie solidaire.

Actuellement, le démarrage d'une coopérative ambulancière est rendu très difficile si vous n'êtes pas syndiqués (CSN). Les ambulanciers syndiqués n'ont qu'à confier un mandat à leur syndicat. Celui fera appel à l'expertise du groupe conseil mce Conseils pour l'expertise technique, économique et coopérative, ainsi qu'au réseau de finance solidaire issu de la CSN (FondAction, caisse d'économie solidaire, Filaction) pour obtenir les capitaux requis.

2) La gestion au quotidien

Il est important de trouver le bon modèle pour assurer un meilleur équilibre entre les parties prenantes dans une coopérative ambulancière. Trois acteurs clés interviennent, i.e. les travailleurs syndiqués, les (mêmes) travailleurs coopérateurs et le gouvernement. Un 4e acteur, le financier (réseau CSN), est également impliqué. Les difficultés d'une bonne gestion au quotidien sont accrues dans la mesure où nous observons une certaine confusion entre le syndicat et la coopérative. Le gouvernement est impliqué par l'entremise des pratiques professionnelles. La gestion au quotidien de ces entités est donc plus complexe alors que les plus grosses coopératives regroupent plus de 200 membres.

Alors que les revenus sont garantis (par l'État), il importe de garantir un bon contrôle des dépenses pour assurer la pérennité de la coopérative.

3) L'expansion du modèle

La 3e phase implique l'expansion du modèle. Les outils (réseau CSN) qui furent mis sur pied ont permis de fournir l'expertise technique, l'encadrement conseil, autant au plan économique que coopératif, et le financement. Il est donc parfaitement réaliste d'envisager l'expansion.

La formule coopérative est avantageuse, autant pour le gouvernement que pour les ambulanciers. Les autres acteurs du milieu de la santé changent leur perception des ambulanciers. Ces derniers deviennent de plus en plus des partenaires au sein du réseau alors l'efficacité des interventions s'accroît.

Alors qu'il y a encore de l'espace pour la consolidation impliquant les entreprises privées (familiales), il est également possible d'envisager le secteur connexe du transport adapté, actuellement inefficace parce que mal organisé. L'inefficacité du secteur du transport adapté a des répercussions sur le secteur ambulancier lorsque ceux-ci sont appelés en remplacement alors que le transport ambulancier est plus coûteux.

Financement Capital régional et coopératif Desjardins

Le rôle des financiers dans le développement coopératif est fondamental. Nous entendons régulièrement des intervenants citer l'absence de capitaux comme étant une cause majeure du «non développement coopératif». Au-delà des acteurs et modèles dont nous avons présenté les pratiques dans les deux premières sections, cette dernière section revisite cette question des pratiques, mais d'un point de vue de financier cette fois. Quelles sont leurs pratiques, et comment s'harmonisent-ils avec celles des développeurs? À cet égard, il importe de mentionner que le Québec a vu se développer plusieurs acteurs financiers dédiés au financement coopératif au cours des 20 dernières années. Ceux-ci ont une approche respectueuse du développement coopératif, et travaillent en partenariat. Voyons l'approche privilégiée par Capital régional et coopératif Desjardins.

Capital régional coopératif Desjardins (CRCD) accorde un financement minimal de $250 000 pour chaque projet coopératif qu'il accepte de financer. Le financement accordé n'est aucunement lié à des garanties et complète le financement requis après que les financiers classiques aient accepté de s'impliquer.

En raison de leur politique interne, les secteurs coopératifs financés par CRCD touchent principalement les secteurs agricoles, forestiers et manufacturiers. Ils ne financent pas les coopératives de consommation à moins que celles-ci opèrent plusieurs points de services. Les secteurs et projets coopératifs non couverts par CRCD peuvent trouver un financement auprès des autres instances du réseau Desjardins, ex. les CFE (centres de financement aux entreprises).

Les types de financement possibles sont l'équité (et quasi-équité), les débentures non convertibles, le capital privilégié et les dettes. Ils offrent donc une gamme d'outils qui couvrent bien les besoins actuels des coopératives. CRCD peut également s'associer avec ses partenaires tels le RISQ, FondAction, Filaction, la caisse de solidarité, Investissement Québec...

Plutôt que l'insuffisance de fonds, c'est davantage la qualité des projets coopératifs qui limite le développement coopératif. Ceci s'explique en partie par le fait que le développement coopératif soit davantage tourné vers des projets sociaux depuis quelques années.

Le CRCD finance environ 5 à 6 dossiers par année. Pour ce faire, ils doivent étudier de 25 à 30 dossiers. Les taux chargés sont compétitifs et peuvent fluctuer entre 6¾ % et 13 %. Pour assurer une rentabilité, ils doivent charger des taux moyens d'environ 8% à 9%. Sur les 17 dossiers financés à ce jour par CRCD, il n'y a eu aucune faillite alors que seulement trois dossiers sont jugés plus à risque. Les autres sont de bons à très bons.

Les critères d'obtention du financement

Trois points précis à considérer : (1) vérifier que le marché soit porteur, (2) s'assurer de la compétence de l'équipe de gestion, et, (3) évaluer la vitalité du volet associatif. Ce dernier point est également jugé comme étant très important et fait l'objet d'une analyse systématique.

Il y a une vérification diligente très poussée des dossiers. Le positionnement stratégique de la coopérative est analysé. Le plan d'affaires sera donc validé en profondeur. S'ils pensent qu'il y a un danger pour les membres, ils vont le laisser savoir. Lorsqu'un financement est accordé, un représentant de CRCD est mandaté pour siéger au conseil d'administration de la coopérative. Cette personne sera un expert qui pourra «ajouter de la valeur».

CRCD peut compter sur toute une équipe d'experts en gestion, redressement, développement de marché, communication, etc. qu'ils peuvent mettre au service de la coopérative. Cet apport à valeur ajouté est disponible sans coût additionnel pour la coopérative. Cette équipe d'experts n'est pas disponible chez Investissement Québec alors que FondAction a moins de ressources pour offrir la même qualité de service.

Les dossiers de financement peuvent être réalisés à l'aide de partenaires, i.e. Investissement Québec, FondAction et la caisse de solidarité dans une moindre mesure.

L'analyse du volet associatif reprend celle menée par la CDR, mais avec davantage de profondeur[2]. Ils veulent s'assurer de l'implication des travailleurs et sont présents aux assemblées générales. Ils tiennent à avoir des contacts directs avec les membres. Des rencontres sont donc organisées avec les membres, les dirigeants et les partenaires. Ils veulent s'assurer qu'ils ont affaire à une vraie coopérative. L'outil diagnostic utilisé pour l'analyse du volet coopératif et associatif est très développé.

L'analyse du volet coopératif est très importante car s'il y a des problèmes en cours de route, ils seront appelés à investir davantage. Ils veulent donc s'assurer que les membres pourront (et voudront) également investir dans leur propre coopérative.

Ils ne sont jamais dans le dossier dès le début. Ils ne sont interpellés que lorsqu'il y a un plan d'affaires de monter.

Conclusion

Ce chapitre aura permis d'explorer cette question des pratiques, d'abord d'un point de vue global. Trois grands champs de pratiques furent identifiées : l'animation, la concertation et l'accompagnement. Le contexte dans lequel celles-ci s'appliquent le mieux est évidemment celui d'une région puisque la proximité avec les acteurs est une clé essentielle. La pérennité d'un réseau d'acteurs dédiés au développement coopératif s'avère ici déterminant. En effet, comment assurer que ce travail de base (animation et concertation) se fasse sans une équipe qui y consacre des efforts constants,

---

2 Un «check list» de 7 pages est utilisé pour mener à bien cette validation.

dans une perspective de long terme. Le rôle en amont des acteurs coopératifs (CDR) est donc très important alors que nous avons davantage tendance à focaliser sur les pratiques d'accompagnement.

La deuxième section de ce chapitre nous aura permis d'aborder deux nouveaux modèles coopératifs à l'origine du dynamisme dans le développement coopératif au Québec au cours des 20 dernières années. Les coopératives de solidarité et les coopératives de travailleurs actionnaires sont des moteurs importants du renouveau coopératif, au-delà des modèles traditionnels (consommation, production, travail et habitation). La coopérative de solidarité rend possible une approche multipartite, offrant la possibilité d'impliquer trois types de membres, soit les usagers, les travailleurs et les membres de soutien. La souplesse de ce nouveau modèle lui aura permis de devenir la formule la plus utilisée maintenant, particulièrement lorsqu'il s'agit de faire face à des défis de développement local. Le cas particulier des coopératives de santé (la forte majorité des coopératives de santé créées au Québec choisissent le statut de coopératives de solidarité) illustre bien les possibilités d'une telle formule. Par ailleurs, les coopératives de travailleurs actionnaires offrent l'énorme avantage de permettre le développement coopératif dans des secteurs d'activités économiques souvent inaccessibles à la coopération traditionnel. En effet, les CTA sont conçues pour faciliter le regroupement des travailleurs d'une même entreprise, et permettre l'achat d'actions de l'entreprise pour laquelle ils travaillent. Avec une telle formule, il devient donc possible d'envisager le développement coopératif dans des activités plus exigeantes en matière de capitalisation.

Ces deux nouveaux modèles requièrent des pratiques de développement distincts et qui débordent des pratiques de base. D'où l'importance d'en décrire les particularités. Le troisième axe mentionné dans cette deuxième section concerne la conversion des entreprises privées en coopératives (de travail habituellement). Là également, des pratiques distinctes sont essentielles. Le rôle clé des acteurs syndicaux et partenaires associés s'avère déterminant dans un tel contexte. L'exemple des coopératives ambulancières illustre bien la complexité de tout ce processus. Nous pouvons ainsi observer non seulement la conversion d'entreprises privées en coopératives, mais également la réorganisation d'un secteur économique dans sa quasi-totalité.

Finalement, ce chapitre aborde également la question des pratiques de développement coopératif du point de vue d'un financier. À cet égard, il est intéressant de noter l'importance accordée au volet associatif et à la vitalité coopérative.

Section Two:
Financing Co-ops

Chapter Six

Social Capital and Financing Co-op Start-Ups

Marty Frost

When a group is trying to start a co-operative to serve a common need or a community need, few problems will be more complex or difficult than raising the necessary financial capital to launch and grow their co-op. Financial capital will, in general, take two forms: equity capital and borrowed capital. Equity capital is generally received in one or more forms of capital investment – buying shares in the co-op is an equity investment. Borrowed capital is received as loans of one type or another, or as operating credit – supplier accounts, leases, and so on.

Equity *capital* is generally the first financial capital invested by the members and other investors, before any borrowed capital is sought. Generally divided into a number of shares in the co-op, equity capital represents the ownership of the co-operative and carries the highest level of risk. In the event of failure or dissolution of the co-op, holders of equity capital will be paid out last; in the event there are not sufficient funds from dissolution of the assets to pay out everyone, equity capital may not be repaid.

The Relationship between Financial Capital and Social Capital

The purpose of equity capital investment in a co-operative is to provide cash to launch a business or economic activity that will benefit the members. When a co-operative's economic activity generates profits that exceed what is needed to provide sufficient financial reserves, the excess is generally returned to the members based on the level to which each member has used the services of the co-operative. Members, in fact, "receive limited compensation, if any, on capital subscribed as a condition of membership."[1] Co-ops, after all, are created to serve members' needs, not to serve invested capital. Often this arrangement of a limited return on capital investments will influence offerings of equity capital by non-members. In addition, the offered terms and conditions on such equity capital may not be competitive with other forms of investment, perhaps even other forms of investment with less risk than a business start-up. This does not create an investment environment that will attract large amounts of equity capital, particularly from non-members.

Financial capital dominates our economic culture. Those in our culture, who are very wealthy, for the most part gained their wealth through making strategic capital investments in property or in businesses. A smart investment can yield the investor a return that may be in multiples of the original investment, however, in co-ops the return is often low or non-existent. Our economic culture, therefore, is structured such that we expect risk-related financial capital to provide returns that are virtually unattainable in a co-op capital structure, where the initial purpose of the capital investment is to provide a service to its members, and where the members are the primary beneficiaries. The very words "...limited compensation, if any, on capital subscribed" can bring an abrupt end to any conversation with a potential investor.

The dominant business model that serves the economic culture is the limited liability corporation, and it is structured for just one purpose – service of the financial capital invested by shareholders. When a limited liability corporation earns profits, it is the owners of the shares that benefit, not the employees, not the users of the company's products or services, but the owners of the shares. Indeed, one of the fiduciary duties of a director of a limited liability corporation is to maximize the benefit to the shareholders. In this case, "benefit" has been defined as financial return.

A co-op is designed not to serve financial capital but to serve the needs of its members. When co-op equity investment is restricted to members,

---

1 The International Co-operative Alliance, Statement of the Co-operative Identity.

it may be enough to offer the "limited compensation, if any," described above. Along with this limited compensation of financial capital goes a package of services or goods that are important to the members and have real, demonstrable economic value. Co-ops by their nature, however, often work to serve those who are under-advantaged. As a result, it is sometimes difficult to raise even a small amount of equity capital from members of a new co-op. For this and other reasons, financial investment in the capital of a co-op by people who are not members is now an option in virtually all jurisdictions in Canada.

As the door has opened to financial investment from the larger community, co-ops that need or choose to include non-member investment in their capital structures are challenged to offer terms and conditions that will attract this kind of investment. This situation will arise particularly in the start-up period. Start-up equity capital is viewed by the market of potential non-member investors as speculative or venture capital; high risk, and therefore deserving of higher returns. Keep in mind that, non-member investors will not receive the intrinsic benefits that the co-op will be offering to its members. Unfortunately, under the conditions of low return on investments and not receiving direct intrinsic benefits, most investors will not even consider investing to start a new co-op.

In trying to make their proposed capital investment more attractive, some co-operatives choose to put forward the value of the work they do as an inducement to invest. For example, a worker co-operative may be designed to provide employment to disadvantaged workers, or a credit union or co-operative food store may be opened in an economically challenged neighbourhood. In cases like this, there is intrinsic value in the connections that are formed between people in the community and economic value for the community in which the co-operative is created. This is described varyingly as community capital, environmental capital, human capital, and more and more frequently, as social capital. With each of these descriptions, the co-op members are choosing to offer an investor not just the direct financial return on the invested capital, but an additional return by way of overall improvement in the welfare of a community, the good of society, or the good of the planet's ecology. This can be an effective strategy for raising capital — more and more potential investors are people who have some awareness of social issues that communities face and of ecological concerns. To use social capital as an effective strategy for raising capital, the co-op members must be aware of these social and ecological benefits, they must learn the language and understand it thoroughly, they must choose what message goes to what "market," and they must design their marketing campaign for raising financial capital as carefully as they plan the marketing plan for their products.

We need to look closely at two terms. Above we talked about equity capital – the financial capital that every business, co-operative, or other enterprise, needs to start-up its operation. The average co-op needs access to financial capital. Then we talked about social capital – the benefits that arise from carrying on the co-op's activities and that accrue not only to the co-op's members but to the community as a whole as a result of the connections made between members and the community. This is what the average co-op has to offer. The challenge facing co-operatives (and other community-based enterprises) is to convince the investing public that the social capital created by the co-operative has an intrinsic and economically measurable value that augments and increases the direct financial return offered on an investment in the co-operative.

To begin, let's ground ourselves with a better understanding of financial capital.

Financial Capital and Co-operatives

The first round of financial capital in a co-op will nearly always be equity capital invested by the members. This will be either in the form of cash or a *share subscription*, a legal commitment to pay cash at the request of the co-op. If the business plan calls for more financial capital than the current members can afford to (or are willing to) invest, the co-op must look to other "markets" for this capital, usually a combination of investment by non-members and borrowed capital.

Going back to our conventional economic culture, when we use the word "capital" in the context of business, people immediately think of money invested in a business, usually a limited liability corporation, either to start it up, or to provide the necessary means for the business to finance its growth and development. Within conventional economic arrangements, the individual or individuals who invest the capital will be rewarded with ownership of some or all of the business's economic value, as represented by their portion of the total shares the business issues. If the business is successful, a person's original investment may be worth multiples of its original value on withdrawal. The economic capital generated by the money and work invested in the business comes back to the owners of the shares.

In the case of a co-op, the economic value of the business will, in large part, be owned collectively. In a successful co-op, if a founding member leaves, the value of their original investment will be essentially what it was at the time of initial investment, although this may be augmented by allocations of the member's share of any distributed surplus or an interest rate that may be applied on the value of the initial investment. The majority of the economic capital generated will stay in the co-operative, hence in the community. It is partly for this reason – the retention of capital in a community – that development of new co-ops will often be financed by an outside party, such as a government department or a sponsoring agency. (I differentiate between funding and financing – the difference being that in some form or other, financing gets paid back, whereas funding does not.) This kind of funding is available because of the recognition of the benefit that co-ops intrinsically provide to their community and society, rather than just providing an economic return to the individuals who may have started the co-op. Such support is usually tied to a specific activity, like co-op incorporation, member development, development of a business plan, and sometimes to some post-launch mentoring.

Borrowed capital is difficult to obtain at start-up. Lenders look for things like solid management, proven track record for the business and product, something they can attach as collateral, the financial systems in place, and enough cash flow to service the debt. Most lenders won't consider lending until at least the first few sales have been made. It takes financial capital to make these first steps, and that capital has to come from member (and possibly non-member) investors in the form of equity investment.

How much investment is needed? That will depend on the state of the co-op's development. If the co-op has not yet hired its management team and not yet made its first business transactions, the members should plan to have at least 50% of their capital already secured before approaching a lender or lenders for the balance. If the co-op has already hired its management team, possibly secured one or two customers or deals, and can provide an accurate financial statement it may suffice to have 30% of the capital on board. Other factors will also enter into the decisions around how much financial capital is going to be needed to launch the business and from whom the capital will come. It is a complex negotiation, and one that has as much to do with the relationship the co-op members are able to build with a lender or investor as it does with the numbers shown on the cash flow forecast or the business plan.

All of this can be ameliorated by other circumstances and creative use of available investing and borrowing models. In the case of one client co-op I worked with, the ultimate financing package consisted of the following arrangements:

- Repayable equity investment funds (This fund was originally set up by a non-profit economic development agency for the specific purpose of investing in the co-op. On repayment, these funds would

be lent out to another community business start-up under the same terms.)
- A repayable equity investment amount contributed by a social investor
- A loan from a credit union secured by the co-op's assets
- Another loan from the same credit union secured by a loan guarantee from the same social investor.

This, combined with equity investment by members and non-members, was enough to complete the launch of the business, which continues to provide invaluable services to its members. It was also negotiated on the basis of strong relationships that the founding members had developed with the lenders and investors.

When approaching lenders, it will seldom serve your purpose to talk about the value your co-op will bring to your community or the social value of the work you do. In this domain, the language is finance. It is a rare lender (though a few exist) that will respond positively to a pitch based on the social capital your co-op will provide. Credit unions, as financial co-operatives, may have a deeper understanding of the way a co-operative will work and may prove positive lending partners. Regardless of this, when you are approaching any lender, in addition to the good work you are going to do, make sure you can convince them you have some assets to secure the loan (either the co-op has them or one or more members have them), the co-op will be able to repay the loan, you yourself have invested in the business, and the co-op has the technical and management expertise on board to make sure the business is a good one. Then, maybe talk about your social capital.

Equity investment from members has to form the core of any capital plan. In most provinces of Canada, equity investment in a co-op can also be accepted from non-members – people who support the purpose for which the co-op is being formed, but who won't necessarily fit the definition of a member as defined by the co-op's bylaws. This is the arena in which the concept of social capital may provide positive returns. Even here, however, it has to be combined with a sound financial plan and most often with a financial return.

Social Capital and Co-operatives

Social capital as a concept is complex and is a whole school for study. Indeed, lots of resources are being applied to the concept of social capital and identifying ways it can be used to overcome problems of isolation and community breakdown through more integrated economic development.

Social capital is defined in "Wikipedia" (the online encyclopedia) as "the advantage created by a person's location in a structure of relationships. It explains how some people gain more success in a particular setting through their superior connections to other people."[2]

Some superb writing has been done on social capital, its place in a democratic society, and its ability to address problems affecting our communities. From the point of view of co-op members, though, the above definition somewhat captures the sentiment. Stated generally, social capital exists in co-ops simply because of the connections that are formed among co-op members as they work, shop, or live at their co-op. Robert Putnam, one of the predominant writers on social capital, identifies two major components of social capital: "bonding social capital," which refers to bringing homogenous groups of people together, and "bridging social capital," referring to bringing heterogenous groups of people together.[3] Members of co-ops are "bonded" through their mutual association to address a common need. Members of co-ops form "bridging social capital" in the ways they act to bring people of different social backgrounds together for the collective good. While it may seldom be articulated in these terms, co-ops, by their very nature, produce social capital as a direct result of how they connect people under different circumstances within any given community.

Social capital theory purports that collective enterprises commonly have the capacity to generate social capital. For example, when applied to community enterprises various writings equate a high degree of social capital with: high rates of labour productivity, a stable workforce, a strong inclination toward innovation, and the longevity of these initiatives. These traits have also been identified as qualities inherent in many co-operative businesses. In business reality though, being right is not necessarily enough. In approaching a potential buyer of the co-op's product or service, it is the qualities of the product or service that must be front and centre. Few customers will buy a product or service because of the social mission or qualities of the co-op - unless the product or service is superior, or at least equivalent in price and quality to what the customer could obtain elsewhere. While few investors will invest in the equity of a co-op because of its social purpose or the benefits it provides to a community, unless the investment meets their expected rates of return and level of security, there is a growing community of investors that will invest because they value a social return as part of the compensation for their investment.

---

2 Extracted from < http://en.wikipedia.org/wiki/Social_capital> (November 2006).
3 Robert D Putnam, *Bowling Alone: The Collapse and Revival of American Community* (Simon and Shuster, 2000).

A few years ago, I had the privilege of working with a group of adults with disabilities, "self-advocates" as they described themselves. The project was hosted by the asssociation that had been providing support to these people for a number of years. The idea was to create a small business that would be run as a worker co-op, of which they would be the member/employees. The association felt there was a "captive" market among similar community groups and agencies that would be interested in their product as soon as they heard that the folks were self-advocates. On assessment, that market had the potential to provide enough revenue to generate a reasonable living wage to support the four folks who would be working members. The project went ahead. One of the members discovered a real love and affinity for marketing and went about her work. Their self-advocacy, they had determined, would be a key part of their marketing. Before long she was completely demoralized by the response she was getting from this "captive" market. Instead of being supported, she found that potential customers were reluctant to give her their business because they doubted the ability of the group to provide a quality product. At one point she stated, "They take one look at me and close the door." Even though the quality of the product was high, the business was unable to meet its sales targets. After a number of years of hard work, and of continued support from the founding agency, the business was closed. The social capital inherent in the co-op was not enough to sustain it in the market of their product.

Another project I had the privilege of working on, has seen a different result on the capital side. A co-op was formed to secure the agricultural intergity of a piece of farm land bordered by a small, but fast-growing, city. The land was small, only 27 acres, hence with limited productive capacity, and a half million dollars was needed to secure the land. In order to avoid the complications of the Securities Act, the capital was structured with membership shares only, valued at $5,000 apiece. We felt the productive capacity of the land would only accommodate the production needs of about five members, and that at very modest scale. Other members would have an opportunity to be involved, but in a limited way – as buyers of product from the land, as participants in co-op hosted market gardens, and in governance issues. The principal "product" the co-op had to offer its members was the security of knowing that for the next 100 years, this piece of land would be preserved for agricultural purposes. Within a couple of months the co-op had received commitments from over 100 people to buy shares in the co-op. In this case, a group of people showed a readiness to invest in the social capital of the co-op with little material return promised.

These experiences are repeated elsewhere, both in co-operative enterprises and in non-profit based enterprises. The social capital inherent in the business is often more effective as a marketing tool for raising financial capital than it is for marketing products and services.

Social capital resides in many resources, institutions, and even practices of communities, but a dominant theme is that social capital is strengthened when people create and interract through their networks. These networks may have their bases in service clubs, social organizations, or economic activity, as in the case of members of a co-op. Ralph Matthews, a professor of sociology at the University of British Columbia, and his colleagues are carrying out strategic research through the "Resilient Communities Project." He comments, "A community that has a dense internal social network structure in which many of its members are also linked to outside activities and groups, is in a potentially strong social network position. If such networks are indeed instrumental to economic development, as Putnam and others contend, then such a community is also well placed to benefit from new economic opportunities than may arise."[4] It is the "bonding" and the "bridging" aspect of social networks that creates the cohesiveness in a community that in turn encourages stability in the economic activities carried out there and the responsiveness of potential investors to new economic opportunities.

Conclusion

What is the message we take from this? Co-ops are producers and repositories of social capital. Active involvement of co-op members in the ownership and governance of a co-operative in itself, produces social capital. Will this assist a group starting a co-op to meet a common need? Only in as much as the founders of the co-op are conversant with the benefits of social capital and the language that surrounds it. Essentially a co-op has two "products" each with its own demands, each with its own benefits. The product or service that a co-op delivers to its customers – be they members or the buying public – has the ability to provide the co-op with operating revenue which contributes to the financial capital of the co-op. It is imperative, therefore, that effective marketing of the co-op's product or service take place such that the co-op can survive. The other "product" of the co-op is the social capital it will create. This too, must be effectively marketed, but the market is a different one. The market for the social capital "product" will be the co-op's members and specific lenders or investors – those who have an expressed orientation toward businesses with a social purpose.

4 Ralph Matthews, University of British Columbia, *Using a Social Capital Perspective to Understand Social and Economic Development*. <policyresearch.gc.ca/page.asp?pagenm=v6n3_art_06>.

The key to successful capitalization then, is to identify to which market you are trying to appeal, and to design your marketing efforts to match the listener. In working with co-op start-ups, I often encourage them to create "modular" business plans for securing investment. All business plan presentations will use about 70% of the modules, the other 30% is taylored for a specific party, and will be changed, based on who the audience is. That helps in ensuring that whether the listener is a potential customer, a conventional lender, or a social investor, they will be hearing the right message, the message they want to hear.

The generation of social capital – as a beneficial and effective outcome for strenthening communities both economically and culturally – should be given a higher profile in social policies governing economic development. Development of co-operatives would be a valuable component of any such development. Until it is better understood, though, generation of social capital is unlikely to receive the attention it warrants. Part of the understanding needs to be in developing ways to measure or quantify the value of the social capital where it exists. "If social capital analysis is to become a useful public policy tool, it is necessary to understand not only what it is and how it works but also the link between social capital and other forms of capital, most notably human capital and economic capital."[5] Putnam and others believe that these links exist.

Putnam notes an "overall decline in social capital" in the U.S. over the past 50 years[6] and has observed inevitable negative consequences for American society. The social capital that exists in co-operatives has real value to our communities and our culture and needs to be fostered and grown. We can only contribute to this to the extent that our co-ops are successful, and they will only be successful to the extent that we can secure enough financial capital to keep them healthy and start new ones where they are needed. Clarity in understanding the social capital we hold, and the financial capital we require, is essential to this task.

---

5 Ralph Matthews, *Using a Social Capital Perspective to Understand Social and Economic Development.*
6 Putnam, "Bowling Alone."

Chapter Seven

Capitalization of Co-operative Development in Canada

Greg O'Neill

C apital financing specifically for co-operative development in Canada has been an uneven experience historically and geographically. A basic assumption for this essay is that the existing array of funds available through government programming, foundation funding, the private sector, and other sources is not effective in supporting co-operative development. The reasons are examined in further sections of this essay. Briefly, governments at all levels, with few exceptions, have moved away from providing capital to developing enterprises of any sort. The rules governing charitable giving under the Canada Revenue Agency prohibit support for co-operatives in which members may derive a "personal benefit" such as employment income or patronage dividends. Private sector financing for new co-operatives is too risk-averse and/or expensive to be effective as developmental investment. Finally, the share capital structure and democratic principles of co-operatives makes accessing venture capital a complex and difficult endeavour.

I have been involved in the creation and management of several co-operative specific development funds. I served as manager for the Co-operative Investor Support Programme, the first fund specifically developed for financing the creation of worker co-operatives in Canada by the Newfoundland Labrador Federation of Co-operatives. Later, I managed the Arctic Co-operative Development Fund (ACDF) for 9 years. This fund was established to provide financing and be the financial arm for co-operatives in Canada's Northwest and Nunavut Territories. I also authored studies for the Canadian Worker Co-operative Federation (CWCF) and La Fédération des Coopératives du Nouveau-Québec (FCNQ) on the creation and expansion of their development funds. In recent years, I have also co-authored a business case for the development of a co-operative financial services network in the Northwest and Nunavut Territories.

I have been an active co-operative developer with various affiliations including the Extension Department of St. Francis Xavier University, the Extension Community Development Co-operative in St. John's Newfoundland, The Newfoundland and Labrador Federation of Co-operatives, Arctic Co-operatives Limited, and as a co-operative consultant and member of various worker co-operatives.

The primary lesson I have learned from this experience is that if co-operatives intend to be an effective and significant alternative in the economy, access to capital specific to the needs of co-operatives and controlled by people with co-operative values is absolutely necessary. Lack of co-operative specific funding is a central dilemma in the development of co-operatives as an alternative to corporate enterprise. If co-operatives intend to infuse the economy with people-centred values, as opposed to capital-centric values, the way in which they are capitalized is vitally important. If co-operatives are forced to become capitalized based on standard capital market conditions then co-ops end up importing capital-centric values into their practice rather than injecting people-centred values into the economy.

Co-ops and Access to Capital

Co-operatives are a legal form of incorporation that are regulated through legislation at the provincial or territorial level. There is also federal legislation that enables the incorporation of co-operatives that operate in more than two jurisdictions. Investment in co-operatives is prescribed by legislation and is generally restricted to those who will use the services of the co-operative. There have been recent changes to legislation that allow for an investor class of membership in co-operatives (solidarity co-ops or multi-stakeholder co-ops), as well as opening the possibility for outside investors as shareholders, but the co-operative principles limit the control that investors may have over the decision making process in co-operatives.

Recent experiences of some co-ops that have tried to mix public shareholding and member shareholding as a means to raise capital through public offerings has resulted in loss of membership control in some large co-ops and the loss of their co-operative status. The prairie wheat pools are a case in point.

Venture capital corporations are not equipped to provide investment in co-operative enterprises; they are designed to service private corporations. Co-operatives typically have limited possibilities for raising private capital while retaining their co-operative nature. A co-operative mechanism that is the equivalent to publicly traded equity investments in corporations has yet to be developed. Nonetheless, non-financial co-operatives in Canada had $6 billion in equity in 2003.[1]

There are co-ops that people are developing to respond to needs that are emerging as a result of changes in local economies as they are negatively impacted by global corporatism and the reduction of services provided by governments. However, it is extremely difficult for many developing and emerging co-operatives to raise capital from external sources. This is because of the high risk associated with investment by the private sector in marginalized communities (a place where new co-operatives can be most effective) and because of additional risks associated with the constraints to success in remote and rural communities.

One strength of co-operatives in terms of ownership and share structure, is in the retention of profits or surpluses in the communities in which the co-operatives provide service. Co-ops allow for equitable participation in the democratic governance of the enterprise and allow people with little or no capital to pool their resources so that what one person could not do individually, a community of people can do. This makes them unattractive investments to private investors, because co-ops are not equipped to distribute profits on shares based on the volume of shares held by an investor.

The fact that the greatest need and opportunity for new and emerging co-operatives will be in marginalized economic circumstances also makes them less likely to be able to acquire equity investment. For example, in a paper prepared for the National Aboriginal Capital Corporations Association by Michael Rice in November of 2001, there was a breakdown of how equity investment in Canadian businesses generally compared to the same type of investment in Aboriginal businesses. Using 1999 figures, the amount of equity investment made in Canadian Businesses was $380 billion. Based

1 See: http://www.agr.ca/rcs-src/co-op/pub/pdf/co-opcan03_e.pdf

on the percentage of population in Canada a proportionate investment in Aboriginal businesses would have been $4.8 billion. The actual investment made by equity investors in Aboriginal businesses was $80 million.

Sources of financing available to other businesses in Canada are not available to new and emerging co-operatives for two main reasons: the co-operative nature of their enterprises and the fact that they are in geographic or economically challenged areas. A self-managed revolving loan fund is required if new and emerging co-operative enterprises are to have fair access to developmental investment.

Co-operatives are different from corporate enterprises in many ways. Primarily, they offer an opportunity for a group of people to collectively meet their needs through providing services to themselves through an enterprise whose ownership they share. They are immune to the flight of investment capital fleeing to ever-higher rates of return. They are a community of interest embedded in a geographic community. They are not transient. Co-operatives that are developing or emerging as a response to the vacuum created by government's retreat from social programme spending and the loss of jobs in manufacturing and primary industry sectors need co-operative-appropriate sources of venture capital.

Co-operative Development Opportunities: A Review of Needs

As the out-migration from rural areas to urban centres accelerates, as our economy continues to move from an industrial to service/information based economy, and as government moves away from its role as intermediary in wealth redistribution larger numbers of Canadians are not able to access the basic services they need. Co-operatives exist to provide services to the increasing number of people who need them. Canada needs more co-operatives. Below are two basic rationales for more co-operative development.

1. Decline in Government Services

Beyond the philosophical and political dimensions of co-operatives as they relate to economic democracy, there is a very practical reason for the support and creation of co-operatives. Co-operatives exist in a special economic niche between state capitalism (state enterprise, crown corporations, etc.) and corporate capitalism. That niche is expanding in Canada. Governments have been engaged in the privatization of state-run industries and businesses and continue to reduce funding to social programmes in health, education, and other social services.

The Canadian Council on Social Development tracks the investment that the Government of Canada has made in Social Development. Some of the key points to consider are that in recent years $8.2 billion has been removed from federal transfers to the provinces. That is a reduction of 30%. This has negatively affected the provinces' ability to deliver services such as health care, education, and supporting social assistance programmes. The Government of Canada now spends only 11.6% of GDP on social programmes, the lowest level since 1950. The analysis does not include the additional cuts made by the Government of Canada on September 25, 2006.

The rise of social co-operatives in many European countries and within Quebec provides a practical demonstration of how co-operatives can be effective in filling the gap. A publication available through the Co-operatives Secretariat entitled *The Co-operative Alternative to Public Service Delivery* provides an excellent starting point for understanding what is possible.

2. Impact of Changes in the Economy

At the same time as government has been stepping back, a number of economic factors have added to the need for more co-operative development. Since the 1970s, the transformation of the economy from a manufacturing/industrial base to a service/information technology base has left many people in rural Canada, and many urban residents, behind. The flight of capital investment as a result of economic globalization has also left its mark on many communities in Canada.

The following excerpts from various studies and reports lend support to the assertion that Canadians in rural and urban environments are being negatively impacted by the changes in government policy and increased global trade.

Example One: Employment in manufacturing has declines for the past four years (2002-2006). Statistics Canada reported the sector had lost 11,300 jobs in August 2006 for a total of 87,000 jobs lost since the beginning of the year. ... Businesses may be responding to the challenges of a higher currency and international completion by investing in machinery and equipment to raise productivity.[2]

Example Two: The forestry industry has been especially hammered lately as both structural and cyclical adjustments have changed the competitive nature of Canadian wood fiber and paper products. Information in a report produced by Natural Resources Canada [3] lists 46 plant closures. For the most part these are closures in communities that are single industry towns, and in many cases the sole major employer.

Example Three: Similar circumstances are being experienced in other Canadian industries. Most recently, the auto manufacturing industry has been

2 Don Ogden, CFA Vancouver, Canada, October 16, 2006: Research Department of
  Raymond James Ltd.
3 Natural Resources Canada – The State of Canada's Forest

significantly downsized in Canada. Job losses in the auto industry will likely be in the 10s of thousands in Canada with Ford, GM, Volkswagen, and others all downsizing and restructuring.

Example Four: There is an ongoing crisis in farming in Canada. In 2004, Canadian farmers' Realized Net Income from the markets (Market Net Income – a measure that subtracts out government payments) fell to negative $10,000 per farm.[4] The only year worse than 2004 was 2003, when per-farm Market Net Income was negative $16,000.

Compared to family farms the profit picture for the other links in the chain could not be more different. For the agribusiness corporations dominant in Canada, 2004 was the best year in history; overall, profits hit record highs. In fact, no other agribusiness related sector experienced losses overall, and certainly none experienced losses comparable to those of farmers. Ironically, 2004 was as good for agribusiness as it was bad for farmers.[5]

Example Five: The decline in the fishery and other primary industries has caused an increased exodus from rural Canada into urban centres, accelerating the shifting nature of Canada's population. Based on census data, Canada's rural population has dropped from being 49.1% of the total population in 1961 to 38% in 1996 and it is continuing to decline.

This is creating a two-fold problem: the exodus of the best and the brightest from rural communities and the gradual disintegration of rural infrastructure (social, physical, and economic), and straining many cities' ability to accommodate the influx of people.

Our cities are already unable to meet the housing, employment, and other needs of groups of people already there. See Table One for examples of current unmet social needs.

The marketplace is not meeting the needs of these groups, and government programmes are inadequate. This lack of services and opportunities has created a huge potential for co-operatives throughout Canada.

Co-operatives are an effective tool in serving these diverse needs. Arctic Co-operatives Limited and FCNQ are incredible success stories in Aboriginal Canada. Federated Co-operatives Limited and Co-op Atlantic are delivering essential services in many rural communities in Western and Atlantic Canada. Co-operatives such as the Multicultural Health Brokers Co-operative in Edmonton are gaining momentum in the immigrant communities. Unique social or neighborhood co-operatives, such as the Depanneur Sylvestre[6] in Gatineau, are providing examples for revitalization of inner city neighbor-

---

4 *The Farm Crisis & Corporate Profits: A Report by Canada's National Farmers Union* November 30, 2005).
5 *Ibib.*
6 For more information see: http://depanneursylvestre.net/

Group	Indicator	Average for Group	Source
Immigrants	Poverty Rate	35.8%	*Stats Canada – July, 2003*
Youth	Unemployment Rate	12%	*Stats Canada – The Daily, December 1, 2006*
Seniors (Unattached Women)	Poverty Rate	41%	*Statistics Canada Table 202-0802 – Cat. no. 75-202-XIE. "Persons in low income before tax, by prevalence in percent."*
People with Disabilities	Poverty Rate	31%	*Statistics Canada, 1996 (custom tabulations)*
Lone Parent Families	Median Income	$29,500	*Statistics Canada, median total income by family type*
Aboriginal People	Average Income	$21,435	*Statistics Canada, 2001 Census data*

Table One. Indicators of Unmet Social Needs

hoods. Young people are developing co-operatives that reflect their values; intriguing examples are the Haymarket Café in Calgary and the Mondragon Café in Winnipeg, as well as La Siembra Co-operative in Ottawa. There is a growing movement among seniors to develop co-operative housing. Childcare co-operatives are providing an essential service to single parents and low-income families. Social co-operatives are creating a new approach to engaging people with disabilities in creating opportunities for meeting their own needs, and so on.

The list of possibilities is limited only by the breadth of imagination and creativity found among groups engaged in the development of these new co-operatives. However, the realization of the possibilities is limited by a lack of capital.

How can the capital needs for co-operative development be met?

Examples of Effective Canadian Co-op Development Funds

Outside of Quebec, there are a small number of funds dedicated specifically and completely to the development of co-operatives in Canada. The experience of co-operators in accessing those funds is instructive in several ways. We can learn from their successes and mistakes and find a basis for a model for a national fund that could provide capital financing to new and emerging co-operatives.

Three co-op specific funds are summarized below.

Arctic Co-operatives Limited – Arctic Co-operative Development Fund (ACDF)

Arctic Co-operatives Limited is a service federation owned and controlled by 35 community-based co-operative business enterprises in Nunavut, the Northwest Territories, and northern Manitoba. Arctic Co-operatives Limited coordinates the resources, consolidates the purchasing power, and provides operational and technical support to community based co-operatives, which enables each co-op to provide a wide range of services to local member owners in an economical manner. As the financial arm of the co-operative movement in northern Canada, the mission of the Arctic Co-operative Development Fund is to provide financial services to the member owners so they can help each other achieve and maintain financial stability, sound business practices, and operational growth.

In the case of ACDF, the members, who are also members of Arctic Co-operatives Limited, are able to access equity financing (preferred share or other types of interest-free, long-term investments with flexible repayment options), working capital financing (such as financing for inventory purchasing or bridge financing for development projects), and long-term debt financing (mortgage financing for asset purchasing or long term low-interest loans for debt restructuring). The fund is managed by Arctic Co-operatives Limited; the Board of ACL is the Board of ACDF.

The Government of Canada and the Government of the Northwest Territories provided a contribution of $10.2 million to Arctic Co-operatives Limited to establish the NWT Co-operative Business Development Fund, now known as the Arctic Co-operative Development Fund. Through the co-operative administration of that fund, the Arctic co-operative system has been able to develop a very successful revolving loan fund[7] and stem the flow of interest payments from north to south. In fact, ACDF has been able to turn the original fund contribution over 30 times since 1986. ACDF has grown the capital base of the Fund from the original $10.2 million to over $30 million, through the retention of interest collected on loans made to Arctic community co-operatives.

---

7 A revolving loan fund is a capital fund established to make loans whereby principal repayments of loans are re-paid into the fund and then lent to other borrowers.

	ACDF	Average 28 APIs
Total Revenue	1,934,220	996,083
Interest revenue	1,934,200	383,980
Government Subsidy	0	370,823
Other revenue	0	241,279
Total Expenses	1,028,103	1,078,672
Wage costs	195,275	364,724
Provision for Loan Losses	60,000	213,038
Net Income	906,117	(82,589)
Cumulative loans provided by $	248,107,333	28,343,764
Historical loans written off $	162,057	1,408,927

Table Two. Comparison of ACDF and 28 Aboriginal Financial Institutions

Because ACDF is part of the larger Arctic Co-operatives Limited system, it has been able to operate with very limited costs. It has also been able to achieve a very strong performance in many other areas of fund analysis. The National Aboriginal Capital Corporation Association (NACCA) produced a statistical analysis of ACDF as compared to a total of 28 Aboriginal Financial Institutions (AFI). Table Two highlights some of the areas in which ACDF outperformed other AFIs in terms of operations (revenue and net income) and loan write-offs required. One of the most interesting aspects of ACDF's performance is its total independence of ongoing government subsidization.

ACDF, as a co-operatively-owned and targeted Aboriginal Capital Corporation, has been able to operate without direct government operational subsidy in the most challenging economic environment in Canada and outperform all other AFIs. This illustrates the strength of the co-operative form of organization in terms of stability of business operations, provision of business support networks, and ongoing aftercare and management advisory services. ACDF is a practical model for other co-operative fund development.

Tenacity Works Co-operative Development Fund - Canadian Worker Co-operative Federation (CWCF)

The Canadian Worker Co-operative Federation (CWCF) was founded in the spring of 1991. CWCF membership includes individual worker co-ops, regional federations, co-op developers, and associate members. The worker co-op fund, Tenacity Works, is a $1.5 million investment fund designed to create new worker-owned co-operatives, and to expand existing ones, in all regions of Canada. Tenacity Works is owned and operated by CWCF. The long-term goal for Tenacity Works is a self-sustaining fund which supports the development of the worker co-op sector by making investments and funding technical assistance.

The CWCF board of directors serves as the board of the Fund and makes all directorial decisions, with the exception of the investment decisions. An investment committee reviews and makes final decisions on all applications for financing, approves the investment review process, and provides ongoing advice and support to the board throughout the investment evaluation process.

Tenacity Works has been able to acquire and foster competence in the development of worker co-operatives across the country through the creation of a Worker Co-operative Developers' Network. The network allows the Fund to reach the broad population base it intends to cover. Those who are involved in the Fund as management, staff, directors, and active developers have built up a wealth of development capacity. The ability to maintain a national development capacity is enhanced because of the singular focus of the Fund's investment mandate. The use of a network of related developers has given the Fund a broad reach and a means to match development expertise to worker co-ops in need of service, with very low administrative costs.

The Fund is mandated to make investments in three types of co-operatives: worker co-operatives, multi-stakeholder co-operatives (as long as the workers are a significant class of members), and worker shareholder co-operatives. These can be start-ups/new co-ops, expansions of existing co-operatives, or job rescues (i.e. the creation of a co-operative to ensure the survival of an existing business).

This funding programme allows for two types of investments. The first are conventional "term" loans; the second is a "preferred" loan which requires no repayment of the principal for up to 5 years. It should be noted that, in order to assist the co-operatives in leveraging conventional financing the Fund's security is usually only ahead of the members' equity in order of priority, making the Fund's investments essentially a type of high-risk venture capital.

The evaluation completed on Tenacity Works as a pilot project in 2003 indicated that it met or exceeded all its objectives and allowed for leveraging four times as much investment as was directly placed by the Fund. As the investments are paid back there is more money available to invest, and the

CWCF continues to search for additional sources of replenishment so the fund can become self-sustaining and can meet a broader set of needs.[8]

Ontario Sustainable Energy Association

The members of the Ontario Sustainable Energy Association (OSEA) include a large percentage of co-operatives; in fact, co-operatives are the organizational model of choice for groups developing community-owned renewable energy developments. A list of OSEA co-ops includes: Countryside Energy Co-operative Inc., ecoPerth Hearthmakers Energy Co-operative, Positive Power Co-op, Power-up Renewable Energy Co-op (PURE), Sustainable Energy Resource Group Co-operative (SERG), Superior Renewable Energy Co-operative (SREC), Toronto Renewable Energy Co-operative (TREC), and The Renewable Energy Co-operative North (TREC North).

OSEA has been able to develop a sector-specific fund for community power, starting with a grant from the Ontario Trillium Foundation (OTF) to develop a business model. The OTF recognized the importance of having "venture capital" for these important new initiatives in a capital-intensive and rapidly growing sector.

Eligible community power organizations can access up to $75,000 a year for 3 consecutive years. Other than the OTF, the community power sector relies on smaller grants ($5,000-20,000) from the Community Economic Development and Technical Assistance Programme, the Co-operative Development Initiative, and in some cases, local agencies such as Community Futures Development Corporations.

There are currently over 50 community power projects under development, at an average start-up cost of $500,000 - $650,000 per project. Obviously, the funds available through OSEA are inadequate, but the capital provided has been vital for the birth of new energy co-ops and may leverage the funds required for long-term success.

Other Funding Programmes

There are still many developing co-operatives that don't have access to any funding programmes like the ones described above. They experience the uneven and unpredictable experience of trying to access funds through existing government, private sector, or foundation-based sources of capital. The example above of OSEA is one successful endeavour to provide support to a specific industry in a specific geographical location. As the enterprises

---

8 To apply for support or to learn more about the CWCF and the Tenacity Works Fund, visit their website. http://www.canadianworker.co-op/

are not-for-profit, the group has been successful in accessing foundation funding.

The Federal Co-operative Housing Stabilization Fund is a trust funded through fees paid by the Federal Co-op Housing Programme projects from their capital budgets. A housing co-op with severe short-term difficulties can apply to the Fund for a loan. Co-ops that get this help must report regularly to the Fund administrators and meet the Fund's loan conditions.

A number of funds administered by Credit Union organizations, or set up as Labour Sponsored Venture Capital Corporations, include the support of co-operatives in their mandates but also provide support to other forms of business or social economy enterprises. Access to these funds by new and emerging co-ops has been uneven across the country.

Opportunities for New Co-op Development

What the foregoing demonstrates is that a co-operative's access to development capital can be uneven on both a sectoral and geographic basis. In fact, many emerging clusters of enterprises with high potential for new co-operative development don't have even basic support services for their development. Emerging co-op development opportunities, like the ones listed below, have to access funds for development on an ad hoc basis from a dizzying array of possible sources that may or may not have programme elements that apply to them.[9]

Some emerging co-operative clusters are:
- Various initiatives in the immigrant community that mobilize the immense expertise of individuals whose credentials are not recognized in Canada.
- Co-operatives in aboriginal communities outside of the Arctic, especially among urban Inuit populations.
- Co-operative housing for seniors.
- Childcare co-operatives – to meet a huge unserviced need.
- Youth co-operatives similar to the Haymarket and Mondragon Café, examples that serve the dual purpose of informing urban youth about co-operatives and providing employment to their members.
- A programme for worker-owned co-operatives in forestry, secondary agricultural product processing, and other rural industries.
- The renewable energy sector (see OSEA above).
- Social co-operatives for people with disabilities, seniors, and others.

---

9 A good starting place for identifying available resources for developing co-operatives is CoopZone http://www.coopzone.coop/en/home

- Health care co-operatives.

Each of those areas of opportunity would be ideally served by a distinct support programme tailored to meet the technical aspects of the developmental needs of that form of enterprise. However, there is commonality in the need for capitalization that could be met through a national capital fund for co-operative development.

Towards a National Co-operative Development Fund

A national capital fund for co-operative development may be a focal point for facilitating increased involvement in co-operative development by established co-operatives.

Funds have been established that support the development of co-operatives as one of several types of businesses. Some of these include the Canadian Alternative Investment Co-operative, Vancity Credit Union's CED Funds, and a variety of "community loan funds." While these funds are a very positive and effective element of co-op development in Canada, access to them is limited by geography and type of initiative. The absence of a national, co-operative-specific, venture capital fund means the development of a distinct investment competence for the investment needs and dynamics of co-operatives in Canada is not occurring.

The co-op sector can be creative in approaching the creation of a national fund for co-operative development. It can also look at what has been done in other places.

In some other countries, co-ops are providing capital to support the development of new co-ops. For example, Rainer Schluter, the Director of Co-operatives Europe, in a presentation to the May 2006 CoopZone Forum talked about several initiatives in Europe through which co-operatives provide capital for co-operative development. The most striking example of this is in Italy where according to Mr. Schluter, Co-operative Mutual Benefit Fund collects – by law – 3% of annual profits from all existing co-ops. Co-opfond (Legaco-op) collected 238 millions euros in 10 years and invested 1.5 billion euros in co-op development.

The following excerpt from the Co-operative Grocer provides more detail on the co-operative developement fund in Italy.[10]

> The healthy growth of the co-operative sector in Italy is greatly facilitated by two major financing advantages, both enshrined in national law. The first, which dates to the post-war

---

10 Margaret Lund, "Italy's Co-ops Draw Strong Public Support," *The Co-operative Grocer*.

period, is the fact that any retained earnings of a co-operative organization are not subject to taxation at all. This provides a major advantage for co-operatives over their privately owned peers and has greatly enhanced the sound capitalization of these businesses. Because they have not been subject to taxation, retained earnings can also never be distributed to members; upon the dissolution of any co-operative enterprise, its remaining assets go to help the promotion and development of other co-operatives.

The second more recent innovation, passed in 1992, is the national law which provides that 3% of annual profits of all co-operatives must be contributed to a special fund to provide equity investments and low-interest loans for the growth and development of new co-operatives. This law has proved particularly beneficial in efforts to promote co-operation in the "mezzogiorno," the South of Italy, which is by far the nation's poorest region and where co-operatives are a scarce relative to the more affluent and activist central and northern parts of the country.

While the impressive success of the Italian co-operative movement has much to do with a beneficial legislative environment, the co-ops own willingness to work together is also a key element of their success. Italian consumer co-operatives could not have won the environmental and consumer battles they did in the '70s and '80s if they had not agreed to let their independent identities take a back seat at times and instead exercised their substantial market power in concert.

Balance sheet analysis of 2002 statistics for Canadian consumer co-ops showed $318 million in undistributed surpluses.[11] If 3% of those funds were to be put into a fund for co-operative development, seed capital of $9.5 million would be available.

Some established co-operatives and/or credit unions are already leading by example in the co-operative development endeavour in Canada. Co-op start-ups in Canada require a strategy to access the huge resources of technical expertise, investment capital, and access to markets that exist within the established co-operatives in Canada. A well-known example of this is Vancity Credit Union.[12]

We use our business and financial resources to help non-profits and co-operatives find innovative ways to build and leverage assets for long-term sustainability. This includes advice and financing for community organizations wanting to purchase a building for their own use. Community-owned assets strengthen balance sheets, reduce economic dependence, and provide resources that can be used to further the social or environmental mission of the organization.

---

11 Compiled by Co-operatives Secretariat – http://www.agr.ca/rcs-src/co-op/pub/pdf/co-opcan03_e.pdf

12 The following excerpts are from the Vancity website: https://www.vancity.com.

We support non-profits and co-operatives to develop strategies, plans, and skills for long-term financial sustainability. In 2005, we launched a series of financial sustainability workshops for community organizations to explore ways to diversify revenue, build assets, manage finances, and develop corporate partnerships.

Our goal is to support the development of successful social enterprises. To do that, we draw on business and financial tools from across our organization including grants, loans, and technical assistance. We also build community partnerships to help non-profits and co-operatives move along the path from early stage business development to strong and thriving businesses.

The experience of Vancity, since differentiating itself from the rest of the capital-centric market place through support of co-operative and community development, has been very positive.

Between 1991 and 2005, Vancity provided over $6,000,000 in grants and contributions through its co-op and community development programmes. In the same period, Vancity provided over $20 million in loans through its Co-op and Community Development Programmeme.

How has the commitment of this $26,000,000 in resources to the community affected the bottom line of the Credit Union? Vancity's assets actually grew from $6.9 billion in 2000 to $10.5 billion in 2004 according to its annual report for 2004. Its net earnings grew from $21.0 million to $57.8 million in the same period. The involvement of this credit union in its community has been used very successfully to market the financial services it provides to its members.

One of the projects supported by the Vancity programme is the BC Multicultural Health Services Society for a grant to conduct a pilot project to examine the feasibility of establishing a cross-cultural health brokers' co-operative. Vancity also supported the United Community Services Co-op's Shared Services Plan with a grant to develop, implement, and market a range of shared services and products for non-profits, aimed at reducing costs and improving efficiency and sustainability of non-profits in BC. The BC Co-operative Association also received a grant to promote awareness and use of social co-ops as a model for the design/delivery of social care in BC.

How did Vancity come to provide these services? It happened because members with energy, vision, and passion became involved in the governance of this co-operative and took leadership roles in defining the policies and programmes.

At their core, co-operatives are still democratic institutions that members own. As long as this situation exists there is an opportunity for people with a vision and desire for social change to get involved and make those changes. As developers we need to get involved in established co-operatives in our

2

own communities and work with those co-ops to build a bridge between the resources they command and the needs that exist. Co-op developers and others with vision can become directors in other established co-ops and credit unions and establish policies that support co-operative development so the Vancity experience is replicated all over the country.

There are other Canadian examples of co-ops and credit unions doing similar things. The problem is these examples are isolated in various parts of the country, and there is no standard practice, or embracing of this practice, by the co-operative establishment in general. This results in uneven availability of resources across the country.

The Co-operatives[UK] Programme

In the United Kingdom, Co-operatives[UK] identifies itself as the "apex organization for UK co-operative enterprise, promoting co-operative and mutual solutions, working in partnership with our members to grow a stronger and more successful co-operative movement."

In February, 2006, this organization adopted a guidance document by which its members can assess their performance on social and co-operative development. Among the indicators they chose to assess their performance are the following:
- Member economic involvement
- Member democratic participation
- Participation of employees and members in training and education
- Staff injury and absentee rates
- Staff profile – gender and ethnicity
- Customer satisfaction
- Consideration of ethical issues in procurement and investment decisions
- Investment in community and co-operative initiatives
- Net carbon dioxide emissions arising from operations
- Proportion of waste recycled/reused

Co-operatives in the UK have clearly chosen to see themselves as a part of a movement. By adopting this list of performance indicators, they have positioned themselves as leaders in the social development and environmental stewardship movements. Within the guidance document are specific standards for measuring achievement in the key performance areas.

Co-operatives[UK] chose to evaluate co-op performance using these indicators due to a sense of moral and social responsibility; responding to expectations from society; a belief that organizations have a long-term interest in fostering a healthy community ("enlightened self-interest"); a desire to promote social inclusion; and the knowledge that community interventions involving employees, customers, and suppliers can have direct benefits through increased profitability, stronger company image, reduced costs, better employee morale, and improved customer loyalty.

Co-ops in the Co-operatives[UK] programme measure themselves in terms of meeting the performance indicators – including the proportion of pretax profits a co-operative invests into the community over a one-year period and the proportion of pre-tax profits a co-operative invests into other co-operatives over a one-year period.

Also included in the document are case studies on how specific co-ops measured up in terms of the indicators. The following two case studies are included in terms of investment in community and co-operative initiatives.

The Co-operative Group

In total, the Co-operative Group (including the Co-operative Bank but excluding CIS) contributed £5,816,402 to the community for the year ending in January 2002. This figure was 3.9% of profit before share interest and dividends of £150.1m. A further £2,023,851 was raised from customers, employees, and other organizations levered in as a result of the Co-operative Group's input.[13]

Abbey National

The Abbey National Group reports on the ways in which it supports local communities. In 2001, the Group reported a total contribution to the community in cash and other ways of £3.9 million (a 45% increase over the previous year). It also reported on volunteering hours spent by staff.[14]

There are many other international examples of co-operatives being leaders in the field of social development and the economic democracy movement. What co-operatives in Europe have learned is that leadership by co-operatives, based on co-operative principles and values, can foster the creation of co-operatives to serve the needs of many more people, and at the same time improve the bottom lines for the business of existing co-ops.

Resources for Co-op Development

Successful development of new co-operatives in Canada depends on accessing the necessary resources to do the job. Resources are required for two broad functions: first, technical assistance for supporting the planning, de-

---

13 Social Accountability Summary Report 2002, the Co-operative Group.
14 Abbey National Group, *Corporate Citizenship Report 2001*.

velopment, and post development process, and second, investment capital. The basic types of technical assistance and investment capital are discused in this section.

Technical Assistance

There are many sources of information on the types of support required for developing co-operatives. Within the broad descriptor of technical assistance the required support could be sub-divided into two categories of resources needed prior to start-up. They are group development, or governance, and business development supports. The following table provides a very basic division of the supports required for each of these two aspects.

The table below refers to the broad areas of support required in a start-up situation. This support is provided to the group by co-op development resource people. The services are provided either through a regional co-operative organization staff person tasked with that responsibility (BCCA, for example), a civil servant tasked with that responsibility (Manitoba Government Co-op Development Agency), an employee of an existing co-operative federation (Arctic Co-operatives staff), a non-profit group that provides those types of services (SEED Winnipeg), or by an independent co-op consultant (independent members of the CWCF Worker Co-op Developers Network or CoopZone). The costs of these services may vary by the source of revenues to cover them.

An existing co-op, or a co-op passing from start-up status to operating status, will require revisions to the plans it has developed. As new members

Table Three. Areas where Technical Assistance is Beneficial

Group Development/Governance	Business Development
Membership Assessment, Recruitment, Training, and Group Dynamics	Pre-feasibility Assessment
Incorporation Process – Legal Framework	Feasibility Study
By-law Development	Marketing Plan
Board Development	Operating Plan
Membership, Board, Management Relationship Definition	Financing Plan and arranging Financing Package
Policy Development	Business Plan: Negotiating business relationships (suppliers, financial services, etc.)

join or new directors are elected, ongoing training is required. As the co-op broadens its experience, new policies and an annual planning process will be required. If co-ops are developed by service federations, such as Arctic Co-operatives Limited, these services are provided on a fee-for-service basis through ongoing management advisory services. This "aftercare" is essential in influencing success rates for start-up co-ops.[15]

Technical Assistance Challenges and Opportunities

Most new and emerging co-operatives are not part of a service federation and many are developing in an environment in which the members are marginalized economically and/or geographically. As a result, support for their development is required from external sources.

The Government of Canada has recently set up programming specific to co-operative development. The Co-operative Development Initiative (CDI) is a very interesting experiment in providing resources for co-operative development. The obvious gaping hole in the programme is the lack of investment capital; however, the Co-operative Development Initiative does provide some resources for technical assistance.

CDI grants financial resources based on a formula that requires a percentage of the total funding for development assistance to come from an outside source. That requirement is difficult to meet in some regions of the country.

CDI needs more money and a more direct route from government to group, but despite its flaws, it is the best programme to support co-op development in the 25 years of my experience.

Within the context of access to financial resources to cover the costs of technical assistance, matching resources to needs is a problem that persists in co-op development practice. Not all co-ops can receive the assistance they need. Many independent consultants are not able to access financial resources to work with groups. Within the category of technical assistance resources, there are three specific resource needs that exist: skilled developers with resources, financial resources to pay for consulting services provided by developers, and aftercare service to developing co-operatives.

Skilled Developers with Resources

There is a need for a co-op developer's institute dedicated to the teaching of skills required for developing co-operatives. There are pieces of this resource available in various programmes and institutes across the country

---

15 Aftercare refers to revisiting the development process at crucial times in the co-op's life cycle.

(Coady Institute, British Columbia Institute for Co-operative Studies, Centre for Co-operative Studies at the University of Saskatchewan, and others), but we need a unifying force to bring those resources together and create a coherent programme of skill development.

There are clusters of co-op developers in various parts of the country. Winnipeg, for example has a very dynamic co-op development culture. Other parts of the Prairies have huge gaps in the availability of skilled co-op developers, but not a shortage of groups looking for help or people interested in helping. The capacity available to assist the development of co-operatives needs to be addressed by training people in how to develop co-ops.

There are a small number of business professionals (lawyers and accountants) who specialize in co-operative matters. This cadre of professional resources also needs to be increased. Most of the existing co-op business professionals are associated with larger industry focused co-operative federations, or are part of a larger firm and aren't readily available to, or affordable by, groups in development. Part of a co-op development institute's mandate could be to hold workshops for business professionals on co-op legal and accounting matters.

Financial Resources to Pay for the Costs of Development

The skills and abilities required to help a group of individuals transform into a co-operative business are diverse and complex. This set of skills is not generally valued at a very high level by either those developing the government programmes that provide support to co-op development, or by the established co-operative sector in Canada. The funds available to support those who are engaged in the practice of co-operative development reflect the lack of value placed on co-op development skills. More funds need to be put toward supporting this activity.

Aftercare Services for Developing Co-operatives

New co-op development is generally not occurring within established co-operative federations that provide business support services to their members. In cases where it does occur, the new co-op gets plugged into an established support network and ongoing services are provided, but most co-ops that are developing are outside the realm of the established "service" federations. Unfortunately, most development focused federations and organizations do not provide aftercare or ongoing business support services due to lack of resources.

The result is a great deal of the effort, time, resources, and energy expended in the set up of these new co-ops is lost when these co-ops fold because of the lack of timely advice. Resources have to be allocated to provide for ongoing business advisory services, either through an existing federation focused on development or through an independent developers' entity.

Investment Capital

The second type of resource required for co-op development is capital. The types of investment capital required for developing co-ops can be identified in four broad categories: equity investment, working capital, long-term debt financing, and debt restructuring.

Equity Investment

Table Four shows a general listing of sources of equity capital as an enterprise goes through different stages of growth.

What is missing from this list is a co-op specific venture capital source of equity financing. The co-op development funds discussed in the previous section of this article do provide some equity investment for start-ups within the sphere of their mandate. There is often a big gap between the equity needed and the equity available to co-ops.

Table Four. Sources of Capital for Co-ops

Start up	• Owners/Members • Associate Members • Sympathetic individuals/Organizations • Angels/philanthropists • Government Programmes • Service Federations
Operational Stage	• Private Sector Social Investors • Strategic Partnering

Working Capital

Working capital may be required for several reasons. It is used to purchase inventory of either raw materials or finished goods, and it may be necessary at start-up or on a seasonal basis, depending on the type of enterprise the co-op is involved in. Working capital may also be required to provide cash flow at various times in the co-op's business cycle. A possible use may be to manage accounts receivable or payroll requirements on a short-term basis pending collection of debts owed to the co-op. Bridge financing for a capital project may also be required. In this case, the co-op may be unable to draw funds from a long-term mortgage until stages of the project are completed.

The ability to turn around working capital requests on a short-term basis is crucial to a co-op's success. At start-up, the requirement for working capital is one area that is often underestimated in a co-op's business plan. Start-up is usually too high a risk time in the business cycle for conventional lenders (banks, credit unions, etc.) to finance. This means co-ops end up having to locate and negotiate with non-traditional lenders to access working capital. This takes a long time to arrange, if it is possible at all. Often opportunities for co-op development are lost in the time lag.

Long-Term Debt Financing

Co-ops need to purchase capital assets at start-up and throughout their life cycle. This financing is usually provided by a lender for the purchase of a specific asset (for example, computer equipment), and the lender retains ownership of the asset through a mortgage or other security instrument until the loan is repaid. The strength of a co-op's business plan is usually the determining factor in whether or not it is successful in acquiring this type of financing. Many sources for this type of financing are generally accessible with a good business plan. However, this is not always the case, and the same time delays may apply to acquiring this type of financing as apply to working capital.

Debt Restructuring

This type of financing is provided to co-ops with a high debt-to-equity ratio. Co-ops in this situation may have experienced an operational down-turn and used up equity through increased borrowing to finance operations. In most cases, co-ops in this situation may choose to wind up their operations and dissolve the co-op. However, in some cases the debt load may be serviceable because of new opportunities the co-op has identified, or because of adjustments the co-op is capable of making to operations. For co-ops with a reasonable chance at turning their operations around through a restructuring plan provided by an aftercare service provider, a special kind of financing may be possible.

The Arctic Co-operative Development Fund provided this type of financing to its members. The ACDF practice was to purchase existing accounts payable and long-term debts through issuing low-interest long-term debt (loans) and preferred shares. This practice resulted in many co-operatives being able to stave off bankruptcy, turn around operations, and become successful service providers in their communities. From 1986-2004, ACDF provided $25 million in debt restructuring loans to 31 co-operatives. The co-operatives receiving these loans repaid more than $17 million of the debt refinancing provided, and all but two are still operating.

Developmental Investment Capital

All four types of investment capital described above could be available through one fund administered by the co-operative sector and accessible by all co-operatives.

Community economies across Canada, especially rural communities, are in varied states of maturity. With the deterioration of economies in single industry towns, the out-migration of youth and skilled professionals from rural communities, and a decline in market base, professional and financial services and other basic development infrastructure are often not available. As communities and their economies move through the spectrum of experience from economic underdevelopment to being economically viable, their markets develop and access to financial and professional services increase. For example, towns along the McKenzie River are seeing their infrastructure develop as their economies are impacted by new diamond mining activity, renewed oil and gas exploration, and possible pipeline development. The needs of these communities for developmental investment for enterprise development are replaced by the ability to acquire commercial lending.

Commercial lending is not available to communities where the market remains small and services are limited. Co-operative start-ups in those communities still have a requirement for developmental investment.

In addition, groups within vibrant economies in rural areas and urban centers, such as the groups identified in the first part of this article that are not served by the marketplace, have limited access to the market. Co-operatives are an effective tool to help communities and groups of people within communities create a bridge to the marketplace by providing a means for collective enterprise development for income generation, service provision, or marketing of products.

Groups and communities require access to development capital because commercial lending is unavailable to them.

The practice of developmental investment (the placement of capital for development purposes with minimal expectation of return) differs from commercial lending in three basic ways. First, the purpose of developmental lending is not primarily a return on capital invested but an increase in economic opportunity in the location of the investment. Repayment is expected with developmental investment, but generally there is flexibility in discerning which projects to sponsor, and this evaluation is not the same in commercial lending practices. Commercial lending expects capital to be increased through business activity. Developmental investment expects economic opportunity (employment, income levels, business and administrative skill capacity) of participants to increase as a result of investments made.

Secondly, commercial lending is administered by people with a market perspective based on a set of criteria that has become established practice. Commercial lenders depend on the success of their investments to generate financial returns to increase the volume of funds available for commercial lending purposes and cover the operating costs of their practice. Developmental investment is administered by community-based organizations that have a distinct competence concerning the community and the specific needs for the improvement of the economic welfare of that community. They depend on the character of the investment to a much larger degree and may be part of a practice that includes other services to the community.

Thirdly, commercial lending, with few exceptions, does not consider the social impact of the investments that it makes. It has a single purpose – the increase of the capital available for investment, or a return to the shareholders of the investment firm, commercial bank, or loan fund. Success is measured in strictly financial terms. Investment decisions are assessed by the rate of financial return on the investment made.

Developmental investment has a wider and less defined set of parameters. In most organizations in which developmental lending is being carried on, there is a set of conflicting imperatives. One imperative is the stability and growth of the funds available for developmental lending. A second imperative is meeting the developmental goals established (employment creation, poverty reduction, etc.). Each developmental investment practice deals with this internal conflict in its own way.

A general approach to managing the conflict inherent in developmental investment is the provision of support services to the projects that are financed prior to and post-start-up. This practice provides support to specific enterprises to improve their chances of commercial success and increase the probability of recapturing investments made. The successful developmental investor builds a distinctive competence in a targeted area of investing (co-operatives, for example) and develops mutually supportive partnerships with similar investors or networks with similar service providers.

The specific types of developmental investment capital needed are disscused below.

1) Equity for Start-up

Equity investment in co-operatives is prescribed by legislation and is generally restricted to those who will use the services of the co-operative. There have been recent changes to legislation that allow for an investor class of membership in co-operatives (solidarity co-ops or multi-stakeholder co-ops), but co-operative principles limit the control that non-member investors may have over the decision making process in co-operatives. While these legislative changes have made it possible to raise equity for a co-op from outside of the member class of share capital, it is not easy to do it and retain member control. In contrast to private and public corporations, there are no venture capital corporations that provide investment in co-operative enterprises. Co-operatives typically have limited possibilities for raising private capital.

Equity investment is required at start-up in most cases, because the founding members of most developing co-ops, especially by marginalized groups of people, don't have enough of their own money to start a co-op. As a start-up, the enterprise is probably not going to generate enough cash flow or profit to provide 100% debt financing.

2) Equity for Debt Restructuring

Because many co-ops are forced to start without contributed equity, there are also co-ops in desperate need of debt restructuring because of insupportable interest-bearing debt. These co-ops need ongoing advisory support and the development of strategic recovery plans, but they also need an injection of equity if they are to survive. Developing co-ops need access to funds for debt restructuring.

3) Long-Term Debt for Asset Acquisition

This is a straightforward type of financing related to specific tangible assets with funds specifically for that purpose and secured by the assets purchased. At start-up, especially, traditional lenders do not generally finance asset acquisition. There is a need for a development-focused lender of capital to be in place. With this type of lending included in the mix of financing provided by a co-op development fund, there is a potential for growth of the development fund through interest paid on the loans made.

4) Long-Term Debt for Debt Restructuring

An application for long-term development financing by an established co-op can also present an opportunity for a developer to complete an operational review of an existing co-op. It may provide an opportunity to identify an operational problem in time for a correction to be made. In the right set of circumstances, long term development loan financing can also be part of a debt restructuring package.

5) Working Capital

Working capital loans are generally short-term loans made to enterprises to finance a cash flow shortage. The cash flow shortage is generally a result of non-collection of accounts receivable, the need for large inventory purchases, or poor operational performance. Demands for working capital loans that merit consideration can be generated for several reasons: the seasonality of the enterprise may cause fluctuations in cash flow; expenses can be higher and/or revenue lower because of the effects of a specific season on the business; at start-up, a co-op that is involved in manufacturing or wholesale/retail services may require a purchase of initial raw material or other inventory to start production and sales. These cases, based on the review of the operation, may generate a lending practice that includes working capital loans or lines of credit.

Cash flow deficiencies caused by operational problems need to be considered more carefully. In fact, an application for a working capital loan can be the trigger for an operational review (aftercare) of the enterprise to be initiated. If the right recovery plan can be developed and operational deficiencies addressed, working capital loans can also be part of a debt-restructuring package provided to a specific co-op. For this and other reasons, it is important that the provision of capital through a co-op development fund be linked to a practice of providing advisory services or technical assistance.

Conclusion

When co-op people, members, directors, and employees talk to government or others outside the sector about the creative and powerful work in which we are involved, we always mention our principles and values. We use them to differentiate ourselves from other businesses or enterprises that are engaged in the commerce of our country. When I talk to co-op people from other countries, they are always aware of the huge role that co-operatives play in the Canadian economy, and the role that Canadian co-operatives play in assisting developing countries.

The Rochdale Pioneers, in their laws and objectives included the following:

> That as soon as practicable, this society shall proceed to arrange the powers of production, distribution, education, and government, or in other words to establish a self-supporting home-colony of united interests, or assist other societies in establishing such colonies.

They had a vision of a better world through co-operative enterprise.

Moses Coady, the visionary leader of co-operative development in Atlantic Canada, in his book *Masters of Their Own Destiny*, included a chapter on the future. He said:

> It may be disheartening for most of us to think that the job is a big one. It may be discouraging to realize that the task must be done by the people themselves. It may

be doubted that the so-called ignorant masses are capable of rising to the economic, moral, and intellectual level necessary for the effectual operation of their economic and political machinery. But that is our dream. ... We cannot grant the privilege of political democracy and at the same time withhold the opportunities for economic democracy on which it should also be founded. That would be a contradiction between our fundamental philosophy and our application of it.

Similarly, those of us who enjoy the benefits of the co-operatives to which we belong would be contradicting our own principles to deny the same benefits to those in our country who do not have the same opportunities. We can use the power of what we have co-operatively created to provide new opportunities to dying rural communities, to those suffering within our cities, immigrants, youth, Aboriginal people, seniors, and others who need it. Not to do so would be to deny our own stated beliefs. This is especially true given the fact that we have the means to do it.

Chapter Eight

Co-operative Development and Solidarity Financing

Joël Lebossé

The present article discusses best practices from the perspective of issues related to financing co-operative enterprises. It sketches a brief portrait of the practices developed in Québec over the past 30 years. This portrait focuses both on capitalisation by members and on co-operatives' access to financing sources, debt, and equity.

Following a brief examination of the origins of financial needs and the difficulties encountered in meeting them through traditional banks, this article discusses the specific modalities of public intervention, internal capitalisation, and access to outside financing on the one hand, and, on the other hand, describes how the various actors and their financing activities have multiplied in Québec over the last ten years.

On the basis of this topography of solidarity finance players in Québec (unique in North America), the article discusses how this dialogue and other collaborative practices, which are dedicated to the co-operative sector and other enterprises (i.e., non-profit organization), have taken shape.

Lastly, the discussion focuses on the major aspects of financial risk assessment of co-operative enterprises by the institutions that finance them.

In addition to the typical elements of analysis (production, sales, market, potential, etc.), "solidarity" investors also pay close attention to governance, that is, democratic practices capable of being effective in economic and financial terms and profitable with regard to fulfilling its mission—the collective interest of members and the community.

Analysing financial risk amounts to validating the potential for success and efficiency of a co-operative enterprise that fully meets the International Co-operative Alliance's definition of a co-operative:

> A co-operative is an autonomous association of persons united voluntarily to meet their common economic, social, and cultural needs and aspirations through a jointly owned and democratically controlled enterprise.[1]

Co-operative Capitalisation: A Major Development Issue

A Co-operative Enterprise's Fundamental Need for Capital

Like any enterprise that produces goods and services, co-operative enterprises, be they worker or user co-operatives, must have assets such as production equipment and the funds necessary to finance the production cycle.

The source of the money invested to meet this end initially comes from the enterprise's assets. This start-up fund is necessary. In contrast to companies based on share capital provided by "investors," co-operative enterprises can only rely on social and privileged shares from their members.

A co-operative enterprise's purpose is to serve its members well by providing them with work or by establishing adapted services that meet their needs. As such, the criterion for the members to invest in the enterprise is not particularly high in the initial stages of its creation. Indeed, sometimes the issue is not even raised.

This state of affairs creates certain difficulties, in that even though they are not founded on the same bases as capitalist enterprises, co-operative enterprises must be competitive in their market.

As such, they must have the necessary financial means to produce these goods and services, to promote them, to market them, and to manage inventories and accounts receivable. In this regard, co-operative enterprises must build up sufficient capital to meet these needs.

---

1 ICA: http://www.ica.coop/coop/index.html

Subsequently, and to the extent that this capital appears to be sufficient according to criteria generally applied by financial institutions, in principle they can, like any enterprise, ask banks for loans on their equipment, as well as for a line of credit.

In principle, financing for co-operative enterprises is organized and articulated in the same way that it is for any enterprise. However, the fact that they are co-operatives requires them to overcome two major obstacles.

1) Building Capital

Co-operative enterprises have to build their assets or capital by relying on their members.

Like any entrepreneur, co-operatives must capitalize their enterprise. Since it is often the case that the founding members do not possess the necessary start-up funds, capital has to be built up as the co-operative's economic activities develop. In a workers' co-op, members must convert some of their income into savings invested as "privileged shares." This conversion often represents a significant part of their salary (5% to 10%) that is invested in their co-operative. In the case of consumer co-operatives, patronage dividends may be retained or members may be asked to purchase additional shares.

Since this investment can only have significant effects over time, constituting minimum start-up capital is a problem that is often difficult to overcome in the start-up phase of co-operative enterprises.

Indeed, when co-operatives are created in order to operate an enterprise, they have an immediate need for start-up capital. In order to obtain outside financing, lenders who are in a position to finance investments systematically require a significant amount of member-supplied autonomous capitalisation.

2) Access to Outside Financing

Given the parameters typically adopted by banks, all businesses, especially when they are starting up, have to have start-up capital, because they will never receive 100% of what they need in loans. As such, even in the case of loans guaranteed by the federal government, businesses must have 10% to 30% of the anticipated cost.

Moreover, lenders demand guarantees, even the government and its financial institutions require this. The first guarantee also takes the form of a mortgage on the material that is financed and is very often supplemented by a request for a personal surety by the shareholders. The reason for this second requirement is that, in the event of bankruptcy, the sale of the material used for the guarantee rarely covers the balance outstanding on the loan.

In the case of co-operative enterprises, the personal wealth of the members is rarely sufficient to cover the amount of the personal surety that a lending bank will inevitably ask of them. In addition, it comes as no surprise that individual workers would be quite reluctant to commit themselves to repaying a co-operative's debt, given that they have almost no control over the management decisions that could lead to a situation in which they would have to honour their surety.

Another consideration is that co-operative governance contains an element that is a major source of discomfort for bankers. Bankers generally deal with one or more people, entrepreneurs and shareholders of share-capital enterprises, who hold all the decision-making power. In co-operatives, however, the entrepreneur they deal with is the executive director or general manager who does not control the decisions made during board or general meetings. Indeed, it is even possible that the director will not keep this position for the duration of the loan.

In collective enterprises, it is the co-operative association that is the entrepreneur. As such, the means of governance – the board of directors and management – constitute the decision-making body. Bankers are thus required to deal with people whom the association has appointed at the time when they negotiate with them, and they are well aware that these people can be replaced at any time, either because they decide to leave or are replaced.

In light of these three elements, which are inevitably viewed as not at all typical of the way enterprises are usually organized, financing applications submitted by co-operatives are not that well received by bankers, whose role is to lend the savings placed in their institution while avoiding excessive risks.

There are thus two major obstacles: building autonomous capital and securing bank financing. Whatever the case, a co-operative's members are subject to enormous pressures – they have to make a financial investment, which may be substantial, and they may have to make additional personal commitments.

These elements could be seen as significant constraints to establishing and to developing co-operative enterprises. As such, it is not surprising that issues related to co-operative financing are continually and insistently present at all levels and in all countries where there is a desire to create collective enterprises.

Québec Co-operatives: An Example of Original Practices

In Québec, where co-operative culture is particularly well developed, there was a need earlier than in other regions to find solutions to the financing needs discussed above.

In light of the various initiatives and laws promulgated in Québec with a view to fostering the emergence and development of co-operatives, it is clear that government's desire to support the co-operative movement has never let up. To be sure, this desire has varied in intensity from one period and one government to another since the 1960s. These efforts have focused on different aspects, all of which sought to reinforce the emergence, development, and feasibility of co-operative enterprises.

Incentives for Co-operative Capitalisation

In Québec, the legislation on co-operatives provides a significant fiscal advantage in the form of an income tax credit that is slightly higher (112.5%) than the amount invested in a co-operative by its worker-members.[2] This incentive is quite important in that it makes it possible to considerably limit the economic and financial impact of the "required investment" by members of a co-operative when they lend money to the business that employs them. Unfortunately, this fiscal policy is only recognised for Québec income tax. Indeed, it is a permanent subject of debate and discussion in Canada between the co-operative movement and the federal government.

In the late 1970s, the Québec government created a co-operative development society with a mandate to facilitate the capitalisation of worker co-operatives and to provide them with advisory support. Notwithstanding subsequent institutional developments, the programmes established at the time are still active.

Advisory support is funded in a global manner by the Québec government in a partnership with the Conseil québécois des co-operatives et des mutuelles (CQCM) on behalf of its members. This partnership was renewed for three years in February 2007. Support activities are conducted by the sectoral co-operative federations (funeral homes and housing, for example) and above all by the 11 regional development co-operatives, for which providing this support is the primary function.[3]

Since this time, support for capitalisation has considerably increased in Québec. The Co-operative Development Society's programmes are now more developed and Investissement Québec, a provincial crown corpora-

---

2 Reduced from 125% to 112.5% in 2003.
3 This aspect is described in Christian Savard's article in this publication.

tion, is now its operator. These programmes consist in lending money directly to co-operatives (a bit like a reimbursable "advance") via deductions on workers' salaries. In this way, co-operatives acquire the capital necessary to complete their financing.

This method of financing represents a considerable two-fold advantage. Firstly, it solves the problem of insufficient co-operative start-up capital (or capital required during the development phases). Secondly, the presence of a public financial institution has a reassuring effect on the banks solicited for their other borrowing needs.

It should be noted that the reimbursement of this "advance" has no effect on a co-operative business's repayment capacity, because it is the members who make the repayment via the shares they purchase. This is a very important aspect, because the co-operative enterprise is not indebted to the programme, leaving it free to borrow money from a bank or other lender.

Access to Bank Loans by Co-operatives

Another programme managed by Investissement Québec provides a partial guarantee (50% to 75%, and sometimes as much as 90%) to financial institutions for investment loans, as well as credit lines accorded to co-operative enterprises. The advantage of this kind of intervention is that it reassures the bank (in Québec, these banks are often co-operatives) and gives them a better understanding of how co-operatives operate. In addition, the presence of a public programme enables lenders to reduce their exposure to a potentially high degree of financial risk.

It is very clear that these Québec government interventions have acted as a major lever that has favoured the development of co-operative enterprises over the last 30 years.

Emergence of Other Sources of Financing for Promoting the Co-operative Enterprise Model

The presence of the Desjardins Movement, a major financial institution with which nearly all Québecers have a connection (Desjardins has more than 5 million members), has contributed as much to the natural integration of co-operative reality into Québec society as the co-operative movement in the agricultural sector.

Subsequently, the strengthening and development of co-operative enterprises, which became more "financable" due to public intervention, has also strengthened its own power of influence via its network vis-à-vis political, economic, and social decision makers.

Determining the Effect of Union Involvement for Promoting the Co-operative Model

The union movement's involvement in the emergence of collective enterprises (a sector which is commonly referred to as the social economy) has contributed significantly to supporting the development of co-operative businesses, especially during the 1980s when Québec was going through a major economic crisis.

With more than 300,000 members the CSN (Confédration des syndicates nationaux) is Québec's second largest federation of unions. The CSN has always been active in the co-operative movement. In the early 1980s it increased its support with a view to fostering the development and maintenance of employment in Québec, with particular attention to co-operative entrepreneurship.

In 1971, CSN spearheaded the creation of a credit union dedicated entirely to financing collective enterprises. This financial institution (Desjardins Solidarity Credit Union) has become one of the most important credit unions in the Desjardins Movement, and its entire development has been conducted by providing services exclusively to collective enterprises. In contrast to most financial institutions, its in-depth understanding of the co-operative movement and other components of the social economy has enabled it to operate as a lender in conditions of risk and with success rates that largely surpass those achieved by habitual banking practices with private enterprises.

In 1987, the CSN initiated the creation of a consultation group whose primary mandate was to provide high-level support to workers, particularly with regard to helping them form co-operatives.[4] It needs to be understood that the 1980s were a decade of major crisis for Québec businesses. Skyrocketing interest rates hit these businesses hard and tens of thousands of workers found themselves out of a job.

In this context, collectivities and local communities also took steps in reaction to the devastating effects of this crisis. In retrospect, we can see that this movement, which emerged out of a very dynamic and particularly proactive civil society, was the origin of many collective enterprises. These new enterprises, owned by the communities that brought them into the world, initially sought to meet the economic and social needs of their sec-

---

4 MCE Conseils (Mantien et Création d'Emplois – Maintaining and Creating Employment), which are still very active.

tor or community. They were constituted as not-for-profits (NPOs) and as co-operatives. Subsequently, the political and social context of the second half of the 1990s and the growing strength of this movement created a very favourable situation for its own development.[5]

It goes beyond the scope of the present discussion to enter into the details of the global development plan of what has since come to be known as the "social economy." However, it should be noted that it included projects and public financing programmes that sought, among other things, to strengthen the technical support provided to businesses, and to develop their access to financing.

Among these initiatives, the Québec government opted to favour the development of the social economy through a new capitalisation tool for collective enterprises (co-operatives and NPOs). The tool in question is the Réseau d'investissemnt social du Québec or RISQ (Québec Social Investment Network), created in 1997. This venture capital organization is dedicated exclusively to financing small collective enterprises (less than $50,000). It has $10 million in capital – given freely to it by the banking sector and a few major Québec enterprises.

During the same period, the CSN maintained its commitment to supporting Québec's economic development by creating a worker fund in 1996 – Fondaction, the CSN fund for co-operation and employment. Its desire to invest in capitalizing co-operative enterprises is made manifestly clear. It is also explicitly indicated in its constitutive law. Fondaction CSN currently has over a half a billion dollars in capitalization assets.

Fondaction has since created two operators specialized in financing co-operative enterprises – Filaction (fund for local investment and support of community funds) and a co-operative financing fund. These two funds have $16 million for capitalisation loans to collective enterprises. Their specific function consists in providing venture capital in the range of $50,000 to $500,000. They serve to complement RISQ (less than $50,000) and more important venture capital organizations ($500,000 and more).

It must be stressed that Québec's solidarity financing players work in close collaboration with one another to create conditions of accessibility to financing for collective enterprises (capitalization for the most part), this is illustrated by the way in which a certain number of its tools have been fashioned. One example of this is the co-operative financing fund - its capital comes from Fondaction CSN and from RISQ, who have turned its management over to Filaction.

---

5 *Osons la solidarité*, report issued by the Québec government's social economy work group (November 1996).

The community credit funds and other micro credit funds in Québec are also significant solidarity financing players. They provide modest loans to small businesses operated by autonomous workers, as well as collective enterprises. One of Filaction's mandates is to supply capital to these micro credit funds.

The most recent financing initiative (2007) intended for collective enterprises is the Fiducie du chantier de l'économie sociale (Social Economy Work Group Trust). It is made up of a significant capital contribution from the Canadian and Québec governments and funding from Québec's two worker funds (including Fondation CSN). The Trust's goal is to provide patient capital, that is, capital that is reimbursed over a very long period of time, to collective enterprises with a view to considerably improving their autonomous development capacity. In all likelihood, the Trust will have around $45 million in investment capital over the next five years.

Over the last ten years, other spheres of Québec society have also become significantly involved in facilitating financing for collective enterprises. For example, the Québec government allows a portion of local investment funds managed by autonomous economic development agencies (local development centres) to be dedicated to the social economy. Generally speaking, this takes the form of grants that do not exceed $50,000 per project.

In addition, in the early 2000s, the Desjardins Movement created Capital régional et coopérative Desjardins, a venture capital fund dedicated in part to co-operatives. Its financing for co-operatives is in the same range as that provided by Fondaction CSN. It targets larger enterprises and has a capital fund of $572 million.[6]

Dialogue and Synergy

The foregoing has made it clear that the financing potential for Québec's collective enterprises, co-operatives in particular, is considerable.

Among other things, the interactions of financial backers with these enterprises are based on active dialogue. Not only are their respective financing packages complementary, but solidarity financing players have very rooted collaboration practices. It often happens that a financing application submitted by a collective enterprise to one of these parties is treated in close communication with other solidarity financing bodies.

The players all know one another and know what the others can provide to a business within the framework of their respective investment policies, their specificity, and their constraints. As such, regardless of whether it is the first financial institution approached by a collective enterprise, it will

6 2006 Biannual Report.

automatically verify the possibilities of financing by the other solidarity financing organizations. In this way, the financing round for the enterprise is greatly facilitated to be sure the smallest groups successfully meet their needs by limiting themselves to one or two financing institutions. For greater financial needs, it is typical to see three or four solidarity financing and local development institutions working together to complete the financing arrangements. These complementary interactions and practices are illustrated in the figure "Steps of Solidarity Financing," which can be found at the end of this article.

How to Evaluate a Collective Enterprise's Chances of Success and Financial Risk

In recent years, the dialogue among solidarity financing institutions described above has produced other effects that go far beyond partnerships in financing rounds.

RISQ-initiated discussion forums, intended to strengthen concerted action among the various partners involved in financing collective enterprises (including local development agencies), have led to a conclusion shared by all, namely, the risk assessment and methods of financial analysis of collective enterprises cannot be accomplished with the tools used for evaluating traditional enterprises. In-depth economic, social, and financial analysis requires a distinct approach and know-how.

Financial institutions dedicated to co-operatives and NPOs each have very significant expertise in this regard. In 2001, six of these institutions decided to create a tool for transferring their know-how and knowledge.[7] They also invited the participation of two consultancy firms as well as the Division of Co-operatives, Department in Québec's Ministry of Economic Development.

This effort took some time and was accomplished in a concerted manner with many other partners, all of whom are very involved in supporting the emergence and development of co-operative enterprises and NPOs. Their work gave rise to the *Guide for Analysis of Social Economy Enterprises*, devoted entirely to understanding the balance between an enterprise's economic management and the fulfilment of its mission. It lays out and explains all the parameters to be evaluated while identifying the social, economic, and financial criteria and indicators to be used in an assessment. In short, an assessment looks into all aspects of the enterprise, ranging from governance

---

7 RISQ, Investissement Québec, Caisse d'économie solidaire Desjardins, Fondaction CSN, Filaction, and the Division of Co-operatives, Ministry of Economic Development, with the support of MCE Conseils et Pythagore, a specialised firm in the social economy sector.

needs in their sector or community. This mission must always form the basis of decisions with regard to managing the enterprise.

What I have noticed as a financial partner of many collective enterprises is that the more democracy plays a role in the concrete practice of governance, the more the enterprise's decisions are coherent with its mission.

All enterprises must at one time or another cope with difficulties—financial losses, decreases in activities, productivity problems, etc. Participatory management practices which involve transparency, and which have developed solidarity among the directors and the workers, are very precious. The board of directors and the workers are able to come together to find solutions which would be impossible in a privately-owned enterprise. In difficult situations, there is often a need for volunteer work and motivation based on a feeling of belonging, such that everyone in the enterprise pitches in and, as a result, the enterprise extricates itself from a critical situation.

In contrast, when all managerial decision making is centred on issues related to productivity and the enterprise is managed along traditional lines, mobilization is very difficult. The reaction of workers and the community to a crisis will not give rise to this kind of solidarity, which is indispensable in surviving moments of difficulty.

Democratic Tools: Information Transparency

A few solidarity financing players in Québec have come to the conclusion that, while it is always necessary to verify the quality of governance, it is also important to provide support in terms of training and information. As such, we decided to jointly invest in creating simple information tools intended for administrators and directors of collective enterprises.

Écosol,[9] a production co-operative, was created in 2005 by Filaction, the Co-operative Financing Fund, the Desjardins Solidarity Credit Union, and RISQ in partnership with a public relations company that had been associated with us for many years. This company was active in providing information service and online management tools for administrators, presidents, and executive directors of collective enterprises.[10]

Firstly, a management chart, personalized for each enterprise, was designed in such a way that it can be available to the enterprise and its members after only 30 minutes of monthly data entry. The main monthly figures, revenues, and expenses, and cash assets, comparisons with the previous year and with forecasts, economic indicators of productivity and economic and social performance, and indicators about the democratic life of the enterprise yield a three-page report, largely in the form of graphs, which is sent

9 Économie solidaire (Solidarity economy)
10 www.ecosol.coop

to grounding in the community, partnerships, conditions of production of goods and services, human resources, equipment, and organization, before turning its attention to financial issues.[8]

The Guide, which is based largely on many training sessions offered in every region in Québec, has been widely distributed within Québec. These sessions are intended for all developers, analysts, and bankers who wish to understand the best way to finance the collective enterprises in their community or sector. More than 1,000 copies of the Guide have been distributed in two years, and its teachings have reached hundreds of development and financing professionals. Indeed, the Guide has become required reading in several Québec universities.

The creation of these tools within a very active collaborative framework involving social economy financial institutions has contributed to strengthening collaborative ties since 2004.

Governance of Collective Enterprise: A Major Issue

I refer the reader to the contents of the Guide, which discusses all the aspects mentioned above in great detail. As a representative of a solidarity financing institution, I would like to discuss a few issues that the authors of the Guide have identified as being major elements in analysing the conditions of success of a collective enterprise.

In contrast to reference works in the field of analysing enterprises, the Guide stresses the importance of the service mission in relation to members and the community. In light of their many years of accumulated experience, all the Guide's authors agree that the quality of governance is the most important element.

It is important to stress the fact that in a collective enterprise, the entrepreneur is the association and thus, the people that represent it.

Governance includes, above all, managerial ethics and quality, as well as democratic practices. As such, the complementarity of expertise on the board of directors and the quality of the information it has, the relevant sharing of roles between the board and the administration, and the frequency of meetings and their content are all key parameters for assessing the reliability and efficiency of the management of an enterprise, collective enterprises in particular.

A co-operative enterprise (like that of a NPO) is created to fulfil a mission for the benefit of its members, to provide them with work or access to goods and services in conditions that are better adapted to their specific

---

8 The *Guide for Analysis of Social Economy Enterprises* is available in French and in English at RISQ Montreal.

each month by email to recipients designated by the enterprise (ideally, all the administrators).

Other reasonably priced, online decision-making tools will be available in the spring of 2007. These include a self-diagnosis of all the enterprise's functions (inspired by the analysis presented in the Guide), which the enterprise's executive director, the treasurer or accountant can carry out in real time and without help on their own computer.

In addition, Écosol will soon offer the possibility for presidents and directors of co-operative enterprises and NPOs to join a mentorship network. In line with the social economy, this mentorship, which must be viewed as a private relationship between two individuals in which the more experienced individual provides support for the less experienced member, can be focused on issues related as much to governance as to managing the enterprise's mission and to the main operational, technical, and strategic functions related to the enterprise's executive direction or presidency.

The goal always remains the same, namely, to make it possible for administrators and directors to regularly receive strategic information. This is an essential condition to operationalising collective intelligence for the benefit of the project and of the community it serves.

Québec's Way of Doing Things: Target Public Interventions, Mobilization of Civil Society, and Dynamic Collective Entrepreneurship

Money is always key to the success on an entrepreneurial project, whatever its form, history, or status. Financial capital (equity) must be built up for the start-up and must continue to be built in line with the co-operative enterprise's phases of development. What Québec has done over a few decades has been to mobilize pubic funds and direct them towards professional, targeted financial interventions adapted to co-operatives. Civil society, in particular the CSN and the community movement, work closely to complement and strengthen the financial means necessary for this capitalization.

While the state's involvement is necessary, it can only be effective if the concerned social movements exercise their capacity for pressuring and influencing it, and if they use their considerable potential for innovation and initiative. The tools made available for co-operative development in Québec (very often accessible to other collective enterprises) are as much financial as technical in nature: accompaniment/support and adapted management tools.

A co-operative project's potential for success is considerably enhanced when technical accompaniment and financial instruments are available.

In Québec, statistics show that twice as many co-operative enterprises as traditional enterprises survive the critical first five years of existence. As noted above, this is due to the extraordinary capacity for providing support displayed by the co-operative enterprise community. It is an inestimable "competitive" advantage. The tools developed in the Québec social economy model have been successful and innovative by stressing the social dimension as much as the financial dimension.

Electronic bibliography

- http://www.fondaction.com/ for Fondaction CSN
- http://www.filaction.qc.ca/ for Filaction
- http://www.filaction.qc.ca/FFC/ for the Fonds de financement coopératif
- http://www.cecosol.coop/ for the Caisse d'économie solidaire Desjardins
- http://www.fonds-risq.qc.ca/ for the réseau d'investissement social du Québec, publisher of Guide for Analysis of Social Economy Enterprises
- http://www.capitalregional.com/ for Capital régional et coopératif Desjardins
- http://www.investQuébec.com/ for Investissement Québec
- http://www.rqcc.qc.ca/ for the réseau québécois de crédit communautaire
- http://www.acldq.qc.ca/ for the centres locaux de développement
- http://www.reseau-sadc.qc.ca/ for the sociétés d'aide au développement des collectivités
- http://www.ecosol.coop/ for Écosol
- http://www.chantier.qc.ca/ for the Fiducie du chantier de l'économie sociale

Steps of Solidarity Financing Dedicated all or in part to Financing Collective Enterprises

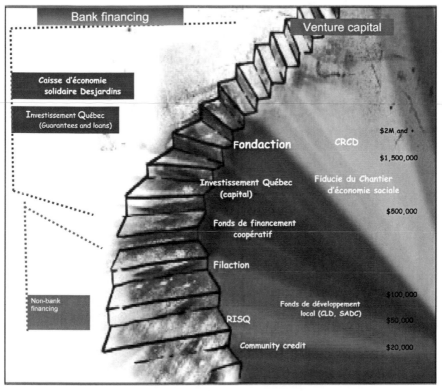

Bank Financing of Collective Enterprises
- Caisse d'économie solidaire Desjardins: Medium- and long-term loans and lines of credit.
- Investissement Québec: Guarantees for financial institutions and direct lending to enterprises from $10,000 to several million dollars.
- Community Credit: Microcredit of a few thousand $, up to $50,000 (on average $15,000 to $20,000).

Venture capital
- RISQ: $20 000 to $50 000.
- Fonds de développement local: $5,000 to $125,000, depending on each Fund's potential.
- Filaction: $50,000 to $500,000, et Fonds de financement coopératif: $100,000 to $250,000.
- Investissement Québec: capitalisation programme, from a few tens of thousands of dollars to $500,000.
- Fiducie du Chantier de l'économie sociale: $50,000 to a maximum of $1,500,000.
- Fondation CSN: $250,000 to a few million dollars.
- Capital régional et coopératif Desjardins: $200,000 to a few million dollars.

Développement coopératif et finance solidaire

Joël Lebossé

L e présent article aborde la question des meilleures pratiques à partir des questions relatives au financement des entreprises coopératives. Il trace un portrait rapide des pratiques développées au Québec dans les trente dernières années, autant sur le soutien à la capitalisation par les membres que sur l'accès pour la coopérative aux sources de financement, dette et équité.

Après un rapide tour de piste sur l'origine des besoins financiers et les difficultés à trouver des réponses auprès des banques traditionnelles, il aborde d'une part les modalités spécifiques de l'intervention publique aux différents niveaux, capitalisation interne et accès au financement externe, et d'autre part, décrit comment se sont multipliés les acteurs et leurs interventions en financement au Québec dans les 10 dernières années.

À partir de cette géographie des acteurs de la finance solidaire québécoise, assez unique en Amérique du nord, il présente comment se concrétisent les pratiques de concertation et de collaboration de ces financiers solidaires, dédiés au secteur des coopératives et autres entreprises collectives (connu sous l'acronyme OBNL pour Organisme à but non lucratif).

Enfin, il propose quelques repères sur les points majeurs de l'évaluation du risque financier dans une entreprise coopérative par les institutions qui les financent. Au delà des aspects habituels d'analyse d'une entreprise (production, ventes, marché, potentiels, etc) l'analyse d'un investisseur « solidaire » est très axée sur la gouvernance, celle d'une pratique démocratique capable d'être efficace au plan économique et financier et rentable quant à la réalisation de sa mission, à savoir : l'intérêt collectif de ses membres et de sa communauté.

Faire une analyse du risque financier, revient en fait de valider le potentiel de réussite et l'efficience d'une entreprise coopérative répondant pleinement à la définition de l'ACI.

> «Une coopérative est une association autonome de personnes volontairement réunies pour satisfaire leurs aspirations et besoins économiques, sociaux et culturels communs au moyen d'une entreprise dont la propriété est collective et où le pouvoir est exercé démocratiquement[1]».

La capitalisation des coopératives, un enjeu majeur pour leur développement

l'Incontournable besoin de capital d'une entreprise coopérative

Comme toute entreprise qui produit des biens et des services, les entreprises coopératives, qu'elles soient de travailleurs ou d'usagers doivent pouvoir disposer des actifs, notamment les équipements de production et aussi les liquidités nécessaires au financement du cycle de production.

L'origine de l'argent investi pour ce faire, est dans un premier temps ce qu'il est convenu d'appeler l'avoir d'une entreprise. C'est la mise de fonds nécessaire. À ce titre, et contrairement aux entreprises constituées d'un capital-action apportée par les « associés-investisseurs » l'entreprise coopérative ne peut compter que sur les souscriptions de parts sociales et privilégiées en provenance de ces membres.

Le propre d'une entreprise coopérative est de rechercher à bien servir ses membres en leur offrant une situation de travail, ou en mettant en place des services adaptés correspondant à leurs besoins d'usage. De ce fait, le critère de capacité d'investissement en argent de la part de ses membres n'est pas prioritaire dans la démarche initiale de création d'entreprises et même parfois, il n'est pas évoqué.

---

1 Extrait de la déclaration de l'ACI : Association coopérative internationale.

Cette état de fait créée une difficulté particulière car l'entreprise coopérative, en dehors du fait qu'elle est fondée sur d'autres bases que l'entreprise capitaliste, est de la même façon en situation de concurrence et de compétition sur le marché économique à qui elle s'adresse.

Elle doit donc disposer des moyens financiers nécessaires à la production de ces biens et services, à leur promotion et à leur mise en marché, à la prise en charge des inventaires et à celle des comptes à recevoir. L'entreprise coopérative doit donc se constituer un capital capable de faire face à ses besoins.

Par la suite et seulement si ce capital apparaît suffisant selon les critères généralement retenus par les institutions financières, théoriquement elle pourrait, comme toute entreprise, faire appel aux banques pour des emprunts sur les équipements et même pour disposer d'une marge de crédit.

Théoriquement, le financement d'une entreprise coopérative s'organise et s'articule de la même façon que toute entreprise. Cependant le fait d'être coopérative l'a conduit à devoir dépasser deux écueils majeurs.

1) La constitution du capital

Les entreprises coopératives doivent donc constituer leur avoir, leur capital en faisant appel à leurs membres.

Comme tout entrepreneur, celles-ci doivent d'abord compter sur elles-mêmes pour capitaliser leur entreprise. Comme fréquemment, les membres fondateurs d'une coopérative disposent d'assez peu de capacités de mise de fonds, le capital ne peut se constituer qu'au fur et à mesure du développement des activités économiques de la coopérative. Les travailleurs de la coopérative doivent alors détourner une partie de leurs revenus afin de la constituer en épargne investie sous la forme de parts privilégiées (l'équivalent des actions privilégiées) et c'est souvent un effort important que de prélever une part de son salaire qui va parfois jusqu'à 5 à 10 % et l'investir dans sa coopérative. Pour les coopératives d'usagers, c'est l'épargne des membres qui leur est confiée.

Malgré tout, comme cette souscription ne peut avoir des effets significatifs qu'avec le temps, la constitution du capital minimum de départ reste un problème souvent difficile à résoudre dans les situations de démarrage d'entreprises coopératives.

En effet quand la coopérative se constitue pour opérer l'entreprise, c'est immédiatement qu'elle a besoin des mises de fonds. Inévitablement, pour obtenir du financement externe, un montant significatif de capitalisation autonome par ses membres est systématiquement exigé par les prêteurs capables de financer les investissements.

2) l'Accès au financement externe

Les paramètres habituels retenus par les banques font que toute entreprise, surtout au moment de son démarrage, doit disposer d'un capital de départ car on ne lui financera jamais 100 % du besoin. Ainsi, même pour des prêts garantis par le gouvernement fédéral, l'entreprise doit disposer de 10 % à 30 % de la dépense envisagée.

Par ailleurs, les prêteurs exigent des garanties, même l'État ou ses instruments financiers. La première garantie est toujours constituée par une hypothèque sur le matériel financé, mais elle est très souvent complétée par une demande de caution personnelle des actionnaires de l'entreprise. La raison est qu'en cas de faillite de l'entreprise, la vente du matériel en garantie couvre rarement la totalité du prêt restant à payer.

Dans le cas d'une entreprise coopérative, il est rare que le patrimoine personnel de chacun des membres soit suffisant pour que leur caution personnelle qui va inévitablement leur être demandée, représente la valeur recherchée par la banque à qui elle demande un prêt. De plus, on peut comprendre que chacun des travailleurs aura une lourde hésitation au moment de s'engager personnellement à rembourser la dette de la coopérative, en considérant qu'il n'a quasiment pas de contrôle sur les décisions de gestion qui pourraient l'amener à honorer sa caution.

De plus, il y a dans la gouvernance d'une coopérative un élément majeur d'inconfort pour le banquier. En effet, il fait généralement affaire avec une ou plusieurs personnes, entrepreneures et actionnaires d'entreprises à capital-action, qui disposent de l'ensemble du pouvoir de décision. Alors que dans la coopérative, l'entrepreneur avec qui il discute en est seulement le directeur, il ne dispose pas du contrôle des décisions dans l'assemblée générale et il est même possible qu'il ne conserve pas ses fonctions pendant toute la durée du prêt.

Dans l'entreprise collective, c'est l'association coopérative qui est l'entrepreneur. C'est donc la gouvernance, à savoir le conseil d'administration et la direction générale, qui forme l'organe de décision. Le banquier doit donc faire affaire avec des personnes qui sont titulaires de mandats donnés par l'association au moment où elle négocie avec lui et il sait que ces personnes peuvent à n'importe quel moment être remplacées du fait de leur départ volontaire ou de leur éviction.

On ne peut que constater qu'avec ces trois éléments inévitablement perçus comme très atypiques par rapport à l'organisation habituelle d'une entreprise, une demande de financement par une coopérative n'a pas vraiment un effet motivant pour un banquier (et c'est un euphémisme) qui rappelons-nous a le mandat de prêter l'épargne que nous lui avons confiée en évitant de lui faire prendre des risques démesurés.

Deux écueils majeurs donc, constituer le capital autonome et obtenir du financement bancaire. Dans tous les cas, les membres de la coopérative sont soumis à des pressions énormes, ils doivent renoncer à une partie de leur salaire pas toujours très élevé et prendre des engagements personnels démesurés.

On peut considérer que ce sont des facteurs très contraignants qui freinent la constitution et le développement des entreprises du mouvement coopératif. Ce n'est donc pas le fait du hasard si la question du financement des coopératives revient de façon permanente et insistante à tous les niveaux et dans tous les pays où la volonté de constituer des entreprises collectives est là.

Le Québec coopératif, un exemple de pratiques originales

Le Québec, où la culture coopérative est particulièrement développée, a donc dû, plus tôt que d'autres, chercher des solutions à cet ensemble de questions reliées aux besoins de financement.

À la lecture des nombreuses initiatives et des lois émises au Québec visant à favoriser l'émergence et le développement des coopératives, il est clair que la volonté gouvernementale de soutenir le mouvement coopératif ne s'est jamais démentie. Bien sûr, l'effort a pu être d'une intensité variable selon les périodes et les gouvernements successifs depuis les années 60.

Les efforts ont porté sur différents aspects, visant tous à renforcer l'émergence, le développement et les conditions de viabilité des entreprises coopératives.

l'Incitation à la capitalisation des coopératives

Au Québec, la loi sur les coopératives prévoit un avantage fiscal significatif c'est-à-dire un crédit d'impôt qui est légèrement supérieur (112,5%) au montant investi dans leur coopérative par ses membres travailleurs[2]. Cet incitatif est très important car il permet de limiter considérablement l'impact économique et financier de ce geste « d'épargnant obligé » que posent les membres d'une coopérative quand ils prêtent à l'entreprise dans laquelle ils travaillent.

Malheureusement il faut souligner que cet effort fiscal n'existe que pour l'impôt provincial du Québec. C'est d'ailleurs un sujet permanent de débats

---

2 Réduit de 125% à 112,5% en 2003.

et de discussions au Canada entre le mouvement coopératif et le gouvernement fédéral.

Le gouvernement du Québec a pris l'initiative à la fin des années 70 de constituer une société de développement des coopératives dont les mandats étaient, d'une part, de faciliter la capitalisation des coopératives de travail, et d'autre part, de leur donner du support conseil.

Par-delà les évolutions institutionnelles intervenues depuis, les programmes mis en œuvre à l'époque sont toujours actifs.

Le support conseil est financé de façon globale par le gouvernement dans un partenariat entre le conseil québécois des coopératives et des mutuelles (CQCM), au nom de ses membres. Cette convention vient d'ailleurs d'être renouvelée pour trois ans au début février 2007. Les activités de support sont réalisées d'une part par des fédérations sectorielles de coopératives (funéraire, habitation, par exemple) et surtout par les 11 coopératives de développement régional dont c'est le mandat majeur. Cet aspect est décrit dans un autre article du présent ouvrage, il est signé de Christian Savard.

Depuis, le support à la capitalisation s'est beaucoup amplifié au Québec. Les programmes de la société de développement coopératif de l'époque sont bien plus développés qu'alors et c'est aujourd'hui Investissement Québec, société d'État, qui en est l'opérateur. Ces programmes consistent à prêter directement de l'argent aux coopératives (un peu comme une « avance » remboursable) par les prélèvements sur les salaires des travailleurs. La coopérative dispose ainsi du capital nécessaire pour compléter sa ronde de financement

Ce mode de financement est un atout considérable à deux titres. D'une part, il vient résoudre le problème d'insuffisance de capital de démarrage des coopératives (ou lors des phases de développement), d'autre part, la présence d'une institution financière publique a un effet rassurant pour la banque sollicitée sur les autres besoins de crédits.

Il faut souligner que le remboursement de cette « avance » est sans aucun effet sur la capacité de remboursement de l'entreprise coopérative puisque ce sont ses membres qui remboursent par leurs souscriptions au capital. C'est un aspect très important car elles laissent ainsi à l'entreprise coopérative toute sa marge de manœuvre pour s'endetter auprès d'une banque.

l'Accès au crédit bancaire pour les coopératives

Un autre programme, toujours géré par investissement Québec, consiste à donner une garantie partielle, de 50 à 75 % et parfois jusqu'à 90 % aux institutions financières, pour des prêts d'investissement et même pour des marges de crédit accordés à une entreprise coopérative. L'avantage de ce type d'intervention est que ça met la banque (au Québec se sont souvent des coopératives financières) en confiance et en situation de mieux comprendre, par l'expérience, le fonctionnement d'une coopérative. L'intervention d'un programme public lui permet finalement de réduire sa perception d'un risque financier potentiellement élevé.

On peut affirmer sans conteste, que ces interventions de la puissance publique québécoise ont eu un effet de levier majeur sur le développement des entreprises coopératives dans les 30 dernières années.

Émergence d'autres sources de financement pour la promotion du modèle de l'entreprise coopérative

La présence du mouvement Desjardins, institution financière majeure avec laquelle presque tous les Québécois ont une histoire (Desjardins compte plus de 5 millions de membres), autant que l'importance de la coopération dans le milieu agricole, ont contribué à intégrer naturellement la réalité du fait coopératif dans la société québécoise.

Par la suite, le renforcement et le développement d'entreprises coopératives, devenues mieux finançables grâce aux interventions publiques, a aussi produit un renforcement de sa propre capacité d'influence via son réseau auprès des décideurs des milieux politique, économique et social.

l'Effet déterminant de l'implication syndicale pour la promotion du modèle coopératif

L'implication du mouvement syndical dans l'émergence des entreprises collectives (qu'il est convenu aujourd'hui de nommer le secteur de l'économie sociale) aura été pour beaucoup dans le support au développement des entreprises coopératives, en particulier au détour des années 80, en plein cœur d'une crise économique majeure au Québec.

La confédération des syndicats nationaux (CSN) est la deuxième centrale syndicale en importance au Québec et elle compte aujourd'hui plus de 300 000 membres. Elle s'est historiquement beaucoup investie aux côtés du mouvement coopératif. Au début des années 80 elle a renforcé son soutien, notamment pour aider à transformer en coopératives de travail des entreprises vivant des difficultés majeures, en vue de sauver les activités économiques et les emplois qui s'y rattachent.

Pour ce faire, elle a pris des initiatives très originales. Elle a pris l'initiative de la mise en place de différents outils d'intervention économique en vue de favoriser le développement et le maintien de l'emploi au Québec avec une préoccupation particulière pour la forme coopérative de l'entrepreneuriat.

Elle a été à l'origine de la création en 1971 d'une caisse d'économie (coopérative financière), entièrement vouée au financement des entreprises collectives. Cette institution financière (la Caisse d'économie solidaire Desjardins) est aujourd'hui l'une des plus importantes du mouvement Desjardins alors que tout son développement a été réalisé au service des seules entreprises collectives. À la différence de la plupart des institutions financières, sa compréhension profonde du mouvement coopératif et des autres composantes de l'économie sociale lui ont permis d'exercer son métier de prêteur dans des conditions de risque et avec un taux de succès très au-delà de la pratique habituelle des banques auprès des entreprises privées.

Plus tard en 1987, la CSN a initié la création d'un groupe de consultation dont le mandat premier était d'apporter du support technique de haut niveau aux travailleurs, notamment en vue de les aider à se constituer en coopérative[3]. Il faut comprendre que les années 1980 ont été des années de crise majeure pour les entreprises au Québec. La montée vertigineuse des taux d'intérêt frappait les entreprises en jetant à la rue des dizaines de milliers de travailleurs.

Dans ce contexte, les collectivités et les communautés locales ont elles-aussi pris des initiatives en réaction aux impacts dévastateurs de cette crise. Avec le recul, on a pu constater que ce mouvement, issu d'une société civile très dynamique et particulièrement proactive, est à l'origine de nombreuses entreprises collectives. Ces nouvelles entreprises, propriétés de la communauté qui les a vus naître, visaient d'abord à répondre à des besoins économiques et sociaux dans leurs milieux. Elles se sont constituées sous la forme d'OBNL et en coopérative. Plus tard, le contexte politique et social de la deuxième moitié des années 1990 et la force croissante de ce mouvement ont créé une situation très favorable à son propre développement[4].

Il n'est pas dans notre propos ici de rentrer dans le détail du plan global de développement de ce que l'on appelle depuis « l'économie sociale », mais il faut savoir qu'il contenait des projets et des programmes de financement public visant entre autres à renforcer le support technique auprès des entreprises et a développer leur accès à du financement.

Parmi ces initiatives, le gouvernement du Québec a choisi de favoriser le développement de l'économie sociale par un nouvel outil de capitalisation des entreprises collectives (coopératives et OBNL). Elle s'est traduite par la création du Réseau d'investissement social du Québec (RISQ) en 1997, organisme de capital de risque entièrement dédié au financement de petits projets d'entreprises collectives (moins de 50 000 $). Cet organisme a été

---

3 Aujourd'hui toujours très actif (M. C. E. conseils, pour Maintien et Créations d'Emplois).
4 Osons la solidarité, rapport du chantier de l'économie sociale au gouvernement du
   Québec novembre 1996.

capitalisé à hauteur de 10 millions de $, dont une part provenant d'un apport à titre gratuit du secteur bancaire et de quelques grandes entreprises québécoises

De son côté, et dans les mêmes années, la CSN a continué son engagement pour soutenir le développement économique au Québec avec la création en 1996 d'un fonds de travailleurs : Fondaction, le Fonds CSN pour la coopération et l'emploi. Sa volonté d'investir dans la capitalisation des entreprises du mouvement coopératif y est clairement affichée. Elle est aussi inscrite explicitement dans sa loi constitutive. Aujourd'hui, Fondaction CSN détient une capitalisation supérieure à un demi milliard de $

Fondaction prit ensuite l'initiative de créer deux opérateurs spécialisés dans le financement des entreprises collectives. Il s'agit de Filaction, le fonds pour l'investissement local et l'approvisionnement des fonds communautaires et du fonds de financement coopératif. Dotés de 16 millions $, ces deux fonds rendent disponibles des prêts de capitalisation aux entreprises collectives. Leur fonction particulière consiste à offrir du capital de risque à l'intérieur d'une fourchette d'investissement de 50 000 à 500 000 $. Ils se situent l'un et l'autre en complémentarité avec le RISQ (moins de 50 000 $) et les intervenants financiers en capital de risque plus majeurs (un demi-million de dollars et plus).

Il faut souligner que les acteurs québécois de la finance solidaire travaillent en étroite collaboration pour créer les conditions d'accessibilité du financement, principalement en capitalisation, pour les entreprises collectives, comme l'illustre la façon dont se sont constituées un certain nombre de ses outils. Le fonds de financement coopératif en est un exemple : son capital vient d'une part de Fondaction CSN d'autre part du RISQ. Ils en ont conjointement confié la gestion à Filaction.

Les fonds de crédit communautaire ainsi que les autres fonds de micro-crédit au Québec sont aussi des acteurs significatifs de la finance solidaire. Ils rendent disponible du crédit de montants modestes aux petites entreprises aux travailleurs autonomes et aussi aux entreprises collectives. Filaction a parmi ses mandats une fonction d'approvisionnement en capital de ces fonds de micro-crédit.

La dernière née des initiatives de financement (2007), auprès des entreprises collectives est la Fiducie du chantier de l'économie sociale. Elle s'est constituée d'abord par un apport en capital significatif de la part des deux niveaux de gouvernement (fédéral et provincial), ainsi que d'un financement en provenance des deux fonds de travailleurs du Québec, dont Fondaction CSN. L'ambition de la Fiducie est d'offrir du capital patient, c'est-à-dire remboursable à très long terme, aux entreprises collectives en vue de renforcer considérablement leur capacité autonome de développement. Elle devrait disposer d'une capacité d'intervention de l'ordre de 45 Millions de $ sur les cinq prochaines années.

D'autres sphères de la société québécoise se sont aussi impliquées de façon significative dans les 10 dernières années pour faciliter le financement des entreprises collectives. Par exemple, le gouvernement du Québec a accepté qu'une partie des fonds d'investissements locaux gérés par des agences de développement économique autonomes (les centres locaux de développement)   soient dédiés à l'économie sociale. Généralement il s'agit de subventions qui ne dépassent pas 50 000 $ par projet.

Par ailleurs, au début des années 2000, le mouvement Desjardins a pris l'initiative de constituer un fonds de capital de risque dédié en partie aux coopératives : Capital régional et coopératif Desjardins. Son offre de financement auprès des coopératives se situe dans la même fourchette d'intervention que celle de Fondaction CSN. Elle vise les entreprises de taille plus importante. Ce Fonds est capitalisé pour un total de 572 Millions de $[5]

Une pratique de concertation et de complémentarité

Au travers de ce rapide portrait, on peut constater aisément que les entreprises collectives du Québec, notamment les coopératives, disposent d'un potentiel de financement très important.

Mais en outre, la pratique des intervenants financiers auprès de ses entreprises est fondée sur une de concertation active. Non seulement l'offre financière de chacun est complémentaire des autres, mais en plus les acteurs de la finance solidaire ont des habitudes de collaboration très ancrées. Il est fréquent qu'une demande de financement déposée par une entreprise collective auprès de l'un des intervenants soit traitée en concertation étroite avec les autres financiers solidaires.

Nous nous connaissons bien entre nous et savons ce que chacun peut apporter à une entreprise dans le cadre de ses propres politiques d'investissement, ses spécificités et ses contraintes. De ce fait, quelle que soit la première institution financière sollicitée par une entreprise collective, son réflexe est de valider les possibilités d'intervention financière des autres financiers solidaires. La ronde de financement pour l'entreprise en est grandement facilitée. Bien entendu, les plus petits projets réussissent à combler leurs besoins en se limitant à un ou deux financiers. Pour des besoins financiers plus conséquents, il est habituel que trois à quatre intervenants de la finance solidaire et du développement local se concertent et s'impliquent dans la réalisation du montage financier.

---

5 Rapport semestriel 2006 .

La démonstration de cette complémentarité et de nos pratiques de partenariat est représentée par l'illustration baptisée entre nous « l'escalier de la finance solidaire ». (joint en fin d'article).

Comment évaluer les chances de réussite d'une entreprise collective et donc ... son risque financier

La concertation entre financiers solidaires telle que décrite précédemment a produit dans les dernières années d'autres effets qui dépassent largement le partenariat dans les rondes de financement.

À l'initiative du RISQ, des tables de discussion visant à renforcer la concertation entre les partenaires impliqués dans le financement des entreprises collectives, ce qui inclut les agences de développement local, ont produit un constat majeur, partagé par tous : l'évaluation du risque et les modalités d'analyse financière d'une entreprise collective ne peut se réaliser avec les outils utilisés pour l'évaluation des entreprises traditionnelles. L'analyse approfondie sur les plans économique social et financier suppose une approche et des savoir-faire particuliers.

Les institutions financières dédiées aux coopératives et OBNL détiennent chacune une expertise très significative en la matière. Six de ces institutions ont pris la décision de constituer un outil de transfert de leur savoir-faire et de leurs connaissances en 2001[6]. Elles se sont également associées deux firmes d'experts-conseils et la direction des coopératives, organe ministériel du gouvernement du Québec.

C'est un travail de longue haleine qui a été réalisé de façon concertée avec de nombreux autres partenaires, tous très impliqués dans le support à l'émergence de développement des entreprises coopératives et OSBL.

Il a donné naissance à un guide d'analyse des entreprises d'économie sociale, entièrement voué à la compréhension de l'équilibre entre la gestion économique de l'entreprise et la réalisation de sa mission. Il énonce, explique et enseigne l'ensemble des paramètres à évaluer tout en précisant les critères et indicateurs sociaux, économiques et financiers à retenir dans une évaluation.

Celle-ci aborde tous les aspects qui vont de la gouvernance, à l'ancrage dans le milieu et aux partenariats, aux conditions de production des biens

---

6 RISQ, Investissement Québec, la caisse d'économie solidaire Desjardins, Fondation CSN, Filaction, direction des coopératives du ministère de développement économique. Avec le support de MCE Conseils et de Pythagore, firme spécialisée du secteur de l'économie sociale.

et services, aux ressources humaines équipements et organisation, avant d'aboutir à la partie financière de l'évaluation[7].

Sa diffusion a été très large au Québec. Elle s'est surtout appuyée sur de nombreuses sessions de formation offertes dans toutes les régions, en direction de tous les développeurs, analystes et banquiers désirant mieux connaître la façon pertinente de financer les entreprises collectives dans leur région et leurs milieux. Plus de 1000 exemplaires du guide ont été distribués en deux ans et les formations ont touché plusieurs centaines de professionnels du développement et du financement. Le guide fait même partie aujourd'hui des ouvrages de référence obligatoires dans plusieurs universités du Québec.

La réalisation de ces outils dans un cadre de concertation très actif entre institutions dédiées au financement de l'économie sociale, a encore renforcé les pratiques de collaboration depuis 2004.

La gouvernance de l'entreprise collective : un enjeu majeur

Je renvoie le lecteur au contenu du guide lui-même, qui aborde de façon très détaillée l'ensemble des aspects évoqués jusqu'ici. Je désire maintenant, du point de vue du financier solidaire que je suis, faire état de quelques enjeux qui sont apparus unanimement aux auteurs comme vraiment majeurs dans leur travail d'analyse des conditions de réussite d'une entreprise collective.

À la différence des ouvrages de référence en matière d'analyse d'une entreprise, ce guide insiste beaucoup sur l'importance de la mission de service aux membres et à la communauté. Tous les auteurs du guide s'entendent, au titre de leurs nombreuses années d'expérience cumulées, pour considérer que parmi les clés du succès d'une entreprise collective, c'est la qualité de la gouvernance qui en est certainement le plus important.

Nous voulons le souligner, dans une entreprise collective l'entrepreneur c'est l'association et donc les personnes qui la représentent.

On entend surtout par gouvernance, l'éthique et la qualité de la gestion ainsi que des pratiques démocratiques. Ainsi, la complémentarité des expertises dans le conseil d'administration et la qualité de l'information dont il dispose, la pertinence du partage des rôles entre la direction et le CA, la fréquence des rencontres et leur contenu, sont autant de paramètres qui vont être déterminants pour évaluer la fiabilité et l'efficience de la gestion collective d'une entreprise, notamment coopérative.

Une entreprise coopérative (comme c'est le cas pour un OBNL) est constituée pour réaliser une mission au bénéfice de ses membres, leur offrir du travail ou leur donner un accès à des produits ou des services dans des

---

7 Le guide d'analyse des entreprises d'économie sociale est disponible en français et en anglais auprès du RISQ à Montréal.

conditions les mieux adaptées à leurs besoins spécifiques dans leur milieu où leur communauté. C'est cette mission qui doit toujours être au cœur des décisions relatives à la gestion de l'entreprise.

Ce que nous constatons comme partenaire financier de nombreuses entreprises collectives, est que plus la démocratie joue bien son rôle dans la pratique concrète de la gouvernance, plus les décisions prises par l'entreprise sont en cohérence avec sa mission.

Toute entreprise doit un jour affronter des difficultés : perte financière, baisse d'activité, problème de productivité, etc... Des pratiques de gestion participative impliquant de la transparence, ayant su développer de la solidarité interne entre administrateurs et travailleurs, sont très précieuses. Le conseil d'administration et les travailleurs sont capables de se mobiliser pour trouver des solutions qui seraient impossibles dans une entreprise à propriété privée. Il est fréquent dans les situations difficiles de faire appel au bénévolat, de s'appuyer sur la motivation reliée au sentiment d'appartenance pour que chacun dans l'entreprise mette l'épaule à la roue et que ce collectif entrepreneurial sorte d'une situation critique.

À l'inverse, quand toutes les décisions de gestion sont centrées sur les questions de productivité et que l'entreprise est gérée selon les modes des entreprises traditionnelles, la mobilisation est très difficile et la réaction des travailleurs et du milieu ne permettra pas cette solidarité indispensable pour passer au travers des périodes de difficultés.

Les outils de la démocratie : la transparence de l'information

Avec quelques intervenants de la finance solidaire au Québec, nous sommes arrivés à la conclusion qu'il fallait toujours valider la qualité de la gouvernance mais aussi faire en sorte de lui donner du support en termes de formation et d'information.

Nous avons ainsi décidé d'investir conjointement dans la réalisation d'outils simples d'information destinés aux administrateurs et aux directeurs d'entreprises collectives.

Écosol, pour économie solidaire, coopérative de producteurs, est née en 2005 de l'initiative de Filaction, du fonds de financement coopératif, de la caisse d'économie solidaire Desjardins et du RISQ, avec la complicité et le partenariat d'une entreprise informatique associée de longue date à nos activités. Elle a conçu des services d'information et des outils de gestion en ligne pour les administrateurs, les présidences et directions générales d'entreprise collective[8].

_____

8 www.ecosol.coop

Premièrement, un tableau de bord de gestion conçu pour être disponible auprès de l'entreprise et de ses membres après seulement 30 minutes de saisie mensuelle d'informations, personnalisée pour chaque entreprise. Les principaux chiffres du mois, revenus et dépenses, la situation de liquidités comparés à l'année précédente et aux prévisions, les indicateurs économiques de productivité et de performances économiques et sociales, les indicateurs sur la vie démocratique, forment un rapport de trois pages, principalement sous la forme de graphiques, qui est adressé mensuellement par courriel aux destinataires désignés par l'entreprise, idéalement tous les administrateurs.

D'autres outils d'aide à la décision, accessibles en ligne pour un prix très modique, seront disponibles dès le printemps 2007 : un autodiagnostic de l'ensemble des fonctions de l'entreprise, très inspiré de l'analyse telle que présentée dans le Guide ; un outil de projection sur les besoins de financement et surtout de capitalisation, que le directeur, le trésorier, où le comptable de l'entreprise peut réaliser en direct et sans assistance à partir de son propre ordinateur.

De plus, Écosol offrira prochainement la possibilité pour les présidences ou les directions d'entreprise coopérative ou à but non lucratif de s'inscrire dans un réseau de mentorat. À l'image de l'économie sociale, ce mentorat, qu'il faut comprendre comme une relation privée entre deux personnes, l'une plus expérimentée appuyant l'autre moins, peut porter autant sur les questions relatives à la gouvernance, à la gestion de la mission qu'aux principales fonctions opérationnelles, techniques et stratégiques de direction ou de président de l'entreprise.

Le but poursuivi reste toujours le même, faire en sorte que les administrateurs, et tous les décideurs de l'entreprise disposent d'une information stratégique de façon régulière. C'est une condition incontournable pour que l'intelligence collective soit opérante au bénéfice du projet, de la communauté qu'il dessert.

La façon de faire au Québec : une intervention publique ciblée, la mobilisation de la société civile et un entrepreneurship collectif dynamique ...

L'argent reste toujours la clé de la réussite d'un projet d'entreprise, quel qu'en soit sa forme, son histoire et son statut. Le capital financier (l'équité) doit pouvoir être réuni lors d'un démarrage et doit continuer à se construire au fur et à mesure des étapes de développement de l'entreprise coopérative. Ce que le Québec a su réaliser en quelques décennies, c'est mobiliser des crédits publics pour les destiner à de l'intervention financière profession-nelle, ciblée et adaptée aux coopératives. La société civile, notamment le mouvement syndical CSN et le mouvement communautaire, travaillent de très près pour compléter et renforcer les moyens financiers nécessaires à cette question de capitalisation.

L'implication de l'État est incontournable, mais elle ne peut être efficace que si les mouvements sociaux concernés exercent autant leur capacité de pression et d'influence auprès de lui qu'ils usent de leur très grand potentiel d'innovation et d'initiative. Les outils rendus disponibles pour le développe-ment coopératif au Québec (accessibles très souvent aux autres entreprises collectives) sont autant financiers que techniques : accompagnement et sup-port, et outils de gestion adaptés.

Pour réussir un projet coopératif, quand des moyens d'accompagnement technique et des instruments financiers sont disponibles le potentiel de suc-cès est considérablement renforcée.

Au Québec, Les statistiques montrent que les entreprises coopératives sont deux fois plus nombreuses que les entreprises traditionnelles à passer la dif-ficile étape des cinq premières années de vie d'une entreprise. Comme nous l'avons souligné précédemment, c'est en raison de la capacité extraordinaire de soutien de l'association et de la communauté à la mission de l'entreprise collective. C'est un avantage « concurrentiel » inestimable. Pour conserver cet avantage, les coopérants doivent investir dans leur vie associative. Les outils développés dans le modèle québécois d'économie sociale ont innové en mettant une emphase aussi importante sur cette dimension sociale, que sur celle plus traditionnelle de la capitalisation.

Bibliographie électronique
- http://www.fondaction.com/ pour Fondaction CSN
- http://www.filaction.qc.ca/ pour Filaction
- http://www.filaction.qc.ca/FFC/ pour le Fonds de financement coopératif
- http://www.cecosol.coop/ pour la Caisse d'économie solidaire Desjardins
- http://www.fonds-risq.qc.ca/ pour le réseau d'investissement social du Québec : éditeur du guide d'analyse des entreprises d'économie sociale

- http://www.capitalregional.com/ pour Capital régional et coopératif Desjardins
- http://www.investquebec.com/ pour Investissement Québec
- http://www.rqcc.qc.ca/ pour le réseau québécois de crédit communautaire
- http://www.acldq.qc.ca/ pour les centres locaux de développement
- http://www.reseau-sadc.qc.ca/ pour les sociétés d'aide au développement des collectivités
- http://www.ecosol.coop/ pour la coopérative de services en ligne Écosol
- http://www.chantier.qc.ca/ pour la fiducie du chantier de l'économie sociale

L'escalier de la finance solidaire dédiée en tout ou partie au financement des entreprises **collectives**

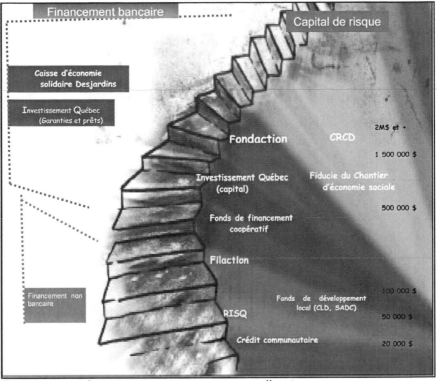

Financement bancaire aux entreprises collectives

- Caisse d'économie solidaire Desjardins : prêts à moyen et long termes et marges de crédit
- Investissement Québec : Garanties auprès des institutions financières et prêts directs aux entreprises de 10 000 $ à plusieurs millions de $
- Crédit communautaire : micro-crédit de quelques milliers de $ jusqu'à 50 000$ (moyenne de 15 000 à 20 000$)

Capital de risque

- RISQ : de 20 000$ à 50 000$
- Fonds de développement local : 5 000$ à 125 000$ selon le potentiel de chaque Fonds
- Filaction de 50 000$ à 500 000$, et Fonds de financement coopératif : de 100 000$ à 250 000$
- Investissement Québec : programme de capitalisation , de quelques dizaines de milliers de $ à 500 000$
- Fiducie du Chantier de l'économie sociale : de 50 000$ à un maximum de 1 500 000$
- Fondation CSN : de 250 000$ à quelques millions de $
- Capital régional et coopératif Desjardins: de 200 000$ à quelques millions

Section Three: Working Together to Make Co-ops Work

Chapter Nine

Good Governance

Lynn Hannley

C o-operatives are membership based organizations and the long-term sustainability of a co-operative is dependent upon the robustness of its governance system. Within co-ops, governance pertains to all the decisions that must be made to set-up and operate the co-op and encompasses all the various ways those decisions will be made. From my perspective as a developer, instilling good practices of governance from the outset is vital to the health of a co-op because initial patterns and processes tend to be perpetuated by members as the co-operative develops and evolves.

Among the many definitions of governance, I think the following two are useful in developing a framework for defining good governance:

Governance means the process of decision-making and the process by which decisions are implemented (or not implemented).

> Good governance has eight major characteristics. It is participatory, consensus oriented, accountable, transparent, responsive, effective and efficient, equitable and inclusive, and follows the rule of law. It assures that corruption is minimized, the views of minorities are taken into account, and that the voices of the most vulnerable in society are heard in decision-making. It is also responsive to the present and future needs of society.[1]

---

1 United Nations Economic and Social Commission for Asia and the Pacific, Human Settlements, What is Good Governance. Available at: www.unescap.org (Cited May 2006).

Governance is the task of defining the goals and standards of an organization and ensuring that there are effective management and other structures that will enable the organization to achieve these goals and standards.

There are four key elements to good governance in housing co-ops:
- *That the co-op maintains high ethical standards,*
- *That the co-op has strong systems of accountability to its members,*
- *That the co-op has proper systems to ensure effective operations, and*
- *That members work together to achieve democratically agreed objectives[2]*

In examining these two definitions, we see governance includes:
- Defining goals and standards,
- Making decisions, and
- Ensuring effective systems are in place to implement decisions in order to achieve agreed to objectives.

The characteristics of good governance are:
- It is participatory,
- There is a consensus oriented process for decision making,
- Participants work together,
- There is accountability and transparency,
- There is a way to evaluate the effectiveness of the decisions and the process is efficient, and
- There is a built in capacity to be responsive to the present and future needs of the members and the organization.

In this paper, I will use the components of the definition and the characteristics of good governance to develop a framework that can be used by co-operatives to facilitate governance.

Different types of co-operatives have different governance requirements as a result of both the nature of the co-operative business and the relationship of members to the co-operative. For example, consumer co-operatives are owned by the members who use the services and, more often than not, the employees who provide the services cannot serve on the board. Worker co-operatives, on the other hand, are owned and operated by members who are employees. Housing co-operatives, while technically a type of consumer co-operative, have specific needs that must be addressed in the design of the governance framework because of the 24/7 nature of the service provided. Multi-stakeholder co-operatives also have specific needs arising from the mixed nature of their membership and the specific nature of the business.

---

2 Code of governance for housing co-operatives: Confederation of Co-operative Housing, February 2001, Available at: http://www.cch.coop/coopinfo/codegov.html

A multi-stakeholder community forestry co-operative may well have different governance requirements than a community health care co-operative. Regardless of the specific needs of the co-operative, key characteristics of a good governance model include the characteristics named above.

The Participatory Element of Good Governance

Put Members at the Centre

As member owned and operated organizations, the role of the member is key to the success of the co-operative. Co-operatives[UK] has developed a good framework for what "member at the center" means, how that translates into both member rights and responsibilities, and ensuring clarity of roles and expectations for all parties involved. Although developed for consumer co-operatives, this framework can be transferred and adapted to other types of co-operatives.

Over the years, co-op clients that I have dealt with have used various tools to develop clear definitions of members' rights and responsibilities. It has been my experience that when the member rights and responsibilities are clearly articulated, members find it easier to become engaged in a meaningful way with their co-operative. A co-operative can be operating successfully even if there is a lack of clarity around the roles of the members, however, the co-operative's on going viability may be at risk. What I think is useful about the Co-operatives[UK] material is it provides a comprehensive framework to build on; for example it includes the members' right to voice an opinion and be consulted on key decisions affecting the society, access to member education and training opportunities, and the right to be informed of their rights. Incorporating these rights into the governance structure will have a significant impact on how a co-operative operates.

The inclusion of member responsibilities, such as holding the board to account by questioning and criticising its actions and decisions where necessary and ensuring the continuance of their society as a co-operative organization, will have a positive impact on the interaction between members and their co-operative.

> The governance of co-operative societies originates from their members. As member-owned businesses, co-operatives should seek to involve members as much as possible in the governance of the business. The way this can be achieved is by ensuring that members are aware of their rights and responsibilities, and by ensuring a sufficient dialogue is maintained between the society and the members.

Members have the right to:
- Be involved in the democratic decision making within the society by:
  - Attending members' meetings,
  - Voting in society elections,
  - Standing for election (subject to qualification) and participating in the democratic process,
  - Voicing an opinion and being consulted on key decisions affecting the society, and
  - Making proposals to improve the society's activities;
- Share in the benefits arising from the trading success of the society;
- Have access to member education and training opportunities;
- Have access to information which should be provided in keeping with co-operative values and heritage;
- Be informed of their rights; and
- Enjoy equal treatment with other members.

Members have a responsibility to:
- Abide by the rules of the society;
- Use the services of the society;
- Not act to the detriment of the society;
- Accept that their co-operative is a distinctive membership organization;
- Acknowledge and subscribe to the values and principles set out in the Statement of Co-operative Identity of the International Co-operative Alliance;
- Ensure the continuance of their society as a co-operative organization;
- Hold the board to account by questioning and criticising where necessary its actions and decisions;
- Encourage others to join the society and use its services;
- Learn more about the society, its values, structure, and aspirations;
- Take an interest in the governance of the society, vote in director elections, and attend Annual General Meetings where possible;
- Seek and develop useful means of exchanging information within the society and make use of occasions or routes of communication to provide for this exchange; and
- Inform the society of local events, conditions, and opportunities that might affect the operation of the society.

The exercise and discharge of these rights and responsibilities in a responsible fashion will ensure that the identity of the society as a co-operative is maintained.[3]

Membership in a co-operative is a two-way street and the exercise of both rights and responsibilities by the members is key to ensure the ongoing success of a co-operative. Co-operatives will fail if their members have no

---

3 Good Governance, Corporate Governance, Volume Two: Appendices to the Code of Best Practice, Co-operativesUK, May 2005 p .2.

sense of ownership and do not exercise their rights and responsibilities. One example of a long-term co-operative that failed, in part as a result of the members not exercising their rights and responsibilities, is Rice Growers Association (RGA) operating in California.[4] The RGA closed down in 2000 after 80 years of operation. In the 1980s, it had 80% of the total California rice crop and only 5% when it closed in 2000. A survey was conducted to determine the causes for the co-operative's closure. The survey found many members felt they did not have to be involved in the governance of the co-operative to benefit from its operations - the free rider approach. In addition, members thought they did not have to be involved because there were others who were looking after the affairs of the co-operative.

As a developer, I have been involved with many co-operatives over the years. One thing I have found is that member participation is very high during the development and early operational stages of a co-operative. Unless the members appreciate that their involvement has a direct impact on the success of their co-operative once the co-operative is up and running, the level of participation often goes down. A reduction in the level of participation can be accelerated if a co-operative is operating without any financial difficulties; members may have the sense of the organization operating on automatic pilot.

A sustainable co-operative is one in which the members have a true sense of ownership, and thus, think they should participate in directing and controlling the organization. It is important to find ways to ensure members develop this sense of ownership and do not become "free-riders." One of the recommendations from the study of the RGA to deal with lack of membership engagement proposed that the board engage the members and management regularly and solicit input from the membership.[5] This recommendation echoes the member's right to "voice an opinion and be consulted on key decisions affecting the society" identified by Co-operatives[UK].

It is important for co-operatives to be intentional in their approach to engaging the members in the governance of the co-operative. The concept of member engagement needs to be built into the governance ethos and framework. In 2003, Co-operatives[UK] embarked on a "Governance and Participation" project for the purpose of developing and enhancing ways and methods in which organizations across the social economy sector could actively involve members in governance of their co-ops. As part of the pro-

---

4 Jennifer Keeling, "Lesson from a Failed Co-operative: The Rice Growers Association Experience," *Update*, (Agricultural and Resource Economics, University of California: Giannini Foundation), Jan/Feb. 2004.

5 *Ibid.*

Table One: Ways Two Co-operatives Incorporated Participatory Governance

Ethical Consumer Research Association Publishing Ltd.

- Worker co-op – 12 workers (10 members, 2 on probation)
- Operated a successful business since 1987

Oxford, Swindon & Glouster Co-operative Society

- Consumer Co-operative
- Covers a geographical area of 5 counties – 84,000 active members, 3,834 staff
- 85 food stores
- 8 motor dealerships
- 28 funeral homes
- 13 Travel business outlets
- Property management
- Co-operative nursery
- Amalgamation of two failing societies that were not responsive to members
- Increased member involvement is central to the way co-operative does business

Participatory Processes of each Co-ops

- Different types of co-op meetings to accommodate and manage the decision-making process
- This allows members to participate at various levels
- Minutes of all co-op meetings are circulated to all members
- Members' meetings start with open dialogue which allows members to raise issues and set the agenda
- If a co-op member's participation is considered inadequate, the co-operative first considers the training needs of the individual, ensureing the members has knowledge, understanding, and confidence to contribute to the decision-making process
- It brings in external resources to help members deal with issues they cannot resolve

- Quarterly society members' meetings – held over three evenings at a different location each evening
- Society members are given an update and have the opportunity to discuss the matters before voting
- Other forms of communication include:
  - Newsletter
  - Member education council
  - Member groups
  - Web site
  - Store based information
  - Training seminars
  - Conferences
- Society carries out broad range of consultations with members, staff, and other stakeholders, including other co-operatives and suppliers.

cess, it looked at a number of different co-operatives to review how they had incorporated participatory governance. Table One provides an overview of the practices of two of these co-operatives; the first is a smaller worker co-operative and the second is a large consumer co-operative. In both cases, the co-operatives have placed significant importance on member engagement and have developed systems that enhance the overall participation of their members. These two examples illustrate that, regardless of the size, it is possible to engage the members in a meaningful way.

As part of its Governance and Participation project, Co-operatives[UK] developed a series of workshops and a Development Toolkit, which includes a participation section with the following:

- Participation Stocktaking — enables users to evaluate their own mechanisms and resources for participation and provides ideas on how to improve participatory governance.
- Participation Methods – an inventory of tools and mechanisms to improve participation in an organization and guidance on good practice and considerations.

A good governance framework must be focused around the members and actively involve them in establishing the organization's overall goals and objectives and in the governance of the co-operative. In order to effectively accomplish this, a co-operative must ensure its members have adequate knowledge and skills. Initial and ongoing membership education is key.

Member Education

The Rochdale Weavers recognized the importance of education and actually allocated 2.5% of their net revenue to member education; this was after paying expenses and setting aside business expansion funds but prior to the allocation of profits to its members. In its 1937 review of the Co-operative Principles, the ICA found most of its members continued to allocate funds for education, with such funding varying from 1 to 5 % of net revenue. Unfortunately, today many co-operatives do not allocate adequate resources towards member education. In addition, a number of those that do often limit such expenditures to the education of board members.

One example of an effective member education process resulting in greater member participation is that set up by Home for Change Housing Co-operative, one of the groups included in the Co-operatives[UK] case studies. Unlike many housing co-operatives, all of the members are part of the governing body. The work of the co-operative is carried out on a voluntary basis through a number of working groups, with the assistance of a paid staff. The majority of members are actively involved in the working groups. All new members must be nominated prior to being accepted as a member and must attend at least three general meetings, participate in one working committee, and attend indoctrination sessions before they can be nominated. These sessions include: co-operative history, what is a co-operative, background on Homes for Change, working groups, the structure of the co-operative, overview of the work areas within the co-operative, working co-operatively, different working situations, skills required, and completion of a basic skills audit. The co-operative also provides training to its working groups on such things as: chairing meetings, participation in meetings, effective planning, managing volunteers, and Information Technology (IT) skills. With its focus on both co-operative education and skills training, the co-operative is able to *"harness the expertise and abilities of its members to effectively manage and govern the Co-operative."*[6] Education alone is not enough; for a co-operative to successfully harness member's expertise and abilities, it needs a strategic member engagement plan.

Strategic Plan for Member Engagement

A strategic plan will enable a co-operative to determine what it should be doing to engage its membership, what resources it requires, and how it should implement its plan. Depending upon the size and the nature of the co-operative, the strategic plan could be initiated by either the board or the membership. It is important that a co-operative clearly identify whose responsibility it is to undertake the work. A strategic plan has to be specific to an individual co-operative, take into account the members' strengths and weaknesses, and the limitations that might impact member engagement. It is important that the strategic plan is grounded in reality and not based upon expectations that cannot be met. The strategic plan should include both formal and informal ways of involving the members in the co-operative. The informal ways of involving members could include: socials, recreational events, specific social justice or environmental projects, and other community projects. Members of co-operatives should not underestimate the value of breaking bread and celebrating together; for these activities facilitate community and community is an essential building block of co-operation and vice versa.

Nurturing a Consensus Orientation

Although co-operatives are described as democratic organizations, a model based upon democratic majority rule is not necessarily appropriate within a

---

6 The Development Toolkit, Case Studies, Co-operatives[UK], Governance and Participation Project, Available at: www.co-operatives-uk.coop (Cited December 2006, p. 24-26).

co-operative context. A model based upon consensus, creating community, and valuing the input of each participant is much more effective in a co-operative context.

> *What makes consensus so good is that it allows everyone in a group to contribute to and own a decision, without it being dominated by those who shout the loudest. It is a better system than majority voting as it tries to avoid the alienation of minorities that major-ity rule can create. It values everyone's opinion equally and works towards conclusions acceptable to all. With consensus everyone in the group must agree to a decision for it to become effective!*[7]

Consensus does not mean everyone must be completely satisfied with the final outcome or that everyone agrees with the outcome. The decision, how-ever, must be acceptable enough that everyone will commit to support the group in choosing it. Consensus decision making:

- Stresses group members work together to co-operatively develop a decision,
- Focuses on group unity, not the majority of votes, and
- Is based upon the belief that every member is considered important and needs to be heard.

There are three essential ingredients in the consensus decision making pro-cess:

- Decisions must be made with the community's best interest in mind,
- Everyone takes responsibility to speak their point of view and to listen to others, and
- Everyone agrees not to hinder the implementation of the decision.

As a developer, I recommend the use of a consensus decision making model to all the groups that I work with, regardless of whether they are co-op-eratives or not. The process I use to ensure participation during a meeting to enable the group to achieve consensus involves a "four card system." I have found the use of this card system enhances the quality of the group's discussion process and has the impact of mitigating domination by a few. The cards used during the discussion period include:

- Green card – used to indicate a desire to participate in the discus-sion.
- Yellow card – used for clarification or specific information require-ments; the yellow card takes precedence over green.

---

7 People and Planet – Groups Guide Consensus. Available from the World Wide Web <http://noncms.peopleandplanet.org/groups/guide/guide.consensus.php>. (Cited January 2005).

- Purple card – used for process purposes (group off topic, a break required); the purple card takes precedence over green and yellow.

I have found the nature and tone of the discussion is much more congenial and co-operative when the cards are used. I think that one reasons for this is that the playing field is leveled since every card is equal.

When it is time to make a decision, cards used to determine consensus include:

- Green – indicates agreement,
- Yellow – indicates standing aside (that the individual does not support the decision but will let it pass), and
- Red – indicates standing in the way or blocking the decision.

After the discussion of a proposal and initial test for consensus is taken, those who indicate they are standing aside are then asked why they do not support the proposal. This gives those who are in a minority the opportunity to put forward their concerns in a non-confrontational milieu for further review and discussion. If, after the second round of discussion, there are individuals who do not support the decision, but are not blocking the decision and could live with the decision, consensus has been achieved. However, if a proposal makes a few people, even one person, deeply unhappy, then there may be a valid reason for that unhappiness, and the group needs to review the decision. If there are individuals who cannot live with the decision or are blocking it, no consensus has been achieved and the proposal must be re-submitted. Effective consensus decision making often requires:

- A comprehensive proposal or background information to inform the discussion, which preferably should be circulated in advance of the meeting,
- A facilitator whose role is to facilitate the discussion, keep the meeting focused and moving,
- A timekeeper to ensure the meeting follows the time allocated for each item,
- A card-watcher to identify the order and priority of the speakers, and
- A scribe or note-taker to record the decisions.

Some groups also like to have a process person. I have found it is also useful to have participants check-in at the beginning of the meeting and check-out at the end. Checking-in effectively serves two purposes. It allows the individual to focus their mental and physical energy on the meeting by bringing themselves into the here and now. It also lets the individual communicate any personal circumstances that may have an impact on how they interact with the group. Check-out provides an opportunity to evaluate the meeting and identify what might be modified to improve the overall process. Check-out also brings closure to the meeting.[8]

It has been my experience that both the meeting dynamics and decision making process improves significantly using the consensus model. Some might argue such a model is designed only for small intimate groups. I have successfully used this specific card model with larger non-intimate groups. While it may be difficult to use such a model with hundreds of members, the following principles can be used to develop more effective consensus building decision making models with any size group:

- Unity of purpose,
- Co-operation,
- Trust,
- Differences are valued,
- Feelings are valued,
- Equal power, equal responsibility,
- Common ownership of ideas,
- Respect for time and process, and
- Willingness to learn new skills.

Transparency and Accountability

Pre-requisites for transparency and accountability include:

- Agreement on a set of operating rules and regulations, often referred to as bylaws (or rules) and policies;
- Clarity regarding the roles of the members, board, committees, and the staff;
- Skilled and informed board of directors; and
- A means of ensuring adequate information is available to plan, manage, and govern the affairs of the co-operative.

Together these guidelines create a formal framework that transforms a group of individuals working together into a corporate body - separate from themselves - their co-operative. A new developing worker co-operative brought the significance of this distinction home to me when one of the members indicated how excited he was that they now needed bylaws and rules to guide their operations. For him, this was indicative of the fact that they no longer were just a group of individual personalities but members of a co-operative that would continue to exist as members came and went. Formalization of structure is important, otherwise an organization becomes amoeba-like, a constantly changing entity based upon the influence of the dominant personalities within the group.

8 Facilitator's Toolbox, Member Manual, Prairie Sky Cohousing Co-operative Ltd., July 2000.

Within each sector there are sample bylaws and policies that can be modified to meet the specific circumstance of an individual co-operative. However, a group can't just take a set of sample bylaws and policies and adopt them. It must tailor the bylaws and policies to its specific needs, thereby creating living documents, and ones that reflect their specific circumstances. The key in assessing these various options is having a good grounding in the nature and type of co-operative, the scope of the proposed business venture, and an understanding of how various options play out in real life. A skilled developer can take a group through this process.

Leadership and Delegation - A Skilled and Informed Board of Directors

In most cases, the members of a co-operative divide up the tasks necessary to govern and manage its operations. The division of tasks results in the delegation of duties and authority to various parties. The most common structure used is one that includes a board and committees, where the board is delegated the responsibility to oversee the day-to-day ongoing operations of the co-operative. While there are standard duties and responsibilities that all boards have, co-operative boards have additional responsibilities, which are aptly described in The Code of Best Practice for Consumer Co-operatives.

> The board has a direct responsibility to ensure that the society carries out its commitment to be a bona fide co-operative. The board must have a commitment to adhere to the International Co-operative Alliance's Statement of Co-operative Identity and to support co-operatives in other sectors. The board should always ensure that in running the business, the management executive maintains the society's co-operative values and standards, and they should ensure the society's obligations to its members and others, in particular employees, customers, suppliers, and the community, are understood and met.[9]

For the most part, members of the board are members of the co-operative who sit as unpaid volunteers (or are paid a limited stipend) and often have a limited business or board background. In many cases, it maybe difficult to get members to serve on the board and sometimes the commitment of those elected to the board is erratic. Being on a co-operative board can be a very challenging experience - particularly if the board is operating with limited human and financial resources. Regardless of its limitations, a board should undertake an analysis of its skill set and experience and ensure directors have access to necessary training to enable it to carry out its delegated duties. It has been my experience that a board that does not do

---

9 "Appendices to the Code of Best Practice," Good Governance, Corporate Governance, Volume Two (Co-operatives^UK) May 2005 p. 6.

this is more likely to exhibit less transparency. This is, I think, in part due to over compensating for being "in over their heads" and a concern about being found out.

It is essential that co-operative developers effectively inculcate their co-operative clients with the need to continuously develop skills and build capacity within the group. The co-operative sector has a role to play in such skill and capacity development by enabling boards to access the necessary resources and training and by providing training on governance delivered by professionals well versed in co-operatives. Such sessions must be delivered at times and locations that encourage, rather than inhabit, participation; volunteer board members will rarely be able to get time off work to participate in a training session. An example of an effective practice is the training sessions developed and delivered by the co-operative housing sector that focus on skill development, group process, and general technical awareness. These sessions are delivered by instructors certified by the Co-operative Housing Federation of Canada and are delivered during the evening or on weekends. Fees for these courses are reasonable.

It is highly unlikely a board will have all of the skills and knowledge it requires to discharge its responsibilities. As part of their business planning and thinking, co-operative members should take steps to ensure that members and directors have the resources to engage the skills that are needed when they are required. If the board does not have the complete skill set and cannot acquire the skills through training, then it should consider contracting out for those skills. I have encountered groups that are reluctant to hire out and attempt to undertake the work on their own. This is an attitude that seems to stem from a specific interpretation of "self-help;" that is, members or the board have to do it themselves on a voluntary basis, regardless of their skill set. It is important that members understand that it is okay to hire out and that their co-operative does not become less of a co-operative for doing so.

Succession Planning

Succession planning is also an important component of ensuring transparency and accountability. An effective practice is to identify potential board members well in advance and, if necessary, provide them with preparatory training and mentoring. This process should start months before the actual election of new directors. Unfortunately, in many co-operatives, the board is running around at the last minute trying to find members to stand for election; in some instances individuals with limited skills and resources are elected by acclamation. One effective way of addressing this is for a co-operative to emphasize and formalize its members' rights and responsibilities contract with the co-operative - every member has a responsibility to ensure the continuance of their co-operative.

Summary – A Framework to Facilitate Good Governance

The following are elements of a framework that can help guide the implementation of good governance practices in a co-op.

- Members are the key element of the framework and a clear description of the members' rights and responsibilities helps ensure that the members actively engage in the governance of the co-operative.
- It is important to provide the members with education and training that will enhance their understanding and participation.
- Work together to develop and implement a strategic member engagement plan.
- Decision making models should focus on group unity over a majority rules approach and value the views of each individual.
- Clearly articulated bylaws and policies should reflect the specific needs of the co-operative and be clearly understood and supported by all members.
- Define the roles and job descriptions for the various parties (members, board, committees, staff, and outside contractors engaged in management).
- To ensure the co-op has skilled and informed board members, there is a need for ongoing board education and training, as well as the ability to access resources as required.
- Procedures should be in place to provide the members, board, committees, and staff with the information required to properly manage and govern the co-op.

In my many years of experience as a co-op developer, I have observed that when co-op members are able to take the time to develop and implement governance models built upon these elements, the economic health of the co-operative is enhanced, as is members' satisfaction with their co-operative. In cases where the governance is not a priority, the long term viability of the co-operative is jeopardized, members leave the co-operative, board members resign, the economic health of the co-operative takes a nosedive as does its members overall satisfaction. As I have discussed in this paper, good research has been undertaken on co-ops and governance practices, and we now have many years of experience to draw on. In addition, there are now more tools and resources available within the co-operative sector that can be used to enhance governance practices.

While I have learnt many things over the years, three key lessons, with regard to co-operative governance are:

1. It is important to formalize corporate structure, governance systems, and decision making processes within the co-operative. It is often very tempting for members to operate informally. This is especially true if members know each other. In some circumstances, members are reluctant to formalize their governance systems, believing that such formalization is anti-co-operative.

2. It is important to have a decision making process that fosters consensus and co-operation. When I started out as a developer, the only decision making process that was used was the majority vote system. Little was know about consensus building models and there were few tools available. One method used to foster community was to require a higher than majority vote to carry decisions, particularly those decisions deemed to be significant by the group. While this approach increased the degree of agreement, there still were winners and losers. A consensus building model works to ensure members who do not agree with a decision can live with it and do not feel they have lost.

3. It is import that the members and the board act intentionally. Things do not just fall into place by chance, members don't just participate because they somehow perceive this to be a good thing, and members aren't always seeking out board positions. Strategic planning is important to ensure a co-operative can develop and implement a governance system that will ensure the ongoing sustainability of the co-operative.

Developing a system to improve the overall governance within a co-operative and enhance the operations of the co-operative is worth the investment in the long run.

> Improving the governance of an organization is about making an organization more effective, resilient, and strengthening its purpose. For any organization, good governance and arrangements can contribute to its overall success. In the longer term, good governance can contribute to enabling the group to take on new challenges, meet community needs, and grow and develop into a valuable resource for local people."[10]

---

10 Co-operatives[UK], Governance and Participation Project, Overview Improving Governance. Available at: www.co-operatives-uk.coop/NewVentures/gp/overview (Cited December 2006).

Chapter Ten

Co-operative Development in Canada: The Emergence of Programme Delivery Partnerships

Glen Fitzpatrick

Co-operative development in Canada has a long history that has seen a variety of approaches to the provision of support services for newly developing enterprises. At different points in the past, in various regions of the country, co-op development services have been delivered by charitable foundations, religious organizations, provincial governments, unions, existing co-ops, and community development agencies. These co-op development supporters have had a variety of motivations, some spiritual, some practical, and some political. All, however, have had to address the issue of finding the resources to deliver the support services required to assist people in forming co-operatives.

In recent years, a new focus on co-op development partnerships has emerged as a way to address this resource capacity issue. These partnerships involve engaging the support of a number of stakeholders to access the resources required to assist newly emerging co-operatives through start-up and initial operations. The need for these partnerships has, to some degree, been a result of the lack of resources available from within the Canadian co-op sector to support new developments. Therefore, development practitioners and groups engaged in establishing new co-ops have had to look elsewhere for assistance. Much of this new interest in partnerships is centered on accessing government support for co-op development, based on the rationale that co-ops are a tool for generating employment and economic development, particularly in rural communities.

Co-operative Development Partnerships in Canada

Today, at the community level, "Project Development Partnerships" are often formed to establish a team of resource people and/or agencies to help facilitate development of a co-operative enterprise. These partnerships are structured to meet the individual needs of a specific project. They tend to be informal and usually remain in place until the co-operative is operational. Such a partnership may, for example, include a provincial co-op development association to provide organizational advice, a local community development agency to assist with business planning, and a provincial government agency to fund member-training activities.

In Newfoundland, for example, an e-commerce co-operative was recently established to assist small business operators to market their products through a jointly owned website. The Mariner Opportunities Network (a regional development agency in the Harbour Grace/Carbonear region) developed the technology required. Financial support was provided by the Atlantic Canada Opportunities Agency (a federal government regional development organization), and advisory support was provided by the NL Federation of Co-operatives (the province's co-op development agency). Such project partnerships are common across the county, particularly in rural communities.

At a broader level, partnerships are also being established by organizations to deliver programmes and services that promote the co-op business alternative and ensure availability of support services for multiple co-op development projects on an ongoing basis. These "Programme Partnerships" tend to be more formal in nature than project partnerships. They are often implemented at the national or provincial level and ensure the availability of advisory and/or financial support services to assist projects at the community level.

In Quebec, for example, such a partnership has been implemented where the co-op sector and the provincial government are working collaboratively to deliver a co-op development strategy that provides support services through a network of co-op development centres across the province. At this point, it is probably the most advanced of any programme partnership in Canada, and it has accelerated the number of co-op incorporations in Quebec in recent years.

Both Project and Programme Partnerships are generally based on the common interests of the participating agencies. When money is involved there are usually formal agreements, in the form of contracts or memorandums of understanding, that ensure clarity and commitment to partner roles and responsibilities. Partnering agencies often have different rationales for becoming a co-op development project or programme partner. For example, a federal government agency may wish to facilitate development of a particular industry sector, a provincial government may be interested in job creation, and for a co-op association growing the sector may be the priority. These differing priorities must be understood and accepted by all if the partnership is to be successful.

Who are the Partners?

In Canada, both Project and Programme Partnerships tend to be established between agencies that share a common interest in supporting new co-operative development as part of their respective mandates. Some examples follow.

Provincial Co-operative Associations

These provincial associations have differing levels of capacity to provide development support services across the country. Where they do provide assistance, they have become important points of contact for people interested in developing a potential co-operative enterprise, providing advisory services and assisting with coordination of the project. They are often an important communications link with other potential partners such as government, industry associations, and the existing co-operative sector, all of whom may be in a position to assist with the project. These associations exist in most provinces across the country but are most active in British Columbia, Ontario, Quebec, Nova Scotia, and Newfoundland and Labrador.

Government Programmes and Services

Both provincial and federal governments are active in the co-op development process, providing community development, business support services, and financial support. Their support tends to be primarily based on the role co-ops can play as a vehicle to create jobs and stimulate economic growth. Therefore, government is often engaged in supporting co-operative development projects. Though seen primarily as a source of grants and financing, government can also play an important role in the provision of information and expertise that is often under-rated in the co-op development process. The best examples are found in Quebec and Newfoundland and Labrador.

The Existing Co-operative Sector

Many existing co-ops and sector federations play an important role in assisting the development of new co-operatives, particularly from an industry specific perspective. In such circumstances, the new co-operative benefits from the knowledge, resources, and expertise offered by the existing co-operative, often free of charge. The existing sector also benefits in that the new co-operative will join a federation or partner with the existing sector in other ways, thereby contributing to long term growth and success.

This approach is well established in other countries as a preferred method for the development of new co-operatives. It is an approach also favored in Quebec, which has a number of sector federations that work in partnership with a network of regional co-op development centres to address both start-up and operational requirements. There is potential for greater application of this approach in other parts of the country as a more cost-effective and mutually beneficial model for new co-operative development in Canada.

Private Consultants

Many co-op developers across the country are employed by co-op sector organizations, community development agencies, and government. However, some developers operate independently as consultants, offering their services on a fee-for-service basis to developing co-ops. These consultants undertake a variety of tasks that usually complement the skills and resources provided by other partners working with the developing group. Their roles often tends to be technical in nature, focusing on specific deliverables such as business and marketing plans, training and research, and industry assessments. Many of these consultants align themselves with other co-op developers through provincial networks. Work is ongoing on the establishment of a national network to enhance communications and skills development across the country.

Community Development Organizations

There are many regional development organizations across Canada that provide financing and resource support for co-operative development projects. Whether they are economic zone boards in Newfoundland and Labrador, or regional development councils in Quebec, these organizations are important "players" from a socio-economic perspective. Generally speaking, these organizations are supportive of co-operatives as a community owned business alternative. Their mandates vary significantly, and some are more knowledgeable about co-operative development than others. However, their potential role as resource supports for co-op development projects should be acknowledged and encouraged for both Project and Programme Partnerships.

Emergence of Programme Partnerships

The partners described above have traditionally been, and continue to be, the primary resource supports for Project Partnerships. More recently, however, we have seen these same stakeholders becoming engaged in the establishment of Programme Partnerships that make a range of co-op development services available on an ongoing basis. At the national level, such Programme Partnerships have been initiated by the Co-op Housing Federation of Canada, the Canadian Co-operatives Association, and the Worker Co-op Federation of Canada. Co-op associations in Nova Scotia, Quebec, Newfoundland and Labrador have established provincial Programme Partnerships. All of these Programme Partnerships have been successful in facilitating new growth in the co-op sector in Canada.

The development of Programme Partnerships in Canada differs substantially from Project Partnerships. It usually requires a more formalized, longer term relationship than is required for a Project Partnership, and usually involves larger capital contributions. As with project partners, programme partners also have important roles to play. Roles and responsibilities must be negotiated amongst programme partners within the context of a programme structure and service delivery plan that reflects the interests of all.

From this perspective, it is critical that co-op developers (and the co-op agencies they may represent) recognize and respect the differing mandates and motivations of other potential partners when seeking to engage them in new programme development. Federal and provincial governments, for example, must comply with a variety of organizational restrictions, evaluation, and reporting requirements. Co-operative agencies initiating Programme Partnerships must be sensitive to these requirements and flexible in their ability to respond. This requires that they bring good negotiating, diplomatic, and programme planning skills to the table; skills that often differ from those required to support Project Partnership initiatives.

Building Programme Partnerships

The negotiation of Programme Partnership agreements and the delivery of related services has, therefore, become an increasingly important dimension of the work undertaken by co-op developers in Canada. Individuals are required with the skills to initiate these partnerships, develop the programmes, and deliver the services. They are needed within the co-op sector, including provincial associations, sector federations, and other agencies with a commitment to co-operative development. They are also needed within government and the community development sector to build awareness of the unique benefits of co-operative development and foster an environment supportive of Programme Partnership initiatives.

This means it is critical for the co-op sector, and those currently engaged in providing support services for newly developing projects, to reach out to potential partners outside the sector and invite them to be part of the solution in terms of facilitating the growth and development of the co-op sector across the country. This will require a commitment from the existing sector to do its part in supporting co-operative development programming at the federal and provincial levels. It will also require existing co-op developers to take an inclusive approach that will build knowledge and awareness within these potential partner organizations and encourage them to play a more proactive role in supporting new developing co-operative enterprises.

Formalizing Agreements

As previously mentioned, short term Project Partnerships, particularly those involving government and the co-op sector, often require contractual agreements that cover terms and conditions of funding contributions to support specific co-operative development activities. Such partnerships are currently being implemented between provincial and federal governments, provincial co-op associations, and co-op sector federations across the country.

Recently, however, we have seen the development of new, more comprehensive agreements that cover a broader range of multi-sector co-op development activities, including co-operative policy development, promotional activities, financial support, delivery of development advisory services, and aftercare support. In many cases, these Programme Partnerships are long-term agreements that include financial arrangements and allocation of resources to achieve mutually agreed upon objectives.

In such cases, it is therefore advisable and often required that partners sign on to formalized agreements, which outline roles and responsibilities and results to be achieved. Typically, these programme agreements take the form of contracts and memorandums of understanding which outline in detail all aspects of the co-operative development programme and how it will be delivered. Such partnerships have recently been established in Quebec, Nova Scotia, Newfoundland and Labrador.

In Newfoundland and Labrador, for example, the provincial co-op association is currently partnering with the provincial government's Rural Development Department to deliver co-op development services through its regional offices across the province. The Federal government is providing funding support to facilitate development of this new relationship, which is now entering its third year of operations and is generating positive results. This partnership enables the provincial association to expand the availability of co-op development services in the province, while at the same time furthering the department's mandate to help create small businesses in rural communities.

Programme Partnerships often require that existing co-op organizations forgo some autonomy and control of a development programme in order to access support of other organizations. Co-op developers need to recognize that establishing and maintaining Programme Partnerships can be a balancing act where differing opinions, philosophies, mandates, and objectives must be acknowledged in the interests of service delivery. Personal views and philosophies must often be put aside in the interests of bringing about consensus on a programme initiative. This includes allowing all partners to play a role in the decision making process.

This does not mean those committed to co-op development must sacrifice their particular personal view points in order to access resource supports that may be available from other organizations. Rather, it means developers need to recognize establishment of new co-op enterprises often generates benefits that fit with the mandates of many community development agencies in Canada that are engaged in such activities as job creation and development of rural communities.

It is important, however, that the integrity of the co-op model as a democratic, community-owned business enterprise be maintained as a cornerstone of the Programme Partnership development process. The new co-ops developed through Programme Partnerships must remain autonomous businesses, owned and controlled by the members. It is the role of existing co-op sector organizations that are proposing Programme Partnerships to act as guardians of the co-op principles, and ensure they are a fundamental part of the service delivery continuum.

However, co-op organizations should not be overly concerned about other potential partners wishing to subvert the process to the detriment of co-op development objectives. Clarification of roles and responsibilities should address such a possibility early in the planning process. In any case, most agencies want the co-op sector involved in order to legitimize the process and share the work load. But in all cases, the issue of how co-op development should be undertaken and who should deliver on different aspects of the development process should be open to consideration, depending on the particular circumstances involved.

For more extensive, long-term partnership agreements, it is sometimes advisable to engage the services of an external facilitator to ensure all potential partners have equal opportunity to put forward and, if necessary, provide a supporting rationale for their perspectives on an appropriate service delivery agreement. This will also ensure the resulting agreement fully reflects the substance of the discussions and consensus reached regarding elements of a potential agreement.

Conclusion

The move towards partnerships as a means of increasing the level of resource support to facilitate co-operative development in Canada has been accelerating in recent years. In addition to supporting co-operative development projects at the community level, co-operative development agencies are also recognizing the need for co-op developers to have expertise in partnership negotiation, strategy development, programme delivery, and management of partner relations.

In other words, the skills required to create and maintain an effective regime of support services for co-operative development in Canada now go beyond the capacity to deliver on the generally accepted "steps" in the co-operative development process. The development and delivery of Partnership Programmes is now an important part of the work currently undertaken by those engaged in the co-op development field.

In Canada, the increasing engagement of government and community development partners is creating greater understanding and broader awareness of the benefits of the co-operative business option. This is resulting in a broader acceptance of the model and consequently resulting in increasing numbers of co-operative development programmes and projects. These new partnerships may therefore, be signaling a new era of collaboration between the co-operative sector and other agencies engaged in the community development process, which can potentially place co-operatives in the forefront as a socio-economic development tool for rural communities across the country.

Chapter Eleven

Co-operative Practices and the Experience of a Regional Development Co-operative

Christian Savard

The co-operative movement is well established in Québec and its growth in semi-urban and rural areas is a phenomenon which delights local elected officials. However, it is not well established in all of Québec's seventeen administrative regions.

The goal of this essay is to present the factors which contributed to the success of the development approach of the Centre-du-Québec/Mauricie (CD-CQM) Development Co-operative in its territory.

A brief description of the socioeconomic development actors in Québec will be presented first, followed by a profile of the CDCQM and co-operative development practices.

Development Actors in Québec

Regional County Municipalities (RMCs)

Québec's territory is divided into seventeen administrative regions, which includes close to 86 regional county municipalities (RMC). An agreement exits concerning the role of RMCs and their responsibilities with respect to local development, as well as operating conditions. The RMC may take any measure necessary in order to promote local development and entrepreneurship support in its territory. To this end, it may offer a complete range of front-line services to businesses and guarantee their financing. Each RMC also develops a local action plan for the economy and employment that considers the five-year development plan set out by its territory's Conférence régionale des élus (CRE) [Regional Conference of Elected Officials]. Each RMC oversees the implementation of this plan. Taking into account national and regional directions, strategies, and objectives, each RMC must develop an entrepreneurial development strategy. Finally, an RMC may act as an advisory body to its territory's Centre local d'emploi (CLE) [Local Employment Centre]. In order to fulfill these mandates, the RMC entrusts the exercise of its jurisdiction to a "Centre local de développement" (CLD) [Local Development Centre].

Regional Conference of Elected Officials (CRE)

In each administrative region, a CRE is instituted and is the Québec government's privileged partner in the area of regional development. Each CRE has as its principal mandate the evaluation of planning and development bodies, at both the local and regional levels, which are either partially or fully government-funded; promotion of co-op development with partners in the region; and, where appropriate, advising the Minister for Development in the region.

The CRE develops a five-year plan which defines general and specific development goals for the region with a view to sustainable development and, according to the principles of equality and parity, considers political involvement of youth and women.

This five-year development plan must also consider the regional strategies and objectives with respect to labour and employment as determined by the territory's Regional Council of Labour market partners and the plan for significant economic development issues adopted by its territory's metropolitan community. The CRE may enter into specific agreements with government ministries or organizations and, where appropriate, other partners. The CRE carries out all other mandates as assigned by the Minister.

Actors in Mauricie and Centre-du-Québec

In Mauricie, there are six RMCs: the RMC of Maskinongé, the Town of La Tuque, the Town of Shawinigan, the RMC of Mékinac, the RMC of Des Chenaux, and the Town of Trois-Rivières. In the Centre-du-Québec, there are five RMCs: the RMC of l'Érable, the RMC of Arthabaska, the RMC of Drummond, the RMC of Bécancour, and the RMC of Nicolet-Yamaska. Each of the eleven organizations has a CLD and there are two CREs (Mauricie and Centre-du-Québec). All of these organizations are linked with the Ministry of Municipal and Regional Affairs, which has two quite distinctive regional directorates. Over and above the development activities at the territorial level, the Canadian government has seven organizations (Community Futures Development Corporation) sponsored by Canada Economic Development (CED)[1], which operate in the more rural locations.

This is a concise presentation of the front-line partners who guide, support, and work side by side with Québec entrepreneurs.

Co-operative Development Organization in Québec

Some Historical Points

Co-operatives represent an important part of Québec's collective heritage. In fact, starting in the late 18th century, mutual benefit societies facilitated the development of a certain social partnership in the face of adversity. Mutual fire insurance companies arrived in the mid-19th century, and several other types of co-operatives made their appearance at the turn of the 20th century. The birth of caisses populaires [credit unions] during this era is the best known example.

The current co-operative movement took shape over time, beginning in 1937-1939, principally as a response to the urgent needs caused by the economic crisis raging at the time. Québecers once again demonstrated their spirit of social partnership and took the situation into their own hands by creating co-operative grocery stores, forestry co-operatives, etc., in order to meet their basic needs. Twenty-two consumer co-operatives and seven fishers' co-operatives were created in 1939 alone. As for agricultural co-operatives, sixty-one were incorporated in 1938, and at least forty more per year would spring up over the next seven consecutive years.

In 1951, the Conseil de la coopération du Québec (CCQ) [Québec Co-operation Council], the true flagship of Québec co-operatives, was created.

1 For more information visit http://www.dec-ced.gc.ca/

In 1963, at the request of the co-operative movement, the government undertook a complete overhaul of the Co-operative Syndicates Act, which dated from 1906. In order to acknowledge the diverse needs of different types of co-operatives, it created two complementary laws: the Co-operative Associations Act and the Savings and Credit Unions Act.

These new acts confirmed the importance of the role that the government had conferred upon the Conseil de la coopération du Québec in the future; the CCQ would be required to advise the Provincial Secretary with the creation of each new co-operative. The CCQ would also receive an annual subsidy to be used for creating a committee and participating in the official acknowledgement of co-operatives.

In order to manage this new co-operative legislation and to offer improved support to the co-operative movement, the Québec government created the Co-operative Branch. Established in 1963, the Co-operative Branch was set-up as an administrative unit, within the Department of the Provincial Secretary, to deal specifically with co-operatives. It would later become the Co-operatives Directorate.

In the summer of 1968, the government created a new ministry, that of Financial Institutions, Consumers, and Co-operatives. The Act by which this new ministry was created enshrined the distinction between co-operatives and traditional businesses. It also provided for the appointment of a deputy minister who would be responsible specifically for co-operatives within this new ministry, which also housed the Co-operative Branch.

Finally, the government established a partnership with the co-operative movement through the creation of the Société de développement coopératif (SDC) [Society for Co-operative Development], whose mission it is to promote the creation and development of co-operatives with the goal of ensuring the population's increasing participation in economic activity, promoting the economic development of the regions, and creating jobs in these regions.

This organization would receive 25 million dollars between 1977 and 1984, of which 22 million would come from the government. It is interesting to note that the SDC is principally managed by administrators named by the Conseil de la coopération du Québec.

In accordance with the order of February 1985, the Direction des coopératives of the Ministère de l'Industrie et du Commerce (MIC) [Co-operatives Directorate, Ministry of Industry and Trade] financed the first regional development co-operatives in order to promote the growth of co-operative entrepreneurship.

The amendments to the Co-operatives Act in 1985 and 1997 must not be overlooked. They created two new types of co-operatives - worker-shareholder co-operatives and solidarity co-operatives, which had a significant impact on the future of co-operation.

The Co-opératives de développement régional (CDR) [Regional Development Co-operative] network

In order to cover the entire Québec territory, there are eleven regional development co-operatives whose mission it is to promote the creation and development of co-operative enterprises, thus contributing to the sustainable development of the regions they serve. Their territorial delimitation follows the geographical layout of Québec's administrative regions; six CDRs cover two regions. CDRs are administratively autonomous and formed a federation in 1998 to unite and represent them. In 2003, the total CDR group numbered 1,050 co-operative members from all economic regions, a 4-million dollar turnover, and approximately fifty employees with a total payroll of 2 million dollars. The network contributed to the creation of the great majority of new co-operatives in Québec (213 over the last two years), generating more than 10,000 new jobs created and sustained per year.

As a privileged partner of the Ministère du Développement économique, de l'Innovation et de l'Exportation (MDEIE) [Ministry of Economic Development, Innovation, and Export] the CDR network receives most of its annual revenue from the Ministry for the creation of co-operative enterprises and jobs. Enshrined in a memorandum of understanding, which is renewable every 3 years, the CDR network receives approximatly 60% of their budget, for an annual available amount of 3 million dollars.

The Centre-du-Québec/ Mauricie Development Co-operative: Ten Years of Action

The Region

The Centre-du-Québec Development Co-operative serves a large territory which includes the Centre-du-Québec and Mauricie regions.

The territory covers a very large area which includes the towns of Drummondville, Victoriaville, and Plessisville to the south, and Trois-Rivières, Shawinigan, and La Tuque to the north. There are close to 485,000 people living in eleven regional municipal counties (des Chenaux, Maskinongé, Mékinac, La Tuque, Shawinigan, Trois-Rivières, Arthabaska, Bécancour,

Drummond, Érable, and Nicolet-Yamaska). The population lives in rural, semi-rural, and urban areas. The territory includes several post-secondary institutions, including colleges and universities, health centres, and private airports.

The Mauricie region (administrative region 04) is characterized by the preponderance of industry related to resource development and manufacturing. Production of pulp and paper and related products constitutes the most significant portion of the manufacturing labour market. Generally speaking this region is identified in Québec as being a resource region.

For its part, the Centre-du-Québec region (one of seventeen administrative regions) principally hinges on the agro processing industry and the manufacturing sector. It is identified as a central region. In this area, 40.5% of sectors involve blue-collar jobs (construction, manufacturing industries) while 10.5 % involve post-secondary training (instructional services, chemical industry).

A Brief History of the CDCQM

Founded on June 6, 1996, by a group made up of thirty-two co-operatives, the CDCQM was the result of a long process of discussion and studies undertaken by the Conseil régional de développement (1984) which at that time included Mauricie and Centre-du-Québec.

From the very beginning, the CDCQM had a team of administrators who were well known in their field. Among them was the founding president, Mr. Jacques Lemieux, who at that time was also the vice-president of the Québec-Appalaches CDR, which was adjacent to our territory. We must also highlight the participation of Mr. Jean Marineau of the Co-operative Affairs Directorate in the Fédération des caisses Desjardins du centre du Québec [federation of credit unions], who contributed some of his "co-operative soul" to our CDR.

On December 12, 1996, the first executive director took up his duties at the CDR. The CDCQM, which started out with 32 members, now numbers more than 125 as of 2006. Since its creation, it has contributed to the creation of more than 160 co-operatives, which have in turn contributed to the creation of many jobs.

The Co-operative Movement in the Region (Sectors and Co-operative Forces)

In the early days of the CDR, the Centre-du-Québec and Mauricie regions were not recognized as areas which were particularly favourable for the development of co-operatives. In 1997, there were 285 co-operatives

– approximately 8% of all co-operatives in Québec. They were distributed among the following sectors: financial co-operatives (52%), housing co-operatives (18%), producer co-operatives (11%), consumer co-operatives (12%) and worker-shareholder co-operatives (7%). In geographical terms, 155 co-operatives were located in Centre-du-Québec and 134 in Mauricie. More specifically, there are a higher number of producer co-operatives in Centre-du-Québec because of its agricultural capacity, while there are more worker-shareholder co-operatives in Mauricie.

Nine years later, the total number of co-operatives is approximately 250 (126 in Centre-du-Québec and 125 in Mauricie), and this is the case despite the strong increase in the number of new co-operatives. The reason for the decline in total numbers is primarily due to a wave of mergers of financial co-operatives. The significant new growth has been in the number of worker-shareholder co-operatives, which has grown from 19 to 50 and the creation of 26 solidarity co-operatives, a new model which was implemented in 1997 in Québec.

Resources

The Team

The CDR relies on a team of seven to provide services to its clients: an executive director, three co-operative development advisors, two youth collective entrepreneurial development officers, and an administrative assistant.

Finances

Over the last three years, the CDCQM has been able to rely on average revenues of $593,000 to cover expenses. However, over the last ten years of its existence, it has been able to generate surplus funds, which have provided it with a general reserve of $284,000.

The Economic Model Supporting the Sustainability of the CDR

Revenue and Cost Structure

The CDR's financial model is unique in Québec in that it resembles a public-private partnership programme (PPP). It is virtually the only programme in Québec in which revenues are variable and linked to an accounting system based on job creation. In fact, the CDR is a co-operative that occupies the border between public and private.

The Centre-du-Québec/Mauricie CDR gained 77% of its revenue over the last 3 years from the Québec government's Regional Co-operative Development Programme. The other 33% came from co-operative facilitation activities through the services provided (start-up/follow-up) and the co-operative structure. The members of the CDR support their organization financially by paying an annual membership fee of $100 for co-operatives with three or more employees and $25 for all others.

Government Programmes

A large portion of the CDRs' funding comes from the Co-operative Development Assistance Programme, which is part of the Québec government's Ministère du Développement économique, de l'Innovation et de l'Exportation (MDEIE) [Ministry for Economic Development, Innovation, and Export]. A partnership agreement between the Conseil de la coopération du Québec (CCQ) [Québec Co-operation Council] and the MDEIE confers upon the CCQ the mandate to administer and manage financial assistance for co-operative development for the purposes of the CDR Assistance Programme, which represents approximately 3 million dollars for all 11 CDRs which cover the Québec territory (seventeen administrative regions).

Under the agreement, the Conseil provides the CDR with financial assistance in order to allow it to provide the programme's services according to the three following components:
1. Promoting co-operatives
2. Providing technical services to promoters of new co-operatives
3. Providing specialized support and follow-up services to existing co-operatives.

Component 1: Promoting Co-operatives

An amount of $88,000 per economic area (or $176,000 for the CDCQM) is reserved for co-operative promotion and dialogue about co-operatives in the area. This aid is available on the condition that CDR activities on the whole generate at least $650,000 of self-sustaining income.

Eligible projects are:
- co-operative promotion activities involving the general public and specific clientele,
- providing tools and information to officers of CLD and other economic development organizations in order to support the emergence of new co-operatives,
- development activities involving the territory's co-operatives, and
- participation in local and regional activities related to economic development.

Components 2: Providing Technical Services

An amount of $88,000 per economic area is also available for the provision of technical services to help promote new co-operatives (Component 2) and for the provision of support services and follow-up with existing co-operatives (Component 3).

Financial assistance is provided for the following specialized services:

- activities promoting awareness of, and providing support for, the co-operative principles to promoters and members,
- legal assistance in creating the co-operative constitution, assistance in drafting the co-operative's regulations, and general support for the start-up of the co-operative,
- assistance in making the eligibility request to the Co-operative Investment Plan, and
- support to the enterprise for a maximum period of 2 years, or until it becomes the responsibility of its federation.

The method of compensation for this component is contingent upon the fact that the new co-operative be operational and that an external auditor be able to show that the jobs created have been filled for a minimum of 10 weeks during the year of its creation.

Generally speaking, each co-operative receives $3,000 in revenue for each job created, plus $600 for sustained employment. Under this component, the CDCQM has a potential $176,000 for job creation through new co-operatives.

Component 3: Providing Support and Follow-up

The provision of support services may include the following:

- Activities related to associative operations (such as legal and associative compliance);
- Action and recovery plans;
- Support for implementation of methods for evaluating associative operations;
- Support for implementation of a day-to-day management system and for associative opperations;
- Assistance in the co-operative training of managers and administrators;
- Activities related to economic operations such as:
  - Analysis and action plan,
  - Delivery of specialized support and mentoring services,
  - Recovery assistance, and
  - Assistance in hiring strategic personnel;

- Value-added activities;
- Assistance in implementing best business practices; and
- Specific activities related to taxation, accounting, finance, marketing, processing, production, human resources, governance, communication, quality management, technology, and R&D.

A maximum amount of $5,000 may be allocated per intervention in a co-operative. Generally speaking, the CDCQM has received approximately $30,000 of intervention funding annually through this component over the last 2 years.

Other Programmes

In 2006, a pilot agreement was signed by the CDCQM and Canada Economic Development for the provision of specialized technical services to co-operatives under the Mesure de développement des compétences en économie sociale [Social Economy Skills Development Programming]. This allows for the use of resources dedicated to co-operative support for 1 year ($95,000). The agreement also provides for the development of three management guides intended for co-operatives.

Since 2004, the CDCQM has also had the opportunity to benefit from financial assistance from the Québec government through the "Défi de l'entrepreneuriat jeunesse" [Youth Entrepreneurship Challenge] programme. This assistance, worth $50,000 per economic region, allows for the hiring of a staff person responsible for promoting collective entrepreneurship to youth, particularly through the Jeunes Co-op [Youth Co-op], Coopératives jeunesse de services [Youth Service Co-operatives], and Ensemble vers la réussite [Together For Success] programmes.

The Pool Required to Achieve Sufficient Critical Mass

According to our practices of the last ten years, we do not believe that there is a correlation between sufficient critical mass and the number of co-operatives which have been started. Co-operative growth is more a question of organizational and operational effectiveness, credibility, and the presence of adequate skills and know-how.

Here is some socio-demographic data which will help illustrate this point. The Centre-du-Québec and Mauricie areas cover 3.1% of Québec territory. With 6.5% of the Québec population, 7.2% of businesses, 6.1% of jobs, and 6.1% of investments. With 7.5% of co-operatives these areas have one of the most modest critical masses.

More specifically, the Mauricie region has an area of 39,736 km², a population of 261,089 (2001), 7,885 businesses, average disposable family incomes of $18,815 (2001), and investments of $1,344,341,000 in 2002.

The Centre-du-Québec region, for its part, has an area of 6,986 km², a population of 222,208, 8,545 businesses, disposable family incomes of $18,381 (2001), and investments of $1,006,350,000 (2002).

Overall, co-operatives only represent 1.5% of all businesses in both economic regions.

Essential Tools for Co-operative Development and CDR Action

Expertise

The quality of the people who occupy key positions in the organization is a major factor in the success of the CDR. In fact, the president, the executive director, and the advisors must possess the required profile in terms of skills and attitude, as well as a strong commitment to the values and goals of the organization. Considering the similarity between the CDR and a private enterprise, entrepreneurs-developers must be sought who can lead a team and have healthy business practices in the area of general management. These developer-types are often B.A. qualified, already have business experience, and display superior interpersonal skills. They must have a mastery of the various management tools and have a passion for their work which is contagious. They are often very committed to their geographic area and are motivated by their love of creating. What stimulates them is not so much the promise of profits but the concrete results their commitment brings.

Member Pool

A good member pool can certainly help to create a climate which is more conducive to the creation of co-operatives but these members will not necessarily create new organizations. A better approach would be the skillful advising of intermediary organizations in business creation (CLDs, accountants, lawyers).

Community Involvement

Having roots in the regional economic development structures is one of the CDR's great strengths. On this topic, let us note that the CDR, through its personnel or the members of its board of directors, sits on more than 20 representational bodies in the territory and more than 7 at the national level.

Moreover, the CDR has developed a good relationship with a large number of regional agents and with the Desjardins credit union network. Below is a list of several organizations where the CDR is present (on committees or boards of directors): the Centre local de développement de Shawinigan (CLD), the Société de développement économique de Trois-Rivières (Economic Development Corporation), the CLD of Bécancour, the CLD of Nicolet-Yamaska, the Société d'aide au développement des collectivités de Bécancour-Nicolet-Yamaska (Community Futures Development Corporation), the Comité régional d'économie sociale de la Mauricie et du Centre-du-Québec (Social Economy Regional Committee), the Conférence régionale des élus de la Mauricie (Regional Conference of Elected Officials), the Corporation de développement agroalimentaire forêt du Centre-du-Québec (Agroprocessing and Forestry Development Corporation), the Forum jeunesse Mauricie (Youth Forum), the Comité relève de la Mauricie (Nominating Committee), and our territory's chambers of commerce.

At the national level there are: the Conseil québécois de la coopération et de la mutualité (Québec Council for Co-operation and Mutuality), the Chantier de l'économie sociale, the Groupe d'économie solidaire du Québec (Québec Economic Solidarity Group), the Fédération des coopératives de développement régional du Québec (Québec Federation of Regional Development Co-operatives), and the Fondation pour l'éducation à la coopération (Foundation for Co-operation Education), among others.

Principal Types of Co-operatives

Québec legislation contains a wide range of types of co-operatives adapted to the reality of promoters of collective enterprises, for example: consumer co-operatives, producer co-operatives, worker co-operatives, worker-shareholder co-operatives, and solidarity co-operatives.

a) Consumer Co-operatives

This type of co-operative provides goods and services to its members for their personal use. It is present in several sectors of activity, such as savings and credit, food, purchasing, etc.

This type of co-operative lost much of its popularity over the last several years; however, it was the catalyst which produced financial co-operatives, such as the caisses populaires, in Québec. During the last 10 years in our territory, it constitutes 4 % of new co-operatives. Some successful examples include: Coopérative d'aide domestique de la MRC Maskinongé (Housekeeping Services Co-operative), Coop de services de santé Robert-Verrier (Health Services Co-op).

b) Producer Co-operatives

This type of co-operative brings together producers who enjoy economic advantages by procuring goods and services necessary for the practice of their occupation or their business. These services can be found in sectors such as agri-processing, business consulting services, groups of self-employed workers or businesses, etc.

Several co-operatives of this type can be found in the agricultural sector: the Coopérative d'utilisation de matériel agricole (CUMA) [Agricultural Equipment Users' Co-operative] and the Coopérative d'utilisation de main-d'œuvre agricole (CUMO) [Agricultural Labour Co-operative]. These co-operatives represent approximately 19% of all business licences granted. Examples of such co-operatives are the Coopérative de producteurs en développement économique de Bécancour (Economic Development Producers' Co-operative), the Coopérative de producteurs porc Ultra (Ultra Pork Producers' Co-operative), the Coopérative du marché de Drummondville (Market Co-operative), the CUMA de la canneberge (cranberries), the Incubateur coopératif de St-Léonard d'Aston (Co-operative Incubator), and the Coopérative de services aux artistes du Bas-St-François (Artists' Services Co-operative).

c) Worker Co-operatives

The goal of this type of co-operative is to provide work for its members. The workers own the co-operative to which they belong. It is involved with such diverse fields as: forestry, retail, leisure, culture, tourism, etc.

It is the most popular type of co-operative in Québec, representing 46% of the business licences granted in our territory. Some examples include: the Coopérative de soutien à domicile et d'entretien Haute-Mauricie (Home Support and Maintenance Co-operative), A à Z Organisation d'événements – coopérative de travail (Event Planning – Work Co-operative), the Coopérative des travailleurs Les habitations APEX (susainable building workers' co-operative), the Coopérative de travail Brasserie artisanale Le Trou du Diable (Brew Pub workers' co-operative), and the Coop de travail Drainomax.

d) Worker-Shareholder Co-operatives

Through this type of co-operative, the workers in a business become shareholders of the business and thus participate in its development, decision-making process, and share in its profits. This co-operative is an effective way to ensure the returns, expansion, and development of a company. This type of co-operative can be found in sectors, such as production, high-end technology, manufacturing, etc. This type of co-operative represents close to 7% of cases. In our opinion, this is one of the models with the greatest potential to meet the turnover needs of manufacturing businesses in Québec. Some examples are: the Coopérative de travail sur métaux Mégapro (200 employees) [Metalwork Co-operative], la Coopérative de travailleurs actionnaire de Métal Grenier, la Coopérative de travailleurs actionnaire de Confection Aventure, and la Coopérative de travailleurs actionnaire de Savik Super-Chrome.

e) Solidarity Co-operatives

This co-operative includes all of the following: members who use the services provided by the co-operative, members who are workers in the co-operative, and all other people or organizations who have an economic or social interest in the co-operative achieving its goals; the latter are called support members. It is present in home care and services, recreotourism, and local development sectors.

This type of co-operative has become the most popular over the last several years. It represents more than 25% of the business licences granted in our territory. Some solidarity co-operatives are: the Coopérative de solidarité en services immobiliers – Habitations populaires du Québec (Real Estate Services), the Coop de solidarité en milieu collégial – Buffet Margelle 2000, the Coopérative de solidarité de la Maison familiale rurale de la MRC Maskinongé (Rural Family Guest House), the Coopérative de solidarité en développement local de Villeroy (incubateur), the Coopérative de solidarité en développement local de Gentilly (golf club), and the Coopérative de solidarité d'aide domestique de Shawinigan (Housekeepers' Co-operative).

Expertise Required by Advisors

In order for development advisors to fulfill their responsibilities in an optimal manner, they must possess the following knowledge, abilities, and skills:

- In-depth knowledge of the principles, procedures, and practices of co-operative development, including the laws and regulations governing the constitution and operation of co-operative organizations.
- In-depth knowledge of the principles of administration, principles and practices of co-operative management, and their application to the creation and development of commercial and community service enterprises.
- Very good knowledge of the co-operative sector at the regional level, of its problems, priorities, and management practices.

- Very good knowledge of the principles and practices related to community development and collective economic development, as well as the development agencies and organizations of the region.
- Very good knowledge of the government, community, and business development; technical support; and management programmes and services; etc., which developing co-operatives could access.
- Very good knowledge of the instruments, procedures, and techniques used to present, promote, and deliver information.
- Ability to communicate effectively and clearly.
- Ability to organize and facilitate public meetings, seminars, workshops, etc.
- Ability to work with community groups, sector groups, producer and consumer groups to assist them in focusing on priorities in the area of development and to complete steps in the organization and business development and planning process.

Results and Performance

Over the 1997-2005 period, 154 co-operatives were created in all sectors of economic activity, which allowed for the creation and sustaining of 1,369 jobs in Centre-du-Québec and Mauricie. On average 66 requests for information were made per year, for an average creation of seventeen co-operatives per year, or the equivalent of one co-operative per 3.88 files opened.

Globally speaking, we are observing a decrease in the number of open files (one granted for every three open files) over the last two years. As for the most active types of co-operatives, they can be broken down into the following: consumer co-operatives (3%), worker-shareholder co-operatives (7%), producer co-operatives (19%), solidarity co-operatives (25%), and worker co-operatives (46%).

The Centre-du-Québec and Mauricie are experiencing a sharp increase in the creation of solidarity co-operatives: 31% in 2004, 40% in 2005, and 50% in 2006.

The survival rate for co-operatives in our territory is comparable to that of the province of Québec. It reaches 64% after 5 years and drops to 46% after 10 years, compared with rates of 36% and 20% for other types of businesses.

The Ingredients of Our Success

Complicit Governance

CDCQM's 10-year history demonstrates the stability and commitment of its board of directors. Of the 32 administrators who have come and gone in this time, three have remained for at least 10 years: the president, vice-president, and secretary-treasurer. The officers had the required profile, having already performed management and president roles at the professional level, and they personified co-operative values and goals. One important policy in the co-operative's creation was the restriction of board of director positions exclusively to member co-operatives. Finally, the board banked on a manager who was well known and had credibility in the field of regional development; he created a team of professionals that performed, was motivated, complemented each other well, and was client-driven.

A True Strategic Plan: Finding a Mission and a Vision

In order to better position itself on the ground, the CDR implemented a strategic planning exercise in 2001 that allowed it to adapt its mission, vision, and work plan.

The CDR's mission is to become the resource of choice in co-operative matters. It actively participates in socio-economic development by offering services related to the creation and sustaining of co-operatives in the territory. Its vision is to be known and recognized as the hub for consulting services for the start-up and follow-up of co-operatives, while valuing co-operative education, co-development, and access to capital, thus facilitating the territory's socio-economic development.

An Aggressive Communication Strategy

The CDR developed an aggressive communication plan with the aim of showing its strengths and defining its image. The following are the larger goals, which underpin the actual methods used.

a) To make the CDR, its services, and its role known in the region
   Key Message: "Co-operative development is our business"
   Methods:
   • A monthly newsletter "Le Lien-Coop" [Coop-Link],
   • Annual co-operative tournament (alternating between the two regions),
   • Visits from co-operatives and socio-economic partners,
   • Representations,

- Annual General Meeting, and
- Communiqués, press conferences, web site.

b) To make co-operation known, highlight its value, and promote it

- Annual Co-operative Merit Gala,
- Special section – weekly and daily regional newspapers,
- Co-operative directory,
- Flyers and brochures,
- Management guides,
- Training workshop,
- Relève Coopérative Week,
- Media review, and
- Calendar.

c) Mobilize co-operatives around the CDR and recruit a significant membership

- Member loyalty programme,
- Participation in other Annual General Meetings,
- Visits, and
- Develop roots in the region through participation on the boards of directors of strategic organizations.

d) A challenging awareness campaign

Promoting youth's awareness of co-operation was an important aim of the organization. We felt that it was important to introduce youth to the values underpinning the co-operative principles in order to counter their exodus to the large urban centres. In 10 years, more than 5,000 youth have been introduced to co-operative values through diverse co-operative education projects: the Coopérative jeunesse de services (CJS), Jeune Coop, Ensemble vers la réussite (EVR), and Relève Coopérative Week. In addition, each year, we have honoured a youth initiative during our annual gala. In 2001-2002, we benefited from a very effective provincial Youth Secretariat initiative, the Audace programme [Audacity]. The latter allowed young entrepreneurs starting up their co-operatives to access financial assistance.

e) Providing services adapted to the needs of groups

The CDR offers services to the promoters of new co-operatives and exist-ing co-operatives. Developing co-operatives can receive start-up support, follow-up, and coaching services for the first year. Existing co-operatives can access training on associative operations, professional coaching, and consulting services (analysis, customized training, negotiation, financial analysis, and accounting). More specialized services are also offered (taxation, mediation, legal assistance) in collaboration with other specialists.

There is a strong spirit of community among all CLDs in the territory and a will to work together to prepare the files. Generally speaking, the CLD will develop the business plan and the CDR will address the associated component and the financial aspects related to the co-operative.

f) An integrated offering of financial methods

Québec is fortunate to have an integrated financing offer available to co-operatives. The CDR is at the heart of this great network and makes these programmes accessible to a local clientele. Here is a brief list of facilitative resources:

- The Co-operative Investment Plan,
- Les mesures d'Investissement Québec [Investment Measures],
- The support of the Desjardins Movement,
- Solidarity financing: Fondaction, Filaction, etc.,
- CLD and CFDC local and regional programmes, and
- Other resources which are available to SMEs.

Conclusion

Active for 10 years, the CDCQM has met the challenge of starting up many co-operatives and developing roots in the regional economic landscape. The strength of our organization rests in the abilities and attitudes of our human resources (senior management and core staff) who have shown so much patience and learned to move with the flow of business and social environment issues. The strategic positioning of our organization at the crossroads of economy and society has made us a tool for building the economy. We owe our success to the participation of local stakeholders and their ability to organize the sustainable development of their community by taking the co-operative path. Our communities understand that co-operation is a principle which aims to reconcile economic and social development, the protection of the environment, and conservation of natural resources.

Coopérative de développement Centre-du-Québec / Mauricie (CDCQM)

Christian Savard

L e mouvement coopératif est bien développé au Québec et sa crois-
sance dans les milieux semi-urbains et ruraux est un phénomène qui
fait le bonheur des élus locaux. Mais, ce constat n'est pas établi dans
les 17 régions administratives du Québec.

L'objectif de cet essai est de vous présenter les facteurs qui ont contribué
au succès de la démarche de développement de la Coopérative de développement Centre-du-Québec / Mauricie (CDCQM) sur son territoire.

Dans un premier temps, une brève description des acteurs du développement socio-économique au Québec est présentée suivi d'un portrait de la
CDCQM et des pratiques de développement coopératif.

Les acteurs du développement au Québec

Municipalités régionales de comté

Le territoire québécois est divisé en 17 régions administratives, lesquelles comptent près de 86 municipalités régionales de comté (MRC) une entente concernant son rôle et ses responsabilités en matière de développement local ainsi que les conditions d'exercice. La MRC peut ainsi prendre toute mesure afin de favoriser le développement local et le soutien à l'entrepreneuriat sur son territoire. À cette fin, elle peut offrir l'ensemble des services de première ligne aux entreprises et assurer leur financement. Par ailleurs, elle élabore un plan d'action local pour l'économie et l'emploi en tenant compte du plan quinquennal de développement établi par la Conférence régionale des élus (CRE) de son territoire et veille à la réalisation de ce plan. Elle doit aussi élaborer, en tenant compte des orientations, stratégies et objectifs nationaux et régionaux, une stratégie en matière de développement de l'entrepreneuriat. Enfin, elle peut agir en tant qu'organisme consultatif auprès du Centre local d'emploi (CLE) de son territoire. Dans le but de réaliser ces mandats, la MRC confie à un « Centre local de développement » (CLD) l'exercice de sa compétence.

Conférence régionale des élus

Dans chacune des régions administratives, une « Conférence régionale des élus » (CRE) est instituée et est l'interlocuteur privilégié du gouvernement du Québec en matière de développement régional. Chaque conférence régionale des élus a principalement pour mandat d'évaluer les organismes de planification et de développement au palier local et régional, dont le financement provient en tout ou en partie du gouvernement, de favoriser la concertation des partenaires dans la région et de donner, le cas échéant, des avis au ministre sur le développement de la région.

La Conférence régionale des élus établit un plan quinquennal de développement définissant, dans une perspective de développement durable, les objectifs généraux et particuliers de développement de la région et en tenant compte en priorité de la participation à la vie démocratique de la région des jeunes et, selon les principes de l'égalité et de la parité, des femmes.

Ce plan quinquennal de développement doit aussi tenir compte des stratégies et des objectifs régionaux en matière de main-d'œuvre et d'emploi déterminés par le conseil régional des partenaires du marché du travail de son territoire ainsi que du plan des grands enjeux du développement économique adopté par la communauté métropolitaine de son territoire. La Conférence régionale des élus peut conclure, également, avec les ministères ou organismes du gouvernement et, le cas échéant, avec d'autres partenaires, des ententes spécifiques. La conférence régionale des élus exécute tout autre mandat que lui confie le ministre.

Acteurs dans Maurice et Centre-du-Québec

En Mauricie, on compte 6 territoires de MRC ou ville : MRC de Maskinongé, Ville de La Tuque, Ville de Shawinigan, MRC de Mékinac, MRC Des Chenaux et Ville de Trois-Rivières, alors qu'au Centre-du-Québec, on compte 5 territoires de MRC : MRC de l'Érable, MRC d'Arthabaska, MRC de Drummond, MRC de Bécancour et MRC de Nicolet-Yamaska. Chacune des onze organisations a un CLD et le tout est complété par deux Conférences régionales des élus (Mauricie et Centre-du-Québec). L'ensemble de ces organisations est en lien avec le ministère des Affaires municipales et des Régions qui a deux directions régionales bien distinctes.

Venant compléter les actions de développement territorial, le gouvernement canadien compte sept organisations (Société d'aide au développement des collectivités) parrainées par Développement économique Canada (DEC) qui intervient dans les localités plus rurales.

Voilà, de façon très succincte, les collaborateurs de première ligne qui accueille, accompagne et côtoie les entrepreneurs du Québec.

L'organisation du développement coopératif au Québec

Quelques éléments historiques

Les coopératives représentent une partie importante du patrimoine collectif du Québec. En effet, dès la fin du 18e siècle, les sociétés de secours mutuel permettent le développement d'une certaine solidarité sociale face à l'adversité. Les mutuelles d'assurance incendie arrivent au milieu du 19e siècle et plusieurs autres types de coopératives font leur apparition au tournant du 20e siècle. La naissance des caisses populaires, à cette époque, est l'exemple le plus connu.

Le mouvement coopératif actuel prendra forme progressivement à partir des années 1937 à 1939 surtout pour répondre aux besoins pressants découlant de la crise économique qui faisait alors rage. Les Québécois font encore une fois preuve de solidarité sociale et se prennent en main en créant des magasins d'alimentation coopératifs, des coopératives forestières, etc., pour combler leurs besoins de base. Vingt-deux (22) coopératives de consommateurs et sept (7) coopératives de pêcheurs naîtront en 1939 seulement.

Quant aux coopératives agricoles, soixante et une (61) sont incorporées en 1938 et il y en aura ensuite au moins quarante par année pendant sept années consécutives.

C'est en 1951 que naîtra le Conseil de la coopération du Québec (CCQ), véritable « tête de réseau » de l'ensemble des coopératives du Québec. En 1963, à la demande du mouvement coopératif, le gouvernement procède à une refonte en profondeur de la Loi sur les syndicats coopératifs qui datait en 1906. Pour reconnaître la diversité des besoins des types de coopératives, il crée deux lois complémentaires : la Loi sur les associations coopératives et la Loi sur les caisses d'épargnes et de crédit.

Les nouvelles lois confirment l'importance accordée par le gouvernement du rôle du Conseil de la coopération du Québec : à l'avenir, le CCQ devra donner un avis au secrétaire de la province lors de création de chaque nouvelle coopérative. Le Conseil recevra une subvention annuelle pour créer un comité et collaborer à la reconnaissance officielle des coopératives.

Toujours en 1963, pour gérer la nouvelle législation coopérative et offrir un meilleur support au mouvement coopératif, le gouvernement du Québec crée, au sein du Secrétariat de la province, une unité administrative spécialement destinées aux coopératives : le Service aux coopératives qui allait devenir éventuellement la Direction des coopératives.

À l'été 1968, le gouvernement créé un nouveau ministère : celui des Institutions financières, des consommateurs et des coopératives. La loi qui créé ce nouveau ministère, consacre la distinction entre les entreprises coopératives et les entreprises traditionnelles. Elle prévoit également la nomination d'un sous-ministre associé, chargé spécifiquement des coopératives, à l'intérieur de ce nouveau Ministère dont relèvera également le Service aux coopératives.

Le gouvernement établit finalement un partenariat avec le mouvement coopératif en créant la Société de développement coopératif (SDC) qui a pour mission de favoriser la création et le développement d'entreprises coopératives en vue d'assurer une participation accrue de la population à l'activité économique et de favoriser le développement économique des régions et la création d'emplois dans ces régions.

Cette société recevra 25 millions de dollars de 1977 à 1984 dont 22 millions de dollars viendront du gouvernement. Fait intéressant, la SDC est majoritairement dirigée par des administrateurs désignés par le Conseil de la coopération du Québec.

En vertu du décret de février 1985, la Direction des coopératives du ministère de l'Industrie et du Commerce (MIC) finance les premières coopératives de développement régional afin d'accroître l'entrepreneurship coopératif.

Par ailleurs, il ne faut pas passer sous silence les modifications apportées à la Loi des coopératives en 1985 et 1997 créant deux nouveaux types de coopératives : travailleurs actionnaires et solidarité, qui modifieront significativement l'avenir de la coopération.

Le réseau des coopératives de développement régional (CDR)

Pour couvrir l'ensemble du territoire québécois, il existe onze (11) coopératives de développement régional ayant comme mission d'accroître la création et le développement d'entreprises coopératives contribuant ainsi au développement durable des régions desservies. Leur délimitation territoriale épouse le découpage géographique des régions administratives du Québec; 6 CDR couvrent deux régions. Les CDR sont autonomes dans leur administration et se sont données une fédération, en 1998, pour les regrouper et les représenter. En 2003, l'ensemble des CDR comptait 1 050 membres coopératifs en provenance de toutes les régions économiques, un chiffre d'affaires de 4 millions de dollars, une cinquantaine d'employés avec une masse salariale de 2 millions de dollars. Le réseau avait contribué à la création de la grande majorité des nouvelles coopératives au Québec, soit 213 pour les deux dernières années, générant plus de 10 000 emplois créés et maintenus par année.

Partenaire privilégié (mandataire) du ministère du Développement économique, de l'Innovation et de l'Exportation (MDEIE) pour la création d'entreprises et d'emplois coopératifs, confirmé dans un protocole d'entente renouvelable à chaque 3 ans, le réseau des CDR retire la majeure partie de ses revenus de cette entente (environ 60 %) selon ses résultats annuels de création de coopératives et d'emplois pour un montant annuel disponible de 3 millions de dollars.

La coopérative de développement Centre-du-Québec/Mauricie : en action depuis 10 ans

La Région

La Coopérative de développement régional centre du Québec dessert un grand territoire qui regroupe les régions Centre-du-Québec et Mauricie.

Le territoire couvre une très grande superficie touchant les villes de Drummondville, Victoriaville et Plessisville, au Sud, et Trois-Rivières, Shawinigan et La Tuque, au Nord. On compte près de 485 000 personnes réparties en onze (11) territoires de municipalités régionales de comtés (MRC) (des Chenaux, Maskinongé, Mékinac, La Tuque, Shawinigan, Trois-Rivières, Arthabaska, Bécancour, Drummond, Érable et Nicolet-Yamaska). La population vit en milieu rural, semi-rural et urbain. Le territoire comprend plusieurs maisons d'enseignement post-secondaire tant collégial qu'universitaire, des centres hospitaliers et des aéroports privés.

La région de la Mauricie (région administrative 04) se caractérise par la prépondérance des industries liées à l'exploitation et à la transformation des ressources naturelles. La production de pâtes et papiers ainsi que de produits connexes y fournit la part la plus importante de l'emploi manufacturier. De façon générale, elle est identifiée, au Québec, comme région ressource.

Pour sa part, la région du Centre-du-Québec (région administrative 17) s'articule, principalement, autour de l'agroalimentaire et du secteur manufacturier. Elle est identifiée comme région centrale. Les secteurs sont issus des savoirs moyens (construction, industries manufacturières) à 40,5 % tandis que les savoirs élevés (services d'enseignement, industries chimiques) obtiennent 10,5 %.

Bref historique de la CDCQM

Fondée le 6 juin 1996 par un groupe formé de trente-deux (32) coopératives, la CDCQM a été le résultat d'une longue démarche de concertation et d'études pilotées par le Conseil régional de développement 04 (1984) qui comptait, à ce moment, la Mauricie et le Centre-du-Québec dans ses rangs.

Quoiqu'il en soit, la CDCQM a vu le jour avec une équipe d'administrateurs reconnus dans leur milieu. Parmi eux, le président-fondateur, M. Jacques Lemieux, qui à l'époque exerçait la fonction de vice-président de la CDR de Québec-Appalaches, qui était contiguë à notre territoire. Soulignons aussi la présence de M. Jean Marineau, de la direction des Affaires coopératives à la Fédération des caisses Desjardins du centre du Québec, qui a transmis un peu de son « âme coopérative » à notre CDR.

Le 12 décembre 1996, le premier directeur général a fait ses débuts à la CDR. Comptant 32 membres à ses débuts, la CDCQM en regroupe maintenant plus de 125 en 2006. Depuis sa création, elle a contribué à la création de plus de 160 coopératives contribuant à la création de nombreux emplois.

Le mouvement coopératif dans la région (les secteurs et forces coopératives présentes)

Dans les débuts de la CDR, les régions Centre-du-Québec et Mauricie n'étaient pas reconnues comme un milieu particulièrement propice au développement de coopératives. En 1997, on comptait 285 coopératives, environ 8 % de l'ensemble des coopératives au Québec. Elles étaient réparties de la façon suivante : coopératives financières (52 %), coopératives d'habitation (18 %), coopératives de producteurs (11 %), coopératives de consommateurs (12 %) et coopérative de travailleurs – travailleurs actionnaires (7 %).

En terme géographique, on en retrouvait 155 au Centre-du-Québec et 134 en Mauricie. De façon plus particulière, les coopératives de producteurs sont plus nombreuses au Centre-du-Québec en raison de son potentiel agricole alors qu'on retrouve plus de coopératives de travailleurs – travailleurs actionnaires en Mauricie.

Neuf ans plus tard, le nombre total de coopérative est d'environ 250 (126 au Centre-du-Québec et 125 en Mauricie) et ce malgré un fort accroissement de nouvelles coopératives. L'écart est dû principalement à une vague de fusion au sein des coopératives financières faisant chuter leur nombre de près de 50 %. Les principaux faits saillants sont l'accroissement significatif du nombre de coopératives de travailleurs – travailleurs actionnaires qui sont passées de 19 à 50 coopératives et la création de 26 coopératives de solidarité, nouveau modèle mis en place en 1997 au Québec.

Les ressources

L'équipe

La CDR compte sur une équipe de 7 personnes pour assurer ses services à la clientèle : 1 directeur général, 3 conseillers en développement coopératif, 2 agentes de développement de l'entrepreneuriat collectif jeunesse et 1 adjointe administrative.

Les finances

Au cours des trois dernières années, la CDCQM a pu compter sur des revenus moyens de 593 000 $ pour des dépenses moyennes de 595 000 $. Cependant, elle a pu au cours de ses dix années d'existence générer des excédents qui lui permettent de compter sur une réserve générale de 284 000 $.

Modèle économique sur lequel repose la pérennité de la CDR

La structure de revenus et de coûts

Le modèle économique des CDR est unique au Québec en ce sens qu'il s'apparente à un programme de partenariat public-privé (PPP). C'est pratiquement le seul programme au Québec où les revenus sont variables et reliés à une reddition de compte basé sur la création d'emplois. En fait, la CDR est une coopérative qui se trouve à la frontière du public et du privé.

La CDR Centre-du-Québec / Mauricie a tiré 77 % de ses revenus du programme d'aide aux coopératives de développement régional du gouvernement du Québec au cours des 3 dernières années. L'autre 33 % provenait des activités d'animation coopérative des services offerts (démarrage-suivi) et de la structure coopérative. Les membres de la CDR supportent financièrement leur organisation en souscrivant une cotisation annuelle de 100 $ pour les coopératives de 3 employés et plus et de 25 $ par année pour les autres.

Programme gouvernemental

Une grande partie du financement des CDR provient du programme d'aide au développement coopératif qui origine du ministère du Développement économique, de l'Innovation et de l'Exportation (MDEIE) du gouvernement du Québec. Une entente de partenariat entre le Conseil de la coopération du Québec (CCQ) et le MDEIE confie au CCQ le mandat d'administrer et de gérer l'aide financière pour le développement coopératif dans le cadre du programme d'aide aux CDR qui représente environ 3 millions de dollars pour l'ensemble des 11 CDR qui couvrent l'ensemble du territoire québécois (17 régions administratives).

En vertu de la convention, le Conseil verse à la CDR une aide financière en vue de lui permettre de fournir les services compris dans le programme selon les trois volets suivants :

1. Promotion coopérative
2. Prestation de services techniques aux promoteurs de nouvelles coopératives
3. Prestation de services d'accompagnement et de suivi spécialisé aux coopératives existantes.

Volet 1 : Promotion coopérative

Un montant de 88 000 $ par région économique, donc 176 000 $ est versé à la CDCQM pour la promotion coopérative et la concertation des coopératives en région. Cette aide est conditionnelle à la réalisation par l'ensemble du réseau des CDR d'activités admissibles pour au moins 650 000 $ de revenus d'autofinancement.

Les projets admissibles sont :
- les activités de promotion coopérative auprès du grand public et de clientèles particulières,
- l'outillage et l'information des agents des CLD et des autres organismes de développement économique afin de supporter l'émergence de nouvelles coopératives,
- la réalisation d'activités de concertation de coopératives du territoire, et
- la participation aux activités locales et régionales pertinentes en développement économique.

Volet 2 : Prestation de services techniques

Un montant de 88 000 $ par région économique est aussi prévu, donc 176 000 $ pour la CDCQM pour la prestation de services techniques aux promoteurs de nouvelles coopératives (volet 2) et la prestation de services d'accompagnement et de suivi spécialisé aux coopératives existantes (volet 3).

L'aide financière au volet 2 est versée pour les services spécialisés suivants :
- la sensibilisation et l'accompagnement des promoteurs et membres à la formule coopérative,
- l'aide légale à la constitution de la coopérative,
- l'assistance à la rédaction des règlements de la coopérative et le support à la mise en marche du fonctionnement coopératif,
- l'aide à la demande d'admissibilité du régime d'investissement coopératif, et
- le soutien à l'entreprise démarrée pendant une période maximum de 2 ans ou jusqu'à son accompagnement par sa fédération.

Le mode de rémunération pour ce volet est conditionnel à ce que la nouvelle coopérative soit en opération et qu'il puisse être démontré par un vérificateur externe que les emplois créés ont au moins été occupé pendant 10 semaines au cours de l'année de sa création.

De façon générale, un statut procure 3 000 $ de revenus et chaque emploi créé, un montant variant de 1 000 $ à 3 200 $ selon le nombre d'emplois créés dans la nouvelle coopérative et de 600 $ pour les emplois maintenus. Selon ce volet, la CDCQM dispose d'un potentiel de 176 000 $ pour des nouvelles coopératives avec emploi.

Volet 3 : Prestation de services d'accompagnement

Quant au volet 3 concernant la prestation de services d'accompagnement, il peut prendre la forme suivante:

- Activités liées à la vie associative telles que : bilan de la conformité légale et associative;
- Plan d'action et redressement du fonctionnement associatif;
- Support à l'implantation de mesures d'évaluation de la vie associative;
- Support à l'implantation d'un système de gestion courante et de renforcement de la vie associative;
- Aide à la formation coopérative des gestionnaires et administrateurs;
- Activités liées à la vie économique telles que :
  - Diagnostic et plan d'action,
  - Dispenses de services d'accompagnement spécialisés et de mentorat,
  - Assistance au redressement, et
  - Assistance à l'embauche de personnel stratégique;
- Activités à valeur ajoutée;
- Assistance à l'implantation des meilleures pratiques d'affaires;
- Activités spécifiques liées à la fiscalité, la comptabilité, la finance, le marketing, l'exploitation, la production, les ressources humaines, la gouvernance, les communications, la gestion de la qualité, la technologie, la R&D.

Un maximum de 5 000 $ peut être alloué par intervention dans une coopérative. De façon générale, la CDCQM réalise environ 30 000 $ d'intervention annuellement dans ce volet depuis 2 ans.

Autres programmes

En 2006, une entente pilote est intervenue entre la CDCQM et Développement Economique Canada pour la prestation de services techniques spécialisés aux coopératives en vertu de la « Mesure de développement des compétences en économie sociale ». En effet, celle-ci permet l'engagement d'une ressource dédiée à l'accompagnement des coopératives pour 1 an (95 000 $). L'entente prévoit la conception de trois guides de gestion à l'intention des coopératives.

Depuis 2004, la CDCQM a aussi l'opportunité de bénéficier d'une aide financière du gouvernement du Québec dans le cadre du programme « Défi de l'entrepreneuriat jeunesse ». Cette aide, de 50 000 $ par région économique, permet la création d'un poste d'agent chargé de promouvoir l'entrepreneuriat collectif auprès des jeunes, notamment les programmes Jeunes Coop, Coopératives jeunesse de services et Ensemble vers la réussite.

Bassin requis pour atteindre une masse critique suffisante

Selon notre pratique des dix dernières années, nous ne croyons pas qu'il y ait une corrélation entre une masse critique suffisante et le nombre de coopératives démarrées. C'est plutôt une question d'efficacité organisationnelle et opérationnelle, de crédibilité et la présence de compétences adéquates et de savoir-faire.

Quoiqu'il en soit voici quelques données socio-démographiques. Les régions Centre-du-Québec et Mauricie couvent 3,1 % du territoire québécois en terme de superficie. Avec 6,5 % de la population du Québec, 7,2 % des entreprises, 6,1 % des emplois, 6,1 % des investissements et 7,5 % des coopératives, elles ont une masse critique des plus modestes. De façon plus détaillée, la région Mauricie a une superficie de 39 736 km^2, une population de 261 089 habitants (2001), 7 885 entreprises, des revenus disponibles de 18 815 $ (2001) et des investissements de 1 344 341 000 $ en 2002.

Quant à elle, la région Centre-du-Québec a une superficie de 6 986 km2, une population de 222 208 habitants, 8 545 entreprises, des revenus disponibles de 18 381 $ (2001) et des investissements de 1 006 350 000 $ (2002).

De façon globale, les coopératives ne représentent que 1,5 % de toutes les entreprises des 2 régions économiques.

Outils essentiels à la base du développement coopératif et de l'action de la CDR

Expertises

La qualité des personnes occupant les fonctions clés dans l'organisation est un élément majeur du succès de la CDR. En effet, la présidence, la direction générale et les conseillers doivent posséder le profil requis en terme d'habiletés et d'attitudes de même qu'un engagement indéfectible aux valeurs et objectifs de l'organisation. Considérant la similitude avec l'entreprise privée, on doit retrouver des personnes entrepreneurs-développeurs capables d'animer une équipe et ayant de saines pratiques de gestion pour ce qui touche les directions générales. Ces développeurs-types sont souvent des bacheliers s'étant déjà lancés en affaires dotés de grandes habiletés relationnelles. Ils maîtrisent les divers outils de gestion et dégagent une passion contagieuse. Ils sont souvent très engagés dans leur milieu où le goût de créer les animent. Ce n'est pas tant l'appât du gain, mais celui des résultats concrets de leurs implications qui les stimulent.

Bassin de membres

Un bon bassin de membres peut certes aider à créer un climat plus propice à l'émergence de coopératives, mais ce ne sont pas eux qui vont nécessairement créer de nouvelles organisations. C'est plus l'habileté à informer les organisations intermédiaires de création d'entreprises (CLD, comptables, avocats) qui constitue la bonne démarche.

Pour la CDR, nous estimons qu'un taux de membership des coopératives du territoire de 50 % est fort révélateur de leur niveau de mobilisation. De ce fait, à la CDCQM, on retrouve un taux d'adhésion de 52 %, ce qui équivaut au paiement d'une part sociale de 100 $ au début et par la suite d'une cotisation annuelle de 100 $.

Implication dans la communauté

L'enracinement dans les structures régionales de développement économique est une grande force de la CDR. À ce sujet, notons que la CDR, par le biais de son personnel ou de ses membres du conseil d'administration, siège à plus de 20 lieux de représentation sur le territoire et plus de 7 à l'échelle nationale. De plus, la CDR a développé une bonne complicité avec un grand nombre d'intermédiaires régionaux et avec le réseau des caisses populaires Desjardins. Mentionnons ici quelques organismes où la CDR est présente (sur des comités ou conseils d'administration) : Centre local de développement de Shawinigan (CLD), Société de développement économique de Trois-Rivières, CLD de Bécancour, CLD de Nicolet-Yamaska, Société d'aide au développement des collectivités de Bécancour-Nicolet-Yamaska, les comités régional d'économie sociale de la Mauricie et du Centre-du-Québec, la Conférence régionale des élus de la Mauricie, la Corporation de développement agroalimentaire forêt du Centre-du-Québec, le Forum jeunesse Mauricie, le Comité relève de la Mauricie et les chambres de commerce de notre territoire.

À l'échelle nationale, citons le Conseil québécois de la coopération et de la mutualité, le Chantier de l'économie sociale, le Groupe d'économie solidaire du Québec, la Fédération des coopératives de développement régional du Québec, la Fondation pour l'éducation à la coopération, entre autres.

Principaux types de coopératives

La législation québécoise contient une gamme variée de types de coopératives adaptées aux réalités des promoteurs d'entreprises collectives : la coopérative de consommateurs, la coopérative de producteurs, la coopérative de travail, la coopérative de travailleurs actionnaires et la coopérative de solidarité.

a) Coopérative de consommateurs

Cette coopérative fournit des biens et des services à ses membres pour leur usage personnel. Elle est présente dans plusieurs secteurs d'activités comme : l'épargne et le crédit, l'alimentation, le regroupement d'achats, etc.

C'est une formule qui a perdu beaucoup de sa popularité au cours des dernières années. C'est la formule qui a engendré les coopératives financières au Québec avec les caisses populaires. Au cours des 10 dernières années, dans notre territoire, on la retrouve dans 4 % des statuts émis. Voici quelques cas : Coopérative d'aide domestique de la MRC Maskinongé, Coop de services de santé Robert-Verrrier.

b) Coopérative de producteurs

Cette coopérative regroupe des producteurs qui bénéficient d'avantages économiques en se procurant des biens et des services nécessaires à l'exercice de leur profession ou à l'exploitation de leur entreprise. Ces services se retrouvent dans des secteurs comme : l'agroalimentaire, les services-conseils aux entreprises, le regroupement de travailleurs autonomes ou d'entreprises, etc.

On retrouve plusieurs coopératives de ce type dans le secteur agricole : Coopérative d'utilisation de matériel agricole (CUMA), Coopérative d'utilisation de main-d'œuvre agricole (CUMO). Ces coopératives représentent environ 19 % de tous les statuts émis. Citons : la Coopérative de producteurs en développement économique de Bécancour, Coopérative de producteurs porc Ultra, Coopérative du marché de Drummondville, CUMA de la canneberge, Incubateur coopératif de St-Léonard d'Aston, Coopérative de services aux artistes du Bas-St-François.

c) Coopérative de travailleurs

Cette coopérative a pour but de fournir du travail à ses membres. La coopérative appartient aux travailleurs qui en font partie. Elle se retrouve dans des domaines aussi diversifiés que : l'industrie forestière, le commerce de détail, les loisirs, la culture et le tourisme, etc.

C'est le type de coopérative le plus populaire au Québec avec 46 % des statuts émis dans notre territoire. Voici quelques exemples : la Coopérative de soutien à domicile et d'entretien Haute-Mauricie, A à Z Organisation d'événements – coopérative de travail, Coopérative des travailleurs Les habitations APEX, Coopérative de travail Brasserie artisanale Le Trou du Diable, Coop de travail Drainomax.

d) Coopérative de travailleurs actionnaires

Par le biais de la coopérative, les travailleurs d'une entreprise deviennent actionnaires de celle-ci et participent ainsi à son développement, aux prises de décision de même qu'au partage des résultats. Cette coopérative constitue un moyen efficace pour assurer la relève, l'expansion, le développement d'une compagnie. Elle se retrouve dans les secteurs tels que : la fabrication, la haute technologie, le manufacturier, etc.

Dans près de 7 % des cas, ce type de coopérative est utilisé. À notre avis, c'est un des modèles qui possède le plus de potentiel pour répondre au besoin de relève des entreprises manufacturières au Québec. Voici quelques exemples : la Coopérative de travail sur métaux Mégapro (200 employés), la Coopérative de travailleurs actionnaire de Métal Grenier, la Coopérative de travailleurs actionnaire de Confection Aventure, la Coopérative de travailleurs actionnaire de Savik Super-Chrome.

e) Coopérative de solidarité

Cette coopérative regroupe à la fois des membres qui sont utilisateurs des services offerts par la coopérative, des membres qui sont travailleurs de la coopérative et toute personne ou société qui a un intérêt économique ou social dans l'atteinte de l'objet de la coopérative, qu'on appelle membre de soutien. Elle est présente dans les secteurs tels que : les soins et services à domicile, le récréotouristique, le développement local, etc.

C'est la formule la plus demandée au cours des dernières années. C'est plus de 25 % des émissions de statuts sur notre territoire. On retrouve : la Coopérative de solidarité en services immobiliers – Habitations populaires du Québec, la Coop de solidarité en milieu collégial – Buffet Margelle 2000, la Coopérative de solidarité de la Maison familiale rurale de la MRC Maskinongé, la Coopérative de solidarité en développement local de Villeroy (incubateur), la Coopérative de solidarité en développement local de Gentilly (club de golf), la Coopérative de solidarité d'aide domestique de Shawinigan, etc.

Expertises requises des conseillers

Pour bien assumer ces responsabilités, les conseillers en développement doivent posséder les connaissances, les compétences et les habiletés suivantes :

- Une connaissance approfondie des principes, des processus et des pratiques de développement coopératif, y compris les lois et les règlements qui régissent la constitution et l'exploitation des organismes coopératifs.
- Une connaissance approfondie des modèles d'administration, des principes et des pratiques de gestion des coopératives, et de leur application à la création et au développement d'entreprises de services commerciaux et communautaires.
- Une très bonne connaissance du secteur des coopératives établies à l'échelle des régions, de ses problèmes, priorités et de ses pratiques de gestion.
- Une très bonne connaissance des principes et des pratiques liés au développement communautaire et au développement économique des collectivités, ainsi que des agences et des organismes de développement de la région.
- Une très bonne connaissance des programmes et des services gouvernementaux de développement communautaire et d'entreprise, de soutien technique et de gestion, etc. auxquels les coopératives en développement pourraient avoir accès.
- Une très bonne connaissance des instruments, des processus et des techniques de présentation, de promotion et de diffusion de l'information.
- La capacité de communiquer efficacement et clairement.
- La capacité d'organiser et de diriger des réunions publiques, des séminaires, des ateliers de travail, etc.
- La capacité de travailler avec des groupes communautaires, sectoriels, de producteurs et de consommateurs, pour les aider à se concentrer sur les priorités en matière de développement et à franchir les étapes des processus de développement et de planification organisationnelle et d'entreprise.

Résultats et performance

Au cours de la période 1997-2005, il s'est créé 154 entreprises coopératives dans tous les secteurs d'activités économiques qui ont permis la création et le maintien de 1 369 emplois au Centre-du-Québec et en Mauricie. De façon générale, il s'est traité, en moyenne, 66 demandes d'informations annuellement pour une création moyenne de 17 statuts coopératifs par année où l'équivalent de 1 statut pour 3.88 dossiers ouverts.

De façon générale, on observe une diminution du nombre de dossiers ouverts (1 statut pour 3 dossiers ouverts) depuis 2 ans. Au niveau des types de coopératives les plus utilisées, elles se répartissent de la façon suivant : coopératives de consommateurs (3 %), de travailleurs actionnaires (7 %), de producteurs (19 %), de solidarité (25 %) et de travail (46 %).

Au Centre-du-Québec et de la Mauricie, la création de coopératives de solidarité est en forte hausse en 2006, 50 %; 2005, 40 % et 2004, 31 %.

Le taux de survie des coopératives sur notre territoire rejoint celui du Québec. Il atteint 64 % après 5 ans et passe à 46 % après 10 ans, comparativement à 36 % et 20 % pour les autres types d'entreprises.

Les ingrédients de notre succès

Une gouvernance complice

L'historique des 10 ans de la CDCQM met en évidence la stabilité et l'engagement de son conseil d'administration. Parmi les 32 administrateurs qui se sont succédés depuis ce temps au conseil, trois ont franchi les 10 ans, dont la présidence, la vice-présidence et le secrétaire-trésorier.

Les officiers avaient le profil requis ayant exercé des rôles de direction et de présidence au niveau professionnel et personnifiant bien les valeurs et objectifs d'une coopérative. Un point majeur à la création de la coopérative a été de réserver les postes du conseil d'administration exclusivement à des coopératives. En dernier lieu, le conseil a misé sur un gestionnaire qui était reconnu et crédible dans le milieu du développement régional qui s'est entouré d'une équipe performante complémentaire, entreprenante, dédiée à la clientèle.

Une véritable planification stratégique : se donner une mission et une vision

Afin de mieux asseoir sont action naissante sur le terrain, la CDR a réalisé un exercice de planification stratégique en 2001 qui lui a permis d'ajuster sa mission, sa vision et son plan de travail.

Comme mission, la CDR souhaite être la référence en matière coopérative. Elle participe activement au développement socio-économique en offrant des services liés à la création et au maintien de coopératives sur le territoire. Elle se donne la vision d'être connue et reconnue comme le carrefour de services-conseils pour le démarrage et le suivi des coopératives tout en privilégiant l'éducation coopérative, la concertation et l'accès au capital en permettant ainsi le développement socio-économique du territoire.

Une stratégie de communication agressive

La CDR s'est dotée d'un plan de communication agressif visant à mettre en valeur ses forces et de préciser son image. Voici les grands objectifs qui soutendent les moyens d'actions déployés.

a) Faire connaître la CDR dans la région, ses services et son rôle

Thème: « Le développement coopératif, c'est notre affaire »
  Moyens:
  * Le bulletin mensuel « Le Lien-Coop »;
  * Tournoi annuel des coopératives (alternance dans les 2 régions);
  * Visites des coopératives et des partenaires socio-économiques;
  * Représentations;
  * Assemblée générale annuelle; et
  * Communiqués, conférence de presse, site Web;

b) Faire connaître, mettre en valeur et promouvoir la coopération
  * Gala annuel du Mérite Coopératif;
  * Cahier spécial – hebdos et quotidiens régionaux;
  * Annuaire des coopératives;
  * Dépliants et brochures;
  * Guides de gestion;
  * Atelier de formation;
  * Semaine de la Relève coopérative;
  * Revue de presse;
  * Calendrier

c) Mobiliser les coopératives autour de la CDR et recruter un membership significatif
  * Programme de fidélisation des membres;
  * Participation à d'autres assemblées générales annuelles;
  * Visites;
  * Enracinement dans la région par la participation au conseil d'administration d'organisations stratégiques.

d) Un travail de sensibilisation en amont

La sensibilisation des jeunes à la coopération a été une cible importante pour l'organisation. À notre avis, il était important d'initier les jeunes aux valeurs entourant la formule coopérative pour contrer leur exode vers les grands centres urbains. En 10 ans, ce sont plus de 5 000 jeunes qui ont été initiés aux valeurs coopératives par les divers projets d'éducation coopérative : Coopérative jeunesse de services (CJS), Jeune Coop, Ensemble vers la réussite (EVR) et la Semaine de la Relève coopérative. De plus, à chaque année, nous avons honoré une initiative jeunesse dans le cadre de notre gala annuel. Au cours des années 2001-2002, nous avons pu bénéficier d'une initiative provinciale très efficace, du Secrétariat à la jeunesse, le programme Audace. Celui-ci permettait, aux jeunes entrepreneurs qui démarraient leur entreprise coopérative, de bénéficier d'une aide financière.

e)   Une prestation de services adaptés aux besoins des groupes

La CDR offre des services aux promoteurs de nouvelles coopératives et aux coopératives bien établies. Aux coopératives en voir de formation, on retrouve le support au démarrage, le suivi et l'accompagnement pour la première année. Aux coopératives existantes, elle offre : la formation sur la vie associative, du coaching professionnel, des services-conseils (diagnostic, formation sur mesure, négociation, analyse financière et comptabilité). De plus, des services plus spécialisés sont offerts (fiscalité, médiation, assistance légale) en collaboration avec d'autres spécialistes.

Par ailleurs, il existe une étroite complicité avec tous les CLD du territoire pour œuvrer ensemble au montage des dossiers. Généralement, les CLD développent le plan d'affaires et la CDR le volet associatif et les aspects financiers reliés à la coopérative.

f) Une offre intégrée de mesures financières

Le Québec profite d'une offre intégrée de financement à l'intention des coopératives. La CDR est au cœur de ce grand réseau et rend accessible ces programmes adaptés à une clientèle locale. Brièvement, voici les mesures facilitantes :
* Le Régime d'investissement coopératif;
* Les mesures d'Investissement Québec;
* Le support du Mouvement Desjardins;
* La finance solidaire : Fondaction, Filaction, etc.;
* Les programmes locaux et régionaux des CLD, SADC;
* Les autres mesures qui s'adressent aux PME.

Conclusion

En action depuis 10 ans, la CDCQM a réussi le défi du démarrage d'une coopérative et son enracinement dans le tissu économique régional. Ce qui a fait la force de notre organisation, c'est la compétence et les attitudes de nos ressources humaines (dirigeants et permanents) qui ont patiemment appris à vivre au rythme des préoccupations des gens d'affaires et des milieux sociaux. Le positionnement stratégique de notre organisation à la croisée de l'économie et du social, nous a rendus acceptable comme outil de construction de l'économie. La participation des intervenants locaux et leur capacité à organiser eux-mêmes le développement durable de leur communauté par la voie coopérative sont responsables de notre succès. Nos communautés ont compris le sens de la coopération comme une formule visant à réconcilier le développement économique et social, la protection de l'environnement et la conservation des ressources naturelles.

Section Four: Collaborative Strategies for Addressing Specific Needs

Chapter Twelve

Co-op Development With an Immigrant and Refugee Co-op

Melanie Conn and Gulalai Habib

Malalay[1] is the name of the Afghan Women's Sewing and Crafts Co-operative based in Burnaby, B.C. whose members are immigrant and refugee Afghan women. Under the sponsorship of Immigrant Services Society (ISS)[2] of B.C., the co-op has moved from its beginnings as a grassroots community initiative in 2003 to operating out of a well-equipped workshop and meeting space as an incorporated co-operative. Mainly funded by grants until now, the co-op is moving towards more self-sustainability in 2007.

Gulalai Habib is an experienced immigrant settlement counselor and new co-op developer; she is also a founding member of the Afghan-Canadian

---

1 Malalay is the name of a legendary Afghan woman who fought against the British occupation raising the flag in front of exhausted troops during a battle which resulted in victory for her people in 1919.

2 Immigrant Services Society of B.C. incorporated in 1972. Since then, the organization has developed considerable expertise and experience in the delivery of services and programmes for immigrants and refugees. For more information visit the ISS website: www.issB.C..org.

Women's Network of B.C. since 2000. Melanie Conn is an experienced co-op developer who has worked with diverse groups but was not familiar with the Afghan community when she first became a consultant with this project. Gulalai initially coordinated the co-op in a volunteer capacity; she was seconded from ISS to work part-time as a Community Economic Developer with the co-op in 2005, when funds were obtained to support the project. This paper explores how co-op development principles and practices were adapted to the Afghan immigrant and refugee community as an example which could be replicated in other immigrant and refugee communities.

Section One presents the context for the formation of Malalay, specifically information about ISS and the Afghan community in the Lower Mainland of British Columbia. In Section Two, we explore the development process with the group. Section Three presents lessons for co-op developers, immigrant-serving organizations, and government.

The Context for the Development of Malalay

Immigrant Services Society of B.C. (ISS)

The increased level of poverty and the settlement pattern of new immigrants in Burnaby highlighted the need for a focus on community participation, capacity building, and economic development projects. In 2003, the *Afghans Together* programme of ISS created an opportunity for the Afghan community to discuss their ideas and encouraged individual members to provide leadership support by contributing their knowledge and experience in community economic development. Among many ideas one was to start a sewing and crafts group with women in the community.

To fulfill the dream the community faced enormous challenges. These included: a lack of organizational, administrative, and management capacity; limited knowledge around project development and its process; lack of experience in the area of community development; limited knowledge of Canadian legal requirements; limited access to outside agencies; lack of leadership capacity; and a high level of community complexity, including the issue of trust among the war-affected Afghan community.

During 2004 and 2005, advocacy efforts for the sewing group were expanded. *Vibrant Burnaby*, a partnership of community service organizations, provided initial funds for two training sessions related to developing a co-operative enterprise. ISS, with its interest in alternative labour market strategies and community capacity building, took on the incubation of the overall coordination and implementation of the project. A new focus of the

Canadian Community Economic Development Network (CCEDNet) on the development of co-operatives and social enterprises in urban immigrant communities created the momentum for a partnership between the two organizations and accelerated the progress of the project over the next two years. DevCo, a co-op development a co-op development training and consulting organization, started to work in tandem with ISS to develop project proposals and expand funding opportunities for the co-op.

Despite the risk involved in taking on a new bottom-up approach to development, and the need to constantly adapt to the changing requirements of the project, ISS became a major player. The organization received two-year funding from Vancity Community Foundation and one year funding from Status of Women Canada, which provided the main financial resources for the project. ISS also made successful proposals to the Unitarian Church of Vancouver, the B.C. Co-op Association, Women Futures, and other organizations.

An Advisory Committee was established including representatives from CCEDNet, Vancity, DevCo, Vibrant Burnaby, Status of Women Canada, B.C. Co-op Association, Afghan Women's Network, Afghans Together, and Malalay members. The Committee provides guidance and support for the co-op, helps members establish networks in mainstream and immigrant communities, assists in creating awareness about the co-op with the general public, and ultimately, helps the co-op's members advocate for policy and programme changes.

ISS's vision is to build partnerships with the CED sector and to explore community development that is about much more than material benefits and focuses instead on the sum of people's own aspirations, efforts, and learning to better themselves materially, socially, intellectually, and spiritually.

The Community

The Afghan community in the Lower Mainland of British Columbia has increased significantly over the last five years. As an indication of this growth, consider that in 1999 there were a total of 200 government-sponsored refugees, whereas ISS served over 2000 Afghan refugees in 2006.

The community suffers from nearly three decades of war. Over two million Afghans have been killed in wars during that time. They are the largest refugee population in the world. Since 1978, more than 6,700,000 Afghans have fled from armed conflict, finding refuge in neighbouring countries. The death of so many young and able-bodied men has left over 500,000 war widows, women with disabled family members, and a large number of unmarried girls who are responsible for their families. The close-knit

Afghan family system and their traditional resilience means that despite the intensity and longevity of their suffering there are, overall, few beggars or prostitutes among Afghan society. We have also seen the same determination to make a better life in the commitment of women to the co-op.

Afghans present the classic profile of a war-torn community. The most essential requirements for sustainable development hardly exist: stable communities, shared long-term aspirations, income-earning opportunities, adequate health care, and education. These factors are not to do with culture but with war and living as refugees and new immigrants. The primary factors affecting any attempt to do sustainable development work with Afghans are the community's experience with war, the uncertain refugee environment, and the resulting inadequate community capacity to move forward.

Afghan Women

Afghan women who have become part of the local Lower Mainland community continue to face immense obstacles and hardship. Life in Canada is not easy for them as a result of language barriers, economic hardship, the loss of their cultural values, and treatment as "second-class citizens" in everyday life. Afghans comprise 27% of government-assisted refugees in B.C., and among that group 37% are families with single parents, mostly mothers who have lost husbands in the war and who are now the breadwinners for large families with an average of six children.

Many Afghan women immigrants and refugees have lived for five to twenty years in under-equipped refugee camps in Iran, Pakistan, Russia, and India. In Canada, the majority live on income assistance programmes or are members of low-income families. Traumatized by the war, many women are widowed; they frequently experience depression and are isolated within the larger community. Circles of support constituting elders, families, and friends have been eroded.

The women fled uncertainty and dependence, arriving in Canada with a dream of being active and successful role models for their children. However, living for decades in an environment of war and refugee camps has created low self-esteem, low motivation, and extremely limited opportunities for utilizing their previous skills and qualifications, or acquiring new ones. Almost 98% of the members of Malalay are receiving social assistance benefits, and their financial dependence on government intensifies their reduced sense of self-worth.

Low literacy as a result of little or no normal education in the war zones and inadequate education in refugee camps makes learning a new language and the integration process slower for these women than for other newcomers. ESL professionals explain that learning a second language is based on a person's knowledge of their first language. Therefore, simple daily activities, such as using transportation facilities, the banking system, shopping, attending medical appointments, interacting with the school system, accessing services, and understanding their rights, involve enormous struggles.

Raising children in an environment where their cultural values are constantly challenged by Canadian values creates family conflict. Women are alarmed at the shift from status-focused behaviour to freedom-focused behaviour, from a social emphasis on age to a focus on youth, and from duties towards family/clan to the rights of each individual. The lack of language-specific resources to help deal with family issues and cultural shock has made it very difficult for the women to develop coping skills.

Marginalized within a marginalized community, these women are troubled by their inability to contribute to the family income. As well, the lack of recognition of the value of their unpaid work has greatly reduced their status in the family, in the Afghan community, and in society at large. Poor health conditions and limited health education and awareness intensify their settlement difficulties. There are no culturally appropriate centres where women can have access to education, information, and other resources, as well as opportunities for meetings and discussion. There are also no social gathering places for isolated and marginalized immigrant women to ease their loneliness and learn about opportunities.

The Afghan community is relatively new in Canada and most of the women have limited knowledge of basic modern western technology, such as computers, cars, telephones, elevators, transit facilities, and banking equipment, in addition to their lack of English language ability. Most employment programmes do not know how to define the knowledge immigrants and refugees have acquired through generations of survival in often inhospitable conditions; they definitely do not incorporate this information in the conceptualization and design of programmes.

Although traditionally Afghan women have been involved in production and income generating efforts for their families, marketing has been a role for men in the community. Women's knowledge of business and enterprise is limited. The challenges of doing business in the competitive multicultural environment of Canada are major and compounded by the lack of facility in English, minimal economic assets, and social isolation.

The Members of Malalay

Malalay is a diverse group in terms of ethnic background, language, religion, age, education, mental and physical ability, marital and social status, rural and urban experience, duration of settlement in Canada, and many other important factors. The women all face huge barriers to settlement as already described: lack of English skills, little formal education, no formal work experience or training, and no knowledge of the Canadian work force and its norms. As a result, their participation in political, social, and economic aspects of life in Canada has been passive and isolated. Despite the barriers, the women recognized that their talents in sewing and crafts were a potent source of income. They have pinned their hopes on achieving economic independence through the co-op to help them regain their active and empowered roles.

One of the many strengths women brought to the initiative was that the collective and group approach was a familiar structure for them; they could see it as a way to take control of their lives and to begin moving from a passive, dependent role to an active, engaged role in their communities.

In Afghan culture, co-operation is a social obligation. In common with many other poor communities, members know that survival in a subsistence economy depends primarily on co-operation and mutual support within the kin group. The extended family is the primary source of social welfare. Anyone in receipt of a regular income is duty-bound to contribute to the common family fund; dereliction of this duty is despised and, for the vast majority of Afghans, unthinkable. If a family member cannot contribute, this has an important bearing on their status in the family.

Another positive element for the co-op was that sewing and crafts are traditional and culturally accepted roles for women in the segregated and hierarchical social web of Afghan society. In keeping with the overall strategy of working within the culture, meeting with elders and influential community members (men and women) in a central mosque was the first step to gather community support for this project.

Malalay defined its membership as "low income Afghan women" while acknowledging the important contribution made by supporters and advisors. As word about the co-op has spread, more women have begun to inquire about joining. A few months after moving into their workspace the group decided to close membership and establish a waiting list. In general meetings it is common to see new faces, women who want to join in the future when more work is available. In the meantime, members understand the isolation of newcomers, and women are welcomed to enjoy the co-op as a social gathering place and networking opportunity.

The Co-op Development Process

For the purpose of this reflection on our practice, we are focusing on how the significant contextual issues for members have been integrated into the co-op development process. Our framework references three key areas of member participation: Governance, Finance, and Operations. Each section includes a discussion of specific challenges and what we learned.

Since we are writing this paper "in the middle of the story," we also identify many of the development challenges still faced by the co-op.

Our conclusion presents suggestions for how our experience can be utilized by other co-op developers, immigrant-serving agencies, and policy-makers.

The Development Process Begins

The development process began in the summer of 2004 with a series of information sessions about co-ops held over a period of six months in the library of an elementary school and at a community centre in the East Burnaby neighbourhood where most of the members lived. Usually 14 to 25 women attended, although not everyone came to each session.

The group had already been operating on an informal co-operative basis. One member, who had lived in Canada for more than twenty years and had operated a home-based upholstery business on Vancouver Island, supplied the women with large amounts of fabric and sewing supplies. Many of the women made small items such as bags, scarves, and pillows which they exhibited as a group at community events and craft sales, others sold imported items such as Afghan jewellery and other products.

The goals of the initial development phase were to explore the objectives women had for increasing their income through a more formal co-operative enterprise and to provide information about co-op structures for governance, finance, and operations. Eventually, the plan was for the co-op to be incorporated under the provincial Co-operative Association Act.

All the co-op information sessions required the services of an interpreter fluent in Dari, the women's common language. Interpretation during meetings and translation of most documents have been two of the most important ways to increase members' active participation throughout the co-op development process. An additional benefit has been the creation of job opportunities for four Afghan women to learn, practice, and provide interpretation skills.

Since the sessions were also an important opportunity for women to discuss other matters relating to settlement, such as problems accessing services or other resources, the co-op information component was often a fairly brief element of the meetings. However, over the span of several sessions, the outline of the co-op began to take shape.

As with many emerging co-ops the easiest topic to discuss was related to the products and services the women would offer. In this case, the women said they wanted to market their dress-making skills within the Afghan community, they wanted to sell products they were already making to the community at large, and they wanted to explore the potential of accessing large contracts (e.g. curtains, futon covers, school uniforms) for the group to produce collectively. Some members were also interested in selling imported items through the co-op. The women envisioned that the co-op would acquire the sewing equipment required to expand their operations, as well as a workshop space with office and other business support.

Member Development

We knew the women were excited about the opportunity to earn some income by using their skills. We also anticipated that the process for translating their vision into action would require much patience and creativity. Sessions with the group often included a discussion of co-ops as member-owned and member-operated enterprises, different in fundamental ways from companies with one owner or employer. While the women appreciated the idea of a co-op as a way to enjoy more of the fruits of their labour than as employees, it became clear that most had no personal frame of reference for a formal structure for carrying on business, to say nothing about a co-op approach to governance. In fact, many of the women saw Melanie at first as a government representative who would provide work contracts and other resources for the group, rather than as a consultant who could assist them in developing their project. In a similar way, the line between the coordinator's role as an employee of ISS and as the CED/coordinator of the co-op was difficult to clarify.

Although we explained that our roles were to help the co-op become self-managed, we realized these areas would need to be explored in the context of practical operations. We wrestled with the challenge of clarifying and supporting "member ownership and control" for many months. In fact, the whole effort of the development process has been to experiment with various methods, structures, and other interventions to empower the members.

In the next three sections, we explore governance, finances, and operations of the co-op. In relation to governance, we focus on the incorporation process as a way to apply the principle of member ownership and control. The section on finance explores the importance of transparency and hands-on experience to build knowledge, trust, and member responsibility. In the section on operations, we discuss the use of project coordinators as a way to build teamwork and the hiring of a business consultant to provide direct assistance.

Governance

The idea of fitting the fluid, informal, and lively dynamic of the group into a legal framework for incorporation seemed like an extremely daunting challenge. It turned out to be even a lengthier process than anticipated to find the structures that worked best for the group. Although the scheduled date for submitting the incorporation documents was changed many times, the co-op was incorporated in August, 2006.

Meetings, Quorums, and Minutes

In the course of two years of focused co-op development with Malalay, there have been dozens of meetings with the group. Meetings were scheduled for three hours, at the same time, and in the same place whenever possible, great efforts were made to ensure that women were informed about them. However, the majority of the group would generally not gather until an hour or longer after the scheduled time and every new arrival was greeted by all members of the group. In the last half hour women would still be arriving. As a result, much less information could be covered than anticipated and it was difficult for the group to make decisions about their structure.

Most groups need a period of adjustment to make the transition from an informal, social approach to a more structured one. However, there were unique circumstances with Malalay; often family responsibilities that needed attention arose at the last moment, appointments with settlement workers or social assistance workers had priority over co-op meetings, serious health problems interfered with attendance, those who depended on public transportation to get to the meetings might not have bus fare or would miss their connection. Given the challenges of their daily lives, the commitment of so many women to attend the meetings regularly was a clear sign of success. And the greetings, tea, and catch-up conversation were balm for their souls – the *social capital* that will ultimately make the co-op grow and survive.

After one or two months in their new space, a few of the women began to express some frustration about revisiting discussions and decisions made in previous meetings. This was the ideal time to introduce the concept of a *quorum* as "the number of members required to be present at a meeting for decisions to be made." After much discussion, a quorum was set at ten members. Once the membership list was confirmed, the number was revised as "a majority of the members." Over time, women began to arrive before the meeting was scheduled to begin in order to set out the refreshments, there were still delays but more business was accomplished.

For the first while, the CED worker took notes from meetings which were translated into Dari and distributed. At the time of setting the quorum, we suggested that the women take turns as minute-takers with her support. She presented a simple template for recording: topics discussed, decisions made, and actions to be taken. Taking minutes was not an easy task, even for the educated members, for some of them had lost many skills in the years of living in refugee camps away from formal settings.

Equal participation of all members has been a challenge. Members with low literacy skills and new arrivals tended not to think of themselves as capable of participating in decision-making. They saw their contribution mainly to serve other members by making tea and cleaning up after meetings. This gradually changed as the women gained a clearer picture of the purpose of the co-op and its difference from the traditional structure where elders are in charge or from their memories of Afghanistan with political and warring authorities imposing decisions.

Sessions were planned to give women the opportunity to share and learn about themselves and others, to consider the lifetime barriers associated with their role as women, and to talk about their dream of a new life in Canada. Their openness provided inspiration for renewed efforts to work collectively.

The support of settled immigrants was an additional strength of the project. However, it has been important to attend to the dynamics between new and settled immigrants in ways that leave room for the growth, empowerment, and leadership of newcomers. Realizing the effects of war and the need for enormous trust building efforts, group guidelines were developed in order to create an atmosphere where each woman could find her voice.

Board of Directors

It was necessary for the co-op to have a board of directors if it was to incorporate. We also thought the co-op would function more efficiently if a smaller group took responsibility for the oversight of the co-op. Most importantly though, the establishment of the board would represent the beginning of a transition from the co-op as a "project" of ISS to an incorporated entity that would manage itself and plan its own future.

The concept of the board of directors was introduced very early in the co-op development process. As with many groups, the members of Malalay were in no hurry to move from the "group of the whole" into one with smaller units, whether committees or a board of directors. They preferred large meetings where everyone was involved in making decisions and plans. The idea of the board was more challenging for two reasons. The first was that most members were not familiar with formal corporate structures for doing business, which meant that a great deal of information had to be translated and interpreted for presentation.

The second, and more fundamental challenge, was the concern shared by most members that the board would be an elite power group within the co-op. In a community where trust-building is a long-term and painstaking process, it was extremely important for members to have a very clear idea about the responsibilities of the directors and how members would continue to be the "supreme authority." While many groups take considerable time before they are ready (i.e. willing) to delegate responsibility to some of its members, the process has been especially lengthy and intense with Malalay.

One way we handled the need for clarification was with a document written in clear English and translated into Dari called: "What does it mean to be a board member?" (Appended to the end of this article.) While the document did not resolve all the concerns, it has provided a basis for talking about the board and its role. It also helped to reduce the anxiety of women who may have been fearful about taking a seat on the board.

The discussions about the board continued for many months. Eventually, the impetus for choosing the co-op's first directors arose from a frustrating experience; members were unable to open a co-op bank account because they were not incorporated. There was a surge of new energy to get on with the process and the need for interim directors became an immediate concern. Given the lack of experience of the women with democracy in Afghanistan, the coordinator suggested they use a secret ballot to ensure that each woman was able to exercise her right to vote without fear. To eliminate any embarrassment for women who were not literate in Dari, a unique ballot was created that showed photos of all members. Women were asked to circle the faces of the five women who they thought would be the best "representatives" on the board.

Melanie acted as a scrutineer with Monica Mueller, who had been involved with the co-op for several months in various volunteer and paid roles. Every circled face was noted and we announced the results at the same meeting where the voting took place. For the most part the women seemed satisfied with the process, although one member expressed her concern that the secret ballot was not a good idea. In case her concern was that the ballots were incorrectly counted, they were filed at the office rather than being destroyed as is customary. Over the next four months there was increasing acceptance of the elected directors. In November 2007, there will be another election at the first Annual General Meeting of the co-op. This will give the group an opportunity to build on the first experience in a context of more familiarity with the role of the board.

Board Meetings

The five new interim directors have met weekly since July, 2006. The learning curve has been steep and is ongoing, involving everything from taking minutes to developing a rudimentary bookkeeping system, to addressing conflicts within the larger group. One of the main challenges has been to establish a reporting system that facilitates efficiency and still allows membership participation in decision-making. The process has been for the board to present a summary of its discussions and recommendations at the weekly general meeting. The role of the board is a work in progress.

In some instances, the process has worked fairly well, such as the hiring of the business consultant. We presented our rationale for the business consultant to the board and a detailed job description was prepared; the board reviewed and approved the description, which was then presented to the members. As a first step, the board also recommended interviewing Monica because she had already been working with the co-op as a volunteer ESL teacher and in delivering some training classes around marketing. With the membership's agreement, the board interviewed her and recommended hiring her for two days a week.

Frequently, however, the members re-hash board discussions and the structure seems to slow down decision-making rather than to streamline it. As a result, the directors have sometimes felt frustrated and confused about their role. We are still looking for the right balance in a structure that empowers members and also builds the board's capacity to fulfill its responsibility. We anticipated that the most effective way for the directors and the membership as a whole to become comfortable with a more structured way of managing the co-op would be by experiencing it. We will be assisting the whole group to look at some specific ways to review and revise the role of the board as the co-op approaches the date for the first Annual General Meeting, where there will be an election of directors for longer terms.

Finance

There are a host of administrative and planning issues relating to financial matters that require attention in any co-op (e.g. accessing funds for capital expenses, bookkeeping, budgeting). It is often challenging for members to focus on financial issues, especially if their work experience has been informal and very small-scale. From the beginning, the role of ISS with Malalay has included financial oversight; the organization has been the official applicant for any large grants and has taken responsibility for bookkeeping, accounting, and monitoring. However, with incorporation of the co-op came the need to increase the knowledge and skills of members in many areas relating to finances. The directors especially needed to be able to carry out their fiduciary responsibility as trustees of the co-op. We also knew a successful process would involve both trust-building and hands-on experience handling money.

Knowledge

Many immigrant women have limited experience in the financial management of an organization. Their economic situation is not always the relevant factor in their ability. For example, a woman living in poverty needs to manage her limited funds with great care and skill, while a more affluent woman may be less attentive. For Malalay members, cultural factors were particularly significant; women are mostly responsible for managing the family's finances. But even when there was a willingness to move into more activity around financial matters, Malalay members face the additional challenge of learning about the requirements of various Canadian systems. Given that their involvement in financial matters inevitably demanded literacy in English, the challenges have been considerable.

One helpful resource was the offer by Vancity Credit Union to deliver a series of four sessions on Financial Literacy, including the Canadian banking system in Canada, budgeting, credit, and simple financial tips.

A second contribution to building women's ability to participate in financial and other aspects of the co-op was a series of weekly ESL sessions over a period of five months. It is impossible to over-estimate the importance of the sessions, which were offered by Monica as a volunteer. The sessions not only enabled women to interact to a greater degree with customers and suppliers but also greatly increased their ability to work with Monica when she was hired later as the business consultant.

Trust-building

We learned that knowledge on its own was not sufficient to build women's ability to handle financial matters; trust among group members was crucial. The best example of the relationship between knowledge and trust was the experience of opening a bank account prior to the co-op's incorporation. The credit union required two individuals to open personal accounts as a first step; the next step was for them to open a group account with the two individuals and any others as signers. Arrangements were made many times to follow through with the plan but they were not implemented. After several weeks, we discovered that women in the group were unclear about the process and they were extremely uneasy because they thought two individuals were going to have control of the co-op's money. Once we clarified the procedure and explained that the two women would not be using the collective account, the group easily gathered to open the group account. It was an important lesson to move very slowly and be absolutely transparent when money is involved.

During the past months, members of Malalay have also been actively engaged in several sessions about conflict resolution and effective communication. While putting the lessons into practice is expected to take some time, the members now have a foundation to build effective communication within the group and can more easily discuss financial matters or other issues.

Practice Handling Money

ISS has been administering payment of major expenses for consultants, staff, and overhead, while the co-op has mainly handled money related to sales. The board decided to rotate the responsibility for tracking expenses and payment among teams of two directors for two month periods with overlap of one director to the next team for continuity. Previously, the system of financial tracking was based on individuals reporting income and expenditures, but written records were often not completed. While the new process has many bumps, the directors have begun to learn what is involved in fulfilling the responsibility and have been open to Monica's patient demonstration of basic bookkeeping. We anticipate that as the directors' confidence grows, the systems will function more smoothly.

While everyone involved with Malalay (ISS, consultants, members) understands the transition to self-management will be a lengthy process, we have identified some significant steps to help the process move forward. One step was for the board to meet with the Director of Immigrant Settlement Services to discuss the overall budget for the co-op. The preparation of the documents for the meeting took many hours of our time to clarify every line item and to arrange for accurate translation into Dari. At the meeting, the Director talked about ISS's role to ensure that the co-op had the services, expertise, and other support needed to be successful, explaining where those items were represented in the budget.

As well, he explained that as part of the plan was to assist the co-op's transition to increased self-management, ISS would transfer a portion of funds to the co-op's account. The directors will then have the opportunity to handle specific expenses, including bus tickets for members, office and cleaning supplies, equipment repair and maintenance, telephone, rent, and utilities. We expect that the experience of "learning by doing" will require much support but will ultimately be a huge step in building the confidence of the directors to handle more aspects of the co-ops finances in the future.

One goal of the meeting was for members to receive explicit information about how funds that were obtained by ISS on behalf of the co-op were to be allocated. However, it has been difficult for the directors who attended this meeting to communicate the information to the members when they were asked about budget items. There is still a great deal of discussion that needs to take place to completely de-mystify the co-op's finances and the role of ISS.

Operations

In co-op development, the operation of the business – production of a product or delivery of a service – is where "the rubber hits the road." After more than three years of talking about the co-op, the members of Malalay were eager to get down to sewing in earnest.

The transition from planning to production has been very gradual and involved many steps: finding an appropriate workspace, acquiring the equipment for more sustained and large-scale production, learning about the apparel industry and the Canadian market for clothing and craft products, establishing procedures and policies for production and sales, learning about marketing, and recently, working with a business consultant to provide on-site expertise and teaching.

Workspace and Equipment

Some of the women had sewing machines at home and were already accustomed to making items for sale at exhibitions along with others in the group. The group had also taken on one or two large contracts arranged by one of the members. But for Malalay to have an identity as an enterprise, we knew it was imperative for the co-op to have its own space to work. We developed a matrix with the women to rate potential locations and it became clear that a space within walking distance of the Edmonds area of Burnaby, where most of the Afghan community resides, was the highest priority, weighted higher even than the rental cost. ISS spent many weeks looking for an appropriate space, constantly challenged by zoning and cost barriers. Finally, a location was found in the basement of a dental clinic at the heart of the desired area; the co-op moved into its new space in August, 2005.

The women eagerly planned how to use the warren of small rooms, including one to be reserved for childcare. With the co-op within walking distance for most of the women, the need for on-site childcare has been reduced; however, members trained in Child Safety and First Aid have arranged to be present when needed. Very quickly the space became much more than a place to sew. Women congregate for tea and conversation, as well as to work, celebrations of religious holidays are held on a regular basis, as well as International Women's Day and New Year's events. Sharing information, networking about community events, and food distribution also takes place at the co-op.

Equipping the workspace was the next significant step. Several of the members went on a field trip to Mason Sewing Machine Company where they tried out a number of the machines. It was a pleasure to see one woman, who had always presented herself very shyly, sit down confidently at an industrial machine and demonstrate how it worked. With a generous donation from the Unitarian Church of Vancouver and financial support by Vancity Community Foundation, the shopping list was submitted and within a few weeks the machines and other necessary equipment arrived.

Production

Initially women worked on small individual projects, but an opportunity soon arose for them to produce a significant number of tote bags for a local organization. This was a chance for them to create a systematic structure for working together and to learn in a practical way about pricing and payment. Many discussions ensued: rates were set for different aspects of production (cutting, sewing, ironing), accommodation was made for those who sewed the complete bag at home, and a price per bag was proposed.

The contract resulted in two important lessons. First, it became clear that it was necessary for specific members to closely coordinate each contract. The group decided that project coordinators would be involved through-out the entire process of future contracts from the initial discussions with customers about design and price, through monitoring the quality of items before delivery. The second decision was for members to make it a priority to work together as a team in the co-op space rather than at home on a piece-work basis.

The lessons were underlined by a visit to the manufacturing facility of Maiwa Handprints, a well-known fabric import and design company in Vancouver.[3] The owner has more than twenty years of experience in sup-porting artisans in many countries to produce fabric for production of Maiwa clothing designs. She readily agreed to host a tour of the facility and fifteen women attended. In the process, she identified the essential features involved in production: consistent sizing, very high quality stitching, careful finishing, and attention to customer specifications. She also explained how assembly production was a faster and better approach than piece-work, of-fering to assist the group in developing their own system. The women were excited about the visit and their first-hand look at the top-quality products.

---

3 For more information on Maiwa Handprints see: <http://www.maiwa.com/about.html>

Income from Production

Income to the co-op from production has been minimal, about $2,500 during 2005-06 over a twelve-month period. In the year or so since Malalay moved into its workspace, a number of dressmaking and alteration jobs have been taken on by individual members. In those situations, the policy is for members to give 10% of the total price to the co-op. Some small contracts involving several members have also been completed, e.g. making ten futon covers for ISS's Welcome House (a residential unit for government sponsored refugees in B.C.). Where a team of members produce a product, the percentage to the co-op is 10-15% depending on the overall price. Establishing both policies required many months of discussion and were based on the women's experience of working together.

Co-op members also recognize the importance of the work that supports production, such as cleaning, office administration, on-site childcare, and coordination. The current budget includes line items for cleaning and childcare, there is also a considerable amount allocated for professional coordination and consultation. However, it has been a point of contention for a few members that office and member coordination does not yet get compensated.

Since the first meetings, the group has discussed the challenges of sharing a small amount of work among 14-18 members who are eager to supplement their incomes. Nevertheless, it is still frustrating for members that the process has been so slow.

Even when Malalay is able to provide more opportunities to its members for paid work, most will need to deal with government policies that constrain them from earning income while receiving government benefits.

Marketing

Until recently, sales had been based more on the initiation of customers than on members' own marketing efforts. Community members would drop in with clothing to be altered or designs to be produced. There has also been support from the non-profit sector (e.g., the organizers of the Canadian CEDNet annual conference purchased pillows and bags as gifts for presenters).

Based on advice and experience with other co-ops, we thought the co-op could acquire more work if their clothing and craft products were targeted to specific markets. Soon after the co-op moved into its new space, we placed a brief note about it in *Threads*, the bi-weekly e-newsletter of the B.C. Apparel Association. One response was from a young designer who offered to create a cotton shawl for women to make. She generously requested nothing more than credit for the design, which had a vaguely Afghan look. This gave the women a chance to use their new embroidery equipment. She met with them on several occasions to consult about the design; a dozen shawls were produced but, unfortunately, most did not sell at the exhibitions and sales the women attended.

We turned to Monica Mueller, who several of the women knew from ESL classes, and asked if she would consider doing a short series of sessions on marketing. Monica is also an experienced businesswoman and agreed to design the sessions, focusing on a product she thought had some good potential - a pet pillow with a liner of aromatic, relaxing herbs. Four to six women (including three board members) attended the sessions, which took them out of the comfort zone of the Afghan community and introduced them to some basic marketing concepts.

Monica taught by doing. Women accompanied her to pet stores and fabric stores. Here they learned about negotiating price-volume deals and identifying good quality. She also taught in English, which complemented the ESL classes.

Business Consultant

As the first series of marketing sessions drew to a close, we began to consider the idea of providing more intensive expertise to the whole group, not only in relation to marketing but in other elements of business management. We thought the budget could be adapted to allow a business consultant to work part-time with the group for about six months.

When we raised the idea at a board meeting in June 2006, there was immediate interest and, we think, some relief. There was also some discussion about whether the expertise could be found within the group. With assistance from the owner of Maiwa, a job description was drafted for a consultant "to assist the co-op to manage the business side of the co-op." It was clear that this was a strategy to help the members make the transition to self-management.

In a fairly short time, and with many interruptions due to holidays and other matters, Monica has assisted co-op members to better understand the project coordination role, to develop a simple bookkeeping system, to open a group bank account, and to take a more proactive approach to move production ideas and activities forward. As the chair of the East Burnaby Business Committee, she has also been able to help the co-op identify itself as a local business and to consider ways to contribute to the community.

There are some new contracts underway and a number of ideas for products for spring. Co-op members are becoming more familiar with the characteristics of a systematic approach to production and administration. As with other elements of the co-op's development, to ensure that each step is integrated before moving on to the next one the process of learning cannot be hurried. Given the commitment and eagerness of the group in response to Monica's patient support, we are confident that a great deal will be accomplished over the next six months.

While the achievements of Malalay have been significant for its members and, by extension, for the Afghan community and the community at large, the process has been very slow. We know that strengthening the foundation from which women can move towards greater social and economic independence will need more than the two years of concerted effort already invested.

As we look ahead to the end of current funding for the co-op on March 31, 2007, we are planning to access more resources to ensure the group will continue to get the support it needs and deserves.

Implications

What have we learned that can be useful for other co-op projects with immigrants and refugees? In this section we generalize from our specific experience with Malalay and present some implications for 1) co-op developers and CED workers, 2) immigrant-serving organizations, and 3) government and funders.

For Co-op Developers and CED Workers

- The co-operative development process needs to be adapted to ensure that it is culturally appropriate for immigrant and refugee co-ops and that women with low-literacy and English skills can fully participate and benefit from the process.
- It is imperative for a developer who is not familiar with the language and/or the culture of the co-op members work closely with a colleague who understands the cultural issues of the community and is experienced in the community development process.
- The current information about co-ops and co-op development is in English and focused on a population familiar with Canadian (Western) structures and systems; materials need to be adapted for each group (i.e. demystified, translated into the language of the group).
- Interpretation is essential for meetings, especially in the initial stage of the development process. Trained interpreters in the area of CED and co-op development will be an asset.
- The role of developer and CED worker as advisor, enabler, and coach may be too indirect or subtle to be effective, especially in the first stages of the process. The group will be seeking clear direction; us-

ing a "facilitative" process can be construed as not helping enough, in other words, "Just tell us what to do!"

- The relationship can be complicated when the developer is an outsider; they may be seen as giving advice that is out of sync with the community.
- Previous definitions of flexibility will be superseded by the experience; patience is required, as well as openness to new ideas.
- Falling in love with the group is a hazard of sorts but a most enjoyable one. It can be extremely rewarding for a developer who is an outsider to learn about another culture in a very meaningful context.
- The role of a CED worker is to give people the confidence that they have the ability to develop themselves. At the same time, they need to challenge perceptions from within the culture. Well-trained workers, working within their own cultural context, are in a much better position to challenge perceptions than outsiders. The role of outsiders is to ask the questions of the workers but not to provide the answers; these must be provided by people reflecting on their own context and values.
- Discussions on cultural values need to be a regular and normal part of the process of running a development programme and not ignored or left aside as "too sensitive." In this way, a thinking, questioning, experimenting cadre of workers can be created who are true catalysts for change within their own culture.
- The formation of immigrant co-ops must bring "rights" into the consciousness of its members. It means equal access to what limited services are available. The process requires a commitment to training co-op developers within immigrant and refugee communities who have a detailed understanding of social relations, especially of the complex gender relations in traditional societies where values clash most obviously with "foreign" values.
- The CED worker is in the best position to: facilitate a process of change in the community, examine how far programmes are relevant to immigrant's values, engage the community in a dialogue that seeks understanding with their values and can therefore lead to capacity building, and identify and link the appropriate outside expertise for the community.
- In immigrant lead co-operatives there could be a conflict zone where community concepts of co-operation, culture, poverty, and the nature of social values meet. Influential factors in the community such as age, social and economic status, differences related to

the number of years of settlement and integration in a new country, and different refugee experiences (e.g. new immigrants from liberal societies in comparison with those who lived for years in conservative societies) can all contribute to a positive circle of inter-dependences or a conflict of values and barriers for individual growth and independence. Of all people, receivers of aid and assistance tend to be most disempowered, because they are caught in a vicious circle where negative social attitudes contribute to low-self-esteem that produces a type of behaviour, which in turn fosters negative social attitudes. The only way out is for people on income assistance to start the process of change in themselves.

- For war affected communities, the co-op model needs to be re-examined and adapted based on the community's history, complexities, values, and motivation factors.

- Settlement counselors/CED workers have the advantage of starting within an established trusted relationship with clients and community members. They can work from within the culture and, at the same time, have a non-affiliated position in the community under the umbrella of the immigrant servicing agency. However, the down side is that settlement counselors/workers are often perceived as leaders in their respective community, and it can be difficult to separate one's professional life from one's personal life.

- In a war affected immigrant community, being the bridge between the community and the implementing agency, as well as dealing with financial matters, has enormous challenges. The CED worker needs to be highly committed and dedicated to the change process in the community and be prepared to manage the risks of their involvement, especially when involving smaller ethno-cultural communities where CED workers will often find themselves working in an area that is not fully understood. They must also be prepared to handle the lack of job security due to the lack of long-term funding opportunities. In dealing with many dynamics in the community, the CED worker will need a firm position of support and back up, especially when dealing with the complexities of a community affected by low levels of literacy and a lack of experiences in organizational settings and other concerns, such as disrupted trust due to experiencing years of war, instability, and corruption.

- Coordination of immigrants and refugees co-operatives requires mixed skills of community development, group facilitation, project management, CED experience, and business management, in addition to bi-lingual/bi-cultural expertise.

- The need for documentation and recognition of the project in the formation stage is essential for smooth transition to the next development phases. This will help volunteers from the initial stage to be adequately recognized and be prepared to accept their equal role among other members of the co-op during the next developmental stages.

For Immigrant-Serving Organizations

- A women-centred co-op can provide a significant opportunity for immigrant and refugee women to achieve equality within the broader Canadian society, as well as within their own community, as they address and mitigate many of the obstacles they face. Meeting and working together on self-identified goals and gaining strength and support from one another gives them hope in their ability to take control of their own lives.
- The participation of an organization such as ISS in a specifically Muslim co-op helps to create positive images of immigrant women in a social climate where their communities are racially profiled. This reflects the need for a shift in immigrant serving agencies entering sensitive areas of social and community issues, such as religion, race, and culture, which are traditonaly left untouched. Creating opportunities for dialogue, networking, and capacity building can lead to empowerment of margilaized segments of the community and change unrealistic images.
- Co-operative development is not new in Canada; however, co-operative development for immigrants is new and requires explicitly probing and exploring cultural relevance. This task requires ongoing monitoring of co-operatives for immigrants and refugees. The cultural relevance must be built into the co-operative management and implementation strategy. This means co-operative developers and CED workers must be trained as social animators to raise questions, to be objective about their own cultures, and not simply deliver packaged services.
- CED is solutions-oriented rather than problem-focused. CED focuses on building economic opportunities, as well as building the capacity of the individual and the community as a whole. However, CED initiatives require a shift among funders to ensure organizations can move beyond time limited, project-oriented services to focus on multi-year CED programmes. Without this shift, host agencies will spend considerable time reporting on small, time limited grants.

- Sponsoring agencies must understand true CED work is a multi-year initiative that requires a risk management strategy. The agency needs to ensure the sponsored community economic initiative reflects the agency's mandate/mission.
- Immigrant serving agencies have generally emerged in response to a specified need and the subsequent availability of funds, rather than as an indigenous movement for development and social justice. Co-ops are self-help initiatives based in local constituencies and require flexibility and adaptability.
- Co-op development cannot be undertaken without appropriately designated staff time. Undertaking CED work, especially in the initial co-op development phase ideally requires a full-time CED worker. The host agency must have a designated bi-lingual, bi-cultural CED worker to initially lead the co-op process. However, being a CED worker is not a usual position within an immigrant-serving agency. Grading the pay scale for the position in relation to other employees can raise questions and concerns among non-CED practitioners, while it may be under-rated in relation to the CED sector. Host agencies must recognize that it is currently difficult to locate full-time, multi-year staffing resources.
- Agencies who wish to embark in CED work will need to assess staff training needs, as CED work is not necessarily the skill set of current employees hired to deliver services.
- The financial systems of host agencies may need to be adjusted to accommodate the co-ops' early development stage (e.g., petty cash accounts, etc.). New regulations of the Canadian Revenue Agency may create challenges and unavoidable bureaucracy that will limit flexibility in some aspects of CED work.
- It is important for host agencies to have an exit vision and strategy to implement after the developmental stage of the project is complete to ensure that all parties, including CED workers and community members, are clear about the extent of support and the process leading to the co-op's eventual full autonomy.
- A partnership with one (or more) experienced CED organizations can help develop projects as an alternative labour market strategy for immigrants and refugees.
- With the leadership of CCEDNet, immigrant co-op representatives have recently come together to form ICAN (Immigrant and Refugee Co-ops Action Network). The goals of the new organization include: analyzing the experience of immigrant co-ops, providing

peer learning support, and making recommendations to expand the sector and ensure its success.

For Government and Other Organizations

- The co-op model can be adapted by any immigrant community in Canada and with the support of government and community agencies, communities can move towards financial independence in creative ways.
- Vancity Community Foundation and Status of Women Canada/B.C. recognized the potential for the co-op to make a significant difference in women's lives; their ongoing, generous, and flexible financial support has been instrumental in the development of Malalay.
- A strategic allocation of multi-year (three to five years) funding is required. Current funding programmes for CED are too small, short-term, and unstable, in other words, unsuited to the inherent long-term process of developing a co-op, which means a host organizations spend significant time looking for funding and reporting.
- Funding is required to adequately cover the host organization's administrative costs and for support staff.
- There are policy issues that impede the success of co-ops and other income-generating projects. One is the dollar-for-dollar "claw-back" of earnings from members who are receiving federal supplements or social assistance benefits in British Columbia. The policies of the Federal Government Refugee Assistance Programme and Provincial Government Welfare and Income Assistance are major barriers for co-operatives and individual members.
- Appropriate zoning and allocation of accessible, affordable community space and effective use of community assets (including space) is essential for the sustainability of co-ops and grass-root projects.
- Banks and financial institutions need to distinguish co-operatives from "private businesses" and "non-profit organizations."
- Recognition of social co-operatives as a vital part of society is essential for creating a healthy and vibrant future for all Canadians.

Appendix One: What does it Mean to be a Board Member

Getting incorporated as an official co-operative means there needs to be a "board of directors" who are representatives of the co-op.

- The board of directors is usually between five and seven people; so that the group is big enough to share the work but not too big to have a discussion and make decisions.
- It is a good idea to have a representative of each co-op committee on the board.
- Directors are elected at the Annual General Meeting; the usual term is two years.
- The board meets regularly between membership meetings to:
  - Discuss co-op matters,
  - Make decisions that must be made before the membership meeting, when necessary, and
  - Prepare information and recommendations for the members to discuss, and for their own decisions.

The overall role of being on the board of a co-operative means working with the other directors to:

- Make sure the co-operative is fulfilling its purpose: to market products made by Afghan women members and others who are associated with the co-operative; to provide space, facilities, and services for training, learning, networking opportunities, and other support as required for its members and others, and
- Help to establish a good foundation for the co-op to succeed in the future.

Being a director does not mean you need to be an expert in financial matters or business, but it is a position of responsibility. Being a director means you have a legal responsibility to do the best you can as an "ordinary" citizen to protect the co-ops assets and to direct it to fulfill its members' objectives. this meens you need to:

1) Make sure you understand the current financial situation of the co-op. For example:

- What is the co-op's budget?
- What are the arrangements with funders and other organizations (e.g. ISS, Lakeview Dental Clinic, etc.)?
- What are the co-op's financial obligations (rent, telephone, and other bills)?

- Are there other financial commitments (such as reports to funders)?
- Consider ways to deal with financial problems the co-op may experience.
- Manage internal and outside donations.

2) Make sure you understand the overall plan for the business. For example:
- What projects is the co-op working on?
- How does the co-op plan to sell its members products (exhibitions, get more contracts, etc.)?
- What is needed to help the co-op succeed (e.g. more trainers)?
- Review co-op plans and adjust them according to new needs and different situations.

3) Help to establish policies for the co-op with the members, support the policies, and make sure they are in the Policy Book.

Policies are supported by the board, but implemented and monitored by the Business Management and Office Committees.
- Examples of Business Management Policies are:
  - How work comes into the co-op and members get assigned to do work,
  - Deciding who will coordinate work contracts,
  - The system for members to get paid for work that gets sold, and
  - Keeping track of when people come in to do work, items borrowed, etc.
- Examples of Office Policies are:
  - Keeping track of the co-op's percentage from all sales,
  - Maintaining the appointment system with customers,
  - Recording all the details of contracts, and
  - Updating the weekly list of workers and their hours.
- Examples of Overall Co-op Policies:
  - Follow meeting guidelines and established work policies,
  - Follow the meeting schedule, and
  - Understand the co-op space systems (alarm, cleaning, inventory, etc.).

4) Represent the co-op by signing official documents. For example:
- Cheques,
- Rental agreements,
- Opening a bank account,

- Grant applications, and
- Other documents.

5) Maintain good communication with members by:

- Organizing the agenda for membership meetings,
- Making sure members all have a chance to ask questions and share their ideas,
- Making sure records are kept and shared with members:
  - minutes of board meetings,
  - minutes of membership meetings,
  - financial records, and
  - list of members.
- Encouraging members to learn about the board and consider being board members in the future.

Chapter Thirteen

Effective Practices in Developing Two Immigrant Women's Co-ops

Joy Emmanuel

The Multicultural Health Brokers Co-op: Interview with Yvonne Chiu

The Multicultural Health Brokers Co-op is a worker co-op comprised of women from various ethnic backgrounds who advocate for community development and provide health promotion services in their communities in Edmonton, Alberta. The co-op members act as health brokers between health institutions and immigrant families; providing one-on-one support to individuals and families. Their services include health education, parenting support, prenatal education, post-natal support, sexuality education, and translation. They also provide consultation support to other service providers regarding cross-cultural issues.

Yvonne Chiu is the Co-executive Director of the co-op. She is both a member and director of the co-op and is one of the lead people in the development of the co-op. She refers to herself as an "indigenous developer" – working from within the evolving co-op and learning as the co-op grows. Below are excerpts from an interview with her in the fall of 2006. Yvonne discusses both internal and external challenges the co-op is dealing with and some of the creative ways they have tried to address these concerns.

YC: I wouldn't call myself a developer simply because I am a member of a local worker co-op. If there is any development work it is purely from the unfolding of our organization and our own efforts to truly live and operate as a workers co-op. In a way, I am a little bit of an "indigenous developer," my learning comes out of my experience with the challenges and the growth issues we have, and from that I have a little bit of insight to share.

Our co-op is called the Multicultural Health Brokers Co-op. This month the co-op will be turning eight years old (November 2006). What we focus on is providing culturally relevant support to immigrant communities: support through family, support through community development, support through policy advocacy. It is kind of a unique organization. If you look at us from a certain angle, we are a service delivery organization extending services from the mainstream institutions to our communities, but in other ways, we are building our own communities to be able to deliver programming specific to our needs. Last, but not least, we are also trying to mobilize our own communities so they can gain some political clout and visibility. We operate on many levels and our practice has become an emerging practice that other colleagues, in other cities, are hoping to adopt.

We are made up of workers who are members of the very communities that we serve. Right now we have colleagues from 15 local communities. They fall into 2 clusters. One cluster is from larger, more established immigrant communities and the other cluster is from very small, emerging communities with a refugee background - from Afghanistan, Sudan, and Somalia. Those colleagues work in communities who have many difficult challenges because of their pre-immigration experiences. That is who we are.

JE: *Tell me a little bit about how you got started.*

YC: We have a humble, very specific beginning. When we first started we were a pilot project of the local public health department. It was very specific for training health educators from different immigrant communities for the purpose of providing culturally and linguistically relevant health education back to our own communities. In fact, it was very narrow; it was looking at maternal infant health.

The interesting part is that even within just that role, we were gaining credibility within the community and with Public Health, our parent organization. In fact, to this day, we still have a contract with them. One of our bread and butter contracts is still with Public Health to provide service in this very specific area. But the interesting thing is, we made a conscious decision in our relationship with them, and this is ten years ago, from the start. We decided that in order to gradually affect change in the system, we needed to have autonomy. My colleagues and I were offered the opportunity to be hired by Public Health, but we turned it down because we felt we needed to have autonomy. That is when we decided to become a separate organization. After exploring maybe four different corporate structural options we ended up being a workers co-op.

Once we became independent, we were simply functioning on one core promise: we will always be guided by our priorities. That is how our work has unfolded to this day, having 3 domains to our operation; on the one hand, we are service deliverers, on the other we are community developers, and on top of that, we are political mobilizers trying to make our communities visible and give them more political potency. By having autonomy and following the people's guide, we have become who we are and what we are.

JE: *How are you structured as a workers co-op? Is it the service providers themselves who are the workers?*

YC: We are still small enough to manage a very direct democratic structure. There are 30 of us who are workers. Following guidelines in the new provincial legislation, we were told at least 75% of the workers must be owner/members. Right now, we have around 75% of us who are co-owners and members of the co-op. We try, as much as possible, to have all 26 of us make policy decisions together. It is really hard - given that we are such a culturally diverse organization. It is really difficult to make policy, and at certain times, operational decisions together, because this means every single one of us has to realize the duality of being a worker, who is going to be impacted by the decision - but also see things as an owner, who needs to have a bird's eye view and a global sense of the well being of our organization and the populations we serve. That duality is very difficult. It is something we need to manage individually and be very conscious of when we are engaging in any kind of business discussion.

JE: *Can you say more about working with that duality?*

YC: I don't think we have yet found a way to do it very well. Many of our business decisions have to be made so quickly because there is urgency out there. We tend to be conscious of this individually, but we have not been able to do much collectively – except for one practice. We have given everyone two different cards with two different colours. We invite people to say, "As I express my opinion I'm coming from a worker's perspective," (a green card) and then when we hold up a purple card, "Now I'm taking an owner's perspective." We have done this, but it is really hard. It requires a high degree of self-awareness. That is the only strategy we have tried and we still don't do it consistently. We are trying to do some organizational development and find ways to move ourselves to the next stage and have a more acute sense of this duality.

JE: *Why would one wear a "worker's hat" rather than the "owner hat?"*

YC: Despite our success in the last few years, we are still struggling with financial security. Most of my colleagues are still working part-time for the co-op while maintaining a day job to survive. Often, when we discuss the hours that are to be distributed among us, it is a very heated discussion. In each community there are different circumstances. When we talk about hours or talk about putting more resources to one community rather than the other, it does require us to sometimes step up a bit, to understand the differences among the communities. I think as human beings our tendency is to really recognize only our own reality. "OK, my community has these issues and I am doing things this way. I need these things to be recognized." That is important, that is a reality, but as an owner you have to step up a little and look at all of the communities. Each community is a little different and the degree of need is a little bit different (for example, refugee vs. immigrant).

So, when we are making a decision, of course it has to start with our own individual sense of reality as we experience it, but once we move on in decision-making we have to balance it out. In this reality of scarce resources, we might have to apply an equity model, where personally I wouldn't get more hours, but another colleague who is desperate in the community would. It is really hard, because I work just as hard, I put in extra hours all of the time. Naturally the inclination is, "I too deserve more." But in the current scenario where we don't have enough resources we have to make decisions that are above one's own perspective and reality.

JE: *I am struck by the fact that you have an organization that is addressing community needs and at the same time you are challenged to address your own needs and create community within the co-op.*

YC: Yes that is right. I guess we just do it at the same time. We have no choice. We have to figure out our own solutions; sometimes it is painful to work through. We are busy and really drained and already serving our community. Sometimes, you run out of energy to find a solution, we just carry on for a while until things get desperate; then we come back to trying to find a way to move forward together.

We are more comfortable with a clear hierarchical structure. Sometimes we want to give up and say, "Just put this policy or this decision in place and we will just have to live with it." In my personal view, because we are operating in diversity it is dangerous to apply only one black and white policy or one way of deciding. It is very animated when you debate and are guided by the principle that we will arrive at the right solution. Most of us grew up in a very hierarchical structure with very clear laws to guide us. We sometimes want to give up. "Let's go for that. Then whoever isn't happy with it, too bad!" There is the temptation to do that. I don't think we have found the best way yet. We just know this is one of our core struggles.

JE: *How do you balance things out to build community amongst the workers? Do you have social events or educational events?*

YC: I think we would do much better if we had more time for joy. We are so serious as a group because we are struggling so much. We are looking and addressing difficult issues in the community on the one hand, and on the other side, we are knocking on doors working with the system trying to affect change. Change comes slowly. We feel like we are running out of time. We want to really make an optimum impact in different areas. We are just too serious. It is not helpful for our relationships. Whenever we come together it is about problems we have to solve.

JE: *Do you still have requests from other women who want to join the co-op? Have you had to set a number on how many members you can have?*

YC: I think a time might come when we have to think about a number or a whole new different way to structure ourselves. There are always people interested in our work and wanting to join us. Some people really understand the complexity of the work and the uniqueness and they are excited because they have this belief in higher ideals. Others join because it is looked upon as an employment opportunity and a way to serve the community, which is very noble. We are now being very thoughtful, even reflecting on our own motivation in terms of bringing more colleagues on. It is actually very important that we are ethical in the sense that we really help colleagues come into our work who really understanding the complexity. It is not just a paying job; it is way more than that. It is about affecting change in the system, it is about taking on the challenge of dealing with the dual tension of being a worker and an owner. It is way more complicated than one might want to take on if you are just interested in an employment situation.

JE: *Are there any models that have been helpful for you in all your challenges? What are your sources of support?*

YC: We have some colleagues who are able to help us. Locally we have a colleague who is a co-op developer. She was the one who got us started over 10 years ago. Whenever we are conscious of a problem, we bring her in. But we are limited in resources. I don't think we are the only ones. Most co-ops don't have enough resources to bring in paid technical people. So we only do it when we are desperate, which might not be the best. We also have a partnership with CEDNet in Victoria.

They are trying to understand the unique challenges around immigrant led co-ops. We are one of their case examples, so they try and help us look for information and other sources of inspiration, because sometimes our heads are down and we don't have time to look up and see who else is similar to us. In fact, it was a colleague at CEDNet who helped us understand that we are probably more like a social co-op.

JE: *You said you wouldn't describe yourself as a developer but what is your role within the organization? How do you help develop the co-op?*

YC: Right now, I am the Co-executive Director. I was originally the project co-coordinator when we were still a pilot project with Public Health.

Because most of my colleagues are really involved in their work, my job has been to try and support them. I look for funding, secure contracts wherever I can, and bring out some of the co-op development issues. My colleague who jobshares with me, she was originally from the Philippines and has a bit of exposure to co-ops from there. She has been leading some of the internal co-op development processes. My work is primarily management, promotion, and then a bit more intuitive co-op development.

JE: *We are trying to learn about the effective practices that help support the growth of new co-ops. As you have mentioned, your co-op is quite unique. Can you tell me some of the lessons you've learned which might be helpful to other co-ops who either are going down the same road, or want to go down the same path as the Multicultural Health Brokers Co-op?*

YC: I think each co-op is different. It would be to our benefit to have some resources to support someone for a period of time to be the internal co-op developer whose time and devotion is put towards the internal development. There are at least four or five dimensions to a co-op that really need that day-to-day attentiveness. It is not just about the governance, the operational structure, or financing. It is very much about human relations. It is about human development. That is usually overlooked when external resources are brought in. It would be wonderful if each co-op actually had resources, perhaps in the initial stages, to have someone focus specifically on the co-op development side who deeply understands and is part of the co-op. Then over time, give this person more and more capacity among the others, so that it is a kind of shared knowledge and perspective. Ideally, we would like to come to a place where every member of the co-op has equal technical know how. It still requires someone who has the time and focused energy to be working and to nurture the growth of the co-op. I do sense there is a need to hire someone – who is internal – and who has the time to study, learn, look at inspiration, and bring it back to help us find unique solutions to work with the members and help them. That would be wonderful.

It is a little bit different from the current model where we import a colleague into the co-op to help us empathetically. That is useful at times. But that person who comes in might cause more problems because they don't really understand and we feel like time is wasted. He or she brings some thinking that this is the way, and because we are not very familiar, we accept it. Then after a while, we realize, "Hey, that isn't what we were looking for." We had that experience, so I think we need internal indigenous attention. I think one might have to really live within the co-op in order to be a truly relevant developer. I mean at different stages of the co-op development, like in the early stage, you would need an external coach and a guide. But after a while it becomes important that the internal development support is actually rooted in a lived experience to know who we are.

JE: *How are you set up as a co-op? Is most everyone in the organization a service provider or do you have different roles?*

YC: All of us adopt the same practice, which is really the Multicultural Health Brokering Practice, which happens to be multi-level. On the one hand, not counting myself, each of my colleagues are frontline deliverers in the community, they are also at times community developers – bringing families together, supporting leaders to work on issues, and inevitably involved in some activities that help mainstream institutions gain more understanding and explore the need for change in those institutions. That is what we have come to call the Multicultural Health Brokering Practice.

It is a lot of work, but they are all interconnected. In fact, operating on those levels is what gives us the hopefulness to carry on. If we just work on the level of the front line with individual families, we see the issues reoccurring over and over again. If we didn't engage ourselves in other levels of intervention - either community development or systemic change – I think we would drown in despair. It is almost a requirement to be involved in those other areas. We are searching for higher levels of change so that we hopefully won't be trapped in dealing with the same issues ten years from now.

We have a board. The board consists of members/workers. It is the same people stepping into different roles. But in administration, we are desperately under-resourced.

JE: *Would it be good to have more administration?*

YC: That is where the actually interesting part is and also where the challenge lies. One of the reasons we don't have a very strong administrative/management team is that most sources of funding, whether it is government or non-government, don't look at that aspect of support for the co-operative. They are willing to pay for frontline service providers and then minimal support for core programming. That is why we have a small team, it is a reflection of the reality of the funding world.

JE: *How are the relations internally between the board/members and yourself as admin/management support? Are you satisfied with how that has been set up and how it has evolved?*

YC: We are in a growth stage; I don't think we have actually found our own expression of how these relationships should be played out. In our first few years it was very hard for our board members, because they were also frontline colleagues and their time was more on that. But now in the last few years, we have colleagues who are working on the board and trying hard to learn the skills. It is going better, but we are still figuring this out. Again it is this core internal dynamic when making a statement or engaging in decision-making - how much of it comes from a place of a worker versus an owner versus a board member. It is a difficult place.

I don't know if there are any processes or tools out there, but maybe it is an area we need development in. It's a lot about nurturing the right relationships within a co-op. There is so much that needs to be done around internal development. I think of all of the organizational types that exist, co-ops require us to be more spiritually mature as human beings than any other organizational format. That takes support and I don't think too many of us realize once you become a member of a co-operative it is about committing yourself to spiritual growth. Because it is about a shared community, it is not about singularly, myself doing well, it is about us all doing well. That part I hadn't seen much support or existing technical resources or even processes for. I think we have a gap in the sector around that. It is really very much about self-leadership development. It is not just about the traditional organizational leadership development, it is about self-leadership for a collective purpose.

JE: *Well said! Could you tell me more about why you went with the co-op model?*

YC: As a group some of us lived together and worked together informally for about 3-4 years before we decided on registering as a formal organization. It was clear to us that because we were a culturally diverse group, we would need a democratic structure to encourage us to look at diversity in a democratic context. We would be bringing forward issues, perspectives, and hopes from our own communities and we needed to learn to negotiate with each other to come up with the right decisions. I don't think any other organizational structure would fit. Also, we are dealing ultimately with social injustice issues and no organizational structure is more explicit than the co-op to do that work.

Now, whether we should have been a worker co-op or some other form of co-op is actually an interesting question. Maybe we would have done things a little different if we had adopted a different type of co-op model. But we knew from the beginning that, unfortunately in our communities, gainful meaningful employment is a core problem – a problem in all immigrant and refugee communities. It was our hope - and it has been our learning - that this will generate economic well-being for ourselves and eventually for others. That is why we chose a workers co-op. We could have been a social co-op, but that is something to reflect on.

JE: *Can you tell me about the relationship between yourselves as a co-op and the Public Health Department? Are they still involved and has that been a healthy relationship? Is there anything you have learned about that relationship that might be helpful to other people starting co-operatives?*

YC: There are two things we have learned. Public Health is the first sector where we feel we gained victory because we have a contractual relationship with them. They continue to offer us funding to extend the services to our communities, but the funding has not increased over the years, even though our work has evolved. The system is structured in such a way that does not operate from the principle of equity. They have only this budget and this is how they divvy it up. They have not responded to emerging issues and to the increased volume that we have brought forth to them. On the one hand, we are successful in that they trust us to do the work, but they have not responded to our changes and intent. We need them to have more attention and provide more resources in our communities, but our efforts haven't actually made a lot of difference. So we are basically successful, in that at least the contract is there annually with the same amount every year, but we haven't achieved what we set out to achieve - which is affect change.

JE: *Do you receive any support from organizations in the co-op sector?*

YC: Occasionally, every so often we get a bit of funding here and there. I feel we haven't been very successful in having a supportive relationship in the co-op sector. Over the years we have gotten some support from The Co-operators and the Canadian Workers Co-op Federation in small amounts, but other than that we haven't gotten much support. There is a provincial co-op association, but they too have difficulty financially. We are so envious of our colleagues in B.C. where the credit unions are so involved; in Alberta that is not the case.

JE: *We are interested in hearing about co-ops that are models others can learn from. From our conversation, I feel there is a lot of richness around your experience that would be beneficial to others. Thank you!*

YC: Thank you!

The International Women's Catering Co-op: Interview with Lee Fuge

The International Women's Catering Co-op is composed of a culturally diverse group of women who have come together to prepare, sell, and provide a wide variety of ethnic foods at local farmer's markets and other community venues in Victoria, B.C. The co-op dates back to the mid-1990s when South Island Women for Economic Survival and The Intercultural Association came together to support the efforts of a group of immigrant women eager to start a business cooking their favourite ethnic foods. Since then, the co-op has operated as a part-time, seasonal business with members originally from countries as different as Ecuador, Iraq, India, Ethiopia, and Holland. Working out of the kitchen at a local community centre, the co-op members make such delicacies as empanadas, buraq, potato chap, fatyir, samosas, pakoras, and a variety of curries.

Lee Fuge is both a member of the co-op and a co-op developer working with several other small co-ops and community enterprises in Victoria. In the interview I did with Lee Fuge in the fall of 2006, she described several aspects of her work with the co-op. Below are excerpts from that interview which offer insights on the developer's role in working with a group who does not have access to major financial resources and face other challenges in society, yet who collectively have skills they can utilize to generate an income – under the right conditions. The excerpts highlight ways the developer can maximize the strengths in the group, find and provide the necessary complimentary resources, promote the social capital of the group, and adopt a "small scale" approach where "a little" can go a long way.

LF: I am a member of the International Women's Catering Co-op (IWCC) and have been for the last eight and a half years, since its inception. IWCC is a worker co-op and is a multi-ethnic co-op of women whose competency with English language and numeracy is, for some, fairly limited. My competency at cooking is fairly limited – so we are a good match. Early on there was an agreement struck that I would look after administrative kinds of things and be the interface with bureaucracy and potential clients. In the last couple of years some of the other members of the co-op have stepped forward and taken on some of those responsibilities. From the developer's side, there are a lot of things that are needed to make the co-op work that come from people other than myself. It's a matter of recognizing who is the appropriate person to take a leadership role in a particular situation and everybody being comfortable with that.

I don't do training session or workshops for the co-op because I think there are people who have the skills to do those things and it is not my strength. I do recognize when there's an opportunity for that sort of training and we do talk through a lot of things. In the first couple of years, we did some co-op development work, but we haven't done any recently.

JE: *Does that mean that they have a grasp of the co-op model now and so it is not needed, or you just have not had time to do more workshops?*

LF: I think at an intuitive level most of the women have a grasp of what co-operation is and what the co-op is about. I think most of the women have come from cultures that are much more co-operative than our own and it's been fairly easy for them to come together. In the kitchen there's the intimacy of being in a really confined work space, but even with language barriers, they are able to produce to a certain standard and in a certain time frame. That kind of experience together over the years has brought everybody to a fairly clear understanding of the value of co-operation.

JE: *If your role is to focus more on the business and keep that going, what is your role as a co-op developer and how does this work as a co-operative rather than a community business enterprise?*

LF: The catering co-op is a seasonal, part-time business. Most of our business occurs in the market season, which runs from the beginning of May to the end of October. We do special events and catering jobs in that time frame. If we were evaluated purely on business results, people would probably discount us because we basically have enough cash flow that we can pay everyone, get the equipment that we need, and have enough money to start the next year. We have relationships in the community that give us access to space and other resources on an as-needed basis, so we're not carrying large ongoing overhead.

In the sense of a business that is driven by the bottom-line, we are not a business's business. But I think the value for the people who are members of the co-op and the other people who work with us is that over the nine years of the co-op's existence, through exposing the broader community to the cultural foods, the women feel that they're getting a part of themselves out to the community. So it's hard to describe, but when people come to the first market of the season and they are saying, "We've been waiting all winter," that's pretty valuable. The business contributes to the psychological well-being of the women who are participating and it's that psychological well-being that is as important as the money. That sounds like a very soft and mushy way to describe what is essentially a small-scale co-operative catering business.

JE: *I hear what you are saying as the value or benefit of the co-operative, but how do you see yourself as a co-op developer in this arrangement?*

LE: In my particular case, and I'm thinking very specifically here to Victoria and a community I've become very familiar with, I think part of the value I have to the catering co-op is I'm well-connected. I know where a lot of resources are. I know a lot of the right people to call if something should come up. I'm familiar with the political systems and I'm familiar with the food and agricultural communities. That package of who I am and how I am connected has proven to be of some value to the co-op.

JE: *As a member and as a developer in this situation, how do you work with the status difference of who you are in our Canadian society and the power differential?*

LE: There is always the challenge of how do you work with that and dispel it so that there is a way that everyone can relate without there being a hierarchy within the organization. When you are on the ground day-to-day it's more of a problem, I think, than when you're the consultant brought in to do a specific project, because you are given a lot of authority, almost by default, certainly when you're dealing with a co-op whose membership is not comfortable with the dominant culture and you're the interface with the dominant culture. That's been a real learning experience for me and it goes on. If someone from the media comes to us and asks about doing a piece on the catering co-op, I usually try not to be involved in the piece, or if I am involved, I always make sure that two or three of the women are there and speaking more loudly than I am. That's just one way that the collective aspect of the co-op can be put forward and the collective ownership and responsibility – both psychological and physical – can be conveyed to the community. Even though my mother is half-Dutch and half-Japanese and my father was of mixed race, I pass as a white woman. Having a white woman stand there, talking on behalf of the International Women's Catering Co-op, doesn't seem very appropriate. So for a number of reasons, I go to great lengths to ensure that if we're given those opportunities, that it's some of the other women who are doing those kinds of things. Having those opportunities has, I think, helped the women who have participated get beyond some of their hesitation of dealing with the dominant culture.

JE:Thinking about critical issues that contribute to the success of new co-ops, what factors do you think have made a difference to the success of the catering co-op?

LF: I think something that is missing in the system is the valuing of the small bits and how their connection can be more significant than the larger pieces. For instance, most people when they're thinking about a business start-up think that you need a significant amount of capital, you need formal planning, you need a lot of resources. But with the catering co-op, it is a matter of working with what's there and trying to leverage what's there into something greater so you don't need the "something greater" up front.

In its first year of operation, the co-op received a grant of $5,500 from Rising Tide and it has never had a bank loan, has no debt, and has no huge investment from any one member. We work with the Fairfield Community Association (FCA) – we pay a monthly rental for the storage of our equipment and we pay a per diem rental when we're using the kitchen. We also do a trade with FCA - we cook for a couple of community events because they give us a discount rate on the kitchen. If we had gone the more conventional route and leased a kitchen space and bought or leased equipment, we would have been in a situation where we would have had to operate every day, which was not something that most of the women wanted to do. We would have had a lot of debt, and we would not have been able to sell at the Moss Street Market, which is the main way we get into the community. The market has a policy that if you have a store front you're not allowed to sell there. We would have missed a lot of opportunities to connect with the community had we simply had a storefront. We also would have stood a very good chance of going out of business in the first five years because that is what often happens to small businesses, and restaurants and food businesses are more vulnerable than most others. Even thought the co-op hasn't provided the level of income that some of the members would have liked, the way it has evolved has fit in with other aspects of their lives, met a certain set of needs, and provided the members a certain status in the community that they might not have had if they were not involved in the co-op.

Typically, there is not much in the way of resources for small co-ops and a lot of co-ops don't succeed because they run out of resources of one kind or another, which is unfortunate and something I would like to see addressed within the co-op sector. There is also a lot of talk about promoting co-ops for different cultural groups. I think it is a matter of looking at the individual situation, seeing what people want, and whether the co-op model is actually something that is workable, considering their expectations and desires.

JE: I'm hearing a "small is beautiful" and "small can really work" theme around the importance of valuing other needs the co-op can meet - not just the bottom line. Thank you.

Chapter Fourteen

Co-operative Development on First Nations Reserves in Saskatchewan

April Roberts

In 2005, I began a contract with the First Nations Agriculture Council of Saskatchewan (FNACS) to deliver a pilot programme developing co-operatives on reserves. As I had no previous experience with co-ops, I knew nothing about developing, teaching, promoting, or providing advice about the traditional co-op model. Even though I did not have this experience, the lessons learnt from my previous work were useful in this new venture. The challenges that lay before me were: to develop an understanding of the traditional co-op model, communicate that understanding to diverse audiences in a way that was understandable, and find commonality between the needs in the community and ways the co-op model could contribute in addressing those needs. Being aware of the prevalent issues on reserves and drawing on other work experiences helped me to identify how the co-op model might fit on reserves.

The initial intent of the co-op programme was to provide assistance in meeting communal goals and objectives, while assisting with creating small agricultural businesses that could be a means to support First Nation communities in becoming more self-reliant through the lands.

It has now been two years since I began working in the co-op sector. I continue to work with groups on reserves to develop innovative ideas for utilizing the resources available, provide on-going support, facilitate access to technical information, and act as an advocate upon request. In all this work, I find I need to continuously redefine my role as a "developer" to meet the changing needs of the diverse groups and communities that I meet along the way.

I feel I have exceeded my own expectations in this work by helping several groups adapt a model that was initially intended for rural communities, introducing some First Nations groups to the co-op sector, assisting communities to participate in self-reliance activities, and helping to promote another tool that can provide additional support towards capacity building in First Nations' communities.

It is my hope that this article will provide some guidance and insight on the stumbling blocks and the possibilities for introducing the traditional co-op model on reserves, thus lending some of my personal experience to future co-op developers wanting to assist First Nation communities in developing co-operatives.

Getting Oriented

In order to work effectively within a First Nation community, one must understand the history of the community and be sure not to generalize First Nation issues that are on reserve; in other words, assume that each reserve is unique – no one likes to be stereotyped. Some of the historical events that have taken place, such as policies that were imposed on First Nations, have had an impact on current generations and will continue to affect future generations of First Nations people. Prior to the individual bands creating their own governance systems in the past few decades, the government policies meant that First Nations people residing on reserve were to adhere to regulations set out in the Indian Act. These restrictive regulations included such things as any Indian wanting to leave the reserve had to get permission from the Indian Agent. The Agent also controlled financial transactions such as selling and purchasing cattle, grain, a load of hay, firewood, lime, charcoal, produce, and buying groceries or clothes. Basic needs were denied and inequality was prevalent in daily dealings.

These policies were enforced into the 1980s; however, the residue of the regulations still negatively impacts the ability of First Nation communities to collectively renew as a nation, stunting their capacity for economic growth.

FNACS was developed out of a need to strengthen the stance of First Nation farmers and producers on primary production, processing, and marketing in the wild rice industry and intensive livestock operations in bison and beef. FNACS is developing a First Nation themed approach to marketing and targeting the organic and natural foods market. It also promotes and encourages the development of agro-forestry, special forestry products, and comprehensive agriculture training and development for youth and adults.

As part of the FNACS commitment to developing a strong, viable, and sustainable agricultural sector for on- and off-reserve, status Indians in the province of Saskatchewan, the Council offers technical support to new and emerging First Nation managed on-reserve agriculture co-operatives. Small businesses allow producers to participate and become self-reliant and sustaining, as opposed to being competitors in larger markets where they have to meet greater demands. Co-operatives bring members together into one large family (supporting the idea of kinship). Shared knowledge and experiences are encouraged amongst co-ops so they can be supported by other communal co-ops with similar issues and strengths.

Due to all the historical changes that have occurred, agricultural co-ops on reserves can by no means generate extreme wealth. These changes have hindered First Nations people in their ability to compete on a large scale against companies or other farmers; there has been a lack of support, people have limited knowledge of working with the lands, they have no equity, and have little participation and experience to draw on within the agricultural sector.

Agricultural co-ops do posses the ability to build capacity; they can help producers, families, and individuals develop practical skills for themselves; members acquire agricultural and co-operative experience to pass on to future generations; co-ops provide members with opportunities for hands-on training; they help people work together; and they contribute holistically to families and communities - all through utilizing a resource that is readily available on reserves - the land.

Some Essential Considerations

I have worked within First Nation communities since completing my post-secondary education in 2002. Working with communities to create co-ops has been insightful and somewhat challenging at times. It has certainly given me a better understanding of the dynamics within First Nation communities at various levels, such as political and communal. There are many things that I have learned and wished someone could have told me when I first started this work.   In reflecting on my experience, I have set out some of those insights in hopes that it may benefit other developers and co-op members

Protocol

Do not assume that all First Nations groups, or communities for that matter, are the same. Each group has been through their own issues, whether it is political, personal, or communal. Understand that although you as the consultant or co-operative developer have been asked to go into a community, your job would not be there unless they had requested your assistance. Do not be too proud or too knowledgeable, the group always has valuable feedback and ideas that can contribute to the process.

Assumptions

Leave your assumptions and "wondering" at the door. Do not assume that you know the community dynamics or needs because you know someone from a neighboring community or have read a few books. The difference from one First Nation's community to another and one individual to another should be compared to a fingerprint, no two are the same!

Process

Keep consistent in your process when attempting to assist a community. You will not have the ability to determine an exact course of action until you go into the community and clarify the viability of an idea that has been generated by the group. However, that does not mean the official process cannot be relayed, such as informing the group or narrowing down the ideas, sourcing the community and its neighbouring communities for support networks, developing a basic structure, establishing the membership, completing the forms, and beginning to identify the processes involved after the business has been formed.

Ensure that the group is completely aware of the process involved in opening a co-op. At the same time, take care while informing the group not to overwhelm them with information. This is where the developer needs to ensure that everyone is speaking the "same" language. Even though you know what you are saying, and it can simply be read, this does not mean that everyone has the capacity to think like you, nor should they be expected to given that all adults learn differently; this is a known fact that should be remembered at all times.

Planning the Business

Do a group inventory (training assets, linkages that could benefit the group), narrow down viable long-term and short-term goals (business plan). When developing the plan, ensure all areas are considered that directly contribute to the co-op (e.g. the market options, economic planning, risk management, board training, membership training, succession planning, professional development).

After-Care

Providing after-care is an essential part of supporting a newly incorporated or developing co-op. Consider that they will not have the initial capacity or networks to stabilize themselves for the first few years. In providing support the co-op developer should be prepared to offer resources and information "tools" in areas that would help the group make educated decisions, such as business planning, vision and goal setting, training options, and financial resources (loans, programmes). Other areas of importance might be providing a list and profile of information on other co-ops, the co-op sector, and other organizations, in particular in this scenario, agricultural organizations that provide facilitator services.

Advocacy

Even after providing all the above information and awareness, advocacy is an activity that is important to ensure that the concerns and voices of the developing co-ops are heard. Advocating on behalf of the co-ops is an important role the developer plays. This means taking the concerns, observations, and new developments of the co-ops to other organizations that might strengthen their goals; thus contributing to the overall success of a group and what they have set out to do.

Lessons Learned along the Way

What do I wish someone had told me about co-op development?

I am grateful for all that I have experienced on this journey of learning about co-ops. There have been many challenges and sometimes self-inflicted stress, because I attempted to accomplish what an experienced co-op developer might do, such as advocating concerns and addressing them. These are actions that cannot be achieved by one person alone against the large industries, companies, and challenges of navigating bureaucracy.

What did I not adopt soon enough as a practice that I now use?

When it comes to helping a community or group identify their goals and discuss their dreams, time has no bearing. Do not rush a group or assume that they know exactly what it is they want to do or that all is going to be accomplished in a few meetings. Be prepared to go back several times to complete visioning exercises or to reiterate information that was already stated. Rome was not built in a day! After every meeting, make sure everyone is on the same page and understands the overall group objectives; clarity now will save a lot of time and frustration in the future. Understand that the group is still in a developmental stage for the first year or two after start-up and do not presume to think that they do not need you for on-going support. You were there to help them start-up and you should be there to help smooth out the bumps in the road along the way.

What did I do that I would not do again?

I would not take a lot of literature, pages of information, and power point presentations that are too wordy or too long out to communities. Ultimately, if I cannot read the information and completely process it to deliver without it being in front of me, then I have no business taking it into communities, expecting that they read it completely, and have a good understanding when they are finished. Developing a level of trust, patience, and common ground is important to any process. If you are willing to go into a community to help develop an economic strategy, leave your "time piece" at home and be willing to talk for hours to answer questions, address concerns, and just communicate in an effort to build a relationship.

Unrealistic Expectations of the Group

It can be challenging to address the unrealistic expectations of the group. Often the potential co-op members think that the co-op will be a money-maker – this is an assumption I encountered on different occasions. It is helpful to address this assumption right at the beginning so that everyone is clear. Those wanting to start a co-op need to realize that creating a co-op is a means to better utilize the resources that they have and by no means is it meant as a way to yield financial wealth on reserves - at least not for the first 5 years. The potential is there, but it is a process that could take 10 years to establish. For example, in New Zealand, the Maori groups developed a 10-year succession plan. It did take 10 years for some groups to have noticeable growth economically; whereas, some groups experienced internal growth as a family.

Take Time to Get to Know the Community

Keep in mind that understanding the dynamics prevalent in the community, being sensitive to the community's needs, and respectful of the needs of particular people involved is very important.

It is always good to have a general understanding of the community when assisting with the start-up of a co-op. As one gets to know the dynamics of the community, one can begin to understand the personalities of the potential members who would like to create the co-op. The co-op developer needs to play many roles and have various skills, such as that of a "mind reader" being aware of body language, having the ability to read a room, the ability to work the group so they can discuss their potential. You are an information outlet, at times you will need to be a motivational speaker, and the list does go on.

Redefining Success

Remember that what you (and others) view as successful may not be what the group views as success. For instance, if you are walking into a community that has limited resources and little employment capacity, just providing a few people with an opportunity to learn about the mechanisms that are involved when establishing a business, or learning something as simple as growing a garden, can be a major accomplishment. Keep in mind that these things may not have been something that individuals would have thought of participating in if it were not for the co-op. The guidelines for thinking about success have to be redefined within the particular context. Celebrate each step, they may not realize that simply taking that first step is a great success.

Your Social Footprint

It is not enough to just walk into a community with the intention of incorporating a co-op. This initiative is something that may enhance the quality of a group or perhaps decrease their ability to contribute to the community. Your actions set off a "ripple effect." Once you set foot in the community, you have started a ripple and you must be aware of what kind of ripples you leave behind when you are absent. The future co-op members have to live in these communities; you do not.

A Word on Resources

In Saskatchewan there are a limited number of sectored organizations and/ or businesses that provide co-op assistance; especially assistance that can be delivered with an awareness of First Nation needs on reserve. However, the resources that are currently available for co-ops are helpful and representatives of various organizations have not only provided information, they have assisted with training needs. For example, the Saskatchewan Co-operative Association (SCA) assisted by providing Co-op Basics Training; a service that the First Nation co-ops were very grateful to receive. However, while some resources are available, there are limited resources within Saskatchewan specifically for smaller co-ops; contracting co-op developers has been used as a way to address this need.

Partnerships

In areas of Saskatchewan, partnerships need to be created between First Nations co-ops and off-reserve organizations, some specifically in the agricultural sector. Partnerships with established organizations could assist with enhancing co-op members' skills and providing useful sector information, such as marketing regulations or potential markets for their agricultural products. For example, where could berry co-ops sell their goods without having to get the product federally inspected? This might mean that the group would need to sell to another community or reserve, thus limiting market prospects. Other organizations may have experience, contacts, and insights that would be helpful to the new co-ops.

Over-Reliance on Government

Total dependence on the government as a financial resource does not allow for self-reliance. The intent is that those involved in the co-op project can eventually move away from dependence on government monies into a state of independence as a collective group.

Raising Capital

Raising the capital that is needed to get underway can be a challenge. On reserves not all people have their own land so they can't use it as collateral. They may also not own machinery. This makes it difficult to raise the capital required to purchase machinery and accommodate other expenses that surface in starting agricultural co-ops. On reserves there are various obstacles that are intergenerational regardless of occupation. Another challenge is that First Nation bands do not technically own the land, it is held in trust by the Crown. This means that in order to sell or purchase land, the groups must first approach Indian and Northern Affairs Canada (INAC).

Government Policies that Complicate Starting First Nations' Co-ops

While the Co-operatives Act is written in such a way as to cover co-op start-ups in many settings and sectors, it is not well suited for reserves and the regulations that govern reserves. One of the complications is that certain aspects of life on reserves are covered under Federal jurisdiction, while others are under Provincial domain. For example, the lands are federal, but the co-op act is provincial. Where do agricultural co-ops on reserve lands fit? There has not been a level of government that has stepped up to say that they are willing to provide assistance to co-ops that are created on federal lands.

Conclusion

The initial objectives of the FNACS programme was to promote, educate, and provide technical assistance for the purpose of incorporating new on-reserve agricultural co-op. Throughout this learning experience, information has been compiled to help identify the possibilities and obstacles for creating co-ops on reserve. Over these last two years, I have spent a lot of time making presentations to farmers, individuals, chiefs, and councils in order to assist groups in making educated decisions about creating co-ops on reserves. Some projects have progressed to a second stage of development; others have not. As I have tried to convey in this article, some problems are cultural due to generations of imposed policies and some challenges are structural, such as that of federal versus provincial jurisdictions. Starting any new co-op can be challenging, but co-ops on reserves have particular hurdles that must be overcome. However, encouraging co-operative ventures can have many social benefits and eventually economic benefits that must be reviewed in light of the particular context outlined in this article. For the co-op developer, being informed about these challenges, being aware of some of the skills and resources you will need, and being mindful of one's own assumptions in taking on this work can help one be more effective in working with all parties involved in the start-up stage of new on-reserve co-ops.

Section Five: Co-operating into the Future

Chapter Fifteen

Blood and Oxygen: Navigating the Valley of Death

Peter Hough

This is a little paper about the biggest challenge in co-op development: how to survive the first three years! Every year approximately
10% of all businesses fail. Businesses in the first three years comprise
the greatest proportion of these failures. Two things are important to note.
First, every year all types and ages of businesses fail regardless of past performance, and secondly, once a business is past the first three years it has
statistically the same chances of failure as all other businesses regardless of
age.[1] So three things are clear: 1) it is not easy to succeed, 2) you cannot rest
on past laurels, and 3) surviving years 1-3 is crucial if the co-op is going to
be around for the long term.

Because this paper is about post start-up of new co-ops, it is primarily
addressed to the co-op entrepreneurs - members, directors, managers, and
staff – that must worker together on a day-to-day basis to make the co-op
a success. It is assumed that although a co-op development mentor may be
present at times, the co-op entrepreneurs are usually facing their immediate

---

1 Paul Ormerod, *Why Most Things Fail* (London, UK: Faber and Faber Ltd., 2005).

choices alone. For co-op development facilitators/mentors, the suggestions contained here may be used as a guide for training and strategic interventions in the pre and post start-up phase.

To begin, it is only fair to emphasize that no matter how hard you try and no matter how smart your work, there is no guarantee of success. Each co-op faces many particular challenges rooted in particular circumstances. These challenges unfold within a broader reality, of which we always have limited knowledge and which can and will influence the outcomes of our activities in ways we do not expect and that are beyond our sphere of control or influence. To have a hope of success, co-op entrepreneurs must constantly expand the limits of their knowledge while institutionalizing and incorporating it into the day-to-day life of the co-op in flexible and effective ways. This approach provides a foundation that can help to minimize the effect of unforeseen changes in a given context or unexpected results of members' actions. In light of this, move forward with respect and humility for the work of yourself and your colleagues regardless of the outcome.

Although there are guides that can assist, it is only in the doing that one gains the experience required to become skilled and knowledgeable in the activity. Co-op development is not adventure tourism but rather real adventure. You are going to go where no one else has gone or can go. Yes, others may have taken similar adventures and you can learn from them, but ultimately you are going to face "new" conditions, experiences, and challenges. Typically, a co-op development facilitator is a guide who can assist you in starting your venture but cannot accompany you all the time or for the whole way. In the beginning you may seek guidance in the decisions you have to make but this is your (ad)venture and the decisions are your responsibility.

In this context, the greatest ongoing challenges are: to determine what are the most important priorities, what needs to be accomplished in order to create a sustainable co-op, and how one ensures that resources are secured and allocated to achieve these priorities. Here we are in a unique situation where there is no simple way to determine priorities and where time and resources always seem (usually are) less than are required to cover all the bases. So what to do?

Stick to the life and death issues – cash and member commitment! Organize and allocate resources based on whether the activity will enhance or deplete these assets; most activities do one or the other. Without both healthy cash flow and strong member commitment and participation the co-op will die.

It seems simple enough, if you run out of cash and can't pay your bills, loan commitments, wages, or buy supplies, etc., you will have to close and you are likely to lose whatever material and financial assets you have acquired, as well as your members' investments. If you lose member commitment or fail to develop it (a common scenario for a start-up co-op) the co-op will die as a co-op, even if by some chance it still continues to function as an enterprise. Its chances of having the strength to face adversity will be severely compromised.

These two assets are complementary, interdependent, and facilitate the development of one another. Neither cash nor member commitment are enough on their own, except in the unusual circumstance where a co-op has no requirement for any resources beyond the members' commitment (for example: a baby-sitting exchange co-op where parents exchange services without any financial compensation).

Committed members provide cash (members' shares) to the co-op; they reduce their personal cash demands to a minimum, if required, for short periods of time; they work collaboratively with others to put in place the required systems for success; and they help confront the many expected and unexpected challenges the co-op faces. Core members take personal and collective responsibility for the things that need to be done. Those who have the best understanding of the co-op processes realize the co-op has a life of its own with its own necessities; they realize these needs must be met if the co-op is to meet the members' needs and they get on with it.

Cash allows the co-op to pursue the fundamental goal for which it was created - meeting the specific needs and aspirations identified by the members. Meeting these needs and aspirations, of course, strengthens member commitment. Having cash provides resources for member development, education, training, etc., which in turn provides the members with a realistic understanding of their co-op and what it needs to do to succeed. A strong cash position is a continuing sign to members that the co-op is doing well and encourages members to think long-term in their relationship to the co-op. This long-term thinking ties the members' future to the co-op and increases their determination and commitment to develop the co-op.

Pre–Start-up Phase: The Ideal and Real World

Before beginning the specific reflections on cash and member commitment, I will briefly focus on the pre–start-up phase. In an ideal world, the key steps in an effective co-op development initiative can be laid out, the resources secured, and the necessary time found to do the work thoroughly. The members' vision for the co-op is developed with the participation of all, from the first glimmers to a clear guide for the specific proposed operational realization. Ideally, all members understand Co-op Principles and Values, their specific co-op's needs, and their roles in meeting them. The necessary capital is secured based upon a clear financial model of the co-op that highlights the key financial relationships, and it is a ready tool to project the consequences of actual results and proposed alternatives. All in all, in an ideal situation, member commitment is strong, the members' expectations are realistic, and the resources are at hand.

In practice, the actual world is usually far messier. Even when the ideal approach is known and appreciated it is often not realized due to circumstances. All the resources needed to carry out the work may not be available. Project timing is often driven by potential members needing a solution now, the closing of real or perceived windows of opportunity, and the normal and often good human impatience to get on with it. Some capital may have been secured but not quite as much capital as is truly needed. There have likely been surprises and questions about fellow members' behaviour and commitment. Judgments likely have been made about key assumptions based upon limited and inadequate information.

In light of this, my reflections assume the co-op entrepreneurs will not have everything neatly in place, they will get surprises - some good but many bad, they will have challenges in all aspects of the endeavour, they will experience difficulties agreeing upon what needs to be done and when a task or step should be completed. They will be creating and learning as they go.

In these challenging circumstances, the members need clear criteria for sifting through the many competing demands on the co-op's limited resources. I suggest recognition of the overarching importance that cash and member commitment have to the success of the co-op can provide the needed criteria to mediate the many, likely conflicting, desires and proposed alternatives of individual members; not a small task in most start-up situations. In making a decision they can ask, "Does this particular demand on co-op resources support the development of member commitment and help generate cash, or is it peripheral to these crucial goals?" If it is peripheral and will deplete the co-op's capacity to reach these goals, it should be set aside.

Cash

In thinking about cash, there are two sub-priorities: generating cash and managing cash.

Generating Cash

Generating cash includes initial and ongoing capitalization (e.g. equity, debt, grants, operating lines, etc.) and securing operational cash (e.g. making sales of goods and services the co-op produces and getting paid for them). Cash is also "generated" (i.e. preserved) by not spending it and by limiting and/or reducing operational expenses.

Managing cash includes knowing how much you have, how much you are spending and/or must spend, and how quickly and from what sources it is being replenished.

I believe the most important tool that can help generate and manage cash is the creation of a financial model of the business. This will enable you to understand the key financial relationships, and it allows you to evaluate your working assumptions by comparing actual results to the model's projected results. More importantly, once the co-op is started, using the model facilitates evaluation of alternative approaches for the future. This will help address such questions as: What happens if we change prices? Get more debt or more equity? What level of sales generates positive cash flow? What happens if we change members' wages, or prices for members' products, etc.? The failure to consider such issues before making decisions has led many co-ops to fail. Conversely, carrying out this type of analysis has allowed successful co-ops to set clear sales targets and margins required to generate a profit.

Of course, the model cannot do this by itself. The members must understand the model and must provide accurate information for input into the model. The co-op must have effective budgeting, accounting, costing, and bookkeeping systems in place as soon as possible; in the ideal world, before start-up. But if not then, it must be a top priority after start-up.

The next key focus is on the priority areas for generating cash. There are three key areas to consider: capitalization, sales, and collections.

The key question for capitalization is: does the co-op have enough capital to reach the point at which it generates positive cash flow through operations? In other words, when is there more cash coming into the co-op through sales than is leaving the co-op in purchases and expenses? Monitoring this through financial reporting and financial modeling allows the co-op to forecast future cash needs based upon current trends (actuals). The key objective is to identify any potential cash shortfalls well in advance of their occurrence. This is crucial, as it is much easier to get additional outside capital well in advance of the need than to convince capital providers to "ante up" at the crisis point. Once a crisis hits, members often become your only alternative, and even with members, a crisis is a bad time to be asking for money - they may not have it or may not be willing to part with it given the circumstances. This points to the importance of member commitment in a cash crisis. It is also easy to see how poor capitalization or inadequate cash management can undercut this commitment by making unexpected demands for additional member investment and raising the question for the members of the co-op's viability.

In the long-term, sales are expected to be the key source of cash from operations. Depending upon the type of co-op, sales may be an immediate focus (e.g. a retail consumer co-op), or it may be a medium term focus for the co-operative that manufactures or processes products. In manufacturing or in processing co-ops, the facilities must be constructed and be put through a trial period. The co-op has to ensure it has adequate production capacity and meets the quality requirements of the market before significant sales can usually be made. Once selling is underway (assuming pre–start-up has included good market research) it is vital to have clear and realistic sales goals, target markets, and promotion plans. Sales results need to be monitored daily or weekly against forecasts, and the co-op must be prepared to adapt quickly to negative or positive results. Are the original assumptions about market pricing and product acceptance proving to be true? Are there things we thought we knew but didn't? How can we get better market information? It is crucial not to stay fixed upon an original concept if it isn't working and to always be looking for, and discovering, new opportunities.

Unless the co-op is being paid in a timely manner for their products or services, making sales won't add to the co-op's cash and will actually reduce it until invoice payments are received. Having clear payment terms and enforcing collection policies and procedures is fundamental to generating cash. The terms, collection policies, and procedures are part of the value package offered by the co-op and must meet the requirements of both the customer and the co-op. It is vital that sales staff understands these policies and are committed to communicating them to the customers - member or non-member.

Cash Management

Cash management is usually thought of as a monitoring process. As noted above, the budgeting, bookkeeping, costing, accounting systems, and procedures are the foundation of cash management. Good records must be kept and the data used with the co-op's financial model to monitor and predict the cash flow of the co-op. This is a foundational priority. It is also a priority that often meets resistance from members who may see it as needless, non-productive, busy work. It is crucial that the board and management take the lead in demonstrating the importance of keeping good records, ensuring data collection systems are truly relevant, and making certain records are as simple as possible to complete.

The two other cash management priorities upon which to focus are purchases (both equipment and service) and controlling expenses.

It is easy to spend money when you have it. In the general excitement and sense of empowerment generated by the start-up, it is sometimes difficult to be disciplined with purchases because there is (or at least often is) significant cash on hand (i.e. the cash needed to cover costs until the co-op generates its own positive cash flow). The problem is that the amount secured is based upon future projections from assumptions that have yet to be proven. You don't really know if the co-op has enough cash. So before you make a purchase you need to ask: "Will it reduce operational expenditures by more than its costs and in what time frame? Will it contribute to increased sales or collections? Or, will it contribute substantively to increasing member commitment, thus generating more member financial participation (i.e. investment from or sales to members, etc.)?" Positive answers should lead to the purchase; negative responses should stop it, or at least delay it until benefits are not exceeded by the financial drain on the co-op. An example of such a decision would be the purchase of a new packaging machine for a production line in a worker co-op. Will the increased efficiency reduce the production costs enough to cover the monthly loan payments required to finance the machine? What effect will it have on worker morale? It may allow for increased wages because of the efficiencies or it may reduce the need for labour. To answer these types of question the financial model can be an invaluable tool.

Controlling and reducing expenses should focus on two areas: how to make the co-op's operations more efficient (i.e. how to produce the co-op's goods or services with fewer resources) and how to reduce the costs of those resources used.

Making the co-op more efficient may involve purchases as noted above. However, many operational improvements can be gained by having members and staff focused as a co-operative team. An active focus on developing an engaged and creative membership and workforce should be a priority. The co-op should always be open to suggestions from any source; suggestions that will be evaluated not based upon who made them, but simply whether or not they can improve the flow of the work. Taking an active and directed focus in this area can lead to large cost reductions during a start-up period for a number of reasons: the co-op staff/membership is just learning how to carry out all the necessary tasks and the first approach is rarely the best; the co-op's level of production (particularly if things are going well) will be constantly increasing and what was effective last week may no longer be the best way to meet the increasing demands; and as members and staff come to realize that there is a true desire and openness to suggestions, the ongoing creative dynamic developed will generate continuous improvements.

Reducing the cost of resources is usually more challenging because it often requires gaining knowledge of factors beyond the co-op's working environment, such as discovering new suppliers or cheaper products which still provide the necessary level of production and quality. However, there are effective ways to do this through reading industry publications, attending industry events, and other research.

Member Commitment

What does the co-op need to do to gain and hold member commitment? I will focus on two areas of member commitment: 1) determining members' needs and expectations, and 2) managing to meet those expectations. At start-up, members clearly have made some level of commitment to the co-op in the belief that it will meet their vision and produce the expected benefits. However, as with the cash on hand, this commitment is usually based upon some clear and some not so clear understandings and assumptions made by the members about the requirements, activities, and expected results of the co-op. The proof will be in the pudding, and members' commitment will be put to the test as the real challenges of making the co-op a long-term success become apparent.

In the ideal world, as noted above, the first step in meeting members' needs and expectations will have taken place during the pre–start-up phase of the co-op's development. The members will have clear expectations of the purposes of the co-op and its practical benefits. They will understand personally why it makes sense to be a member and how they need to support the co-op to make it a success. They will be ready to and expect to participate in the life of the co-op. However, I believe experience shows the commitment of many of the members at this stage of development is very fragile and easily broken.

Members, prior to the co-op start-up, have managed to get by without it. Whether it was buying groceries, finding childcare, or having a job, the members have used other options to meet their needs. These options were likely perceived as inadequate, or else the impulse to start or join the co-op would not have arisen. However, these approaches, their costs, benefits, and familiarity means the members will be comparing the results of the co-op to the prior way of meeting these needs. Will they see an improvement? If it requires more effort and involvement on the members' part, will this effort be equally rewarded?

For the co-op, having the broad vision and goals is fairly straightforward. However, translating vision and goals into detailed operational activities that satisfy the particularities of members' needs is a large next step, and doing this within the financial and other resource constraints is even larger. Here are some examples: The members of a new retail grocery co-op may commit to the co-op because they are convinced the co-operative will provide cheaper groceries and that it will carry all of the items they are used to buying. However, it may turn out that neither of these is the case, particularly in the short term. The competition may undercut prices, and due to resource constraints, the co-op may not have the capacity to have a broad product selection in its early days. Do the members quit buying their preferred products, pay more for them, or do they now make two trips to get groceries, one to their old store and one to the co-op? The new child care co-op may not have the capacity to be open during unexpected shift changes of its members' work schedules. The working conditions and pay in the new worker co-op may not be better than the member's old job, or perhaps the pay is not even enough to cover the workers' regular bills. The workers may feel they are exploiting themselves. It is situations such as these that a co-op faces and must overcome if it is to build and maintain the members' commitment.

There are four priorities upon which to focus:

- Implement systems for receiving and disseminating information from and to members,
- Continue to build an understanding of members needs,
- Build participation in governance and operations with transparent accountability, and
- Continually develop both short-term and long-term operational visions for responding to members' needs (i.e. help members to see where the co-op is going and the progress it is making).

The first element of building member commitment is to create ways for genuine dialogue with members. There needs to be appropriate forums for members to raise questions, make suggestions, and express concerns both individually and collectively. The members need to experience an openness and readiness for dialogue and timely responses. This dialogue, depending upon the co-op, may take place with any or all of frontline staff, managers, directors, or with other members. The members need to know what communication vehicles are available (e.g. newsletters, surveys, websites, email discussion forums, formal meetings), who is responsible for production and content of each form of communication, and who will respond to the members on behalf of the co-op.

The board and management of the co-op need to develop an ongoing approach that generates a greater understanding of members' needs. Although the co-op will not likely have the capacity to meet all the particularities of these needs, understanding and analyzing them may lead to uncovering surprising similarities that become unexpected opportunities for the co-operative. The co-op leadership will also hear quickly of changes in the external environment that are affecting members' needs and that will also affect the co-op.

The ability to continue to generate this deeper understanding of members' needs will, of course, depend upon how well the first priority noted above has been accomplished. Some of the communication vehicles developed should have a clear focus on members' needs. In a small worker co-op, information could be relayed through regular meetings; in larger co-ops member feedback may be gathered through suggestion boxes, formal member needs surveys, and/or member satisfaction surveys; and in all co-ops there should always be a readiness for informal direct dialogue with individual members, directors, and mangers.

Another important priority for building the members' commitment is the governance of the co-op. Members' ownership of the co-op is expressed through its governance structure. Are the members truly in control of the co-op? What authority do they have, and what are the limitations?

Of course, for members to play the appropriate role in governing the co-op requires a thorough understanding of the co-op and its operations. This includes understanding the formal governance processes of the board of directors and the members' roles in governance. It means understanding the financial and market circumstance of the co-op and the options it has for moving forward and the risks involved. It means understanding the roles of management and staff and the authority and responsibility they have and to whom they are accountable.

Achieving this understanding is no small task. Training, standard financial reporting, and clear policies are required. This new knowledge needs to become embedded in the life of the co-op and can only happen by having members participating in the co-op's decision-making. Because of the difficulty of this challenge, a co-op board must be committed to not isolating itself or only giving real authority to staff or others "in the know."

The co-op's short-term and long-term operational vision is vital to developing member commitment. Members need to understand exactly what to expect from the co-op, what it can (and can't) do and why. They need to see how the overall activities are building towards a future that will meet their needs and future aspirations. Having this vision enables the co-op's board, managers, and committees to communicate the results it achieves and enables the members to have realistic expectations against which to judge the co-op's progress. The sense of accomplishment and proof that the co-op is, and will, continue to meet the challenges it faces is the cornerstone for building and maintaining member commitment.

Conclusion

So what does this all mean for trying to deal with the many challenges of the first three years after start-up? Simply put, there is no substitute for good judgment based upon sound information. What I have tried to do is outline what I see as the two over-arching priorities to navigate the "Valley of Death." I have provided some suggestions for key priorities, which can be used as criteria to determine how to allocate limited resources within the co-op. Making good decisions in the hustle and bustle of the everyday life of a co-op is a challenge of far greater magnitude than writing about the process. I hope these suggestions will provide a stimulus for all those co-op members and staff entrusted with this task.

Chapter Sixteen

Co-operative Development in a Competitive World

Russ Christianson

Of all the teachings we receive, this one is the most important.
NOTHING BELONGS TO YOU,
of what there is, of what you take, you must share.[1]

Just over two hundred years ago, an energy, technological, and organizational revolution started in England with the widespread use of coal as a fuel for the steam engine and the invention of the "self-regulating market economy." The industrial revolution quickly spread around the world, along with the free market system, and subsistence agrarian villages were transformed into factory towns and cities with the emergence of slums, child labour, low wages, and pollution. Co-operatives were a response to the social misery caused by free markets, and in 1844, the Rochdale pioneers created the co-operative principles that all co-operatives use today. Before the widespread exploitation of cheap fossil fuels (around 1850), the human population had reached about one billion – the natural carrying capacity

---

1 Curve Lake First Nation, Petroglyphs Provincial Park, Ontario, Canada.

of a solar agrarian economy. By 2000, the population was 6 billion and we were using 125% of nature's yearly output. Clearly, using the world's natural capital (water, soil, forests, fish, minerals, and fossil fuels) faster than it can be renewed is not sustainable. As democratic, innovative, and community-based organizations, co-operatives are playing an important role in transforming the unsustainable economic self-interest of the free market system into a socio-economic system that can sustainably fulfill people's collective needs.

Exposing Cultural and Economic Myths of Competition

Starting co-operative businesses seems to go against the grain of our dominant culture, a culture that celebrates win-lose competition and focuses on the "excitement" of conflict. In recent years, some large established co-operatives have even de-mutualized (the Saskatchewan Wheat Pool for example) as part of their management's strategy to compete globally with large corporations.

Our society's major institutions do not encourage co-operation. Nuclear family groupings and single family homes cut our co-operative ties to our communities and extended "tribal" support systems. Schools and universities have competitive evaluation systems built into their intellectual foundations.[2] Sports teams (amateur or professional) are quickly forgotten unless they win gold. Entrepreneurs and business executives are only successful if they become multi-millionaires. The underlying assumption in all of these examples is that life is a competitive, win-lose game.

Our children's minds, emotions, and behaviours are conditioned with these myths, messages, and images from a very young age. As they progress through life, they experience subtle and not-so-subtle external rewards and punishments designed to encourage individualism and competition.[3] It is difficult to peel back the generational layers of competitive conditioning to get to the intrinsic motivation of co-operation. For many people, it is an awakening, and they become lifelong committed co-operative enthusiasts. In Paulo Freire's words, they develop a *"critical consciousness:"*

---

2 A recent study found that MBA students in Canada and the United States are more likely to cheat than students in other disciplines because they believe it is how the business world operates and because they believe their peers cheat. Sharda Prashad, "MBA Students Likelier to Cheat," *Toronto Star* (www.thestar.com), Sept. 20, 2006.

3 Alfie Kohn, an American author has written two impeccably researched and accessibly written books on these subjects: *No Contest: The Case Against Competition* (1986, 1992); and *Punished by Rewards: The Trouble with Gold Stars, Incentive Plans, A's, Praise and Other Bribes* (1993).

Education either functions as an instrument which is used to facilitate integration of the younger generation into the logic of the present system and bring about conformity or it becomes the practice of freedom, the means by which men and women deal critically and creatively with reality and discover how to participate in the transformation of their world.[4]

Co-op developers have an inherent responsibility to fulfill as adult educators, animateurs, facilitators, and catalysts for change. This article is intended to provide co-op developers and proponents with ideas that expose the cultural and economic myth of competition. In my experience, this myth is the most significant barrier to co-operative development, and it forms the basis of government policies and programmes that favour free trade over fair trade. Our money and consumption-driven culture strongly encourages people to act as self-interested individuals, and as people chase the material dream, their behaviour reinforces the myths that people are naturally greedy and that competition is the natural order of things.

Our Natural Propensity to Co-operate

Co-operative development is a complex activity. It requires the apex of human skill and knowledge in group dynamics, leadership, communication, and social organization. As a co-operative developer it is important to be aware of these dynamics and to know when to observe and when to intervene in the process of group development. This micro level of working with a core group is highly influenced by the macro level – the historical, cultural, social, economic, and environmental influences present in our dominant culture.

As human beings, we are born with the benefits of more than two million years of evolution.[5] Each of us is gifted with a brain that has a substantial inventory of intrinsic knowledge and the ability to master complex tasks, including learning a wide variety of languages. Language allows human beings to communicate in great detail and with efficiency because of shared meaning and understanding. As our ancestors evolved over millions of years, our ability to communicate verbally, visually, and in writing has become more sophisticated. We have created complex technologies like the printing press, radio, the telephone, television, and the Internet to enhance our ability to communicate. The electronic communication tools we all use everyday

---

4 Born in Brazil, Paulo Freire (1921-1997) was one of the most influential educational philosophers of his generation. By the time his seminal work, *Pedagogy of the Oppressed*, was published in English (1972) Freire was already being acclaimed internationally as "the authentic voice of the Third World."

5 Ronald Wright, *A Short History of Progress* (Toronto: House of Anansi Press, 2004) p. 16.

(and take for granted) only became widely dispersed in the last century – a blink of the eye in human evolution.

The reality is that our human brain has evolved over two million years to cope with the social intricacies of face-to-face communication. Reading and interpreting body language, facial expressions, and tone of voice are skills that have been finely honed over hundreds of generations. The use of these social skills to navigate the sea of human relationships is the main determining factor in our species' success.

Indeed, the most recent scientific research in the multi-disciplinary field known as "evolutionary psychology" confirms the way we behave today has its roots in the lives of our tribal ancestors. As science writer William F. Allman states in his book, *The Stone Age Present*:

> The primary adaptation of our species is not hunting, tool making, or language but our ability to co-operate. While the process of evolution is often characterized in terms of dog-eat-dog competition and the 'survival of the fittest,' this recent research reveals that our species' success over the eons is due to the fact that we are the most co-operative creatures on the Earth.[6]

Survival of the fittest is a phrase that is often used to justify the racism, oppression, and exploitation that is built into "free-market" economics. It is a phrase that has been incorrectly assigned to the credit of Charles Darwin, the founder of the theory of evolution. In fact, it was the Social Darwinists Thomas H. Huxley and Herbert Spencer, not Darwin, who "coined this term and used it to justify the ascension of the wealthy elite and the exploitation of the poor."[7]

As a response to Huxley's 1888 essay, entitled "The Struggle for Existence in Human Society," the great Russian philosopher, Petre Kropotkin wrote his classic work, "Mutual Aid." Kropotkin, a Russian aristocrat himself, was a keen observer of nature and human society and spent many years in Siberia studying its geography, geology, and zoology. He also lived with the indigenous people of the region and was greatly influenced by their co-operative, tribal ways. After a lifetime of study, discourse, and observation Kropotkin came to the conclusion that "in the ethical progress of man, *mutual support – not mutual struggle* – has had the leading part."[8]

A century later, David Suzuki, Canada's world renowned geneticist and environmental activist, came to the same conclusion:

---

6 William F. Allman, The Stone Age Present (New York, Simon and Schuster, 1994) pp. 14, 21.

7 *Ibid*, p. 27.

8 Petre Kropotkin, *Mutual Aid* (Boston, MA., Extending Horizons Books, originally published in 1902).

Just as the key to a species' survival in the natural world is its ability to adapt to local habitats, so the key to human survival will probably be the local community. If we can create vibrant, increasingly autonomous, and self-reliant local groupings of people that emphasize sharing, co-operation, and living lightly on the Earth, we can avoid the fate warned of by Rachel Carson and the world scientists and restore the sacred balance of life.[9]

When I talk to people about our natural propensity to co-operate with each other, most people knowingly nod their heads in agreement. It helps set a positive context for their hard work in developing their co-operatives and provides ongoing affirmation for their efforts. As a co-op developer, you will have to use your judgment regarding the appropriate times or "teaching moments" to introduce these ideas to the co-op members. A natural opportunity arises when discussing the co-operative principles and values, or during initial discussions regarding the reasons for starting the co-op.

Co-op developers need to educate themselves and co-op proponents that our current "free market" economic system is a human creation - it is not a natural system. And it has only been around for two hundred years. We need to reinforce our intrinsic knowledge that human beings naturally co-operate, help each other, and share. Co-operation has been, and will continue to be, the most effective survival strategy.

Co-operative Solutions to Free Market Problems

Co-operation is the natural response of self-organizing groups who identify a common need and meet face-to-face to find creative ways to fulfill this need in a mutually beneficial way. As this informal co-operation is formalized in a legal organizational structure, the co-op members will require ongoing education, experiential learning, and the concrete application of the international co-operative principles. The fifth co-operative principle, "co-operative education"[10] affirms the importance of investing in ongoing education to ensure the co-operative's democratic culture is maintained, particularly in the face of our current economic system's undemocratic operation.

---

9 David Suzuki with Amanda McConnel, *The Sacred Balance* (Vancouver, BC, Greystone Books, 1997) p. 4.

10 Principle Five: Co-operative Education, Training, and Information. These are on-going activities within the co-op to ensure that members understand how a co-op works and can play an active, informed role in the life of the co-op. See: www.ica.co-op

Our current economic system originated in England at the beginning of the industrial revolution. As Karl Polanyi detailed in his classic work, *The Great Transformation*,[11] market liberalism was the theoretical response of English thinkers to the massive social disruptions caused by industrialization in the early 1800s. Writers like Adam Smith attempted to provide a moral basis for the theory of market liberalism by defining "economic" rules that justified its core tenet that human society should be subordinated to "self-regulating" markets. As England expanded its empire in the 19th century, these tenets became the dominant organizing principle for the world economy.

Co-operative economics, championed by social reformers such as Robert Owen (a Welsh businessman), provided a more humane and concrete response to the social misery caused by free markets. In 1844, a group of weavers in Rochdale, England, inspired by Owen, started a food co-op based on the co-operative principles they penned. As word of their success spread, co-operatives based on the Rochdale principles were started throughout the world.

After the First World War, the United States and Canada experienced a sustained economic boom, "The Roaring Twenties," which came to an abrupt halt with the stock market crash of 1929. A deep economic depression ensued, and in 1933, the newly elected Democratic President of the United States, Franklin D. Roosevelt, introduced his "New Deal." This brought together a broad coalition of social groups that supported the federal government playing an active role in regulating the economy; Roosevelt regulated capital markets, used fiscal policy to create jobs by building infrastructure, and introduced relief (welfare), unemployment insurance, and social security. In Canada, the Conservative Prime Minister Richard Bennett attempted to implement similar reforms, but like today, the provinces challenged the federal government's right to manage these programmes. Canada's economy was protected from further decline when Britain more than doubled the value of its purchases from Canada.[12]

During the "Dirty Thirties," there was a successful flurry of new self-help co-operatives organized in the United States, including 300,000 members in California's "reciprocal economy."[13] In Canada, several established co-operatives hired organizers to help start new co-operatives of all kinds.[14]

After the Second World War, the citizens of Western democracies ensured that the social programmes and constraints on the "free market" introduced

11 Karl Polanyi, *The Great Transformation: The Political and Economic Origins of Our Time* (Boston: Beacon Press, 1944, 1957, 2000).
12 www.wikipedia.ca
13 Jonathan Rowe, "Entrepreneurs of Co-operation," *YES! A Journal of Positive Futures* (Bainbridge Island, Washington USA: Issue 38, Summer 2006).
14 Ian McPherson, Co-operative Movement, www.canadianencyclopedia.com

during the Great Depression were solidified, and co-operatives began to thrive again. For the next four decades, the world's two remaining super-powers, the free market United States (and its allies) and the communist Soviet Union, competed against each other (in the "Cold War") for world influence, building enormous stocks of conventional and nuclear weapons. By December 1991, the Soviet Union could no longer keep pace, it's highly centralized economy collapsed, and the United States emerged as the world's sole super power. Proponents of "free markets" viewed this as a victory, and every US President, British Prime Minister, and Canadian Prime Minister since has unabashedly promoted market liberalization.

Since Ronald Reagan, Margaret Thatcher, and Brian Mulroney reigned as conservatives in the 1980s, free trade and global competition have been the economic mantra of our governments, transnational corporations, and international financial institutions. Globalization is a code word for a collection of "free market" economic policies, including:

- Unfettered international movement and concentration of capital;
- Corporate and personal tax cuts (mostly benefiting the wealthy);
- Deregulation, including diminished labour and environmental standards;
- Privatization of public assets; and
- Diminishment of the governments' role in the economy.

This emphasis on global competition creates a very challenging political, economic, and cultural ethos within which to develop co-operatives. Even though co-operatives have an excellent track record in Canada, with one in three people being members and a survival rate that is twice as high as conventional businesses,[15] it is an ongoing struggle to gain supportive government policies.

Like the old proverb says, with every challenge there is an opportunity. As the globalized economy leaves more and more people and communities behind, groups all over the world have identified opportunities to meet their needs by co-operating together locally. There are thousands of examples of these local co-operative initiatives, from credit unions in India, fair trade coffee growers in Nicaragua, industrial worker co-ops in Argentina, renewable energy co-ops in Denmark, and forestry co-ops in Canada. The following statistics paint an impressive picture of the worldwide impact of the co-operative model:[16]

---

15 *Survival Rates of Co-operatives in Quebec* (Quebec Ministry of Industry and Commerce and the Co-operatives Secretariat) www.agr.ca/policy/coop. 2000.

16 International Co-operative Alliance, www.ica.coop, 2007; National Co-operative Business Alliance, www.ncba.coop, 2007; and Canadian Co-operative Association, www.cca.coop, 2007.

- In 1994, the United Nations estimated the livelihood of nearly 3 billion people, or half of the world's population, was made secure through co-operative enterprises.
- Over 800 million people in over 100 countries worldwide are members of co-operatives.
- Co-operatives provide over 100 million jobs around the world, 20% more than multinational enterprises.
- In the United States, more than 120 million people (40% of Americans) belong to 47,000 co-operatives.
- There are 132,000 co-operative enterprises in the European Union, with 100 million members, and 2.3 million employees.
- Canada has over 9,500 co-operatives and credit unions, with combined assets of approximately $300 billion, employing over 155,000 people.
- Quebec, a province that has had co-operative friendly policies for decades, accounts for almost 40 percent of all co-operatives in Canada and nearly 50 percent of co-op jobs.

The principles and values of co-operatives provide a positive alternative to the hierarchical business structure favoured by the neo-liberal economy. The table below provides a comparison between the values of the competitive "free-market" and the co-operative "fair-market."

Table One: Value Comparison of Competitive vs. Co-operative Economic Systems

Competitive Values	Co-operative Values
• Self-interest (win-lose)	• Mutual Benefit (win-win)
• Maximize Individual Wealth	• Fulfill Collective Needs
• Short-term	• Long-term
• Global Fear	• Local Empowerment
• Autocratic	• Democratic
• Information Control	• Information Sharing
• Bigger is Better	• Small is Beautiful
• Centralized	• Decentralized
• Status Quo	• Visionary Change

These values provide the underlying motivations for people in their daily activities. The contrast between the competitive values and the co-operative values is startlingly clear. Given the last few years of very public corporate scandals, and the greed exhibited by many corporate officers, it is not surprising that co-operatives enjoy a very favourable public perception. Here are some results from recent public opinion surveys.

In the United States[17]

- 77% of people said co-ops have the best interests of consumers in mind, compared to only 47% for private corporations.
- 76% agreed that co-ops run their businesses in a trustworthy manner and for the benefit of their communities, compared to 53% for publicly traded corporations.

In Quebec[18]

- 75% of the general public view co-ops as a good solution to economic challenges.
- 79% believe they offer better prices than corporations.
- 83% believe that they encourage a hands-on, take-charge approach to the local economy.

If we look at the overall outcomes of globalization, we can easily understand why co-operatives are so positively embraced by nearly a billion people worldwide.

Concentration of Wealth

It should come as no surprise that the wealthiest families (who own the majority of shares in transnational corporations) have been globalization's main beneficiaries. Free trade has resulted in substantial gains for the owners of capital at the expense of wage-labourers. Corporate profits have risen everywhere, while in four out of five developing countries the share of wages in manufacturing value-added is much lower than it was thirty years ago.[19]

Tax Cuts

Not only are corporations and their wealthy owners making higher profits, they are also paying less income tax. For example, since Canada's federal budget in 2000, the corporate tax rate has declined from 28% to 21%, making it significantly lower than the United States (35%). Yet, Canada's business elite continues to lobby strenuously for further tax cuts – using the

17 National Co-operative Business Association survey performed by The Opinion Research Corporation of Princeton, N.J. 2003; See http://www.co-opmonth.co-op/primer/perceptions.html

18 Bruno-Marie Béchard, "A Co-operative Approach for Uniting Our Society," Co-operative Forum, Université de Sherbrooke, March 14, 2006. From: http://www.usherbrooke.ca/accueil/direction/allocutions/2006/forum_co-operation-060314_eng.html

19 Robert Wiessman, "Grotesque Inequality - Corporate Globalization and the Global Gap Between Rich and Poor," *Multinational Monitor Magazine*, July/August 2003. Extracted from: www.thirdworldtraveler.com/Third_World/Grotesque_Inequality.html

usual "globally competitive" argument. In the words of Don Drummond, Chief Economist of the Toronto Dominion Bank, "Canadian corporations are riding a wave of record profits and sitting on an unprecedented pile of cash." So much cash that "it raises questions about whether they need or would make productive use of further tax relief."[20]

Diminished Labour Standards

In the name of trade liberalization and labour market flexibility, corporations, the International Monetary Fund (IMF), and the World Bank have required developed and developing countries to water down their labour standards. Labour market deregulation makes it is easier to hire and fire employees, lower wages, and diminishes collective bargaining standards. Today, a full-time permanent job is an oxymoron. Instead, more and more people live from short-term contract to short-term contract, with no benefits or job security.

Privatization

Privatization of public assets has resulted in fire sale prices, a direct transfer of wealth from the overall population to private owners (transnational corporations and local elites). In some cases, privatization has been marked by extreme corruption, creating a small group of billionaires who have gotten away with stealing the public's wealth. For example, the Russian gas giant Gazprom was privatized for $250 million when Russia embraced the IMF's free market policies. Three years later, Gazprom's market value was $40 billion. In the United States, it would have been valued between $300 billion to $900 billion USD. Other publicly owned oil, mining, and electricity companies were privatized at prices less than a twentieth of their subsequent market value.[21]

The economic reality I have briefly sketched out above is not generally reported in the mainstream media – including television, radio, and print. The Internet and public broadcasters, like the CBC, the BBC, or NPR provide a more balanced approach, but they too are often hamstrung in the belief system of global competition and economic self-interest.

As a co-op developer, I find it essential to have a thorough understanding of the global economic system and its shortcomings. As wealth is concentrated, more people around the world do not have their basic physiological needs met. Co-operatives provide them with a collective do-it-yourself

---

20 Don Drummond, *TD Bank Report*, April 2005.
21 Robert Wiessman, "Grotesque Inequality - Corporate Globalization and the Global Gap Between Rich and Poor," *Multinational Monitor Magazine*, July / August 2003. Extracted from: www.thirdworldtraveler.com/Third_World/Grotesque_Inequality.html

approach to meeting their needs for decent housing, financial services, employment, and a variety of social services, like health care, childcare, and home care. Understanding and communicating this critique of the free market system and the co-operative alternative can provide a powerful motivation for people to meet their collective needs by joining the co-operative movement.

An Example – The Organic Food Sector vs. Big Business Agriculture

One area of co-op development that I've been involved with for the past twenty years is organic food and agriculture. The industrial food system is much like other industries – there are a few very large corporations that control most of the market. Over the past decade, as organic food has become a mainstream consumer item, most large food processors have added organic food product lines. One of their major strategies is buying out pioneering firms who have developed organic brands. For example, in the last seven years, Heinz's 57 varieties ($17 billion USD capitalization) has found room for the buyout or merger of 21 leading organic entrepreneurial companies, including: Hain-Celestial, Westbrae, Imagine/Rice Dream, Health Valley, Arrowhead Mills, Spectrum Organics, Garden of Eatin', Earth's Best, and Walnut Acres.

Cargill ($1.3 billion profit USD in 2003) also has an ownership share in these same companies through Hain-Celestial.

And the world's largest food retailers, including the behemoth – Wal-Mart ($288 billion USD in sales), have all jumped on the organic bandwagon. "Wal-Mart says it wants to democratize organic food."[22] This is an absurd statement given that the Walton family, who owns Wal-Mart, make up five of the top ten wealthiest Americans, with a combined fortune of $100 billion USD. Let's take a couple of minutes to look at the incomes of other middlemen and suppliers in the industrial food market:[23]

- Big Oil – four companies own 75% of Canada's refining capacity (Exxon/Imperial Oil, Petro-Canada, Shell, and Irving) – they are all enjoying record profits with Return on Equity (ROE) between 19% to 32%.
- Big Fertilizer (natural gas) – four companies control 94% of the market, the biggest, Dow Chemical – 23% ROE.
- Big Seed – Dupont (Pioneer Hi-Bred) – 16% ROE.
- Big Drugs – Merck – 34% ROE.

---

22 Melanie Warner, "Wal-Mart Eyes Organic Foods," *The New York Times*, May 12, 2006; www.nytimes.com

23 National Farmers' Union, "The Farm Crisis and Corporate Profits," November 30, 2005, Canada.

- Big Banks — 15 to 20% ROE.

Let me add one more ROE, Canada's small and medium sized family farms, negative 5%.

Paraphrasing Charles Dickens, it is the best of times (for corporations) and the worst of times (for family farms). In fact, it's even worse than the Great Depression for farmers and without government support programmes many more would be bankrupt. As bleak as this seems, the silver lining is the growing importance of the co-operative business structures in organic food. The two largest organic dairy producers in the United States and Canada are co-operatives, owned by farmers. The leading fair trade marketing companies in the United States and Canada are co-operatives, including Equal Exchange, Just US!, La Siembra, and Planet Bean — all worker co-operatives. And, as the public, economic, and environmental pressure mounts in favour of local food production and distribution, co-operatives have the opportunity to play an even more significant role as a decentralized, community-based, and regional business model overtakes the highly centralized "global" business model that is completely dependent on cheap energy.

When writing a feasibility study or business plan for a co-operative, it is important to take these broader economic, social, political, legal, and environmental aspects into account. A thorough analysis of this "situational environment"[24] will form the basis of the business strategy for the co-operative and the long-term sustainability of its business model. The underlying advantage of the co-operative model is the creative collaboration that can be harnessed with a well-designed and facilitated co-op development process.

A well facilitated co-op visioning session[25] with the founding members will often draw out a deep understanding of these issues and the ramifications in their day-to-day lives. The ensuing discussion will provide the group members and the co-op developer with a good overview of the various perspectives the members bring to the co-op and whether they have a shared vision for the co-operative. Having facilitated hundreds of these sessions with start-up groups, I always find the discussion worthwhile and often very inspiring. The visioning process is a powerful tool for organizing co-operatives, testing members' propensity to co-operate, and potentially providing an ongoing source of inspiration that will keep the co-op going when times get tough.

Given the seemingly overwhelming influence of "global competition," it is very useful to help co-op proponents put this in perspective. Nascent co-op member need to understand they are part of something bigger — the world's largest and fastest growing socio-economic movement. Every new

---

24 See: "Co-op Business Plan" in the Tools and Resource section of this book.
25 See: "The Co-op Vision — Facilitator's Guide" in the Tools and Resource section.

co-op that starts up and survives the crucial first five years of operation becomes an important addition to the co-op movement. Newly developed co-ops should be strongly encouraged to join their sectoral or regional co-operative associations – it will open up new and unexpected opportunities for co-operation amongst co-operatives and will usually enhance their business success. Often new, innovative co-ops bring entrepreneurial energy and ideas to the larger established co-ops, while the established co-ops can offer access to expertise, business networks, and capital resources.

Sustainability and Co-operation

Whatever else may be said about the century now approaching an end, it must be recorded as the period in which mankind has done more to poison and destroy the environment than in all previous eras of history. The industrial revolution of modern times, beginning about 200 years ago, started society on the road to destruction and spoilage of the whole human habitat, using the adage 'muck makes money.' The degradation of the environment has gone hand in hand with wasteful use of resources and disturbance of the delicate balances of nature.[26]

While "economic growth" has been the raison d'etre of government economic policy for the past 150 years, we are in transition towards a new understanding. "Sustainability" is the new term that is gathering momentum. Over the past twenty years, since the release of the United Nations' Bruntland Commission Report[27] (the World Commission on Environment and Development) the term *sustainable development* has been used to describe an "ideal" kind of economic development that balances free market economic growth while halting ecological destruction. However, to many (including myself) the term is an oxymoron, because the present scale of global economic development is simply not sustainable. Therefore, I will use the term sustainability. The questions to ask are: What will a sustainable economy look like? And what role might co-operatives play in creating this future?

Before I answer these questions, it is important to look at our current state of ecological and economic affairs and how we got here. Twenty-seven years ago, the International Co-operative Alliance identified the root cause of the severe environmental, economic, and social challenges that our species faces today: the industrial revolution and its supporters' retrospective, theoretical justification – self-regulating markets. In October 2006, Sir Nicholas Stern,

26 International Co-operative Alliance: *Co-operatives in the Year 2000*, London, 1980.
27 United Nations (1987) *Report of the World Commission on Environment and Development.* General Assembly Resolution 42/187, 11 December 1987. Retrieved: 2007-04-10 http://www.un.org/documents/ga/res/42/ares42-187.htm

Head of the British Government Economic Service and former World Bank Chief Economist issued his report, *The Economics of Climate Change*, with this admission "Climate change is the greatest market failure the world has seen."[28]

These are significant and stark words to come from the lips of a neo-classical economist who was born in 1946 and has spent his adult life studying and supporting the "self-regulating" market system. However, as quickly as he provides this courageous admission, he also describes climate change as an "economic externality." This is "economic speak," words that economists use to theoretically justify the public cost of pollution that is a direct result of private market transactions. In other words, the market economy has not factored in, or bothered to measure the short-term or long-term costs of the environmental pollution caused by our energy intensive, consumption-driven, wealth obsessed economic system. Stern thus provides his fellow free market economists the escape hatch they desire – "market forces" can find the solutions to the climate change problem, for example by developing a global market for carbon emission credits. So, while Stern slaps the wrists of his free market colleagues (most of the political, academic, and corporate leaders in the Northern Hemisphere), he also winks at them with his fingers crossed behind his back.

The Stern Review is just one of hundreds of studies, publications, movies, and television documentaries that have come to the same conclusions – the human species is causing the unmitigated ecological destruction of our earth. Perhaps the most significant of these studies is the United Nations' *Millennium Ecosystem Assessment* (Millennium Assessment or MA).[29] Published in April 2005, the MA is the most extensive scientific study ever completed regarding the health of our planet's ecosystem and how it affects human well-being. Four years in the making, it brought together nearly 1,400 experts from 95 countries. The objective of the MA was to assess the consequences of ecosystem change for human well-being and establish the basis for actions needed to enhance conservation and the sustainable use of ecosystems.

The results of the study are unmercifully sobering. Sixty percent of the planet's ecosystems are currently being degraded by human activities. These activities include polluting the atmosphere with excess greenhouse gases, draining freshwater aquifers, over-harvesting our forests and fisheries, polluting our oceans, and introducing alien species to new regions. As a result,

---

28 Nicholas Stern, *Stern Review: The Economics of Climate Change*, October 2006, Executive Summary, page viii.

29 Millennium Ecosystem Assessment, 2005. *Ecosystems and Human Well-Being: Synthesis.* (Washington, D.C.: Island Press).

twenty percent of the world's coral reefs have been lost, forty percent of the planet's rivers have been fragmented, and our climate has been seriously disrupted.

The Millennium Ecosystem study has four main conclusions:

1. Over the past fifty years, humans have changed ecosystems more rapidly and extensively than in any comparable period of time in human history, largely to meet our rapidly growing population's demand for food, fresh water, timber, fibre, and fuel. This has resulted in a substantial and largely irreversible loss in the diversity of life on Earth.

2. The changes that have been made to ecosystems have contributed to material net gains in economic development, but these gains have been achieved at growing costs in the form of the degradation of many ecosystems, increased risks of abrupt collapse of these ecosystems, and growing disparity between rich and poor. Unless they are addressed, these problems will substantially diminish the benefits that future generations obtain from ecosystems.

3. The degradation of ecosystems could grow significantly worse during the first half of this century.

4. The challenge of reversing the degradation of ecosystems, while at the same time meeting increasing demands for food, water, timber, fibre, and fuel, can be partially met under some scenarios that the MA has considered, but these involve significant changes in policies, institutions, and practices that are not currently underway.

The incredible growth of the world's industrial economies and human population (world population has more than doubled since 1960) has been fuelled by cheap fossil fuels (gas, oil, coal, and natural gas). The early 1900s witnessed the birth of the most dramatic century of material and technological progress in the history of human kind. And it was also a century of unprecedented human conflict and suffering and ecosystem and species destruction.

Now, at the dawn of the 21st Century (two hundred years after the beginning of the Industrial Revolution and one hundred years after the beginning of the Petroleum Age), we are facing a looming energy and environmental crisis.

The natural carrying capacity of the earth's ecosystem before the exploitation of cheap oil and gas was approximately one billion people.[30] As we

---

30 James Howard Kunstler, *The Long Emergency – Surviving the Converging Catastrophes of the Twenty-first Century* (New York: Atlantic Monthly Press, 2005) p. 6; and Paul Johnson, *The Birth of the Modern* (New York: Harper, 1991).

come to the end of the Petroleum Age, the following facts provide unprecedented challenges for humanity:

Population Growth
- World population is now over 6.5 billion.[31] Half of humanity lives in abject poverty with income of less than two dollars a day,[32] and one in six goes hungry every day.[33]
- Since the early 1900s, the world's population has multiplied by four and its economy – a rough measure of the human load on nature – by more than forty.[34]
- The rapidly growing gap between the world's rich and poor is the root cause of much of the violence and wars in the world. In 1960, the gap was 30:1, it is now 154:1[35] and 86% of the world's wealth is owned by the richest 20%.[36]
- In the 1960s, humans used 70% of nature's yearly output, in the 1980s it was 100%, by 1999 it was 125%.[37]

Energy Depletion
- The original endowment of oil was about 2 trillion barrels. Since 1850, 50% has been used and the remaining 50% is the hardest to get and the lowest quality.[38]
- At the dawn of the Petroleum Age (1916) each barrel of oil drilled provided an energy return of 28:1, it is now 2:1.[39]
- Worldwide discovery of oil peaked in 1964 and has followed a firm downward trend since.[40]
- The rate of oil use has increased 20-fold in the last four decades.[41]

31 World Bank, *World Development Report 2000/2001: Attacking Poverty*, September 2000.
32 www.globalissues.org/TradeRelated/Facts.asp; and World Bank, *World Development Report 2000/2001: Attacking Poverty*, September 2000.
33 State of Food Insecurity in the World 2005. Food and Agriculture Organization of the United Nations.
34 Ronald Wright, *A Short History of Progress* (Toronto: House of Anansi Press, 2004) p. 30.
35 www.thirdworldtraveler.com/Third_World/Grotesque_Inequality.html.
36 United Nations, from an interview with Linda McQuaid, CBC Radio, September 23, 2000.
37 BBC World News, April 8, 2004.
38 James Howard Kunstler, *The Long Emergency – Surviving the Converging Catastrophes of the Twenty-First Century* (New York: Atlantic Monthly Press, 2005) p. 66.
39 *Ibid.*, p. 67.
40 *Ibid.*, p. 66.
41 Dale Allen Pfeiffer, "Without Oil, Families Will Go Hungry, Not Just Their SUVs," *The CCPA Monitor*, April 2006, p. 22.

- The world has likely passed the point of peak oil production already, or will within this decade.[42] After peak, world demand will exceed world capacity to produce oil and costs will escalate and ripple through the economy, causing rapid inflation.
- Natural gas production is expected to peak within the next decade – by 2014 in Canada.[43]
- Our food system consumes 10 times more energy than it produces in food energy.[44]
- In Canada and the United States, we use 1,500 litres of oil to feed each person each year.[45]

Climate Change

- Our planet is warming and the most significant greenhouse gas is carbon dioxide (CO_2). Carbon dioxide is created every time we burn something or when things decompose, and it is the major cause of global warming (approximately 80%).[46]
- If we continue burning fossil fuels at our current rate, the 21st Century will see a doubling of CO_2 in the atmosphere, from three parts per ten thousand that existed one hundred years ago to six parts per ten thousand. This has the potential to heat our planet by three to six degrees Celsius,[47] resulting in drastic weather changes and the world's oceans flooding all coastal cities (most of which are less than 1 meter above sea level).[48]
- More than half of humanity lives on a coastline or lives within 200 kilometres of one.[49]

The evidence regarding the impact of the global free market economy on the natural world is irrefutable. Our human population has far exceeded the

42 James Howard Kunstler, *The Long Emergency – Surviving the Converging Catastrophes of the Twenty-First Century* (New York: Atlantic Monthly Press, 2005) p.67; and David Goldstein, *Out of Gas* (New York: W.W. Norton & Company, 2004) p. 28.

43 Dave Hughes, a leading energy analyst at Natural Resources Canada, predicts that with all available resources online there will be a shortfall of natural gas by 2014.

44 Dale Allen Pfeiffer, "Without Oil, Families Will Go Hungry, Not Just Their SUVs," *The CCPA Monitor*, April 2006, p. 22.

45 *Ibid.,* p. 21.

46 Tim Flannery, *The Weather Makers – How We Are Changing the Climate and What it Means for Life on Earth* (Toronto: Harper Collins, 2005) p. 28.

47 *Ibid.,* p. 26.

48 *Ibid.,* p. 150.

49 Don Hinrichsen, "Coasts in Crisis," September 1995, from: www.aaas.org/international/ehn/fisheries/hinrichs.htm; and UN Atlas of the Oceans, "Human Settlements on the Coast," from http://www.oceansatlas.org

natural carrying capacity of the earth's ecosystems, and we have accelerated climate change by indiscriminately burning fossil fuels. Our current global economy is not sustainable. "Survival of the fittest" economics is a failure. Our world is on the precipice of ecological collapse. If we continue with competitive free market policies, billions of people will perish this century.

This is not "fear-mongering;" it is a conclusion that has been reluctantly reached by some of the world's best scientific, ecological, economic, and political minds. When we are able to suspend our disbelief and our brains begin to absorb this knowledge, we cannot help but feel our stress levels rise as our involuntary fight or flight survival response reacts. This knowledge will provide the motivating factor, the moral imperative that will be required to initiate the changes we each need to make to move into the future with our children and grandchildren.

A few climate change deniers may remain (although the oil companies recently cut off their funding), but most people realize we have to do something differently. Business as usual is no longer an option. In order to survive and slow down the ecological destruction, we will have to radically alter our patterns of consumption, our belief systems, and how we define success.

To answer the sustainability question, for humanity to move forward into the future with hope for coming generations, we will have to co-operate like our tribal ancestors. This cannot be forced co-operation, like the misled practices of totalitarian or fascist regimes. It has to be voluntary co-operation, based on the natural yearning we all have within us to work together to create something more positive and nurturing than we are able to create as individual human beings. Indeed, even Sir Nicholas Stern acknowledges that we have to co-operate globally to solve the climate change challenge.

Conclusion

When I was twenty-five years old, I made a choice to work on the margins of the mainstream competitive economy. I took a manager's job with a small co-operative food wholesaler, the Ontario Federation of Food Co-ops and Clubs Inc. Over the next three years, I worked together with other dedicated employees, members, and board members to turn the organization around. We did this by shifting the focus from developing conventional supermarket co-ops to supplying organic food to natural food co-ops, buying clubs, day care centres, and small independent retailers. Our goal was to break $1 million in sales. In 2006, the co-op was thirty years old and had over $23 million in sales. This not-for-profit co-operative has become Ontario's premier independent organic and natural food distributor, while dozens of private, for-profit, natural, and organic food distributors have come and gone.

After leaving the food co-op wholesaler in 1988, I worked for a year with a worker co-op in northern Ontario, Kagiwiosa Manomin, that produced Canada's first certified organic fair trade product – wild rice. This project was capitalized by generations of indigenous knowledge regarding traditional wild rice harvesting and processing, years of sweat equity by community members, ongoing long-term support from Canada's Mennonite Central Committee, and a few hundred thousand dollars from the Canadian government. The co-op built a small processing plant on the Wabigoon First Nation reserve, performed and implemented very innovative market research, and broke into co-operative and fair trade markets throughout Canada, the United States, and Europe. Kagiwiosa Manomin still operates today and spurred the development of two other co-operative businesses – a wild-crafted jam processor and a sustainable tree harvesting and planting operation.

Returning to southern Ontario in 1989, I became one of the founding members of a worker co-operative food company. Origins Co-op developed a national brand for certified organic foods and distributed the products through the five co-operative natural food wholesalers across Canada. We also attempted, unsuccessfully, to negotiate distribution agreements with Canada's large established co-operative food wholesalers, Federated Co-operatives and Co-op Atlantic. The managers of these co-op businesses did not see the potential for organic food sales and they were not willing to champion the products by educating their members. Origins Co-op also worked for five years (from 1990 to 1995) to successfully lobby the Ontario Milk Marketing Board to allow a separate pool for organic milk; milk which is now sold under the Organic Meadow label, the subsidiary company of OntarBio Organic Farmers Co-operative (the first start-up co-op I worked with as a Co-op Developer).

In the early 1990s, a group of worker co-op proponents inspired by the Mondragon co-ops founded the Ontario Worker Co-op Federation (OWCF) and the Canadian Worker Co-op Federation (CWCF). In Ontario, we lobbied the provincial NDP government to provide start-up and operating funds for four years to support seven worker co-op developers in five regional centres. The OWCF worked with hundreds of groups to help determine their feasibility, and a good number of the co-ops that proceeded through the entire business development process are still operating today.

During the mid to late 1990s, I worked with a number of Green Community organizations in southern Ontario to develop their business plans and create effective revenue generating and marketing programmes focussed on residential energy and water conservation. In the late 1990s and into the new millennium, this work was complimented by the development of a number of renewable energy co-operatives inspired by the wind farm co-ops in Denmark and supported by the Ontario Sustainable Energy Association and the Ontario Co-operative Association.

After many years of lobbying the Liberal federal government, the Canadian Co-operative Association (CCA) and the Conseil Canadien de la Co-opération (CCC) received a commitment of $15 million over five years (2003 to 2008) to support domestic co-operative development. This followed the Canadian Worker Co-op Federation's (CWCF) successful pilot project, Tenacity Works, which was also funded by the federal government. In Ontario, the Ontario Co-operative Association (On Co-op), the Conseil de la Co-opération de l'Ontario (CCO), the CWCF, and the OWCF worked together to design a province-wide co-operative development strategy. Now in its fifth year, the Ontario project has been very successful in:

- Developing new, innovative co-ops,
- Expanding established co-ops, and
- Providing coaching services to newly developed co-ops in an effort to increase their survival rate.

This strategically integrated approach (in both official languages) is a model for co-operative development, and for leveraging cash and in-kind resources from established co-operatives and other co-op funders – particularly given the small amount of money provided by the federal government (less than $200,000 per year for the province of Ontario). Unfortunately, the demand for the co-op development services has far exceeded the supply.

I provide these few examples of co-operative development from my experience to show that even within a very competitive dominant culture, small groups of people who are dedicated to creating a more humane and ecologically sound economic system can make a difference. Imagine what could be done with co-operatives in a societal environment that is supportive, through:

- Educational institutions,
- Government programmes and regulations,
- Capital funds levered from established co-operatives and senior levels of government, and
- Technical assistance (feasibility studies, business planning, incorporation, governance and board training, management training, and coaching)

In fact, your imagination doesn't have to run wild; all you have to do is study the co-operative systems in Mondragon Spain, Emilia Romagna Italy, and Quebec to quickly understand what is possible.

The reality in our relationships, families, work places, and communities is that those who get along, get ahead. The social glue of co-operation sustains personal and business relationships. The daily give and take of life demands that we share with each other, that we tolerate our differences, and find mutually beneficial solutions to our challenges and conflicts.

This century can be the turning point, or the next "Great Transformation," from a destructive, competitive economy, to a nurturing, co-operative economy. Co-operatives have the potential to experience exponential growth throughout the world, as people come to the realization that sustainability requires co-operation and that co-operatives are a proven organizational model that can successfully fulfill our economic, social, and environmental needs.

> Everything on this planet functions according to the law of nature. Particles come together, and on the basis of their co-operation everything around us, our whole environment, can develop and be sustained. Our own body too has the same structure. Different cells come together and work together in co-operation, and as a result, human life is sustained. In a human community the same law and principle of co-operation applies.
>
> The Dalai Lama

Chapter Seventeen

Making Co-operatives a Best Practice

Lynn Hannley

The Italians have a proverb of unusual sagacity for that quick-witted people, namely: 'They who go slowly go far.' Co-operation has gone both slow and far. It has issued like the tortoise from its Lancashire home in England; it has traversed France, Germany, and even the frozen steppes of Russia; the bright-minded Bengalese are applying it, as is the soon-seeing and far-seeing American; and our own emigrant countrymen in Australia are endeavouring to naturalise it there. Like a good chronometer, co-operation is unaffected by change of climate and goes well in every land. [1]

The co-operative model as refined by the Rochdale pioneers during the last half of the 19th century certainly made its way around the world. Today the International Co-operative Alliance (ICA), founded in 1895, has 230 member organizations from 92 countries active in all sectors of the economy that represent more than 800 million individuals worldwide. The UN estimates the livelihood of half the world's population is made secure by co-operative enterprise.[2] In the USA 47,000 co-operatives

---

1 George Jacob Holyoake. *Self-Help by the People: The History of the Rochdale Pioneers* (London: Swan Sonnenschien and Co, 1907).
2 *Women in Business: The Co-operative Option.* See: www.co-operatives-uk.co-op/live/ welcome.asp?id=886 (cited 27 December, 2006).

have 120 million members – 40% of the population of the country.[3] At least 65% of all Albertans have at least one co-op membership.[4] Mondragon Corporation Co-operativa increased its workforce from 25,322 in 1992 to 78,455 in 2005.[5] All of these statistics are indicators of the significant role co-operatives have played in communities throughout the world, yet for many people they are viewed as a fringe model for use by the poor, not a first choice option – and certainly not mainstream.

In this article, I look at how co-operatives can be made a best practice. I examine the distinct nature of co-operatives, including their quadruple bottom line and the closed loop nature of the organizational accountability framework, and I identify why co-operatives are a good fit both to do business and to deliver goods and services in a responsive and sustainable manner. Unfortunately, in most parts of Canada (outside of Quebec), co-operatives have yet to be appreciated as a viable model for doing business or providing services; let alone as a best practice.

First I examine three reasons why co-operatives are a best practice. Next I bring our attention to seven major barriers that hinder the promotion of co-operatives. In closing, I outline measures to make co-operatives a best practice and summarize why it is important to take this step.

Three Reasons Why Co-operatives are a Best Practices

Three reasons why co-operatives are a best practice include:

First, co-operatives are distinct not only because of the nature of their organizational framework but also because of the existence of sectoral, intersectoral, second, and third tier organizations that nurture and support individual co-operatives, thus creating a system that fosters local ownership and control and also harnesses the benefits of vertical and horizontal integration.

Second, co-operatives, particularly worker and multi-stakeholder co-operatives, offer more effective ways to deliver human services than other types of organizations.

Third, co-operatives have a high level of performance.

3 *The International Movement*. See: www.co-oponline.co-op/about_international.html (cited 28 December, 2006).

4 *White Paper on Co-op Development in Alberta* (Edmonton: Alberta Community and Co-operative Association, 2006).

5 *Frequently Asked Questions: Corporation* (Mondragon Corporation Co-operativa) See: http://www.mcc.es/ing/contracto/faqs1.html [cited 5 November, 2006].

1. Co-operatives are Distinct

Co-operatives evolved in response to the lack of institutional services and models that focused on the needs of the consumers and employees, rather than just on the needs of investors or shareholders. In this section, I look at the evolution of co-operatives and further elaborate on their distinct nature.

Creating the Organizational Framework

In 1844, a group of weavers developed an organization that would transform the way people could conduct business.

> Twenty eight weavers have established their store… and commenced their heroic attempt to stem the tide of competition and exploitation that threatened to overwhelm them, by the simple process of uniting for the common purpose of efficiently doing for themselves, upon a basis of mutuality and self-help, what had hitherto been inefficiently done for them at a cost which impoverished their families but provided wealth for the individual captains of industry and trade.[6]

These weavers not only formed the Rochdale Equitable Pioneers Society Limited, known as the first successful modern co-operative, but also developed an overarching set of values and principles to guide the internal operations of the society and the manner in which it would conduct its business. Their model was not built upon aristocratic philanthropy but on an alternate system of production and exchange based upon human values and needs and the use of capital as a tool to meet the objectives of the co-operative. The following statement from the Rochdale Society's 1860 annual almanac of the rules of conduct gives an overview of what distinguished the co-operative from other forms of organization.

> The present Co-operative Movement does not intend to meddle with the various religious or political differences which now exist in society but by a common bond, namely that of self-interest, to join together the means, energies, and the talents of all for the common benefit of each.
>
> 1. That capital should be of their own providing and bear a fixed rate of interest.
>
> 2. That only the purest provisions procurable should be supplied to members.
>
> 3. That full weight and measure should be given.
>
> 4. That market prices should be charged and no credit given nor asked.

---

6 International Co-operative Alliance, "The Present Application of the Rochdale Principles of Co-operation (1937) See: www.ica.co-op/co-op/1937-01html

5. That profits should be divided 'pro rata' upon the amount of purchases made by each member.

6. That the principle of 'one member, one vote' should obtain in government and the equality of the sexes in membership.

7. That the management should be in the hands of officers and committee, elected periodically.

8. That a definite percentage of profits should be allotted to education.

9. That frequent statements and balance sheets should be presented to members.[7]

Some of these principles and rules of conduct were a response to the social and economic conditions of the day, while others set out the organizational framework that was to be the basis of the successful co-operative model. The emphasis on pure provisions and full weight and measures was a response to the unscrupulous practice of local shopkeepers who adulterated products and cheated purchasers on weights and measures. Not only did this new co-operative way of doing business focus on quality goods and services, but it treated consumers with respect, allowing them to become business partners sharing both the responsibilities of ownership and profits. While the capital for the development would come from the members, only a limited rate of return was to be paid on it and the profits were to be divided up based upon patronage. These patronage dividends were calculated after the payment of all expenses; setting aside capital for the maintenance and extension of the business and reserving funds to be applied for educational purposes. The management of the co-operative was overseen by the members, who were elected from amongst themselves, and the operation of the business was to be open and transparent with regular financial information presented to the members. This was truly a new way of doing business, one that was based on honesty and principles of fairness and gave the consumer power and control. The basis of the weaver's new way of doing business was to form the underpinnings of the co-operative framework and what distinguishes this model from other organizational forms.

This way of doing business was revolutionary. These businessmen didn't adulterate products, putting leafs in tea or chalk in flour. They didn't simply see customers as the way to make a profit at the expense of others. They believed that pooling resources and ensuring everyone benefited was the way to do business. Unsurprisingly, and to the annoyance of

---

7 No Author Identified. *About the Co-op -Origins of the Movement - Rules*, [online]. Co-op Online, [cited 5 November 2006]. See: (http://www.co-oponline.co-op/about_intro _origins _rules.html

other traders, the reputation of the co-op shop was soon established and customers flocked to it certain that they would be served quality products at affordable prices."[8]

Creating a Support System

This new co-operative movement spread and took root in a number of countries with agricultural, artisan, marketing, and consumer co-operatives forming the bulk of the co-operatives. A key event in the evolution of this new way of doing business was the establishment of the International Co-operative Alliance (ICA) in 1895, which had the aim of providing information, defining and defending the co-operative principles, and developing international trade. The formation of the ICA can be described as a most significant act; one that would enable the development and growth of co-operatives and create a system that would allow co-operatives to harness the benefits of vertical and horizontal collaboration. The long term sustainability of local co-operatives would be enhanced through the creation of sectoral and intersectoral associations.

One could view the ICA as a type of trade organization. However, unlike most trade organizations, which mainly focus on enhancing members' market share, the ICA is also focused on promoting and developing the fundamental principles and values that underpin the co-operative model. Over the years, the ICA has carried out several reviews of the co-operative principles and values to determine their application to changing times; once in 1937, again in 1966, and most recently in 1995.

Evolving Over Time - The Quadruple Bottom Line

With each of the ICA reviews some principles were refined, some were discarded, and others added. The 1995 review resulted in a statement of identity, a statement of values, and seven operating principles; one of which is concern for community and includes the environment.[9] It is these values and principles that set co-operative ways of doing business apart, thus making it a best practice for meeting economic and social needs.

These evolving values and principles have resulted in an organizational and business model with a quadruple bottom line:

- The business must be economically viable and sustainable over time.

---

8 *About the Co-op: Origins of the Movement,* [online]. Co-op Online, [cited 28 December 2006]. See: (http://www.co-oponline.co-op/about_intro _origins1.html
9 7th Principle: Concern for Community - "Co-operatives work for the sustainable development of their communities through policies approved by their members." See: http://www.ica.coop/coop/principles.html

- The product or results of the business must meet both the needs of the members and the customers of the co-operative; who may or may not be one in the same.
- Members must be actively engaged in the management and governance of the co-operative.
- The business must be carried out with a concern for community.

Unlike many other enterprises, co-operatives need not operate as isolated businesses; they are part of a co-operative sector with sectoral, regional, national, and international organizations available to provide inspiration and support. Membership in these organizations is voluntary and co-operatives do not have to participate in the sector. However, it has been my experience as a developer, that co-operatives that participate in the sector have a greater chance of success in the long term. It is the capacity to collaborate beyond the immediate setting that has contributed to the co-operative sector becoming a viable, sustainable movement.

Below are two short case studies that illustrate the unique nature of co-operatives and how this translates into benefits for the individual co-op, the sector, and society. Both case studies are from the energy sector. The first one is about local gas, electricity, and water co-operatives in Alberta and highlights how they, and their sectoral and intersectoral federations, provide utilities to rural Alberta. This is an example of how the co-operative way of doing business enabled rural Albertans to create an integrated system that they control. Excerpt Two focuses on the energy programmes of Co-operative[UK], which illustrate how the co-operative sector has a built-in capacity to be leaders in addressing global warming and climate change. The co-operative business model is not just a tool for serving its members; it is also a tool for engaging people in creating positive outcomes for future generations. Both examples illustrate what is possible using the co-operative model.

Example One – The Role of Co-operatives in the Provision of Utility Services in Rural Alberta

The sparse population of rural Alberta made it difficult for rural residents to access utility services. In 1948, rural Albertans addressed this situation and began to provide these services (including gas, power, and water) to themselves through a series of co-operatives. In each instance, local community-based co-operatives were developed in various regions of the province to provide service distribution systems to their members. The first of these co-operatives were the rural electrification co-operatives (REAs), formed in 1948, to provide electricity to rural Alberta; these were followed by gas and water co-operatives. Today there are 63 REAs that provide service for approximately 45,000 people, there are 69 gas co-operatives serving 100,000 members, and 170 rural water co-operatives are operative, ranging in size from 6 to 1,200 connections.

The success of these rural utility co-operatives is due in part to the fact that they formed sectoral federations. The formation of these federations provided the individual co-operatives with a greater capacity to service their members. As opportunities arose, these federations expanded their operations to include utility purchasing and production. Through their federations, co-operative members were able to provide themselves with utility/energy services, and they were able to command lower prices because of their enhanced purchasing capacity. A number of the REA's formed a private electrical company to service their members and are now looking at the production of green energy, including wind and biomass. In 2002, these federations (power, gas, and water) along with the Federation of Rural Municipalities created the Alberta Rural Utilities Association, a cross-sectoral association, to deal with government with one voice for all their members. While urban Albertans are subject to the fluctuations of the utility market place, rural Albertans belonging to this network of co-operatives have created an infrastructure to more effectively control their own destiny.

This example illustrates how use of the co-operative model allowed rural Albertans to access the same level of services as their urban counterparts without paying a significant premium for the services. Through collaboration with other co-operatives, these co-ops were able to provide their membership with added value through greater negotiating capacity in the market place. With a predictable market share, these individual co-operatives and their federations take advantage of opportunities to become more efficient and innovative. As described in its operating principles the Central Area REA (CAREA) states that their bottom line is service to their members - not return on investment to the shareholders.

> At CAREA we have never, nor will we ever, put profit ahead of people. We work for ourselves and our community. We are directly responsible to our members and we are accountable for distribution within our service areas. We are an intervener in the regulatory process on behalf of our members.[10]

Through the formation of the Alberta Rural Utilities Association, the individual co-operatives and the various federations have strengthened the ability to ensure the security not only of their utilities but of rural Albertans. The goal of this Association, whose membership includes the federations, as well as the Federation of Rural Municipalities is "to work together with

10 CAREA, *Company Profile: CAREA Principles*, See: http://www.carea.ca/profile. htm#principles

combined efforts to ensure the government receives a clear message from rural Albertans regarding common issues that affect our utilities and other matters affecting rural utility systems and their consumers."[11]

Example Two – Greening the Co-operative Sector - an Initiative of Co-operatives[UK]

Co-operatives[UK], the Union of Co-operative Enterprises, is an intersectoral co-operative dedicated to supporting and promoting co-operatives through-out the UK. It is extremely active in getting its members to be forward looking and in promoting the co-operative model throughout the country. Amongst other activities, it identified climate change as one area where co-operatives could make a difference and has set up two key programmes: the Carbon Challenge and the Co-operative Energy programme.

The Carbon Challenge

Following a 2001 Co-operative Commission report, which recommended that co-operatives re-affirm their "co-operative difference," ten Key Social and Co-operative Performance Indicators (KS&CPI) were developed to en-able co-operatives to measure their difference. One of these indicators is the net carbon dioxide emissions arising from each co-operative's operations. Co-operatives[UK] believes in the "co-operative difference" and takes advan-tage of the capacity of the co-operative sector to play a significant role in shaping the future.

> Throughout their long history, co-operatives have always sought to improve the quality of life and secure a future for communities through creating a virtuous circle that harnesses the benefits of commercial success for 'more-than-just-profit.'

The Carbon Challenge is one programme developed by Co-operatives[UK] to enable its members to make a difference. Each co-operative is asked to re-duce their carbon dioxide emissions by 20% by 2010. Co-operatives[UK] has prepared a specific toolkit for its members to use and provides information and support to its members. Co-operatives[UK] is encouraging its membership to address a significant issue by acting locally but thinking globally. Global warming and climate changes are seen by the co-operative sector in the UK as being one of the most significant issues this world is facing. In addition to reducing their CO_2 levels, individual co-operatives are asked to challenge their members and suppliers to be part of the process, resulting in local action with ripple effects that will have an impact on a global issue. Co-op-eratives[UK] have a seven step programme that is focused on actual reductions,

---

11 Alberta Rural Utilities Association (ARUA), See: http://www.carea.ca

not just carbon trading. For Co-operatives[UK] this programme is not merely a social add-on but rather part of good business practice. They have identified four key benefits which positively impact the co-ops, the community, and the environment:

- Reducing energy costs,
- Improving competitiveness,
- Developing new business opportunities, and
- Demonstrating business leadership on climate change.[12]

Co-operative Energy

Under its Co-operative Energy programme, Co-operatives[UK] promotes the development of community based co-operatively owned alternate energy projects such as wind, solar, and biofuels.

An example of one such co-operative is Westmill Wind Farm Co-op located in south-east England. Through its five wind turbines, this 100% community-owned wind farm will produce pollution free electricity to power more than 2,500 homes and each year avoid the release of 10,000 tonnes of carbon dioxide, a greenhouse gas that contributes to climate change. Funding for this 5.5 million pound project came from a 3.2 million pound share offer and a loan from the Co-operative Bank. While Co-operatives[UK] promotes the development of energy co-operatives and provides some direct support, the actual development of these co-operatives is facilitied though Energy4All, a more-than-profit organization that is owned by the co-operatives it creates.[13]

- - -

In both of the above case studies, the co-operatives involved certainly meet the quadruple bottom line: the businesses are sustainable, the products and services meet the needs of the members and customers, the members are involved in the management and governance, and concern for the community is demonstrated in the focus and nature of the activity. In both cases, the co-operatives provide direct services on a community basis and, at the same time, are able to achieve their economy of scale through the formation of federations and co-operation with others. The local focus of the co-operative approach to the production and distribution of utilities is quite different than either that of the private "just-for-profit sector" or the major government owned or controlled corporations that generally rely on

---

12 Co-operatives[UK], *Carbon Challenge, Demonstrating the Co-operative Difference*, See: www. co-operatives-uk.co-op/live/cme1136.htm (6 November 2006).

13 Westmill Co-op web site: www.westmill.co-op, (Accessed: 29 December 2006).

centralized control and production and extensive and expensive distribution systems. As we look to the future – one focused on alternate clean energy sources, locally produced and distributed – we can see from both these practical examples that the co-operative model can be implemented as a best practice.

2. Co-operatives as a Best Practice for Delivering Human Services

Changing demographics and the shifting multicultural composition of Canada's population presents new challenges in service delivery, job creation, and other dimensions of daily life. These challenges require a variety of responses that can be effectively addressed using the co-operative model. An aging population will require a range of services, from home care support to housing, with a variety of support services. New immigrants and refugees require a range of services to meet their initial needs and to help them settle successfully yet retain their sense of culture and self-esteem. Both worker and multi-stakeholder co-operatives provide a best practice to address these emerging social issues. Worker co-operatives are owned and operated by their employee members. Multi-stakeholder co-operatives are comprised of a variety of stakeholder groups, including those using the service and those providing the service. Unfortunately, the important role these co-operatives could play has yet to be recognized.

Historically, governments have relied on the non-profit, charitable, or benevolent sector to provide services delivered by non-governmental organizations; as a result, most programmes are designed to accommodate either non-profit companies or societies. These traditional NGOs are based upon the values of benevolence and philanthropy rather than self-help, self-responsibility, and solidarity. The fact that the worker members also govern the co-operative is often seen, by those familiar with the traditional NGO, as a conflict of interest and lacking on the accountability front. However, a close examination of the ethical values and the closed-loop nature of the worker co-operative accountability framework dispels any perception of conflict of interest and a lack of accountability.

Co-operatives currently operate according to a set of ethical values as adopted by the ICA in 1995. Worker co-operatives are not just organized for the benefit of those who work and own the company, they are organized to provide a business, goods, or services within a socially responsible context, and, while providing care for others, the relationship between the worker and the customer can be described as mutually symbiotic. This is particularly true when the services provided are human or support services. The idea of conflict of interest is more applicable to a different set of circumstances; one where personal gain is realized as a result of exploitation of a situation. There is little or no capacity for exploitation of a situation within the worker co-operative context, since the relationship of all members to the business is equal, open, and transparent.

The concept of a business responsive to community needs, while perhaps foreign to those who see most businesses organized along a single bottom line (i.e. the maximization of profits), exists within the co-operative framework and was an underpinning of the success of the Rochdale Equitable Pioneers Society. As discussed earlier, co-operatives, including worker co-operatives, are organized and operate along a quadruple bottom line. The idea that only organizations not operating a business (e.g. a non-profit society) or whose business income is directed towards meeting its benevolent objectives (non-profit company) should have access to community and or government resources to provide community-based services is archaic, and needs to be revisited in the context of a changing society and the need for alternate models. Both worker and multi-stakeholder co-operatives can play a significant role in the provision of community services and bring added-value because of the "closed loop" nature of their accountability framework.

When comparing the organizational framework of a traditional NGO and a worker co-operative we see that although the organizational framework in a worker co-operative differs from the traditional NGO, the accountability framework in a co-operative is more robust in several ways. The charts on the following page provide an overview of the organizational components of both an NGO and a worker co-operative providing services to clients/customers that are funded or contracted by a third party.

The Worker Co-operative Model

The organizational components of both the traditional NGO and the worker co-operative are similar. However, the relationship of the various components differs. An examination of the traditional NGO organizational framework reveals an open-ended system, with the funder at one end and the client at the other end, while the worker co-operative can be described as a closed-loop system.

A traditional NGO is managed by a board of directors, who usually serve without remuneration and are not employees. Sometimes users or clients can be members of the board. In their capacity as trustees and agents, the board members are usually responsible for governance, overseeing effective management, strategic planning, and the long-term financial viability of the organization. Board positions usually have fixed terms and members

Chart One: Organizational Components for a Traditional NGO

Organizational Component	*Traditional NGO Description*
Funder (s)	• Fund the operations/services of the organization • Fund specific projects, can be fee-for-service • Requires the organization to report in accordance with agreements
Organization	• Establishes mission and vision • Develops services • Creates business plan • Is governed or governed and managed by a Board of Directors • May or may not have a membership
Board of Directors	• Elected, appointed, or selected • Specified term • Trustee of the affairs of the organization • Responsible for reporting to funder • Other than their reputation they have no vested interested in the activities of the organization (no financial ramifications – unless negligent) • Responsible for hiring and supervising key staff • Generally no direct relationship with clients served
Staff	• Provide services as required • Ensure that the organization has the funding to maintain itself
Clients	• Receive services in accordance with the organization's policies and procedures

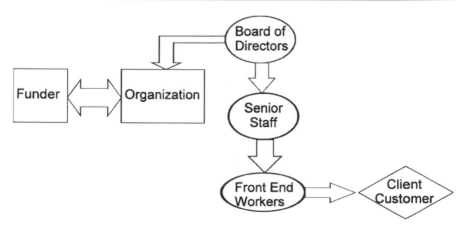

Chart Two: Organizational Components for a Worker Co-op

Organizational Component	Worker Co-operative Description
Funder	• Either provide funding for specific activity or purchasing specific services on a fee-for-service basis • Requires the organization to report as detailed in the contract between the parties
Co-operative	• Consists of members • Operates on a co-operative basis (co-operative values and principles) • Sets out its mission • Develops a business plan • Is governed by a Board
Board of Directors	• Elected by the membership from amongst themselves - can be recalled by the membership • Trustees of the affairs of the co-operative • Responsible for reporting to funder • They have a vested interested in the success of the co-operative – they are part owners • Responsible for membership approvals • Initiate termination of membership • May or may not be responsible for hiring • Direct relationship with client/customer – since as a worker they would be providing services
Staff/employees/workers	• Members of co-operative – owners of business • Provide services as required • All be responsible for providing quality services to ensure ongoing viability
Client/customers	• Receive or purchase services/goods from co-op • In a multi-stakeholder model – could be members of the co-operative

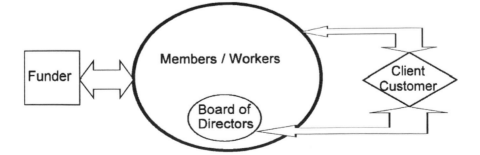

come and go as their terms end. Generally, board members are intensely involved with an organization during their term; however, unless the NGO has a membership, when the term ends the board member leaves and there is little or no ongoing contact or relationship with the organization. Hired staff carry out the day-to-day activities of the organization, which include the provision of services or programmes, securing funding for the organization, and providing support services for the board. Senior management staff usually participates in the strategic planning process; however, other staff, including front-line workers, often do not participate in such planning processes.

In a worker co-operative, all of the members of the co-operative work for the co-operative and, as such, are involved in its day-to-day operations. The board of directors is elected from amongst the workers, which includes both senior management and front-line workers. As trustees and agents, the board members are responsible for the governance and management duties assigned to them by the membership. Responsibilities not delegated to the board are carried out either by the members or committees established by them. Thus, decisions regarding the approach to strategic planning are made with input from the members. Because the board is made up of employee/members, those providing direct service to the clients/customers will often be on the board. Board positions usually have fixed terms and members come and go as their terms end. However, unlike the NGO, ex-board members who continue to work for the co-operative will continue to participate in the affairs of the organization. It should be noted that in a multi-stakeholder co-operative, where the client/customers are also members of the co-operative, the accountability loop is even more compact.

Accountability within an NGO can be described as "structural accountability." The accountability framework is deemed to be inherent in the organizational framework because the board members have no vested interest in the current or ongoing operations of the NGO and the staff are not involved in the governance of the organization. On the one hand, in a worker co-operative accountability can be described as "operational accountability;" it exists as a result of the interplay of the inherent checks and balances that exist within the operational model and because of the overarching co-operative values and principles.

It is interesting to note that since the Enron debacle there has been a shift in thinking regarding the roles of boards of directors and to whom they should be accountable. Traditional thinking within the NGO sector was that the board should be accountable to those providing the funding. New thinking, however, is that the board should be responsible to those that will receive the benefit. This shift in thinking around accountability in the NGO sector to one that is more akin to that found within the co-operative model is described by Hildy Gottlieb:

> Donors and other funders invest in the organization putting money in. But the whole community (including the donors) receives the benefit the organization provides. If the community receives as much benefit/impact as possible the donors will be pleased, which encourages further investment. But the purpose of the organization is not to keep the donors happy; it is to create as much benefit as possible for the recipients of the work the organization does — the community.
>
> Therefore, the board of a non-profit organization is accountable to the community that will receive what the organization provides - benefit, community impact, an improved quality of life.[14]

Looking at these two models, I contend that the worker co-operative's closed-loop accountability framework has the potential to be more responsive to the needs of the customers and is effectively a community driven model. In addition, knowledge and capacity are not lost to the co-operative when a board member's term is up. As owners, the board and staff of a worker co-operative have a greater vested interested in the overall success of the organizations than do the board and staff of the traditional NGO.

The benefits of involving employees in the ownership, management, and governance of an organization are being widely recognized. There is a range of literature on this subject whose benefits are concisely summed up by the Employee Ownership Foundation:

> Those who have experienced first hand the power of employee ownership believe wholeheartedly that economic growth, employee well-being and dignity, and success of the business enterprise are common characteristics of employee-owned companies... [E]xperience and research have shown that employee owners have a different attitude about their company, their job, and their responsibilities that makes them work more effectively and increases the likelihood that their company will be successful. Fundamentally, employee owners are more accountable for their job performance — and their fellow workers' job performance — simply because they have a common stake in the success of their company.[15]

Although the Foundation does not directly promote worker or multi-stakeholder co-operatives, its experience with the positive impact of employee ownership and employee participation in the governance and management

---

14 Hildy Gottlieb, *Board Accountability: A Model for Community-Driven Governance*, Help4 Non-Profits and Tribes Institute, See: www.help4nonprofits.com (Cited 23 June 2005).

15 The Employee Ownership Foundation, *The Importance of Employee Ownership*, See: www. employeeownershipfoundation.org/ownership.asp

of the company reinforces the effectiveness of the worker co-operative model.

After reviewing information regarding the nature of the accountability framework and the co-operative values framework, we can see how the co-operative model, particularly worker and multi-stakeholder co-ops, demonstrate a best practice for the delivery of human services. Below is another short case study that provides a good example of a worker co-operative that provides such services, the Multicultural Health Brokers Co-operative Ltd. (MCHB), operating in Edmonton, Alberta. This worker co-operative provides health brokerage services to 16 immigrant and refugee communities in 23 different languages.

Example Three – Multicultural Health Brokers

The Multicultural Health Brokers Co-operative evolved over time to address the health, education, and social service needs of a variety of cultural groups in a way that was responsive to their specific needs and requirements. In the beginning, a special health team was set up at the Edmonton Board of Health to promote the health of marginalized populations, including immigrants and refugees. As Yvonne Chiu, a member of the MCHB, describes below, ensuring access by immigrants and refugees to services has required a variety of interventions, one of which has been the training of indigenous workers within each of the communities.

> One of the health barriers for immigrant and refugee communities was 'language,' or more accurately, lack of the English language, and one of the innovative projects that was set up, piloted, and evaluated during this time was the Centralized Interpreter Service (CIS).

> A second barrier was 'culture,' or more accurately, a disjunction between the practices of some immigrant and refugee families and the 'traditional practices of mainstream services.' Equality of access to appropriate pre-natal health care was seen as a cornerstone of public health practice. Yet, many immigrant and refugee families were not accessing pre-natal care. This gap led to a collaborative pilot project with Grant MacEwan Community College to equip women of immigrant and refugee communities with the knowledge and skills to provide pre- and post-natal support. In 1994, sixteen women completed the Multicultural Childbirth Educator Training Programme with the hope that they would quickly become a known and respected community resource.[16]

The up-take of the services of the multicultural childbirth educators was not as quick as anticipated. While providing the services to families it became apparent to the educators that because of the complexity of the

---

16 Extracts from an unpublished paper by Yvonne Chiu, January 2005.

circumstances of immigrant and refugee families, a holistic approach was required. Without providing services for the whole family, it was impossible to provide perinatal support. In 1997, the eight remaining educators formalized the concept of "health broker," which recognized the need to provide a bridge between families and the formal health care system. After an extensive review of various organization models and corporate options, the brokers formed a worker co-operative with the mandate "to support immigrant and refugee individuals and families in attaining optimum health through relevant health education, community development, and advocacy support."[17] As Yvonne Chiu indicated, "The co operative model that the MCHB has chosen as an operating structure allows it to live by its principles of democratic governance, direct responsiveness, and accountability, equity, and social justice. It has contributed employment opportunities for a small group of immigrants, mainly women, who have experienced a lack of recognition of foreign credentials directly."[18] From its incorporation in 1999, the co-operative grew to 30 workers in 2005; the workers speak 23 languages and providing services to 16 immigrant and refugee communities.

The MCHB has been extremely successful. It defined and developed the practice of "health broker" and between 2002-2004 it provided pre- and post-natal services to 1,200 families per year. Amongst other activities in this time frame, it also provided intensive home visits for 75 families and bi-cultural parenting couples, as well as early childhood development support to 313 refugee families from eight immigrant countries and services to seniors, school aged children, youth, children with disabilities, and those with mental health problems.

Working closely with the University of Alberta, the MCHB has provided student placement opportunities and worked on curricula for medial students. MCHB is seen as a model to emulate by others across the country. MCHB has been involved in a number of initiatives across the country looking to incorporate multicultural health brokering practice into existing health care services. Most recently, it has teamed up with a number of agencies and organizations including Capital Health, Catholic Social Services, and the Faculty of Medicine to create a New Canadians Health Clinic to provide culturally and linguistically expert, acute and preventative, primary care services to refugees and under serviced immigrants.

The brokers have come a long way from childbirth educators working for the Board of Health to Multicultural Health Brokers; they now operate their own business and collaborate with government and other organization to

---

17 Multicultural Health Brokers Co-operative Web Site: www.mchb.org
18 Extracts from an unpublished paper by Yvonne Chiu, January 2005.

provide culturally sensitive family oriented services. Underlying their success is the adherence to the co-operative principles and values and their sense of accountability to those they serve. The following quote from their website that describes "what they believe in" summarizes this succinctly.

MCHB Co-op is committed to:
* Direct responsiveness and accountability: We are responsible and accountable to the families and communities we serve,
* Equity and social justice: We strive to work for equitable access for those who are marginalized from resources and opportunities in society, and
* Democratic governance: We participate fully in the operations and decision-making of the organization. [19]

3. Co-operatives Have a High Level of Performance

Co-operatives exist in almost every sector of the economy. It is known from studies of the various sectors that co-operatives are generally very successful and bring value. Housing is an excellent example where co-operatives have out-performed other types of providers.

In the past four decades, the co-operative model has been employed across North America and Europe as an effective way to provide affordable housing. Studies in Canada, the U.S., and the U.K. support this claim. A report done in the U.K. by Price Waterhouse for the Department of the Environment comparing co-operatives and other forms of tenant control housing with similar housing associations and local authority developments concluded that co-operatives out-performed other forms of housing. Now in the U.K., many housing projects that were formerly operated by local authorities are either managed by resident-owned co-operatives or have been transferred to resident-owned co-operatives.

Canada Mortgage and Housing Corporation came to the same conclusion through its various evaluations of co-operative housing programmes in Canada. Its 1992 programme evaluation found co-operatives cost 40% less to operate than comparable public housing (owned by the federal or provincial government) and residents had the highest level of satisfaction with their homes. While there are a number of factors that contribute to this difference, one of the more significant was the high level of member participation in management and governance. Non-profit continuing housing co-operatives[20] were identified as a best practice for human settlements

---

19 Multicultural Health Brokers Co-operative see: www.mchb.org
20 In a non-profit continuing housing co-operative, the co-operative continues to own all of the housing and the land. Members either purchase shares or memberships. The shares

at Habitat II because such co-operatives provide affordable housing within mixed income communities, empower low and moderate income people and people with special needs, and involve the resident members in the management and governance of the co-operative. Housing co-operatives are also extremely popular in the U.S. For example, 30% of the housing in New York City is co-operative, the vast majority being limited-equity, affordable housing.

Another example of a high performance co-operative is Mountain Equipment Co-operative (MEC); a retail co-operative conceived in 1971 by a small group of students on a camping trip. Today MEC is Canada's largest supplier of quality outdoor equipment. Operating out of Canada, it is truly an international co-operative that currently has more than 2 million members located in 192 countries. The core purpose of the co-operative is to support people in achieving the benefits of self-propelled, wilderness-oriented recreation. Through its stores across Canada and its web store, MEC provides its members with a range of equipment and supplies at prices which are set to cover costs (including a built-in surplus) and not to maximize profits. Surpluses are allocated to members as patronage shares, which provide MEC with capital to develop and test new gear, to expand the product selection, and to open new stores.

MEC has a very large and committed membership base. Some of the main reasons for its success include selling only quality products, prices members pay are competitive, and surpluses are allocated based upon patronage. I think there are also a number of intangible factors that are also reasons for MEC's success. Promoting healthy outdoor activities and encounters is seen as a "good" thing to do and people like to be associated with organizations that do "good" things. Every person that I have encountered with a MEC membership is extremely proud to be a member. While operating a thriving business is one component of successful co-operative performance, the positive nature of its business and the perceived healthy impact on the community and/or on the environment are also significant. With MEC, these latter factors will continue to attract and satisfy its members as it expands its "green building programme."[21] Not only will MEC be doing a "good" thing but it will be doing it in environmentally-friendly green facilities. By joining MEC and shopping there a member is doing something positive for the environment.

---

are par value shares. When the member leaves the co-operative redeems the share at its original value.

21 MEC is committed to sustainable buildings that are energy efficient, use a minimum amount of water and materials, and fit into the surrounding community.

Another excellent example of a high level of performance arising from the adoption of the co-operative model is the Mondragon group (MCC) of co-operatives in Spain. MCC started when five engineers were encouraged by their local parish priest to set up a factory to make paraffin stoves. From these humble beginnings, it grew into an integrated network of more than 100 co-operatives with combined assets of 18.6 billion euros that provides employment for over 78,000 people in 65 countries around the world - all this within a fifty-year period. MCC was named one of the ten best places to work in Spain by Fortune magazine in 2003. Javier Forcadell Martínez[22] credits the success of MCC to three factors: corporate culture, organizational structure, and a democratic process for strategic planning. According to the study by Forcadell, the co-operative model enables the organization [MCC] to achieve "great effectiveness and provide the impetus for achieving higher levels of innovation and profitability. It enables the organization to create long-term value while achieving the compatibility of its economic, social, environmental, and individual goals."[23]

Co-operatives have a high level of performance and operate according to a set of value and principles that result in a business model with a quadruple bottom line. They work towards improving the quality of life for their members and a secure future for communities and provide an effective way to deliver human services. Yet they are not universally perceived as a best practice. The questions that need to be asked are: Why? What can be done to addresses this issue?

Barriers to Co-ops Being Viewed as a Best Practice Model

There are a number of reasons why co-operatives are not widely viewed as a best practice. I will identify what I perceive to be major barriers that must be strategically addressed within the co-operative sector and by other parties.

1. Lack of Knowledge and Understanding about Co-operatives and the Co-operative Sector

Although a significant proportion of the population belong to one co-operative or another most know very little about co-operatives. Little, if any,

---

22 Javier Forcadell Martínez is a professor of business economics at King Juan Carlos University in Madrid, Spain who has studied MCC extensively.
23 *The Mondragon Co-operative Gives Lessons in Democracy*, Wharton School, See: www. wharton.universia.net, (February 2007).

information is provided in school curricula, including the post secondary system. I think of myself and my colleagues who had no knowledge of the co-operative model when we started out as community development workers. We actually came across the co-operative possibility quite by accident. With the exception of a few government departments that may have had direct dealing with specific co-operatives, there is little knowledge about co-operatives and the co-operative sector in the government. Often even in departments dealing with co-operatives there is a lack of understanding. One example that comes to mind is staff at Canada Mortgage and Housing Corporation (administering CMHC's co-operative housing programmes) telling co-operatives that they should not be joining sector organizations or participating in sector educational sessions and workshops. These comments demonstrate a lack of understanding about the value of inter co op collaboration, as well as the need for ongoing member education.

Even within the co-operative sector itself, co-operatives are often lax at involving their own membership in the operations of the co-operative. In some cases, co-operatives haven't even broadcast the fact that they are a co-operative.

2. Social and Economic System Built Upon the For-Profit and Philanthropic Paradigm

As illustrated in the case of the Multicultural Health Brokers Co-operative, the co-op is respected for the nature and quality of its work and has been extremely successful and effective: however, it has difficulty accessing resources to undertake its work – one of its barriers stems from the fact that it is organized as a worker co-operative. As Yvonne Chiu put it:

> Despite the co-op's outstanding record, it continues to struggle to gain a toehold in the mainstream system as a legitimate resource in supporting immigrant families and communities. The two challenges that it has are:
>
> - The system doesn't recognize that immigrants and refugees have unique needs.
> - Most Albertans, including government, don't understand co-ops and community accountability. Being a board member and an employee is perceived as conflict of interest.[24]

MCHB has been excluded from accessing certain funding because it does not fit nicely into the funding formula boxes. Not only do we need to address the possibility of co-operatives as a "third way" but we also have to confirm the legitimacy of using the co-operative approach.

---

24 Extracts from an unpublished paper by Yvonne Chiu, January 2005.

3. The Perception That Local Initiatives Lack Capacity

I and some of my colleagues have encountered an attitude of skepticism within some communities and organizations towards community-based co-operatives. There seems to be the perception that because the co-operative is owned and governed by ordinary citizens, and not controlled by members of the private business sector, it may not have the where-with-all to develop and manage its business. This situation can become more problematic if those exhibiting this attitude are involved with government or a quasi-government body that might be providing some financial assistance to the co-operative. One example is a housing co-operative which is developing an affordable, mixed-equity residential arrangement, in a small urban area in Alberta. The co-operative received funding from the provincial government under a special programme, which for a variety of very complicated reasons was channeled though the municipality, resulting in the municipality having to account to the Province for the co-operative's use of the funding. The result was micro management on the part of the municipality in areas where it had little knowledge or expertise and delays in funding; all having a negative financial impact on the co-operative. Similar problems had been encountered by co-operatives that received funding under the various Canada Mortgage and Housing Corporation programmes where the programme delivery staff made the co-operative undertake additional work to prove their capabilities, often resulting in additional costs to the co-operative.

Part of the problem is a lack of understanding of the co-operative system and its ongoing supports for individual co-operatives, and another part of the problem is a subliminal culture of colonialism by those who believe they have either "power" or "control over" and do not believe in the concepts of self-help and self-reliance.

4. Democracy is Cumbersome and Time Consuming

One of the arguments against co-operatives is that too much time must be allocated by the members in the governance and management of the organization, thus resulting in a less efficient business operation. There are a number of issues that need to be addressed here, including the lack of understanding of the components and procedures of good governance within a democratic organization and the quantification of the benefits of member participation in the multiple bottom line of the co-op. Done properly, democracy is not cumbersome and time consuming. Mondragon Corporación Co-operativa is a stellar example of what can be done.

5. Lack of Capital - Risk, Start-up, Operational Expenses, and Expansion

One of the major barriers to the development of new co-operatives is the lack of capital. In many instances, members do not have the necessary capital to start up the business. Traditional financial institutions have great resistance in lending to co-operatives. While there is some funding within the co-operative sector, it is extremely limited, both in terms of the dollars available and what the funds can be used for.

6. Lack of Adequate Development Resources

The development of a co-operative is both an extensive and intensive process. The length of time and the resources required depend upon the nature of the co-operative enterprise and the group's internal capacity - both human and capital. A key to the successful development is access on a timely basis to appropriate developmental resources. The current development infrastructure across the country is very sparse and fragmented. In some regions, there is also a disconnect between provincial or regional associations and co-operative developers.

7. The Concept is too Good to be True

In some senses the underpinnings of the co-operative sector, which are its strengths, are also its weaknesses. Looking at the co-operative approach and its support systems, a doubting person may find it hard to believe in the potential anticipated outcomes; whereas co-operators know their model works and delivers the anticipated outcomes. It is essential that the longevity of the co-operative model to date needs to be conveyed to the skeptical so they can see co-operatives have worked and will continue to work in the future.

> Successful co-operatives have been built and developed for over 150 years. Many co-operatives today can trace their roots back to the nineteenth century. This longevity, in comparison with profit-making companies, is a sign of success. During this time co-operatives have managed to maintain their autonomy in creating distinct businesses focused on their members' needs.[25]

---

25 *An Introduction to Participatory Governance in the Co-operative Sector*, A Report commissioned by Co-operatives[UK] on behalf of the Governance and Participation Project, May 2005.

Removing Barriers and Making Co-operatives a Best Practice

Within the sector there are resources that can be used as a starting point for this discussion. One example is the Marketing Our Co-operative Advantage (MOCA) programme that a number of co-operatives have been involved in. In 2005, the National Co-operative Bank (NCB) in the U.S. commissioned a study to determine the impact of the operations of the MOCA programmes. The study found that:

Of the 42 co-operatives interviewed who were marketing their co-operative advantage:

- 53% planned to increase their focus on MOCA and 47% planned to continue the same focus;
- 76% were satisfied or very satisfied with their marketing programme;
- 41% reported business performance above industry average, 54% reported business performance at industry average, and 5% reported business performance below industry average;
- 41% responded that MOCA influences successful business outcomes, while 59% responded that their success is based on, and dependent upon, MOCA.[26]

Amongst other things, the study concluded:

> MOCA does drive successful business outcomes. Quality market research is required for effective MOCA efforts; small co-operatives must collaborate with other co-operatives, either within their region or within their industry, to secure it. The process of identifying and communicating a co-operative advantage is transforming. It brings co-operatives back to their roots, back to basic human ethical values, and in the process makes the co-operative financially healthier and better able to respond to challenges to their co-operative structure and from the emerging global economy.[27]

The co-operative sector, including individual co-operatives, co-operative developers, sectoral, regional, provincial, and national federations, must engage in meaningful dialogue and strategic planning processes to design and implement a plan for co-operative development in the country. A proactive, rather than a reactive, approach is needed if the co-operative sector is to realize its potential. Part of the planning process could look at:

- Marketing the co-operative advantage (both internally and externally). It is possible to build upon the existing tools and experience.

---

26 National Co-operative Bank, *Marketing Our Co-operative Advantage*, Research Report (January–March 2005) p. 2.
27 *Ibid.*, p. 2.

The marketing should not only include members and potential members but should extend to government, the financial sector, and potential co-operative managers.

- The development of curricula (for primary, secondary, and post-secondary) educational institutions.
- The development of tools that could be used to enhance access by the co-operative sector to funding programmes previously accessible only by traditional NGOs.
- The development of a more visible manifestation of supports provided by the sector to dispel the local "lacks capacity" attitude.
- Ways of enhancing and supporting the development capacity within the sector.
- The development of a sustainable system for financing, including risk capital, start-up, operational, and expansion capital.
- The development of opportunities for the existing co-op sector to work collectively on environmental and social issues (e.g. Carbon Challenge in the U.K.).

Why is it Important to Make Co-operatives a Best Practice?

There are a number of reasons why co-operatives should be seen as a best practice. I have been involved in community economic development for a number of years. In many instances, the co-operative is the most appropriate model for our clients to use. The lack of understanding of the co-operative model makes co-operative development very difficult and often artificially prolongs the development process. My colleagues and I spend significant time and resources in "educating" individuals and organizations that our clients are dealing with about co-operatives and their benefits. If co-operatives were seen as a best practice, the time and resources we spend on this education could be better directed to the actual development of co-operatives. I have heard colleagues across the country raise the same issue. For me the reasons for making co-operatives a best practice are three-fold: first, to enhance the effectiveness of co-op developers; second, efficiency of the development process; and third, to create more co-operatives.

As a society, I think we are in a critical period. Globalization, climate change, global warming, depleting natural resources, a non-sustainable social and economic infrastructure, threatened food supply, the increasing gap between rich and the poor − all of these are issues that we are being bombarded with on a daily basis. In some cases, the magnitude of the issues results in overall paralysis and a sense that nothing can really be done. The co-operative model really provides an option to enable individual communities to begin to address these issues at a local level. In fact, it is really the only model that will ensure local empowerment, retention of community wealth, and long-term sustainability. Working together using the co-operative model individuals and their respective co-operatives and federations can accomplish the impossible. Given the issues that we need to address, we need to accomplish the impossible. This is the primary reason for making co-operatives a best practice.

> Co-operation brings a large breath of fresh ethical air to inspire our collective future; in the business world, the economy, society, and in general, our co-operatives put the emphasis on greater responsibility, greater solidarity, and more equity, [which are] core beliefs for a society with more cohesive and solid values.

> Among the assets of the co-operative movement, the notion of the person, the team, participation, responsibility taking, equitable sharing, and democratic management are absolutely fundamental. In every co-op, the members apply values that are universally recognized with the goal of doing business that is centred on the needs of the person.

> Six of the seven co-operative principles show the way for improvement of the human condition: freedom to belong, education, democratic power, autonomy, inter-co-operation, and community engagement. Only one principle deals with the issue of money — as a means and not as an end in itself.[28]

---

28 A *Co-operative Approach for Uniting Our Society,* An Address by Professor Bruno-Marie Béchard, Rector of the Université de Sherbroke, 2006 Co-operative Forum (Quebec City, May 14, 2006.)

Case Studies

The Growth of a National Second-Tier Co-operative Organization

Hazel Corcoran

F ounded in 1990, the Canadian Worker Co-operative Federation (CWCF) is the national federation of worker co-operatives, representing both English and French speaking worker co-operatives in all regions of the country.

CWCF's Vision is: To be a growing, cohesive network of democratically controlled worker co-ops that provide a high quality of worklife and support the development of healthy and sustainable local economies, based on co-operative principles.

CWCF's Mission is:

1. Strengthen our worker co-op members,
2. Support the development of new worker co-ops, and
3. Strengthen the federation and its governance.

CWCF has, from its inception, been focused on the development of worker co-operatives, and on providing services to existing worker co-ops. The worker co-operative sector in Canada may be characterized as an emerging sector, for which CWCF has been successful in designing, developing, delivering, and administering programmes.

At a meeting in February of 1990, representatives of worker co-operatives from across Canada came together for the first time to discuss whether there was a need to develop a national organization to represent their interests. Although worker co-ops had been on the agenda of the Canadian Co-operative Association and the Co-operatives Secretariat, which saw them as having the potential to lead a new wave of co-op development, worker co-operators themselves had little input on the national level and only marginal communication among themselves. It became clear after a couple of days of meetings that there was an opportunity that could only be met by forming a national organization. Further discussion led to outlining the objectives which guided the CWCF in its formation and founding the following year – the spring of 1991, in Antigonish, Nova Scotia.

In its first decade, CWCF was run on an extremely modest budget. For the first two years, its operations were carried out entirely by its volunteer board of directors. For the following eight years, a part-time executive director was employed to guide the activities and coordinate the volunteer efforts of the board members and others. In its first ten years, CWCF was financed through members' and associate members' dues, small fee-for-service contracts, and donations from supporting organizations in the established co-op sector, most significantly the Co-operators Group Ltd.

During this initial decade, CWCF learned two important lessons. One was that it was essential for the fledgling federation to live within its means – although revenues were low, expenses were closely monitored and budgets were generally balanced through holding almost all board meetings by conference call, having most of the work done by volunteers, and by being creative in the use of resources. Through those years, the board president often said, "CWCF has a huge mandate but tiny resources." This meant it was essential to pick the most important things to accomplish. One of the things we focused on was setting the stage for a self-sustaining federation once the sector was large enough and another was lobbying to secure government resources. The second lesson was the importance of perseverance; approximately eight years were spent on lobbying efforts – with little results in that period. In many of those years, substantial efforts were made. We had concluded that the best chance of kick-starting the sector was through government support, and further, that there was a lot that the sector could contribute to communities across Canada. We were not prepared to give up.

In the year 2000, CWCF's long years of lobbying efforts finally resulted in obtaining the pilot project Worker Co-op Development Fund. This began a period of significantly expanding services and the hiring of two full-time-equivalent staff members. The following is a brief description of some of the major accomplishments of CWCF — it should be noted as well that the consistent support of the federal Co-operatives Secretariat over the years has contributed to making many of these accomplishments possible through provision of financing to carry out many studies and projects.

Worker Co-operative Development Fund

"Tenacity Works," the Worker Co-op Fund, is an investment fund whose purpose has been to create new worker co-ops and to expand existing ones in all regions of Canada. The fund was developed as a research/pilot project by the Canadian Worker Co-op Federation and funded by Human Resources Development Canada (as it was called at that time). The objective of the pilot project was to assess the viability of creating a permanent self-sustaining fund to support the development and expansion of worker co-operative enterprises in Canada.

The pilot project was based upon an original proposal developed by CWCF, which outlined an approach for creating a permanent, self-sustaining investment fund. The fund provides 3 key development components. The first component is to assist with each co-op's capitalization by providing up to 35% of the required capital as a foundation to lever the additional required capital from the co-op's members (15% target) and other conventional financial partners. The second is technical assistance, in other words, funding to assist developing co-ops to complete feasibility assessments and business plans. The third component is to assist with the co-op's organizational development and training requirements (incorporation, policies, administrative systems, board training, etc). Throughout the development process, CWCF has taken a tiered approach. The co-op must do well in the feasibility process in order to get support for business planning, then do well in the business plan to receive an investment; and if all goes well, they are eligible for the management after-care and training assistance.

The pilot project was very successfully implemented and has met and exceeded all identified targets. The funds continue to grow and revolve. Over the year 2007, it is expected that approximately $200,000 will be available for loans to worker co-ops.

Worker Co-op Developers' Network

It was apparent to the CWCF that there was a real need for locally-based, worker co-op development expertise that was committed to building the worker co-op sector. In 1997, CWCF carried out a survey of worker co-operative developers and potential developers and found there was interest in creating a Worker Co-op Developers' Network that would provide service to developing worker co-ops and create a forum for information exchange and professional development. However, the resources to do this were not available at that time, but with the creation of the Worker Co-op Fund, CWCF was able to make the Network operational.

There are currently close to 50 people who are members of the Worker Co-operative Developers' Network. The Developers' Network extends to all regions of Canada. It is made up of individuals and organizations that are working at the grassroots level doing worker co-operative development across Canada.

Managing CoopZone

CoopZone is a network of co-operative developers that covers all co-op sectors, not only worker co-ops. CWCF has managed CoopZone since September, 2005 on behalf of the broader co-operative movement, providing a single entry point to co-op development expertise in Canada and a common forum for developers to enhance their practices through information sharing and collaboration.

CoopZone's web site (www.coopzone.coop) contains information on training opportunities, a help wanted forum, and relevant annotated links and resources. The site is bilingual. It is easy to use by readers looking for information, by co-op developers seeking contract opportunities, and by contributors posting new information, links, and requests for technical assistance. As the site becomes more populated with resources, it is increasingly useful to those involved in co-op development. The Network now involves 67 developers, including some who are staff developers in co-op associations or CED organizations and independent developers. CoopZone is a meeting place for everyone involved in development - facilitating communication and collaboration.

RRSP Lobby and Programme

CWCF and the Fédération québécoise des co-opératives forestières lobbied in the 1990s to secure changes that would allow members of worker co-operatives to invest the shares of their co-op in a self-directed RRSP. The lobby was successful and a programme was developed by the CWCF and Concentra Financial (previously called the Co-op Trust Company of Canada) to enable worker co-ops to take advantage of these changes to the RRSP regulation. Co-ops other than a worker co-op (e.g., a producer co-op) are also eligible to take part in this programme as long as they become an associate member of CWCF.

Employment Insurance Brief

Many worker co-ops have difficulties with rulings from Revenue Canada regarding the nature of the employment relationship between the members and the co-op. By working with federal officials, CWCF was able to clarify various options for structuring a worker co-op to ensure that the members have the relationship they desire either an employer-employee relationship (insurable employment) or an independent contractor relationship (self-employment).

Co-operative Development Initiative

After several years of lobbying by the co-op sector, the federal government in 2002 announced the Co-operative Development Initiative, Advisory Services programme. CWCF was chosen by the Canadian Co-operative Association and le Conseil canadien de la co-opération as one of the delivery partners. This programme has allowed CWCF to offer technical assistance to developing and pre-existing worker co-ops, primarily through members of the Developers' Networks.

Documentary: The Take

Canadians Avi Lewis and Naomi Klein made the documentary The Take in 2004 on the Recovered Factory Movement in Argentina. All of these factories are worker co-ops. CWCF aired the premier public showing of the film, with Director Avi Lewis in attendance, at our 2004 conference in Moncton, N.B. CWCF then partnered to host premier releases in other cities, including Ottawa and Calgary. This film has been an excellent tool for education about the worker co-op model as a positive approach for workers in both the global South and North.

Study: Succession Planning Using the Worker Co-op Option

Completed in 2005, this study focused on the sale of a business by a small business owner to its employees as a worker co-op. It documents the information, knowledge, and strategies involved in reaching such a decision, for the owner and for the workers. It explains the functions of a worker co-operative, as well as the various options available to business owners when facing retirement. This approach is potentially very significant due to the large number of retirements by business owners expected in the coming years.

Prairie Labour/Worker Co-op Council

In September 2006, a meeting in Saskatoon was held labour and worker co-op activists to discuss potential collaboration in the face of a series of plant closures in the region. Over two days of intense discussions, leaders from the Prairie Region of the Canadian Labour Congress (CLC) and the CWCF exchanged ideas for advancing the ability of workers and communities to defend their jobs and local economies. Out of this meeting, the Prairie Labour/Worker Co-op Council was created. The purpose of the Council, which is a collaboration of CWCF, Co-op Ventures Worker Co-op, the CLC Prairie Regional office, and other labour organizations, is to facilitate collaboration between labour and worker co-op activists to improve conditions for workers in the region by promoting and facilitating worker ownership.

Participation in broader Co-operative and CED Sectors

On behalf of CWCF, staff and board members have participated on a variety of other boards, including:
- Canadian Co-op Association Board,
- Conseil canadien de la co-opération Board,
- CCEDNet Policy Council,
- Board, Canadian Community Investment Network, and
- International Worker Co-op Federation (CICOPA) Board.

Lessons Learned

In terms of success, the most important factors for CWCF are:

- Building upon the common vision and commitment of the people involved: from board, to staff, to advisors, to worker co-op members, to co-op developers;
- Identifying key services to members, such as the RRSP programme and the Tenacity Works Fund;
- Building links with the broader co-operative sector, other CED organizations, and more recently the labour movement; and
- Maintaining an entrepreneurial culture focused on developing and supporting worker co-ops.

CWCF has a vision to be an integrated service federation, encompassing service to worker co-op members, development of new worker co-ops, and after-care in management and governance. CWCF is a successful example of a sector federation, or a co-op of co-ops, in the long co-operative tradition of sector-specific federations. The leadership at the board level has been extraordinary, notably by the founding president, Mark Goldblatt. Several directors over the years, including Mark, had prior experience with founding another, much larger, sector federation, the Co-operative Housing Federation of Canada. There has been a relatively slow turnover on the board in the first seventeen years of the federation; those who attend the board meetings, whether as board members or invited board advisors, have a high level of mutual respect and trust for one another and work well together.

One challenge for the future, having had little turnover in board or staff since its beginnings, will be to see whether CWCF can continue to do as well once succession in staff and board members begins to happen in earnest. Further, financial resources remain somewhat precarious, with significant dependence on government programming. After funding for the initial CDI Advisory Services programme ends in March 2008, it will be very important for that programme to be renewed and that CWCF continue to participate, or else have a comparable programme in place and accessible by CWCF. If not, then a noticeable reduction in service levels will occur.

There are a couple of lessons which we have learned along the way, although they may at first seem contradictory. First, it is important to have a clear vision towards which the Federation continually strives and that the group supports the mandate which it has given itself. Yet at the same time, the co-op must look for opportunities which allow it to meet its mandate, or be better governed, in ways that may not have been part of the original conception. In other words, a co-op needs to stay true to its vision while remaining flexible in how it is achieved.

The heart of CWCF is the deep commitment to the worker co-op movement, to the co-operative principles, to the development of the co-operative sector, and to commonly agreed upon strategies. Even at those frequent times when it seems that the available resources cannot possibly meet the mandate, CWCF members have found the commitment, drive, and entrepreneurial spirit to make the seemingly impossible, possible. In sum, at CWCF — *tenacity works.*

Case Study Two:
Yellowknife Glass Recyclers Co-op

The Little Co-op that Could

Greg O'Neill

The community of Yellowknife is home to a diverse citizenry. At one end of the spectrum are the oil and diamond company executives living in show homes with all the comforts required to ease through the Yellowknife winter. At the other end of the spectrum are the intrepid houseboaters of Great Slave Lake who have created an alternative community in Yellowknife's historic Oldtown.

The houseboaters are an eclectic mixture of artists, environmentalists, musicians, and those who have chosen to live on the edge-of-the-edge. Their homes float on the water in the summer, and commuting to town is done by canoe or small boats. In the winter, they are encased in the ice, and commuting is done by snow machine or regular motor vehicles that are supported by the thickness of the ice that forms on the lake. It's the time between the two seasons that stimulates the creative spirit and gives birth to many an interesting invention.

One of the citizens of the Yellowknife houseboat community, Matthew Grogono, is a self-sufficient inventor, artist, visionary, mechanic, and activist. About twelve years ago, the city of Yellowknife was considering instituting a recycling programme. During the debate about the programme Matthew asked the mayor and council why the city was not including glass recycling as part of the programme. In response, the mayor challenged Matthew to figure out a way to do it himself if he was so keen on the idea. So, he did.

Matthew and a couple of friends went to the Yellowknife landfill, where scavenging is a popular pastime. (In fact, there is a weekly column in the local newspaper called *Tales from the Dump*.) Matthew and his friends came back to a little workshop he had in Oldtown[1] with an old ringer washer, some discarded electric motors, and a pile of other people's junk. With this material, they built a machine that could polish the rough edges of wine, beer, and other bottles that had been cut down. They then built a machine that could take the cut down, polished glass bottles and stencil images on the outside of the glass.

Some finished products:

For 11 years Matthew ran Yellowknife Glass Recyclers as a sole proprietorship, refining the production process and developing a customer base. Some local artists, fellow houseboaters, and others worked to develop the images that were used for the stencils and over the years an artbank of images was developed. The recyclers became selective in the raw materials chosen to achieve the best end products. However, there was never enough cash to take the business to the next level and never a consistent workforce available to produce in the quantities required to allow the enterprise to achieve its potential. The business was in a catch 22 situation; it did not have adequate cash to hire additional staff to produce the product needed to meet demand and it couldn't meet demand unless it produced more.

As Matthew pondered what to do, he remained active in the community. He was on the board of directors of the Aurora Arts Society, a non-profit organization set up to promote the interests and welfare of local artists. The society had undertaken a study to look at the feasibility of setting up a co-

---

1 Oldtown is the part of Yellowknife where the original southerners who came to mine gold set up camp. It is the site of the first permanent buildings in Yellowknife.

operative as an organization that could administer a centre. Matthew began to think of how this concept might apply to his Yellowknife Glass Recyclers dilemma.

Matthew made the decision to convert his sole proprietorship to a co-operative. He received a grant from the Canadian Worker Co-operative Federation to have a prefeasibility study completed. The glass recyclers had embarked on a voyage of discovery; nothing that would concern a Yellow-knife houseboater. Making the conversion from sole proprietorship was not unlike figuring out how to cross the stretch of space between the houseboat and the shore during the seasons when the surface of the lake was neither ice nor water.

The first challenge was to find a group of co-adventurers. It took some time and a lot of discussion, but an original group of 5 people was organized to form the co-op. The group included people who had worked on and off in the shop over the years and new people who showed up with an interest in both the enterprise and the concept of the co-op. The group needed a business plan and some money. The co-op didn't solve the problem of expansion simply through its creation; it needed a road map to get across the lake. The group expanded to eight members as the discussions went on.

The group received a grant from the government of the Northwest Territories to complete a business plan for the co-op. Some of the issues that needed to be resolved included;

- Valuation of a business that absorbed 11 years of a person's life and was based on inventions that were created and refined, but, at the same time, had never been a big money-maker.
- Defining a production process and ensuring a consistent workforce was available for production.
- Defining a marketing plan to expand the demand for the product.
- Defining a role for Matthew within the new structure that respected his role as the developer and the equality of the other members.
- Finding money to do the above.

The group decided on a value that the co-op was willing to pay to acquire the assets of the business, and they also identified a monthly amount that the co-op would pay Matthew to lease the property in which the operation was housed. It was not an easy thing to do. There was more than one passionate debate on the subject. It is to the credit of all those involved that a final decision was made that respected the integrity of all involved and had a basic fairness to all parties. Matthew received a preferred share in the co-op that will be paid down out of the net savings of the co-operative. This solution guarantees the ongoing productive involvement of Matthew and allows the co-op to repay Matthew over time. If it is a good business enterprise that the co-op is purchasing, then it will generate the cash required to pay down the preferred share. If it doesn't work out, Matthew will get his business back.

The group defined a production process by breaking down the various steps required to make a finished product and then tracked the amount of time required to complete each step. Over a three month period, production workers kept timesheets and tracked the amount of time they committed to production. The time was used as the means to measure labour costs, which was one of the variable costs per unit in the breakeven analysis. The limit of production capacity was determined by how long it took to complete the longest step in the production process. All steps in the production process could be completed concurrently. Suffice it to say that with a constant workforce, the co-op could produce more than enough products to cover the costs of labour and other costs associated with the operation. The workspace and equipment had the capacity to achieve the necessary production.

The co-op members are a creative group. They developed a number of guerrilla marketing schemes to be used in Yellowknife. One creative tactic, the computerized production of $5.00 Grogobucks (gift certificates in the form of money), prompted an on-line warning from Interpol stating that the digital reproduction of currency was a felony. That is when they decided to use Matthew's face on the gift certificates. There were a variety of other schemes that resulted in the Glass Recyclers being in almost every issue of the local newspaper and grabbing free advertising in hotels, bars, and restaurants. The challenge was how to translate that creativity into reaching a market that was greater than the 20,000 residents of Yellowknife.

The co-op was up to the challenge and came up with a strategy to expand the scope of their market. They developed a pricing strategy that has made them very competitive in the market place and allows for enough revenue to generate a healthy surplus. They developed a set of promotional tools:

- A catalogue of items for sale (virtual and hardcopy),
- A secure website for on-line purchases,
- Advertising in selected media,
- An upgrade of the retail Point of Sale equipment to accommodate credit and debit card purchases in their retail outlet, and
- A selected list of potential retailers who would be contacted to carry the product line in other parts of Canada.

They targeted increasing sales in the retail outlet that was part of the operation in Yellowknife. They planned on increasing wholesale and retail sales in other larger centres of the Northwest Territories and Nunavut and penetrating the gift and souvenir markets in large Western Canadian cities by selecting specific retailers to contact and provide promotional materials for wholesale. The key to substantial expansion of retail sales was the development and promotion of a website for secure online purchasing.

The co-op decided to keep Matthew as the manager of the co-op. Matthew reports to a board of directors made up of all the members. Matthew is delegating as much of the responsibility for marketing, bookkeeping, and managing accounts receivable as possible. A breakdown of responsibilities was identified and specific members are taking specific tasks. The group works as a collective and meets regularly to sort out all the unforeseen details of start-up.

The co-op put together a capital plan. The members were able to contribute about 55% of the total capital required and were able to obtain about half of the outside financing they needed. The Canadian Alternative Investment Co-operative made a loan to the co-op. The Co-operators also gave a grant to the co-op.

The lessons learned from this development experience relate to the transitioning of business. There are two transformations taking place simultaneously for Yellowknife Glass Recyclers Co-op. They are transitioning from a sole proprietorship to a co-operative. They are also transitioning from a cottage industry to a full-time business providing primary employment for 3 to 5 people.

The financing of the purchase of the business, from the sole proprietorship to a co-op, was financed by the owner. This created some potential for conflict on both the management/governance aspect of the business, as well as the development of the business. In the first instance, the potential for conflict existed in the expectations of the new owner/members of the co-op to take over and the reluctance of the former owner to relinquish decision making control over the enterprise.

Careful thought was given to identifying the roles and responsibilities of the members/board versus the manager's: Who had what authority and how that authority could be exercised? The drafting of the bylaws laid out the general division of authority between the board (which included all the members, less the manager) and the manager.

The following items were also developed and adopted by the co-op:
- General Manager's job description,
- Position descriptions for: President, Vice-President, Secretary/Treasurer, Director, and
- Terms of Reference for the Executive Committee.

Through a series of meetings, the members of the co-op reviewed and adapted the materials provided. Through that process, they were able to define how they would make decisions within the co-op that addressed both the members' expectations as owners and the former owner's accrued knowledge and abilities in the business operations.

The financial history of the enterprise was not impressive. The business was a break even operation that had provided part of the sole proprietor's annual income. There was also some occasional employment provided to others as described above. Although the potential for growth was obvious, based on the quality of the product that was being produced and the "green" element of the business, the business history of the enterprise would not be attractive to potential investors.

Through drafting of the business plan, the members identified an approach to capitalizing the transition of the business from the owner to the co-op. The initial financing was a conversion of the value of the assets being transferred to preferred shares in the co-op in the owner's name. The co-op then had a structured balance sheet that showed assets of significant value and equity that were a reasonable percentage of the value of the assets. In order for the owner to be able to get his preferred shares paid out the co-op would need to be successful. This layer of financing facilitated the transition of ownership to the co-op.

Another layer of capitalization was required to expand the operation's production and marketing capacity so the co-op could generate enough employment for the members. The members provided "sweat equity" in the form of developing a marketing plan and website. The members also prepared the business plan that was used to approach other lenders. Some of the costs of the business plan were paid through a grant from the NWT government, but a significant amount of time and effort was also contributed by the members. This investment of time, talent, and energy on the part of the members represented an investment in the ownership of the fledgling co-op and consolidated the members' commitment to its success. It also demonstrated to outside lenders that the members were committed to implementing the business plan they had developed.

The commitment of funds by the Canadian Alternative Investment Co-operative and Co-operators was a direct result of this effort on the part of the members. The funds received from these two sources allowed the co-op to take the first steps towards the envisioned expansion. The transition from cottage industry to a business providing secure employment started.

Notwithstanding the need for more investment capital, the co-op has been in business for about six months as of January, 2007. Things are still chugging along. December 2006 was the best sales month ever, and sales for each month the co-op has been operating have been about double what they were for the same month in the previous year. The co-op is still searching for the additional capital it needs to purchase some new equipment required to speed up production and expand its marketing programme, but overall, the fledgling co-op is well underway.

Tools

Developing a Co-op

Russ Christianson

C o-operatives are a well-proven model for doing business and providing for people's needs. They have a very successful track record in Canada, with nearly fifteen million members of co-ops, credit unions, and caisses populaires.[1]

Why Form a Co-op?

This, of course, is the key question. What are the reasons people form co-ops instead of regular corporations? In many ways, co-ops are similar to any business corporation:

- Like corporate shareholders, members of co-ops enjoy limited liability.
- Co-ops can, and do, operate in every sector of the economy.
- Like any business, co-operatives have to meet the needs of their customers (members) to survive and prosper.
- Co-ops and corporations are viewed as "natural persons" under the law, and are therefore able to enter into contractual arrangements.
- Like any business, co-ops need to generate more cash than they spend.
- Co-op's day-to-day business operations are professionally managed like any other business.
- Every province and the Canadian government have legislation that regulates co-operatives and corporations.
- Co-ops can be either for-profit or non-profit organizations.

And, there are some significant differences that make co-ops appealing to many people:

- Co-ops follow the seven principles of co-operation to put their values into practice.

---

1 Co-operatives Secretariat, Government of Canada, Ottawa, 1996.

- Co-ops are democratic organizations. Every member is entitled to one vote, no matter how many shares they own, and proxy votes are not allowed.[2] Many small co-ops make decisions by consensus.
- Co-operatives exist to serve the needs of their members, not to maximize shareholders' wealth.
- Co-operatives can face a much less onerous process for raising capital compared to private corporations.[3]
- Surpluses from operations may be distributed to co-op members based on the amount of use they make of their co-op, not simply on the number of shares they own.
- The survival rate of co-ops is generally much higher than regular businesses (64% versus 36% for all businesses in the first five years of operation in Quebec).[4]   More than 4 out of 10 co-operatives survive more than ten years, compared to 2 businesses out of 10 for the private sector.[5]
- Co-operatives often form federations and associations to further the needs of their members.

Ten Steps to Develop a Co-op

The ten (not necessarily easy) steps to follow in starting a co-op are basically the same as any business:

1. Identify a real opportunity to serve people's needs better.
2. Begin to work with others who share your commitment to the idea.
3. Investigate the financial and market feasibility of your idea.
4. Develop (or hire a consultant to write) a comprehensive business plan.
5. Determine the legal structure that is the most suitable for your business.
6. Incorporate the co-operative.
7. Recruit and educate members.

---

2 Proxy voting may be allowed if members are spread out over a distance. In B.C. the Co-op Act provides for proxies if members live more than 80 kms. from the meeting venue.
3 Co-operatives with more than 25 members must issue and receive approval from the government for its "Offering Statement," while corporations with more than 25 shareholders must follow the much more onerous and expensive process of gaining approval for its "Prospectus."
4 Quebec Ministry of Industry and Commerce and Co-operatives Secretariat, "Survival Rates of Co-operatives in Quebec." Electronic version: www.agr.ca/policy/coop/accueil. html., (2000) p. 15.
5 *Ibid.*, p. 16

8. Organize the first General Membership Meeting and elect the first Board of Directors.
9. Raise the necessary start-up capital, including member investment, outside investors, and lenders.
10.Open for business.

Of course, like any creative endeavour, these steps are not necessarily linear. Depending on your particular situation, some steps may overlap and some may build on others. However, two things have been proven from experience – you will spend less money and you will significantly decrease the risk of your business failing by following these steps.

This "ten-step" list is deceptively simple. Starting a business, whether a co-operative or a private business, is a very complex human activity. It requires perseverance; courage; entrepreneurship; the ability to sell; organizational, interpersonal, and negotiation skills; management ability; and leadership. These qualities are rarely all exhibited by an individual, but a group of people who pool their skills, experiences, and resources will likely find all of these qualities amongst themselves. This is the fundamental reason co-operatives work so well – people work together to accomplish something they could not accomplish as individuals.

You may also be wondering how long this process might take. Well, that very much depends on your group's situation, how often you can meet, how complicated your proposed business is, your group's access to support and resources, and whether your timing and luck are good. Given all of these variables, you can expect to spend many hours over the course of weeks or months before you're ready to open for business.

A final word regarding resources – you do not have to re-invent the wheel. There are many organizations that can provide support for the development of your co-operative. The easiest thing to do is contact a provincial co-operative association or CoopZone (a network of co-op developers).[6]

---

6 For a list for provincial associations check the links page of the Canadian Co-operative Association: http://www.coopscanada.coop/cooplinks. For CoopZone go to: www. coopzone.coop

The Co-op Vision, Purpose, Values – Facilitator's Guide

Russ Christianson[1]

Expectations

- What do you expect from today's session?

Discuss

Facilitator: (read each statement aloud)

- All answers made during this workshop are confidential.
- Every answer is right; this is not a test! Feel free to share your feelings, perceptions, needs, and opinions.
- In writing your responses down, keep your answers short, just a few words or a phrase on the line provided.
- If no answer comes to mind, just leave it blank.
- Please keep your answers to yourself, do not speak them out loud.
- We will have lots of time for discussion.

---

1 The following guide has been generously provided by Russ Christianson of Rhythm Communications. The guide has been slightly modified to fit the format of this book. It is offered here as an example of the steps and kinds of questions which may be helpful to address when working with a new group to clarify their vision for the emerging co-op. It is meant to be used with a matching worksheet where participants can write down their responses. Some questions may need to be adapted to your particular circumstances. Completing this step would be a minimum of a half-day activity.

Meaning

1. What does entrepreneurship mean to you?
2. What does competition mean to you?
3. What does co-operation mean to you?
4. What does personal success mean to you?
5. What does business success mean to you?
6. What does the co-op mean to you?
7. Who are the potential members of the co-op?
8. What needs will the co-op fulfill for its members?
9. What does your business's competition mean to you?
10. What does a co-operatively owned business mean to you?
11. What are the most important skills required to operate a successful co-op business?

Discuss

Ideal Main Role Which Could Be Fulfilled by the Co-op

Facilitator: Please draw a picture of the ideal main role or purpose which could be fulfilled by the co-op. Please use all the crayon colors you consider to be appropriate.

1. Describe the ideal main role or purpose which could be fulfilled by the co-op.
2. What will this ideal main role mean to members or customers?
3. Use up to three words to describe the feelings and emotions you get from your picture.
4. Use up to three words to describe the theme from your picture.

Discuss

Your Vision for the Co-op

Facilitator: Again, thinking in the long-term (ten years or more), please draw a picture of your vision of what the co-op — as a whole — could ideally become in the future. Please use all the crayon colors you consider to be appropriate.

1. Describe your vision of what the co-op could ideally become.
2. Use up to three words to describe the feelings and emotions you get from your picture.
3. Use up to three words to describe the theme of your picture.
4. What will fulfilling this vision mean to the members or customers of the co-op?
5. What barriers might hold the co-op back from achieving this vision?
6. What can be done to assist the co-op in removing these barriers?

Discuss

The Co-op's Chances of Success

1. On a scale from 1 to 10 rate the co-op's chances of success in reaching its vision. (1 is low and 10 is high)
2. Why did your give this rating?
3. How would you improve the co-op's chances of success in reaching its vision?

Discuss - 10 minutes

Mission for the Co-op

1. In point form, write several clear mission statements (how the co-op will reach its vision) for the co-op.
2. What is the most important aspect of fulfilling this mission?
3. What will you do to ensure this mission is fulfilled?

Discuss

Most Important Measurable Objectives (Who does What by When?)

1. Take a moment to review our discussion. From your point of view, what is the most important objective the co-op needs to fulfill in the coming year?
2. What is the second most important objective that the co-op needs to fulfill in the coming year?
3. What is the most important objective that the co-op needs to fulfill in the next three years?
4. What is the second most important objective that the co-op needs to fulfill in the next three years?

Discuss

Next Steps

Discuss

Evaluation

Facilitator: Ask these questions at the end of the session.

1. On a scale from 1 to 10, how would you rate today's session? (1 is low and 10 is high)
2. Why did you give this rating?
3. What specific changes would you make to improve today's session?

Integrating Co-op Values and Principles

Vanessa Hammond[1]

I n the early stage of the co-op's development, it is helpful to review the seven International Co-operative Principles[2] and decide how each principle could be integrated into the co-op in a meaningful and practical way. The co-operative principles are guidelines by which co-ops put their values into practice. You may choose to look at one of the Principles at each board meeting, or do some member education around them at an Annual General Meeting. Another approach is to ask your future members, the youth in your community, how they would like to see them incorporated. Each co-op is unique; each co-op will bring the Principles to life in its own way. Have fun with this. It is not a test with right or wrong answers; it is about finding what is right for your community.

1st Principle: Voluntary and Open Membership

Co-operatives are voluntary organizations; they are open to all persons able to use their services and willing to accept the responsibilities of membership, without gender, social, racial, political, or religious discrimination.

- How will the co-op incorporate this principle? What policies are needed to ensure this principle is part of how the co-op operates?

---

1 Vanessa Hammond is a Co-op Developer in Victoria, B.C. with First Ownership Co-op.
2 http://www.ica.coop/al-ica/

2nd Principle: Democratic Member Control

Co-operatives are democratic organizations controlled by their members who actively participate in setting their policies and making decisions. Men and women serving as elected representatives are accountable to the membership. In primary co-operatives members have equal voting rights (one member, one vote) and co-operatives at other levels are also organised in a democratic manner.

- How will the co-op incorporate this principle? What policies are needed to ensure this principle is part of how the co-op operates?
- How will the co-op balance this with the reasonable interests of specific classes of members such as single individuals, joint members (families or organizations), or investors?

3rd Principle: Member Economic Participation

Members contribute equitably to, and democratically control, the capital of their co-operative. At least part of that capital is usually the common property of the co-operative. Members usually receive limited compensation, if any, on capital subscribed as a condition of membership. Members allocate surpluses for any or all of the following purposes: developing their co-operative (possibly by setting up reserves, part of which at least would be indivisible), benefiting members in proportion to their transactions with the co-operative, and supporting other activities approved by the membership.

- How will the co-op incorporate this principle? What policies are needed to ensure this principle is part of how the co-op operates?
- Consider the share values, annual fees, fees-for-services, and other possible financial commitments that members will have to meet.

4th Principle: Autonomy and Independence

Co-operatives are autonomous, self-help organizations controlled by their members. If they enter into agreements with other organizations, including governments, or raise capital from external sources, they do so on terms that ensure democratic control by their members and maintain their co-operative autonomy.

- How will the co-op incorporate this principle? What policies are needed to ensure this principle is part of how the co-op operates?
- What policies are needed around contracts for providing services, for purchase and supply contracts, for accepting donations, etc.

5th Principle: Education, Training, and Information

Co-operatives provide education and training for their members, elected representatives, managers, and employees so they can contribute effectively to the development of their co-operatives. They inform the general public - particularly young people and opinion leaders - about the nature and benefits of co-operation.

- How will the co-op incorporate this principle? What policies are needed to ensure this principle is part of how the co-op operates?
- What policies are needed related to education of members and non-members about the rights and responsibilities of membership? What education is needed about other topics related to the co-ops activities?

6th Principle: Co-operation among Co-operatives

Co-operatives serve their members most effectively and strengthen the co-operative movement by working together through local, national, regional, and international structures.

- How will the co-op incorporate this principle? What policies are needed to ensure this principle is part of how the co-op operates?

7th Principle: Concern for Community

Co-operatives work for the sustainable development of their communities through policies approved by their members.

- How will the co-op incorporate this principle? What policies are needed to ensure this principle is part of how the co-op operates?

Developing Policies and Procedures

Vanessa Hammond[1]

When you start your co-op, you need to focus on getting all the documents ready for incorporation. You will have various forms to complete (such as the Memorandum of Association and the Rules of Association) that meet the legal requirements and will help you to avoid serious problems. But how will you actually run the day-to-day operations of your co-op?

This is where "Policies" and "Practices" come in.

In different areas of the co-op's operations, the new board/members will be making decisions and developing policies for how to carry out the activities of the co-op. These policy documents are particular to your co-op and can be changed to meet your evolving needs.

Take membership as an example. Your Rules of Association set some limits, or none, on who may become a member. But what are your policies? Do you want to limit the number of new members per year? Do you want members to be able to join at any time or only at certain times of the year? Do you want to hear the voice of youth by having Youth Advisors who may be too young (under 16 in B.C.) to be members and incur all the associated responsibilities but who may have valuable opinions and ideas? Do you want your membership committee to make final decisions about whether potential members meet your criteria, or do you want all applications to come to the board? All of these questions can be addressed through policies. Policies can be changed at a General Meeting but it is helpful to develop policies to guide everyday operations and ensure everyone knows what to expect and that they will be treated the same as others in the same circumstances. The Policy Manual becomes your guide for how to become

---

1 Vanessa Hammond is a co-op developer in Victoria B.C. with First Ownership Co-op

an excellent co-op that meets the needs of your members. Having clear policies will save time and potential problems when members ask, "What should we do about this?"

It is also very important to develop a Procedures Manual where you record all your policies and how they will be implemented. Going back to the example of membership, a Procedures Manual should include: a copy of the final membership policy, the application form, the procedure for moving it expeditiously through the hands of whoever reviews it (the Membership Committee, the Board), and a clear form letter stating, "Welcome … " or "We are sorry, but at present you do not meet our criteria for membership, please contact …. for more information." Your Procedures Manual will save time and effort by answering the question, "Haven't we already made a decision about this?"

Running a co-op takes time and effort. Good Policy and Procedure Manuals will help your co-op make the most efficient use of the energy and enthusiasm of your members.

Co-op Self-Assessment

Russ Christianson

This is a self-assessment in the truest sense. You won't be asked to score a number of questions, total your score, and then be told where you fit on an arbitrary scale that purports to measure temperament, attitudes, or motivations. Rather, it's an opportunity to reflect and talk to friends, family, and potential members of your co-op.

Starting any business requires taking risks. Eighty percent of small businesses fail. There are many reasons for failure, including poor planning, being overly optimistic, lack of adequate investment and cash, poor cost control, personal illness, and plain bad luck.

Co-operatives generally fare better and have twice the survival rate – 40%.[1] This is significantly better than other business models (sole proprietorship, partnership, and corporation), but it still means over half of start-up co-ops fail. Some of the reasons for the better survival rate for co-ops include more cautious and thoughtful decision-making, the emotional support members provide each other, pooling resources and talents, and support from other co-ops and federations.

Like any good business, a co-op requires an excellent business plan, sufficient start-up capital, and the tenacity of its founders. There will be long hours, many meetings, and low pay in the start-up phase. And there will also be break throughs, exciting developments, and the internal reward of accomplishing something important to you and your community.

While many co-ops are profitable businesses, this is not their main goal. If you want to start a business "to get rich quick" (or slowly for that matter), a co-op business is not the right choice. If you want to work together

---

1 Co-operatives Secretariat, *Survival Rates of Co-operatives in Quebec* (Government of Canada and Quebec Ministry of Industry and Commerce, 1999).

with others to fulfill a collective need – say for meaningful work, housing, childcare, good food, joint marketing or purchasing, or filling any other gap in your community – then a co-op may be the right choice.

The main difference between a co-op business and a regular company is democracy. This is both the strength and potential weakness of the co-op structure. It's a strength because it offers people (members) more control over their lives and the potential for making better decisions collectively than individually. It's a weakness because democratic decision-making requires more time, more discussion, and the ability to listen and even change one's mind. This doesn't mean every little decision has to be made by the group. Usually, only long-term policies are determined this way, while day-to-day business operations are clearly assigned to various people, just like any business.

A co-op is for you if: you enjoy working together with other people, you have the interpersonal skills and patience to co-operatively find creative solutions, and you feel confident about managing conflicts.

Over 800 million people are members of co-ops worldwide.[2] They've joined together because they are able to achieve something as a group that they simply couldn't do as individuals.

So, if you still want to continue with this self-assessment, we hope you enjoy the process of reflection. And please be honest with yourself!

1. What is the need you have identified that a co-op could fulfill?
   ☐ Job creation
   ☐ Housing
   ☐ Child Care
   ☐ Food
   ☐ Marketing
   ☐ Joint Purchasing
   ☐ Other

   _____

   _____

2. Are there other organizations or businesses currently fulfilling this need in your community?
   ☐ Yes. Name them:

   _____

---

2 International Co-operative Alliance, 2007.

_____

_____

☐ No. Has one recently failed?

_____

_____

3. Why do you feel a co-op is the right way to fulfill these needs?

_____

_____

4. How many other people are interested in working together with you to start the co-op? What skills and resources do they bring to your group?

Name	Skills	Resources
(your name)		

5. What kind of support can you rely on from your family, friends, and community in starting the co-op?

_____

_____

6. What are your personal reasons for wanting to start a business together with others rather than on your own?

_____

_____

7. What experiences have you had in the past that make you feel confident that you can stick with the start-up when the going gets tough?

_____

_____

8. There will be conflicts in the co-op. How have you dealt with conflicts in the past when you have worked together with people?

_____

_____

9. When you review the list of people and their skills and resources in question 4, how confident do you feel that you have the right people, the right skills, and the right resources?

_____

_____

10.Are there any gaps in skills and resources that you will need other people to fill?

_____

_____

_____

11. What is your strategy to get the ball rolling to start the co-op?

_____

_____

12. Are you ready to spend the next few months getting the co-op going? Do you have the time, energy, and the tenacity required?

_____

_____

13. What do you hope to gain on a personal level from your participation in the co-op?

_____

_____

14. How much money do you personally have to invest in the co-op?

_____

_____

15. What further research or information do you need to access to help you make your decision to start a co-op?

_____

_____

Co-op Feasibility Study

Russ Christianson

A ll right, you have already completed the Co-op Self-Assessment. If you still feel confident that a co-op business is the right thing for you and your group, the next step is to investigate its feasibility. A feasibility study involves gathering, analyzing, and evaluating information for the purpose of answering the question: "Should the co-op go into this business?"

This exercise will build on the Co-op Self-Assessment and delve deeper into the merits and challenges that your co-op enterprise will likely face. The process is designed for your group to share the work, have discussions, and help you screen out business ideas that are likely to fail. The process will also test the group's solidarity and productivity. Put it this way if your group can not confidently and efficiently complete a feasibility study, it's not likely you'll be able to successfully start and operate a business together.

Your Core Business

1. Describe the core business that your co-op will perform on a day-to-day basis.

_____

_____

2. List the products and/or services your co-op will sell.

_____

_____

3. Describe who will use your products and services.

_____

_____

4. Why would someone buy your product or service?

_____

_____

5. List your product/service suppliers.

_____

_____

Competitors

6. In a table like the one below, list your competitors, their strengths, and weaknesses (for example: prices, quality, location, reputation, market share, profitability) and the advantages your co-op will offer compared to your competition.

Competitor	Strengths	Weaknesses	Co-op Advantage

Human Resources

7. In a table like the one below, name the key day-to-day tasks that will need to get done to ensure your co-op's members and/or customers have their needs fulfilled. Now, refer back to question 4 in the Co-op Self-Assessment and put the name of the person who will be responsible for each task.

Day-to-day Tasks	Person Responsible

8. What skills are missing in your group that your co-op will need to get the job done?

_____

_____

9. In a table like the one below, list the staffing positions you will need to complete the collection of tasks listed above. In the second column, list the number of positions and whether they are full time or part time. In the third column, list the amount you would like to pay (be realistic) for each of these positions. In the fourth column, write down the results of multiplying columns two and three. Finally, add all of the rows in column four and total them – this is your initial forecast for salaries and wages. (Note: It is a useful exercise for each member to fill out a "Personal Income and Expense Forecast" as a reality check). Use a pencil (your numbers will likely change as you work through this exercise) and write down your calculations so you know how you arrived at them.

Position Title	Number of Positions	Salary or Wage	Total
		$	$
		$	$
		$	$
		$	$
		$	$
		Grand Total	$

Forecasted Income Statement

The income statement for your co-op is similar to your personal income statement. It starts with revenues and subtracts costs and expenses to result in the "bottom line." To evaluate the financial feasibility of the co-op, you will be looking at what is "likely" to happen. You want to get an overall idea of the likelihood the business will be financially viable – in other words, will the co-op bring more money in than it will spend.

For the purposes of this feasibility, we suggest you use this form, a pencil, and hand-held calculator. Unless you know how to use a computer spreadsheet, the pencil and paper method is much faster, and it's easier to do as a group.

If your co-op looks feasible, you will move on to the next step – the business plan – for which you will need to forecast a "best case" scenario and a "worst case" scenario, in addition to the "likely case." There are many software packages available to write business plans. Most banks and bookstores have these packages. Or, you can use the Canada Business Service Centers' Interactive Business Planner at *www.cbsc.org/ibp*. One thing to keep in mind, these tools will only provide guidance and a format for your plan. There is no shortcut for using your intelligence, creativity, and intuition in writing your plan.

Expenses

Expenses are much easier to forecast than sales. Your group can do research on actual market costs for rent, equipment, insurance, etc. Of course, these costs will grow as the co-op grows, but hopefully not as fast, so the co-op will generate surplus cash from operations.

Sales Forecasts

The approach we suggest for feasibility is to work out your expenses first and then work backwards to determine the level of sales revenue the co-op will require to break-even. Then you can get into the details of how this revenue will be raised. How many products will need to be sold? At what price? How many members will you need? Are there any supply constraints? These are the kinds of questions you want to think about for this step.

Sales forecasting is very intuitive. It's more of an art than a science. Don't hesitate, just take a stab at it, reflect, do some more market research or a member survey, and revise your forecasts and expenses as appropriate. While there is a right answer in adding and multiplying numbers for the forecasts, there is no "right" answer for sales forecasts. There are only forecasts that make sense based on the assumptions you make, and the more reasonable and well researched your information is, the more confident you and others will be in the forecasts. Keep in mind that one of the most common mistakes made by entrepreneurs is being overly optimistic in their sales forecasts. Be conservative and confident in your forecasts.

Profit or Surplus

Most businesses lose money for the first few months (or even years) of operation. However, none will survive unless they generate surplus cash and a profit. You need to think about when your business will become profitable and build this into your financial forecasts.

10. Forecasted Income Statement for the year ending _____.

Item	$ Amount	% of Sales	Assumptions
(1) Sales Revenue	$		
(2) Less: Returns & Allowances	$		
(3) Net Sales (= 1 - 2)	$		
(4) Cost of Goods Sold	$		
(5) Gross Margin (=3 - 4)	$		
Expenses			
(6) Wages & Salaries (including 15-18 % benefits)	$		
(7) Rent	$		
(8) Promotion	$		
(9) Transportation	$		

Item	$ Amount	% of Sales	Assumptions
(10) Utilities	$		
(11) Insurance	$		
(12) Dues	$		
(13) Depreciation (non-cash)	$		
(14) Miscellaneous	$		
(15) Total Expenses (sum 6 to 15)	$		
Net Income or Surplus (5 - 15)	$		

Start-up Capital Required

In order to start the business and generate the level of sales you're forecasting, there will be costs involved. Many of the start-up costs will have to be paid in cash, which means your group will have to raise the money. For-profit co-ops can sell different kinds of shares, and at this point, you don't need to get too technical but simply think about the minimum investment each member will need to make and whom you'll raise the rest of the start-up capital from.

11. Fill in the table below as appropriate to your co-op venture.

Item	*$ Amount*	*Source of $*
Business Plan Consulting	$	
Incorporation and Legal Work	$	
Logo and Letterhead	$	
Membership Drive	$	
Rental Deposit	$	
Leasehold Improvements		
Equipment	$	
Insurance	$	
Wages & Salaries (3 months)	$	
Inventory	$	
Advertising	$	
Other	$	
Grand Total	$	

Summary Feasibility

12.Are there any major questions remaining about your proposed co-op venture?

_____

_____

13.On a scale of 1 to 10, rate how confident your group is in the feasibility of your co-op. (1 is low and 10 is high)

_____

14.Why did you give this rating?

_____

_____

15.What needs to be done to increase your group's confidence level?

_____

_____

Co-op Business Plan Template

Russ Christianson

A business plan is a vital document for any successful co-op. Ideas are simply that until they can be effectively communicated and implemented in a systematic manner. A comprehensive, written document that expresses ideas and assigns specific responsibility to individuals and\or teams within your co-op provides the map for the whole organization to follow. Without a written plan, people go in their own directions, their destinations always moving before they arrive. A co-ordinated effort in a co-operative organization depends upon a written plan that everyone can follow and use as a basis of evaluation for their performance.

Your co-op's business plan should be treated as a living document. As circumstances change, change your objectives to maintain their realism, challenge, and motivational impact. Regularly refer back to the plan and revise it as you gather new information, knowledge, and experience. The document is not written in stone and as your co-op business grows and changes, so should your written plan.

The people who will be responsible for implementation create the most effective business plans. Board members and managers share the responsibility to develop a co-op's business plan and active participation should be encouraged for all employees and other appropriate stakeholders. A plan which is generated by a single person and then forced upon those responsible for making it happen is bound to fail.

Executive Summary

1 The Concept: Vision, Mission, Purpose, And Values

2 Measurable Objectives

3 Situational Analysis
   3.1 The Co-operative Environment
   3.2 The Competitive Environment
   3.3 The Economic Environment
   3.4 The Social Environment
   3.5 The Political Environment
   3.6 The Legal Environment
   3.7 The Natural Environment

4 Marketing Plan
   4.1 Marketing Objectives
   4.2 Target Markets
   4.3 Marketing Mix
      a) Product Mix
      b) Price
      c) Promotion
      d) Place

5 Production
   5.1 Equipment and Facilities
   5.2 Quality Control

6 Organization And People
   6.1 Organizational Structure
   6.2 Staffing
   6.3 Job Descriptions

7 Finances
   7.1 Budget and Financial Control Systems

8 Ownership
   8.1 Capitalization
   8.2 Organizational Structure
   8.3 Projected Return on Investment

Executive Summary

The executive summary is a one-page brief which provides the reader a quick overview of the most salient points in the business plan. It is useful to take a few minutes to review this summary regularly as it keeps the business on track. It may also be used for public and employee relations purposes.

1. The Concept: Vision, Mission, Purpose, and Values

The concept section of the business plan is the foundation of the business. The opening paragraph should summarize: what need will be fulfilled, precisely for whom, and why? Successful co-operatives define and respond to members' and customers' needs and change their business strategy as these needs change.

There are four interrelated pillars to the foundation of a co-operative business:

1. Vision – The vision or dream that members and other stakeholders share for the future of the co-op.
2. Mission – How the co-op will reach its shared vision.
3. Purpose – The underlying purpose fulfilled by the co-op.
4. Values – The Co-operative Principles and values held by co-operatives throughout the world.

Vision

A vision is a picture that vividly represents what the co-operative enterprise can become in the future. Ideally, the co-op will receive vision pictures from all of its stakeholders and commission a professional artist to combine the drawings into one picture for the whole organization (please refer to the visioning exercise earlier in the Tools section). A co-op's stakeholders may include its members, customers, management, employees, and the community. The shared vision and focus of these stakeholders provides the unifying force for the whole organization. The collective vision provides a clear direction upon which to base measurable objectives. Besides acting as a motivating force, significant decisions can be checked for congruence with this vision on an ongoing basis.

Mission

The mission expresses "how to" reach the vision. The mission statement is usually one or two written pages and clearly defines the long-term direction of the co-op. Member and customer service, product quality, employee relations, management style, and competitive positioning are important components of the mission statement. The mission statement is stated in broad terms, which provide guidelines for the detailed results-oriented measurable objectives.

Purpose

The purpose or "raison d'etre" is the co-op's single reason for being; it can be crystalized in one short sentence which articulates the underlying main role of the organization. This sentence can be used on all printed materials of the business, including letterhead, business cards, posters, packaging, and annual reports.

Values

Co-operatives throughout the world share similar values and uphold the seven co-operative principles recognized by the International Co-operative Alliance. Co-operatives are based on the values of self-help, self-responsibility, democracy, equality, equity, and solidarity. In the tradition of their founders, co-operative members believe in the ethical values of honesty, openness, social responsibility, and caring for others.

2. Measurable Objectives

The measurable objectives provide the overall performance standards for the co-op as a whole. This area of the plan clearly delineates who is responsible for achieving specific results by a certain time. The phrase "who does what by when" summarizes this section.

Some examples of measurable objectives are given below:

Description of Objective	Responsibility	Completion Date
2.1 Achieve real sales growth of 10% per annum	Marketing and Sales Manager	Fiscal year-end – Dec. 31, 2007
2.2 Maintain a gross margin of 40%	General Manager and Financial Controller	Ongoing
2.3 Introduce a profit-sharing plan for all employees.	General Manager and Human Resources Manager	Nov. 1, 2007
2.4 Increase market share by 15% this fiscal year	Marketing and Sales Manager	Dec. 31, 2007

Description of Objective	Responsibility	Completion Date
2.5 Reduce operating overhead by 2% per month for six months and maintain the new level	General Manager and Financial Controller	June 30, 2008
2.6 Create eight new products for market testing	Marketing and Sales Manager	Sept. 30, 2009
2.7 Develop and implement a new organizational structure.	General Manager and Human Resources Manager	Jan. 2, 2007
2.8 Achieve a cumulative 10% return on investment over the first five years of operation	General Manager and Financial Controller	Dec. 31, 2010

3. Situational Analysis

The situational analysis evaluates the external environment within which the co-op operates. This analysis identifies the opportunities and the threats faced by your co-op and, in combination with the organizational objectives above, determines the co-op's marketing direction. An intuitive and rational synthesis of your co-op's past, current, and future position is the key to successfully determining the co-op's strategy.

3.1 The Co-operative Environment

The co-operative environment includes all organizations and individuals who have a stake in the success of your co-op. People who share your co-op's vision, mission, purpose, and values and who are willing to participate in making it happen are included within this category. For example, members, suppliers, other co-ops, resellers, employees, and community organizations all provide potential opportunities for co-operation. Opportunities in this environment are primarily related to methods of increasing efficiency, perhaps through strategic alliances, while constraints consist of such things as unresolved conflicts and shortages of materials.

3.2 The Competitive Environment

The competitive environment includes other companies in your industry that are rivals for both resources and sales. Opportunities include offering better value to members and customers, joint ventures, and acquiring competing firms. The primary constraints are the marketing activities of competing firms and the demand constraints for your co-op's products or services.

3.3 The Economic Environment

The effects of local, regional, national, and international economies on your co-op including inflation, unemployment, trade agreements, technological change, and import substitution are included here. International trade offers opportunities for expanded markets but also opens domestic markets to competitors' products.

3.4 The Social Environment

Cultural and social traditions, norms, and attitudes change slowly but have major ramifications over time on how business is conducted. Business practices that are contrary to social values become political issues and are often resolved by legal constraints. Smart co-operatives are social leaders.

3.5 The Political Environment

This comprises the attitudes, beliefs, and values of the public, social, and business critics and other "special-interest" organizations. Product safety, quality, labour practices, conservation, and ethical business practices are issues that may affect member and customer loyalty.

3.6 The Legal Environment

The international, federal, provincial, and municipal laws directed at protecting the public interest and individual rights, provide a myriad of potential opportunities and threats. In the past two decades, much of this legislation has been geared towards creating "free markets" and less government intervention in business. This has allowed global corporations to accumulate astounding levels of wealth, power, and control within oligopoly economic conditions in various industries.

3.7 The Natural Environment

Over the past two decades, the natural world has become a major consideration for our society. There is a built-in link between the economy and the natural environment. The industrial and knowledge economies are only part of what Wendell Berry calls the Great Economy – the ecosystems that sustain the whole web of life and everything that depends on the land and oceans. Businesses that are perceived as being irresponsible environmentally will increasingly pay the price of diminishing sales, increasing costs, and decreasing profits. As organizations realize that the natural environment has limits in the amount of waste and pollution it can absorb and the costs of clean-up mount, opportunities will unfold in providing new technologies and services that conserve energy and treat the environment in a relatively benign manner. Fossil fuel depletion, water contamination, and climate change will be the major forces that effect human populations and economies worldwide in the coming decades.

4. Marketing Plan

Marketing activities must be aligned with organizational objectives. Opportunities are often found by synthesizing information from the situational environments. Once an opportunity is identified, an appropriate strategy must be created to take advantage of it by:
- Establishing marketing objectives,
- Selecting the target market(s), and
- Developing the marketing mix.

4.1 Marketing Objectives

The marketing objectives result from the combination of the co-op's business concept, organizational objectives, and the situational analysis. In some cases, marketing objectives may overlap with the overall objectives. Net income (surplus or profit) or return on investment should be emphasized rather than sales. Marketing is everything your co-op does from the moment of conceptualizing new ideas to successfully meeting the needs of members and customers.

4.2 Target Markets

The success of the co-op's marketing plan will hinge on how well it identifies member and customer needs and organizes its resources to satisfy these needs profitably. The co-op must select the group or segments of potential members or customers it will serve. Effective market research and intuition is critical in this process.

4.3 Marketing Mix

The marketing mix is the set of controllable variables that must be managed to meet the needs of members and targeted customers and achieve your business objectives. The marketing mix is the core of the marketing plan. It is important to maintain your co-op's commitment to your vision and values in the marketing plan. Marketing expenditures should be viewed as long-term investments in the future viability of your co-op and need to ensure consistency in educational and promotional messages.

a) Product Mix

The determination of the products and services you will offer and how you will price them is elemental to your business. In a product-oriented co-op, how you deliver your product and the quality of service you provide is equally as important as the product itself.

b) Price

There are many possible pricing strategies that are possible. You need to determine your price based on competitors' prices, your sales targets, costs, and gross margin. Price can equate with quality in your members' and customers' minds, and yet if you price your product too high with excess margin, your competitors will soon enter your niche and erode your market share and profits.

c) Promotion

The mass media is usually the first thought which enters our minds when we think of promotion. National media outlets are expensive and often ineffective in reaching targeted markets because of the broad coverage offered. Public relations, community action, and point-of-sale advertising are some of the most cost effective forms of promotion, particularly for community-based co-ops.

d) Place

Distribution is often the key element of a successful venture. Making sure your products and services get to your members and customers in an effective and timely manner will determine your co-op's sales, market share, and profitability.

5. Production

5.1 Equipment and Facilities

Depending on the type of operation, you may require an extensive section on production equipment and facilities. A manufacturing or distribution company will require a detailed analysis of the land, building(s), and equipment required to produce its product. A service-oriented company may only require a simple list of office equipment. The capital necessary to acquire the equipment will be an important component of the budget.

5.2 Quality Assurance

This area is crucial for any business, whether product or service oriented. All successful co-ops depend on repeat orders from loyal members and customers. The best way to assure repeat business is by providing value for money and consistently good quality. A good quality assurance system will be based on employees' motivations to create high quality internal checks and balances and on feedback from members and customers. This area has great potential to decrease waste, product returns, and expenses.

6. Organization and People

6.1 Leadership

The board of directors and the management team must provide the leadership and inspiration to motivate the employees and members towards the measurable objectives of the organization. The confidence exhibited by the board and management team, their openness in listening to, and flexibility in implementing, employees' and members' ideas will provide the organizational leadership required to make the business a success.

6.2 Staffing

Ideally, limit the number of employees to people who can consciously agree upon, and contribute directly to, that which your co-op enterprise is to accomplish, for whom, and by when. Each person involved in the business needs to understand and agree with its vision, mission, purpose, and values.

6.3 Job Descriptions

To be effective, people need to clearly understand their responsibilities and their contribution in achieving the goals of the organization. Congruence between the goals of individuals and the organization must be high, and performance that exceeds agreed upon standards needs to be recognized and rewarded. There must be a good match between employees' authority to make decisions and the amount of responsibility they are expected to hold for the outcome of their decisions.

7. Finances

7.1 Budget and Financial Control Systems

There are usually three budget scenarios included in the business plan. Each scenario represents very different outcomes. The first purpose of a budget is to set measurable targets or performance standards for the organization while offering a motivating force for the group as a whole. The second purpose of the budget is to provide a basis for financial control and management decision-making. A monthly comparison between actual results and the budget will give management an idea about what needs to be done next. A third purpose may be providing the financial arguments required to raise start-up or growth capital.

Timely and accurate financial information is a pre-requisite to a successful operation. As new information becomes available, the budget should be updated to reflect appropriate changes. The targeted return on investment will directly influence the budgeting process.

8. Ownership

8.1 Capitalization

While the concept and the human motivations are the key ingredients of a successful business, ideas cannot be implemented without adequate capital. The potential sources of capital include the members, preferred shareholders, suppliers, employees, retained earnings, bank loans, and government grants. Besides the start-up capital required by a new business, all businesses need to set aside a capital pool for contingencies.

8.2 Organizational Structure

The legal structure of the co-operative will depend on the objectives of the members, the size of the business, and the industry. Co-ops can be incorporated as for-profit or not-for-profit organizations. It is useful to show formal reporting relationships in an organizational chart.

8.3 Projected Return on Investment

Every co-operative, whether for-profit or not-for-profit, requires some return on investment. Clear targets should be set to ensure the business provides a reasonable return on the capital invested by members and other shareholders.

Situational Decision Making

Russ Christianson

The most effective style of decision-making depends on the situation. Small co-operatives often make major decisions (like working hours, pay rates, customer service policies, bylaw changes, etc.) using consensus. Why? Because properly facilitated consensus decision-making allows everyone to express their point of view, listen to others, and come to the best decision for the group as a whole. Consensus provides ample opportunity for respectful disagreement and when a decision is reached, it's usually the best solution and people are committed to making it happen. Consensus decreases the chances that people will change their minds after the decision is made, or feel left out of the decision, and therefore unmotivated to contribute to its implementation.

For the hundreds of day-to-day operational decisions in a co-op responsibility needs to be delegated to individuals who are accountable to the group. Everyday routine decisions that are a part of someone's job (for example: returning a customer's call, or counting the cash, and balancing the till at the end of the day) do not require a group discussion; in fact, it would be detrimental to the business and the group dynamic to waste time in a group meeting. Most of these routine decisions will be made unilaterally by each individual. This requires a clear definition and understanding of each person's roles and responsibilities in the co-op. An accountability chart is a useful tool.

For decisions that are less routine, or if a new employee is just learning the job, there may be a need to consult with a supervisor or with co-workers who are affected by the decision. Many managers use the consultative process to gather information and opinions to ensure they make the best decision. And like consensus, consultation takes time. It is not an appropriate method if a decision must be made quickly or on the spot.

Many larger co-operatives use a majority voting system to make long-term policy decisions. As in Canada's political system, the most common understanding of majority voting is 50%-plus-one, but many co-ops require two-thirds or more, particularly for important decisions such as surplus distribution, bylaw changes, or withdrawing a membership. Majority voting is relatively efficient and provides all co-op members an opportunity to vote. However, decisions made by majority can be very divisive over time and, in the end, can require more time than making a decision by consensus in the first place. Majority voting is particularly appropriate with large numbers of co-op members at Annual General Meetings and for formal occasions when motions, seconds, and vote tallies are required. However, smaller co-ops can often use consensus more effectively.

Decision Making Steps

No matter what process is used, decision-making requires choosing between alternative courses of action to deal with a problem. Important steps to consider in the decision-making process include the following:[1]

1. Analyzing the situation. Define what is happening. Get input from others. Be objective rather than emotional.
2. Defining the problem. Don't deal with symptoms but focus on the actual problem.
3. Considering options and developing alternative solutions. (Each alternative must solve the problem.)
4. Evaluating the alternative solutions. Look at both the positive and the negative consequences of each alternative. Some alternatives will have fewer "side effects," or unintended consequences. Get input from others if needed.
5. Making a decision. Make the choice that has the least negative consequences and that solves the problem, accomplishes the purpose, and meets the goal.
6. Implementing the plan and evaluating the decision. Make changes in the plan if needed, again using the steps of the decision-making process.

---

1 Source: www.healthteacher.com/teachersupports/skills5.asp, 1999

Consensus Decision Making

Consensus decision-making is the most effective way to make important decisions with small groups. The process requires direct participation and active listening from all involved and, when well facilitated, leads to better decisions and stronger commitment.

What Is Consensus?[2]

- All participants contribute.
- Everyone's opinions are used and encouraged.
- Differences are viewed as helpful rather than hindering.
- Those members who continue to disagree after full discussion indicate that they are willing to experiment for a prescribed period of time.
- Enough time will be spent that all voices are heard and understood before an effort to finalize a decision is made, however long that takes.
- All members share in the final decision.

Advantages of Consensus

- Members are more likely to support the decision.
- Provides for a win-win solution.
- Facilitates open communication.
- Requires members to listen and understand all sides of the issue.
- Sets the stage for an action - Who, What, Where, When.

Disadvantages of Consensus Decision Making

- Takes more time in a group; the larger the group, the more time may be needed.
- Trust is needed among members to encourage sharing.
- Group leaders must use facilitation rather than control.

Steps in Facilitating Consensus

- Describe and define the problem, situation, or issue.
- Brainstorm a list of alternatives without judging, discussing, or rejecting any ideas. Take only one idea from each person to start.

---

2 Washington State University Cooperative Extension in Spokane County, Adapted from: "Consensus Decision Making, WSU Cooperative Extension Family Community Leadership and 'Consensus,'" in *Community Leadership: Leader's Guide*.

- Review, change, consolidate, rewrite, and set priorities as a group through discussion.
- Make a decision; when it's reached make sure it is written so that everyone can see it.
- Evaluate the results later – revise if needed.

Co-operative Governance

Cathy Lang[1]

What is Governance?

Co-op governance means the processes and structures used to direct and manage the co-op's operations and activities. Good governance helps organizations use their resources more effectively and ensures they are managed in the best interests of their members and principal stakeholders.

Role of the Board of Directors

The main duty of the board is to provide the leadership and overall management of the co-op's affairs, usually together with the senior management.

Board members have important fiduciary and legal responsibilities. Fiduciary means that a director has the responsibility to act for another's benefit rather than for himself or herself. In the case of a co-op, the director's fiduciary duty is to make decisions honestly, in good faith, and in the best interest of the co-operative. Legal responsibilities mean that the directors have a duty to apply with care the skills and experience they bring to the table. The law does not require board members to be experts. But as in all organizations, directors of co-operatives are required to apply their knowl-

---

1 Catherine Lang has worked in management and consulting with social economy organizations for over 25 years. She held the position of Regional Manager of the Canadian Co-operative Association in Ontario and created and directed many of their programs in co-op development, youth, and public education. Through C. Lang Consulting, Catherine seeks to inspire and support innovation and innovators in rural, community, and co-operative economic development.

edge and skills in a way that would be seen as reasonably prudent. This is called the "standard of care."

Directors must act honestly, in good faith, and in the best interests of the co-operative. What is in the best interests of the co-op? In co-ops, members are primarily intersted in maximizing the benefits they receive from membership – taking advantage of the services the co-op provides and, except for non-profit co-ops, sharing its surplus/profit. They also are interested in having a positive impact on their community and the environment.

The key responsibilities of a board of directors includes:
- Member relations and communication;
- Board operations and governance;
- Hiring, monitoring, and evaluating the general manager ;
- Financial planning, policy making, monitoring;
- Comprehensive planning;
- Community, government, and co-op relations;
- Legal aspects; and
- Perpetuating an effective board.

Liability Issues

A co-op, as with any other form of corporation, has an existence in law as a separate person from its directors, officers, members, and shareholders. Contracts signed by the co-op are the co-op's sole responsibility and only its assets may be seized by its creditors – not those of anyone involved with it – unless someone has guaranteed an obligation of the co-op.[2] As long as a director acts in good faith, exercising their *duty of care*, they are not individually liable for the co-op's losses or debts.[3]

Here are some examples of exercising duty of care and fiduciary duties:
- Being well oriented to the Co-operative Act and the co-op's articles of incorporation and bylaws;
- Attending board meetings, or formally sending regrets that are minuted;
- Reading board materials prior to meetings; reading and correcting minutes from previous meetings;
- Asking questions and requesting information needed to make decisions;
- Voting on motions at board meetings and registering your concerns in the minutes; and

---

2 For example, if the co-op had taken out a bank loan and the directors had guaranteed it they would be held responsible if the co-op didn't pay back the loan.
3 With a few exceptions: unpaid wages and remittances being the most common.

- Declaring conflicts of interest, or registering with the board questions of conflict of interest.

Meeting Management and Group Problem Solving

Meeting Rules of Order

A co-op board is responsible for making decisions in the best interest of all members. In order to do so, there are guidelines for making effective decisions using democratic procedures. These guidelines are often called "rules of order." Rules of order are used to try to guarantee the individual rights of members and to ensure that decisions made at general member and board meetings reflect the will of the majority.

Every member has a right to be informed in advance of general meetings, to propose motions, to participate in debates, and to vote. Motions or proposals are suggestions for decisions that the co-op board or members are asked to consider.

A co-op board should strive for consensus on decisions. However, when consensus cannot be reached, especially given restrictions in time, and in order to document decisions of the board, formal voting procedures may be used, following the rules of order. All decisions are noted in the minutes and approved at a subsequent board meeting as accurate. The minutes are legal documents and contain important "organizational memory."

The leadership of the chair, as well as the active and respectful participation of members, is very important in ensuring the rules of order contribute to effective decision-making.

Role of the Chair

Every members' meeting is chaired by a chairperson – normally the president of the board, although meeting chairing can be rotated with other board members. The chair makes sure the individual rights of the members are protected while assisting the board/members to make decisions that reflect the will of the majority.

The functions of the chair include:

- calling the meeting to order,
- ensuring that accurate minutes are recorded,
- conducting the meeting,
- maintaining order,
- allowing motions to be proposed,

- taking votes on motions as appropriate,
- making rulings on questions of procedure, and
- adjourning the meeting.

Any member may challenge a ruling by the chair by raising a "point of order." If this happens the chair must immediately ask members to uphold or overturn the ruling by taking a majority vote.

The chair of a co-op is impartial and cannot argue for or against a proposal while in the role of chair. If the chair wants to make a motion, to participate in a discussion, or to vote on an item, he/she has to turn over the chair to someone else (usually the vice-president or a co-chair) while the item is being considered at the meeting.

The chairperson usually introduces items of business, provides background information, summarizes a discussion, or suggests methods of proceeding with the item at hand. If the vote taken on a motion is tied, the chair may cast one vote to break the tie if the co-ops bylaws allow for this.

Conduct of Business

For most items of business in a co-op, a formal decision by the board is required. Decisions come about as follows:

- a proposal is introduced,
- a proposal or motion is made,
- the motion is discussed and possibly amended, and
- the meeting makes a decision by voting on the motion.

Only one proposal or motion is usually dealt with at a time, except to adjust procedure to make a better decision. It is rare that a meeting starts with debate on a ready-made proposal. The process is usually much more collaborative.

Most board members start discussion with only a vague notion of what concerns them or what kind of action would be appropriate. Although meetings do not usually start with motions, they often end discussion by being able to state a satisfactory motion.

Identifying the Problem or Issue

Discussion at a co-op board meeting will often begin with a comment that a problem seems to exist. Determination about whether and what the problem really is leads to problem solving and proposals for solutions. The process of discussion and decision-making moves an issue from one of an individual member's concern to that of the whole group. The group then attempts to choose an option to deal with the problem that is agreeable to the majority and in the best interest of the whole co-op.

Problem Solving Process

When a particular agenda item is introduced there is often an issue within that agenda item that requires discussion, problem solving, and a decision of the board. The role of the chair, with the board, is to help facilitate effective discussion, problem solving, and decision-making (usually in the form of a motion which is voted on).

Following are steps that can be taken to problem solve a particular issue at a co-op board meeting:

1. Place an issue or problem on the agenda for discussion.
2. Introduce the issue (the chair will ask the director who brought it forward to explain the issue).
3. Check with the members to determine whether there is support and agreement from the group to discuss the issue that it is perceived as a common problem.
4. Make sure to define the problem clearly.
5. Choose a process for discussion and problem solving:
   - Brainstorming,
   - Round robin,
   - General discussion, or
   - Other.
6. Evaluate the proposals that have come from the problem solving discussion.
7. State one proposal to consider as a whole group; ask for someone to second the motion (a supporter) and note both of these names in the minutes.
8. Have the chair or the proposer speak to the proposal (summarize and explain it further).
9. Invite discussion from the group on the proposal.
10. Modify the motion as needed (amendments), requesting this of the proposer and supporter (seconder) as a friendly amendment (if they don't agree then vote on the amendment before proceeding).
11. When all amendments are gathered, the chair will have members vote to include these (or not) in the main proposal.
12. Further discussion is held on the amended proposal.
13. Now it is time to check for consensus. If all agree with the amended motion then it is passed and documented in the minutes; if all do not agree, then any further modifications can be suggested to make it work.
14. If no consensus can be reached, a vote can be called by a member ("calling the question") or by the chair; a majority of votes in favour will pass the motion.

15.The final decision is noted in the minutes by the board secretary.

16.The decision should lead to an action plan.

Role of Board and Management

Authority of Co-op Board

Co-op boards have authority over virtually all aspects of the corporation Much of this authority is delegated or formally passed on by the board to the general manager and her/his team (in co-ops large enough to warrant hiring staff). The board maintains overall responsibility for the co-op at all times.

It is important to know that the authority of the board is collective – individual directors do not have authority unless specific responsibilities are delegated by the board or through bylaws. For instance, if a board makes a decision together, all board members must abide by the decision. And an individual board member should not direct staff to do anything, except where the whole board has agreed to this. This is an area that can lead to difficulties within many co-ops.

Accountability of Co-op Manager

The manager is accountable to the board within the policies and guidelines set by the board. The board is accountable to the general membership for the actions that it has authorized during any period of time.

Role of Board and Management

For most co-ops, the role of the board is to set and monitor policies, ensure financial status of the co-op is in good order, plan for the long-term sustainability of the co-op (strategic business planning), and monitor the performance of the co-op and its operations with respect to these plans in collaboration with the co-op manager.

Following is a brief comparison of the different roles of the board and management:

Board areas:

- Concerned with idea decisions,
- Concerned with long-term decisions, and
- Determines objectives.

Management/staff areas:

- Concerned with action decisions,
- Concerned with shorter and medium-term decisions, and
- Decides how to carry out objectives.

Summary

The board of directors plays a central role in a co-operative's success. In consultation and collaboration with members and management, the board stewards the democratic principles and practices of the co-op. Board members provide leadership, direction, and policy inputs on behalf of members. Good governance, reinforced by regular training and mentoring, is a set of skills and practices that co-op board members can transfer to many other aspects of their lives, including community and business leadership.

Group Process Evaluation Form

Russ Christianson

To analyze your group process, have each member anonymously rate each variable on the scale from 1 to 5.

1. Listening

Members don't really listen to one another, often they interrupt, and don't try to understand others.

1   2   3   4   5

All members really listen and try hard to understand.

2. Open Communication

Members are guarded or cautious in discussions.

1   2   3   4   5

Members express thoughts and feelings openly.

3. Mutual Trust and Confidence

Members are suspicious of one another's motives.

1   2   3   4   5

Members trust one another and do not fear ridicule and reprisal.

4. Attitudes Toward Differences Within the Group

Members avoid arguments, smooth over differences, and suppress or avoid conflicts.	1 2 3 4 5	Members respect and accept differences of opinion and work through them openly without pressure to conform.

5. Mutual Support

Members are defensive about themselves and their functions.	1 2 3 4 5	Members are able to give and receive help.

6. Involvement-Participation

Discussion is dominated by a few members.	1 2 3 4 5	All members are involved and free to participate in any manner they choose.

7. Control Methods

Subject matter and decisions are controlled by the chairperson.	1 2 3 4 5	All members accept responsibility for productive discussion and decision-making.

8. Flexibility

The group is locked into established rules and procedures that members find hard to change.	1 2 3 4 5	Members readily change procedures in response to new situations.

9. Use of Member Resources

Individuals' knowledge and experience are not utilized.	1 2 3 4 5	Each member's abilities, knowledge, and experience are fully utilized.

10. Objectives or Purposes

| Objectives are unclear or misunderstood, resulting in no commitment to them. | 1 2 3 4 5 | Objectives are clear, understood, and receive full commitment from members. |

Business Model Comparison

Russ Christianson

Considerations	Co-operative	Corporation	Partnership	Sole Proprietor
Values	Democratic equality, sharing, community focus, needs based	Hierarchical, profit-focused, maximize shareholders' wealth	Depends on partners' value system	Personal values of owner
Application	Applies to any kind of business or need, no limit in size	Applies to any kind of business, no limit in size	Small businesses & professionals	Usually small businesses
Business Viability	Feasibility Study & Business Plan	Feasibility Study & Business Plan	Feasibility Study & Business Plan	Feasibility Study & Business Plan
Ownership	Three people or more	Individual or more people	Two or more people	Individual
Decision-making	Democratic – consensual or one member one vote	Majority rules – Based on number of common shares held	No formal process	Individual – no formal process
Legal Set-up — Legislation — Cost	Simple to Complex – Co-operative Act – $400 plus	Simple to Complex – Business Corporations Act – $1,000 plus	Simple to Complex – Business Registration – $150 plus	Simple – Business Registration – $150
Profit & Non-profit	Both are possible	Both are possible	Both are possible	Profit-oriented

Considerations	Co-operative	Corporation	Partnership	Sole Proprietor
Capitalization (for-profit)	Flexible – member (voting) shares – preference shares (various classes) – bonds, debentures, loans More than 25 owners – Must issue Offering Statement	Flexible – common (voting) shares – preference shares (various classes) – bonds, debentures, loans More than 35 owners – Must issue Prospectus ($100,000 plus)	Usually limited to partners, family, friends, & bank loans	Usually limited to owner, family, friends, & bank loans
Ease of Start-up	Depends on size, complexity, capital required, teamwork	Depends on size, complexity, capital required, teamwork	Requires team work to be simple & quick	Usually simple & quick
Return on Investment (ROI) (if profitable)	Patronage rebates and unlimited return on preferred shares, no capital gains as shares are par value	Unlimited return on investment, including capital gains on the sale of assets or shares traded on stock exchanges	Unlimited return	Unlimited return
Financial Losses	Shared, & deductible only from co-operative income	Shared & deductible only from corporate taxable income	Shared & deductible from partners' income	Deductible from owner's income
Financial Liability	Limited to member investment	Limited to shareholder investment	All partners' personal assets, can be limited	All personal assets
Tax Implications	Non-profit with social objectives is tax exempt. For-profit is taxable.	Non-profit with social objectives is tax exempt. For-profit is taxable.	Taxable as self-partnership income.	Taxable as self-employment income.
Income Tax	Patronage rebates expensed before taxes (decreases corporate tax), corporate rate usually lower than personal; No income tax on patronage rebates (agricultural co-ops)	Dividends deducted on after-tax income (are not expensed before tax to decrease income), corporate rate usually lower than personal	Income is taxable at personal rate in hands of partners	Income is taxable at personal rate in hands of owner
GST & PST	Both must be collected and paid if applicable	Both must be collected and paid if applicable	Exempt if Status Indian on reserve	Exempt if Status Indian on reserve

Considerations	Co-operative	Corporation	Partnership	Sole Proprietor
Productivity	Powerful combination of shared ownership & decision-making	Depends on management ability & employee relations	Strong internal motivation	Strong internal motivation
Team Work	Built into structure through shared ownership & power	Depends on management but often superficial	Depends on management style	Depends on management style
Survival Rates	Twice as high: 40%+ over ten years	20% over ten years	20% over ten years	20% over ten years
Conflict Potential	Values & structure support diversity of views & conflict management	Depends on management but competitive culture leads to conflict	Depends on partners' temperament & management style	Depends on owner's temperament & management style
Agility	Democracy takes longer but usually results in better decisions & more commitment	Depending on size & management style can be extremely agile	Depends on partners' relationship & management style	Depends on owner's decision-making style
Entrepreneurship (risk taking & innovation)	Depends on size, members' temperament, & organizational culture, often innovative	Depends on size, owner temperament, & organizational culture, often innovative	Depends on owners' temperaments, may be less innovative	Depends on owner temperament, often very innovative
Cultural Barriers	Competitive culture & values lead to negative stereotypes about co-operatives	Well suited to the dominant culture's values of global competition & wealth disparity	Competitive culture & values often lead to conflict	Well suited to individualistic society
Local Economy	Money & jobs stay in local economy	Money goes to shareholders, jobs to cheapest area	Money & jobs usually stay local	Money & jobs usually stay local

Comparison of Non-Profit Co-ops and Corporations

Brian Iler[1]

Non-Profit Co-operatives	Non-Profit Corporations
Limited Liability	Limited Liability
Primary purpose is to provide service to members – this may be educational, social, cultural, economic, or environmental	Primary purpose is to further philanthropic, charitable, educational, scientific, or social objectives
Control by members	Control by members
Business is carried on without the purpose of gain for members, any surplus is retained to further the purposes of the co-op	Business is carried on without the purpose of gain for members
Normally exempt from income tax	Normally exempt from income tax
Each member of the co-op has one vote	Members are generally entitled to one vote but may have multiple votes or no votes
Board members are elected by the membership at the annual general meeting – one member, one vote	Board members may be elected by the membership at the annual general meeting
No share capital – member loans, debentures, and bonds can be issued	No share capital – debentures and bonds may be issued

---

1 Prepared by Brian Iler, Iler Campbell LLP Barristers and Soclicitors.

Non-Profit Co-operatives	Non-Profit Corporations
Membership can be transferred only with board approval	N/A
Bank loans may be negotiated	Bank loans may be negotiated
Regulated under the provincial Co-operative Act. Offering statement required unless exemption available: <35 security holders, <$200,000 capital, investment by members of <$1000 per year	Sale of debentures and other securities exempt from regulation
No surplus may be distributed to members; interest on member loans, bonds, and debentures are usually paid annually or upon maturity	No surplus may be distributed to members
Upon dissolution, co-op must distribute all assets, after payment of debts and liabilities (including member loans), to another non-profit co-operative or charitable organization	Upon dissolution, non-profits must distribute all remaining assets either equally among members or, if charitable, to a charitable organization or, if not a charity, other non-profit organization whose objectives are beneficial to the community

Critical Questions to Accompany the Effective Practices DVD

Joy Emmanuel

T he Effective Practices DVD that accompanies this book provides excerpts from a round table discussion with many of the co-op developers who contributed to this publication. The DVD has been developed as an educational resource that may be used in conjunction with the information in this book for workshops and training sessions. The DVD has two parts: *The Co-op Option* and *Towards a Best Practice Approach*.

Below are a set of critical questions intended to help maximize use of the information set out in the DVD. Critical questions are posed to encourage readers/participants to explore hidden assumptions that may inhibit cohesion within the co-op, address crucial areas of work to build the co-op tap into the collective wisdom within the group. Many of these questions are directed toward members of new co-ops, but questions are also addressed to developers or those who work in some related aspect of co-op development and support.

Part One: The Co-op Option

This 30 minute DVD highlights common challenges new co-op members and developers confront in the start-up period. As the developers noted – it is relatively easy to start a co-operative but, like any new business, it is harder to keep it going. This DVD explores some of the common pitfalls new and optimistic co-op members may not take into account and provides concrete examples of successful co-op development initiatives in Québec and elsewhere illustrating the power of co-operation to create positive change.

Critical Questions for Reflection and Discussion:
- What are the key challenges this/our co-op is facing?
- What options are presented in the DVD that may be helpful?
- What other options and resources are available to assist this/our cop-op?
- How can we work with partners within the co-op movement and other allies to successfully implement the vision of our/this co-op?
- What does the "co-op advantage" mean? How does the "co-op advantage" apply to this/our co-op? How can we actively promote the "co-op advantage" to help ensure the success of our/this co-op?
- What does "co-op culture" mean to us? How can we nurture a more co-operative culture within our co-op? And within our community?

Part Two: Toward a Best Practice Approach

Towards a Best Practice Approach is an hour-long DVD that is thematically broken down into co-op development topics that surfaced in the round table discussion with the developers. The DVD may be viewed as a whole in one setting or segments can be viewed by selecting the chapter option. Below are critical questions to accompany each section of the DVD.

Exploring Best Practices
- What key characteristics are critical to the success of our/this co-op?
- How can we optimize the strengths of the co-op to help us succeed?
- One of the seven principles of the International Co-operative Alliance is co-operation among co-operatives. Putting that principle into practice, are there successful co-ops in other communities that are similar to this/our co-op and from whom we can learn? How can we partner with these co-ops?

- The term "best practice" is used in different sectors of society to refer to ways we can optimize our efforts to accomplish our goals. What does "best practice" mean for our/this co-op?
- As a co-operative, people come together to accomplish tasks and meet their needs in ways that may not be possible on their own. Some developers describe the social interactions "as the most complex and important part of the co-op activities." How would you describe the social interactions of this group?

Challenges of Getting Started

- What are the motivating factors behind the decision to start this/our co-op? If this is a "top-down" co-op formation, have the group members decided that the co-op option is really the right option for them? What practices will ensure new members feel a sense of ownership and responsibility for the co-op?
- What processes and practices have been adopted to move from the way things are to the way members would like them to be in their optimum vision for the co-op?
- How can the "tensions" between the desired outcomes and where the group is at now, be used to constructively and consciously move the group forward?
- Are the roles and responsibilities clearly defined for both the group and the developer?
- The group may be anxious to launch the new co-op business, while the developer may view this as premature and see the need to care for other aspects of developing the new co-op first. How can this "tension" be constructively navigated to ensure healthy development of the co-op?

Decision-making

- What decision-making processes has the co-op adopted?
- Some developers recommend that decisions involving an element of risk or uncertainty be made in a different way than day-to-day operational decisions. Has the group determined the criteria for identifying and making strategic decisions where it is more difficult to know the outcomes?

Leadership and Member Engagement

- What are the leadership practices within the co-op? Is leadership shared?

- In what ways does the leadership style strengthen the group? In what ways do present leadership practices hinder the group?
- In what ways are all members encouraged to express their views and participate in the life of the co-op?
- Are training sessions in leadership development available?
- What processes are in place to help engage new leaders within the co-op?

Securing Financing
- Developers sometimes observe that new co-op entrepreneurs are optimistic and overly confident in their business plans. What "reality checks" can be identified to ensure a solid business plan is in place to support the new co-op?

Raising Capital
- What options are available to the new co-op to help raise the risk capital needed for start-up?
- How can the "social capital" of the new co-op be utilized to help raise the financial capital required for start-up? (See Chapter Six for more on Social Capital.)
- What broader networks in the surrounding community, and beyond, might be engaged to leverage support funds for the co-op?

Challenges for Particular Populations
- What supports are in place to assist people who have been marginalized in our society set up new co-ops?
- In what ways are government programmes supportive of new co-op development? In what ways are these programmes problematic?
- What internal accountability structures are in place within the co-op that address concerns of potential funders and government agents?

Working with Host Organizations:
- What policies/criteria have been set out between the host organization and the new co-op to protect the interests of both parties?
- Is this information clear and acceptable to both parties?
- Has a realistic timeline been determined for which the host organization will maintain their support and involvement?
- How is the host organization acknowledged by the new co-op in ways that respect the goals of the host organization and their support of the new co-op?

Co-ops with First Nations People

- What cultural and social barriers might be operative that:
  - Hinder the development of new co-ops in First Nations' communities?
  - Affect the role the developer plays, how he or she is perceived, and assumptions he or she may have?
- What government policies impinge on the development of new co-ops in First Nations' communities?
- Are the expectations and potential benefits around developing a new co-op clear to all involved? And are they realistic?
- In what ways can new co-ops on reserves complement traditional First Nations cultural and social practices?
- Have practices and policies been identified to ensure new co-ops do not become dependent on the developer?
- What support organizations and established co-ops exist in the broader community that First Nations co-ops could partner with in a learning relationship?

Co-op Development in Québec

- What can we learn from the last 20 years experience of co-op development work in Québec?
- What new models have developed in Québec that might be adopted in communities across Canada?
- What are the benefits of building and supporting sector federations to champion the growth of new co-ops?
- What contributions might academic researchers and co-op studies experts play in strengthening the co-op movement for the development of new co-ops in communities across Canada?
- How can the next generation of co-ops members/leaders be supported? What can be learned from the experience of Québec in the area of encouraging the involvement of youth in the co-op movement?
- How can social events and networking be utilized to promote and support co-op development?
- How can various co-op organizations (provincial associations, large established co-ops, sector federations, etc.) work together to support proactive co-op development?

Creating Partnerships

- What role can economic development agencies and government departments play as partners in developing new co-ops?

- How can these resource partners be more accessible to new co-ops?
- What can be learned from the Québec experience of creating partnerships?
- What best practices can be employed around developing partnerships between new co-ops and multiple stakeholders?

Creating a Development Strategy
- What are the benefits of a broad-based co-op development strategy?
- Who are the players that need to be at the table to create a strategy for co-op development? What might their role be in developing a broader strategy for co-op development?
- What additional resources exist in this community that may be beneficial for supporting the growth of new co-ops? What resources exist in the region?

The Role of the Developer
- At what point is it appropriate for a developer to advise the group that their co-op initiative is not likely to succeed?
- What criteria might a developer use to make this assessment?
- How is this action a best practice in co-op development?
- What responsibilities lie with the developer and what are the responsibilities of the group?

The Role of Government
- What should be the role of government departments in supporting the growth of new co-ops?
- What information would be most helpful to encourage establishment of more government programmes?
- What opportunities exist for co-op development in areas where government has withdrawn services from communities?
- How can new co-ops be developed in these sectors to provide needed services and at the same time ensure governments meet their responsibilities to community residents?

The Role of Established Co-ops
- How can the resources and support of established co-ops be more effectively utilized in the development of new co-ops?
- In what ways can start-up co-ops bring new energy and vision to the table and partner with established co-ops?

- Promoting Co-ops within a Capitalist Economy
- How can co-ops be more effectively promoted within a capitalist economy where the free market economy is contradictory to a co-operative culture?
- What is the "co-op advantage?" How can it be more effectively promoted to illustrate the advantages of co-operatives?
- The free-market economy uses the language of efficiency to promote best practices in business models. Is this the appropriate language for co-operative businesses? Why?

Individualism, Environment, and the Co-op Option

- How is individualism a potential barrier to co-op development?
- How can a more co-operative culture be supported within this/our co-op?
- What internalized cultural biases and assumptions do we have toward co-operation and utilizing the co-op model to meet our needs?
- What opportunities for new co-op development exist within the current environmental challenges our society faces?
- What practices can new and existing co-ops adopt to set higher environmental standards as a best practice for doing business?

Biographies

Lyn Cayo

Lyn is an experienced co-op manager, developer, and co-op consultant who has worked in various capacities with co-operatives in Saskatchewan and British Columbia. As a developer Lyn worked in the Nelson area of B.C. with such co-ops as: Kootenay Bakery Café Cooperative, Nelson Carshare Cooperative, Laughing Coyote Land Cooperative, and Shuswap Log and Lumber Co-op.

Although a book-keeper by trade, Lyn was a co-editor and contributor to *Co-operatives By Design – Building Blocks for Co-op Development* (also published by the B.C. Institute for Co-operative Studies). She is a former editor and contributor to *Blackflash Quarterly Magazine* published by The Photographers' Gallery. She co-wrote the *YouBET* (Youth Business Entrepreneurial) Co-ops Manual. She has contributed articles to the *Co-operative Grocer* magazine and edited several other publications.

Lyn presently lives in the Kootenay region of B.C. and serves on the Advisory Board for BCICS.

Russ Christianson

Russ has been working with co-operative businesses for over twenty years. After completing a Masters of Industrial Relations (MIR) at the University of Toronto in 1983, he became the General Manager of the Ontario Federation of Food Co-ops; together with the board and staff, he helped pioneer the growth and distribution of organic foods in Ontario. Russ was a co-founder of Origins, a worker co-operative that marketed a national brand of organic products in the early 1990s and was instrumental in negotiating a separate pool for organic milk in Ontario.

Russ has worked to promote and develop over one hundred co-operatives in a wide variety of sectors, including agriculture and food, travel, housing, retail, distribution, renewable energy, health, arts, construction, forestry, and manufacturing. In 2003, he was given an award for Outstanding Contribution to the Ontario Co-operative Association for his dedicated service to the co-operative movement.

Russ was a founding member of the Ontario Worker Co-op Federation and is a member of the Pine Ridge Food Buying Club and the Upper Canada Woods Co-op. He lives with his family on a reforested farm north of Campbellford, Ontario.

Melanie Conn

Melanie is a long-time community activist who was born in Toronto, Ontario. She earned her Masters degree at the Columbia University School of Social Work in 1965.

Melanie has been working in community economic development since the early 1970s, in Vancouver, British Columbia. In her work with co-operatives and women's organizations she has developed a highly participatory, CED approach that blends theoretical analysis with a practical application of multiple bottom lines. She is committed to working with others in ways that put the principles of inclusion, respectful collaboration, and mutual responsibility into action.

Melanie is a certified co-op developer and a member of DevCo, a co-operative of consultants where she provides technical and other development assistance for new and established co-operatives of every type. She also designs and delivers train-the-trainer programmes and other curriculum related to co-operatives. She recently completed a feasibility study on marketing models for women-centred social enterprises.

She is also the Director of Simon Fraser University's Certificate Programme for CED professionals, which she designed in response to the need for non-credit professional development opportunities for people working in CED.

Melanie is a founding member and director of the Canadian Women's CED Council, the Chair of the Genuine Progress Index Pacific, and a director of WomenFutures CED Society. She lives in East Vancouver with her partner of thirty-one years.

Hazel Corcoran

Hazel is the Executive Director of the Canadian Worker Co-operative Federation (CWCF), the bilingual association of worker and multi-stakeholder co-ops. For nearly 15 years she has been involved in all aspects of worker co-op development and support, including capitalization, advisory services, and launching the Worker Co-op Developers' Network. Trained as a lawyer and fluently bilingual, she has served the co-operative movement in other capacities, including as Director of le *Conseil candien de la coopération* (1994-2005), Calgary Co-op (1999-2002), Prairie Sky Co-housing Co-op (since 2006), First Calgary Savings and Credit Union (since March 2007), and coordinator of CoopZone through CWCF (starting in 2005). She is a co-founder of the Big Idea Rainbow Foundation, started in 2006, with the goal of spreading the message of co-operatives through popular culture (www.emmett.ca/bigidea).

Originally from New Orleans, she came to Canada to attend university 25 years ago. Hazel understands underdevelopment in a first-world setting. Her commitment to helping build a more co-operative world comes from what she grew up observing in New Orleans.

Daniel Côté

Daniel Côté has been an associate professor at L'École des Hautes Études Commerciales (HEC) in Montréal since 1983. He obtained is Ph.D. from Louisiana State University in 1985. At HEC he has been involved with le Centre de Gestion des Coopératives (1977-2003), and served as director from 1992 to 2003. He teaches courses on business strategy at the graduate and undergraduate levels.

Professor Côté has conducted research on co-operatives for more than 20 years. He has studied different co-operative sectors (mostly agribusiness and finance) and focused on issues such as management, strategy, and entrepreneurship. His main concern has always been the management of co-operatives in a competitive environment. His work focuses on the development of a new co-operative paradigm. He has developed the idea that co-operative leaders have an incentive to strengthen their co-operative identity as it is a source of competitive advantage. His new co-operative paradigm is based on issues of loyalty, mobilization through values, co-operatives as learning organizations, meaning, and legitimacy. His approach to research is very much action based where fundamental ideas and concepts (such as loyalty) are implemented and tested in real life contexts with existing co-operatives. He has published extensively on these issues.

Daniel regularly presents papers at conferences on co-operatives in Canada and internationally. He has also been very involved in training managers and board members of large co-operatives such as the Caisses Desjardins (financial co-operatives) and agricultural co-operatives. In 2004, he received the ACE (Association of Co-operative Educators) award for Outstanding Contributions to Co-operative Education and Training.

He is currently teaching a graduate course on co-operative management for the Masters of Management: Co-operatives and Credit Unions programme at St-Mary's University in Nova Scotia.

Joy Emmanuel

Joy is a senior researcher and project manager at the B.C. Institute for Co-operative Studies. Her background is in Sociology and Adult Education. Before joining BCICS in 2005, she taught part-time for 13 years at St Mary's University, Halifax, N.S. With a strong interest in social justice and alternative economic structures, she has been doing community-oriented research since the early 1990s. She was a founding member of the Nova Scotia branch of the Canadian Centre for Policy Alternatives. She holds certificates in Educational Design and Transformational Leadership. In 1997, she founded Quantum Research and Consulting, which is dedicated to contributing to a more just, caring, and sustainable world.

At BCICS, Joy has been the manager for the Effective Practices project, of which this volume is one outcome. She was the co-ordinator for the 2006 international conference on co-operatives and peace, which brought together participants from 16 different countries. She has published both as a freelance writer and as a community researcher. She is both an editor and contributor to several BCICS publications, including *A Passion for Possibilities: Co-operatives and Communities in British Columbia* (2007), *Co-operatives and the Pursuit of Peace* (2007), a second volume in the Effective Practices series (forthcoming in 2008), and *Adapting to Changing Times: Case Studies of Co-operatives in the 'New Economy' of British Columbia* (forthcoming in 2008).

Joy is actively involved in the co-operative community in the Victoria area. She is a member of several new co-ops and has supported the early development of a regional co-op council.

Glen Michael Fitzpatrick

Glen is from Gander, Newfoundland, and has spent most of his career in the field of co-operative and community economic development. Since graduation from Memorial University in 1977, he has been a teacher, journalist, and community development worker. He began his involvement in the community development sector as a communications officer with the Newfoundland and Labrador Rural Development Council. He became Managing Director of the NL Federation of Co-operatives in 1986, and has since led the organization through an evolutionary process where it has become one of the countries first provincial associations to adopt co-op development as a primary mandate.

Glen has authored a number of articles on co-ops and community development and served in a variety of capacities with regional and national groups engaged in the co-op development process. He is currently a member of the National Advisory Committee for the Federal Government's Co-operative Development Initiative. He is also a member of the Canadian Co-op Association's strategy development committee, which is considering issues related to implementation of a new national co-operatives development strategy.

Marty Frost

Marty Frost is a founding member of FWC Development Co-operative (Dev-Co) and has spent the past 35 years working in and for co-operatives and credit unions. During Marty's ten years as general manager of CRS Workers' Co-operative (Vancouver), the co-op tripled its working membership, quadrupled its sales, and became one of the most successful worker co-ops in the country. Since 1996, Marty has applied his knowledge and experience to the development of a wide variety of co-operative and non-profit ventures through DevCo. In eleven years with DevCo, Marty has facilitated the incorporation of over eighty co-operative ventures, has provided training for co-op boards of directors, management, and members, has assisted in the writing of business plans, assisted with policy development, negotiated contracts, organized conferences, and written a variety of resource materials for co-ops and non-profit enterprises.

Marty has served on the development committee and the executive of the B.C. Co-operative Association and is a director of the Canadian Worker Co-op Federation (CWCF), of which he was also a founding member. He has served on advisory boards to the Ministers responsible for co-operatives at both federal and provincial levels and provided extensive consultation on the Co-op Act of B.C. Marty provided co-operative development services and education in seven provinces and two territories of Canada, as well as in Indonesia, Mongolia, and China, and has received training at the Mondragon co-operative system in Spain. Among his volunteer activities, Marty serves as a director for Aunt Leah's Independent Lifeskills Society and chairs the investment committee for Tenacity Works, the capital fund of the Canadian Worker Co-operative Federation.

Gulalai Habib

Gulalai Habib was born in Kabul, Afghanistan and has over twenty years of involvement as a peace and human rights activist. She has a degree in Civil Engineering and Computer Programming.

Between 1987 and 1999, Gulalai was involved in community development in war zones in Afghanistan, the Middle East, and South Asian regions, working with the United Nations Development Programme. The main focus of her work was on gender in development. Introducing a gender lens to programme evaluation and establishing the first thematic group of UN and NGOs for HIV Aids in Afghanistan were two of her achievements in an extremely restrictive environment for women.

As an activist for peace and human rights with a focus on women's role in peace-building, Gulalai co-ordinated the Afghan Women's Network as a volunteer. Between 1995-1999, the Network provided leadership training at the grassroots level, education programmes among refugee children, and national and international advocacy and awareness raising campaigns for policy change. The Network expanded its independent branches in three cities of Afghanistan and four cities in Pakistan among Afghan refugees. Gulalai moved to Vancouver in 1999 and initiated the formation of the Afghan-Canadian Women's Network of B.C. in 2000.

With over seven years of experiences in the settlement sector in Canada, Gulalai was the co-ordinator of Malalay Co-op and Community Economic Developer at the Immigrant Services Society of B.C. (ISS), a non-profit organization founded in 1972 and the first multi-ethnic immigrant-serving agency in British Columbia. The focus of her work at ISS has been on redefining settlement with a CED emphasis and facilitating the process of sustainable settlement for new Canadians. Gulalai is in the process of completing her certificate for CED professionals at Simon Fraser University.

Gulalai lives with her husband and three children in Burnaby, where the view of Mount Seymour is an invigorating reminder of the Paghman Mountain range in their original home in Kabul.

Lynn Hannley

Lynn Hannley is the Managing Director of The Communitas Group Ltd., in Edmonton, Alberta. The company has been in business since 1972 and acts as a development consultant service primarily in the area of co-operatives and community development. While its development activity is focused in Alberta, Communitas has developed housing projects in the NWT and Nanuvit. Lynn acts as the overall coordinator of the various services, which include Housing Development and Management, Research, Programming and Consultation, Planning and Community Development, and Co-operative and Community Economic Development.

Over the years she has been involved in the development of 59 housing projects - serving a broad range of incomes, whose total value exceeds 300 million dollars, and provides housing for 2,070 households. The majority of the projects are owned and operated by the residents on a co-operative basis. Lynn has provided development services to worker co-operatives and community based co-operatives. She has been involved in research in the area of housing, education, community and co-operative economic development, health systems, and social programmes and policies.

Lynn studied genetics and anthropology at McGill and the University of Alberta. Lynn has served on a variety of boards of directors, including the Co-operative Housing Federation of Canada, Capital City Savings and Credit Union, the Edmonton Task Force on Homelessness (a joint task force of the city of Edmonton and province of Alberta), Home-Ed, and the Edmonton Joint Planning Committee on Housing Research. She is also a published author in areas such as housing, land use, co-operatives, and social policy matters. In 1993, Lynn received the Canada Mortgage and Housing Corporation Award for outstanding contributions to co-operative housing. In 1996, she received the Graham Emslie Award for Contributions to Housing and Community Development from Canadian Housing and Renewal Association, and in 1998, she received the Alberta Co-operative Merit Award from the Alberta Co-operative Council and the Alberta Municipal Affairs.

Peter Hough

Peter is the Financial Officer of the Canadian Worker Co-op Federation (CWCF) and the Fund Manager of Tenacity Works (the revolving loan fund of CWCF). For the past 20 year's Peter has been involved in co-operative development and management. During that time he was Manager of the Community Development Co-op of Nova Scotia (a worker co-op development agency), Executive Director of the Canadian Worker Co-op Federation, and Co-op Development Officer for Arctic Co-operatives Limited. Peter was also manger of the Yellowknife Direct Charge Co-op (consumer co-op) and Just Us! Coffee Roasters Co-op (worker co-op).

Peter is a director and the treasurer of the Canadian Community Investment Network Co-operative, a co-operative of social economy lenders from across Canada. Peter is the participating partner of CWCF in the Atlantic Canadian Social Economy Research Node, administered by Mount St. Vincent University. The research includes looking at financing issues of co-operatives and other social economy organizations in Atlantic Canada.

Peter has been involved in many research projects related to worker co-operatives including: The Co-operative Conversion Research Project, Retiring Small Business Owners, Succession Planning Using the Worker Co-op Option, and a report on establishing a Worker Co-operative Developers' Network in Canada.

Joël Lebossé

Joel has been the director of FILACTION, Québec, since 2001. He is an expert on financing co-operatives and non-profit organizations in the social or community economy. He specializes in micro-financing experiences and local development. He has published numerous papers, and authored a book on financing social enterprises, OECD publications, 1999.

Greg O'Neill

Greg O'Neill grew up in a household on Cape Breton Island where social justice was served with every meal. He believes there is unleashed creative potential in all people that is repressed in the destructive economic environment in which we live. Greg has seen the power of co-operatives as a vehicle for unleashing that potential.

Greg received his co-operative education through the diploma programme at the Coady International Institute, in Antigonish, Nova Scotia, where he became part of a global community of "co-operative change agents" and was inspired by the efforts of his fellow classmates. His associates in the programme were people from India, Africa, South America, the Caribbean, Asia, and other countries and are people dedicated to the service of creating a better world through co-operative development.

Greg spent many years working with Arctic Co-operatives Limited (ACL) as a trainer, business planner, and manager of the Arctic Co-operative Development Fund (ACDF) in Yellowknife. (ACL is the service federation for 35 Inuit and Dene co-operatives in the Canadian Arctic. ACDF is a $30 million fund that is owned by the members of ACL.) He also worked as manager of a fund created by the Newfoundland Labrador Federation of Co-operatives to support development of worker co-operatives during the first years of the cod moratorium.

Greg has been a co-op developer with the St. John's Extension Community Development Co-operative and the Prairies-based Co-op Ventures Worker Co-operative and through his own sole proprietorship, Big Idea Consulting. Greg has developed multi-purpose co-operatives in the Canadian Arctic, worker co-operatives in several regions of Canada, and has completed work for the Canadian Worker Co-operative Federation and La Fédération des Coopératives du Nouveau Québec on the creation and sustainability of co-operative development funds.

April Roberts

April is a co-operative developer with the First Nations Agricultural Council of Saskatchewan (FNACS), based in Saskatoon. For the past two years she has been supporting the development of agriculture co-ops on reserves in Saskatchewan. During this time, she has assisted with the development of a tool kit directed toward First Nations communities interested in setting up agriculture co-ops.

Christian Savard

Christian Savard a fait ses études à l'Université Laval en agronomie et a aussi complété un certificat en administration.

Depuis 27 ans, il est associé au développement économique de son milieu à titre de gestionnaire d'organismes publics. Entre autres, il a œuvré pendant dix ans à la Coopérative de développement Centre-du-Québec/Mauricie, cinq ans à la Direction du développement économique de la ville de Bécancour et depuis six mois à la direction générale de la Conférence régionale des élus de la Mauricie

L'auteur est actuellement directeur général de la Conférence régionale des élus de la Mauricie. Il connaît bien les structures régionales au Québec pour avoir occupé plusieurs postes aux conseils d'administration d'organismes comme la Caisse Desjardins Godefroy, le Centre de santé et des services sociaux Bécancour-Nicolet-Yamaska, la Fondation d'éducation à la coopération, le Centre de la biodiversité du Québec et bien d'autres.

Christian Savard has studied agronomy at Université Laval and also completed a certificate in administration.

For the last 27 years, he has been involved in the economic development of his area as the manager of various public organizations. Some highlights of his experience are: ten years with the Centre-du-Québec/Mauricie Development Cooperative and five years as the Economic Development Directorate of the town of Bécancour.

He is currently a General Manager of the Regional Conference of Elected Officials of Mauricie. He is very familiar with the regional structures in Quebec and has occupied several stations with the boards of directors of organizations like the Case Desjardins Godefroy, the Center of Health and the Social Services Bécancour-Nicolet-Yamaska, the Foundation of Education for Co-operation, the Center of Quebec, and other prominent social economy organizations.

About the BC Institute for Co-operative Studies

Based at the University of Victoria, the British Columbia Institute for Co-operative Studies (BCICS) is a catalyst for research, learning, and teaching about co-operative thought and practice. We seek to understand how the co-operative model functions within different communities and economic contexts to empower people to meet their economic and social needs.

About the Effective Practices Series

Developing co-operatives can be a challenging task. Every step and every decision can be surrounded with questions and an array of options. The Effective Practices series of publications from New Rochdale Press is designed to guide those who endeavour to take on, or support, this collaborative adventure. In this series, we do not provide uniform answers – as no two co-ops are exactly alike – here you will find information to help co-operators make informed choices. In these publications we have documented the insights and experience of other co-operators and co-op developers on how to optimize the use of time and resources, and how to best design the internal structures of the co-op, to create successful and vibrant enterprises.

Publications in the Effective Practices Series

- Co-ops by Design: Building Blocks for Co-op Development – (Eds) Lyn Cayo, Kathleen Gableman, Sol Kinnis
- Effective Practices in Starting Co-ops: The Voice of Canadian Co-op Developers (with DVD) – (Eds) Lynn Cayo and Joy Emmanuel
- Effective Practices in Starting Co-operatives – Two Part DVD
- Effective Practices in Starting Co-operatives (Volume 2) – Joy Emmanuel

For more information on other publications by New Rochdale Press, see the end of this publication.

Effective Practices resources and tools can also be located on the BCICS website at: http://bcics.org/

British Columbia Institute for Co-operative Studies
University of Victoria
University House 2 – room 109
PO Box 3060 STN CSC
Victoria, B.C. V8W 3R4

(250) 472-4539
rochdale @ uvic.ca
www.bcics.org

B C I C S

Other Publications from New Rochdale Press

BCICS actively supports the promotion of Co-operative Studies. As one way to support interest in this growing field, we are pleased to provide a diverse array of publications on co-operative thought and practice. Below is a partial list of recent and forthcoming BCICS publications. To find out more about any of these books or to place an order you may contact us at: (250) 472-4539 or visit our on-line store at: http://bcics.org/catalogue

Co-operatives and Peace Series

Co-operatives and the Pursuit of Peace
(Eds) Joy Emmanuel and Ian MacPherson – $20.00

Co-operatives and the Pursuit of Peace DVD
Forthcoming

People to People: The Co-operative Movement and the Pursuit of Peace
Ian MacPherson and Yehudah Paz – Forthcoming

Co-operative Studies Series

One Path to Co-operative Studies: A Selection of Papers and Presentations
Ian MacPherson – $20.00

Integrated Diversities within a Complex Heritage
(Eds) Ian MacPherson and Erin McLaughlin-Jenkins – (Spring 2008)

Co-operatives and the World of Work
Ian MacPherson – Forthcoming

Effective Practices in Developing Co-operatives

Co-ops by Design: Building Blocks for Co-op Development
(Eds) Lyn Cayo, Kathleen Gableman, Sol Kinnis – $30.00

Effective Practices in Starting Co-ops: The Voice of Canadian Co-op Developers (with DVD)
(Eds) Lynn Cayo and Joy Emmanuel – $30.00

Effective Practices in Starting Co-operatives – Two Part DVD
$ 5.00

Effective Practices in Starting Co-operatives (Volume 2)
Joy Emmanuel – Forthcoming

British Columbia and the Canadian Co-op Movement

Practical Dreamers: Communitarianism and Co-operatives on Malcolm Island
Kevin Wilson – $23.00

A Passion for Possibilities: Co-operatives and Communities in British Columbia
(Ed) Joy Emmanuel – $20.00

Pockets of Co-operation: Co-operatives on Vancouver Island
Eryk Martin – Forthcoming

Adapting to Changing Times: Co-operatives in the New Economy of British Columbia
Joy Emmanuel, Ian MacPherson, Eric Morse, and Ana Maria Perudo – Forthcoming

The Quest for Unity and Distinctive Purpose: A History of the Canadian Credit Union Movement
Ian MacPherson – Forthcoming

Co-operatives and Youth Series

Youth Reinventing Co-operatives: Young Perspectives on the International Co-operative Movement
(Volume One)
(Eds) Robin Puga, Julia Smith, and Ian MacPherson – $22.00

Youth Reinventing Co-operatives (Volume Two)
(Ed) Robin Puga and Ian MacPherson – Forthcoming

Occasional Paper Series

Saanich Organics: A Model for Sustainable Development through Co-operation
Robin Tunnicliffe – $ 4.00

EmPowerment: Learning and Participating in Sustainable Energy Development Co-ops
Fiona Duguid – (Spring 2008)

The Almond Tree Project: A Micro Finance Initiative for HIV/AIDS Sufferers in Ghana
Katie Rollwagen – (Spring 2008)

Theory & Practice: The International Co-operative Alliance and the Second Socialist International
Jonathan Crossen – (Spring 2008)

DAT

Printed in USA

Br